Dr. Strangeglove

ALSO BY WILLIAM J. RYCZEK
AND FROM MCFARLAND

*The Sixties in the News: How an Era Unfolded
in American Newspapers, 1959–1973* (2021)

Baseball on the Brink: The Crisis of 1968 (2017)

*Blackguards and Red Stockings: A History of Baseball's National
Association, 1871–1875,* revised edition (2016)

*Connecticut Gridiron: Football Minor Leaguers
of the 1960s and 1970s* (2014)

*Crash of the Titans: The Early Years of the New York Jets
and the AFL,* revised edition (2009)

*Baseball's First Inning: A History of the National
Pastime Through the Civil War* (2009)

The Yankees in the Early 1960s (2008)

The Amazin' Mets, 1962–1969 (2008)

*When Johnny Came Sliding Home: The Post–Civil War
Baseball Boom, 1865–1870* (1998; paperback 2006)

Dr. Strangeglove
The Life and Times of All-Star Slugger Dick Stuart

William J. Ryczek

McFarland & Company, Inc., Publishers
Jefferson, North Carolina

Library of Congress Cataloguing-in-Publication Data

Names: Ryczek, William J., 1953– author.
Title: Dr. Strangeglove : the life and times of all-star slugger Dick Stuart / William J. Ryczek.
Other titles: Doctor Strangeglove
Description: Jefferson, North Carolina : McFarland & Company, Inc., Publishers, 2021. | Includes bibliographical references and index.
Identifiers: LCCN 2021018197 | ISBN 9781476685533 (paperback : acid free paper) ♾
ISBN 9781476643274 (ebook)
Subjects: LCSH: Stuart, Dick, 1932-2002. | Baseball players—United States—Biography. | BISAC: SPORTS & RECREATION / Baseball / History
Classification: LCC GV865.S88 R94 2021 | DDC 796.357092 [B]—dc23
LC record available at https://lccn.loc.gov/2021018197

British Library cataloguing data are available
ISBN (print) 978-1-4766-8553-3
ISBN (ebook) 978-1-4766-4327-4

© 2021 William J. Ryczek. All rights reserved

No part of this book may be reproduced or transmitted in any form or by any means, electronic or mechanical, including photocopying or recording, or by any information storage and retrieval system, without permission in writing from the publisher.

Front cover image: Dick Stuart was called up to play for the Pittsburgh Pirates midway through the 1958 season (National Baseball Hall of Fame).

Printed in the United States of America

*McFarland & Company, Inc., Publishers
Box 611, Jefferson, North Carolina 28640
www.mcfarlandpub.com*

Table of Contents

Acknowledgments	vi
Introduction: On the Brink of Greatness	1
1. Stuart Might as Well Not Even Take a Bat to the Plate: 1932–1951	7
2. He Has Power, He Has a Good Arm and He Will Give You a Million Laughs: 1952–1954	12
3. Potentially, He Is the Best Hitter in the Pittsburgh Organization: 1955	20
4. The Most Sensational Individual Player in the Capital City's Diamond Memory: 1956	25
5. Jesus, There Goes Dick Stuart: 1957	38
6. Shepard Has a Problem—So Had Miller Huggins with Babe Ruth: 1958—Part 1	53
7. I'm Living in a Dream World at the Moment: 1958—Part 2	61
8. You Can't Blame It All on Stuart: 1959	76
9. The People Came to See Me Hit the Home Run, Not You, Bill: 1960	92
10. I Want This Club to Play Me Regularly or Trade Me: 1961	109
11. He's Too Good a Hitter to Be Kept in Check for a Long Time: 1962	118
12. You Gotta Have the Park: 1963	128
13. It's About Time Stuart Grew Up: 1964	145
14. They've Been Very Impartial Here—They Boo Everybody: 1965	159
15. I'm Not in a Position to Give Anyone an Ultimatum: 1966	174
16. I Don't Think I Could Play Here One More Minute: 1967–1968	188
17. The Old Dick Stuart Is Just That, a Thing of the Past: 1969	197
18. A Nobody: 1970–2002	202
Appendix	213
Dick Stuart Home Run Log	213
Chapter Notes	225
Bibliography	241
Index	243

Acknowledgments

A number of people were helpful in the writing of this book, but there are two in particular that I would like to single out for extra thanks. The first is Laurel Stuart, the wife of Dick's brother Daryl. Dick Stuart is dead, his parents are long deceased, and there are very few people alive who can shed light on Dick's personal and family life. Laurel was kind enough to respond to my letter and answer a number of questions regarding relatives, relationships, and what she knew of Dick's life. One thing she knew, by the way, was that they never called him Dick, always Rich or Richard. Perhaps Mrs. Stuart's greatest contribution was her family photos, which she generously gave permission to print. I cannot thank her enough for her assistance.

The second person deserving of great thanks is my good friend Doron "Duke" Goldman. Duke read every word of my initial draft and provided many helpful suggestions. Duke knows baseball history, he knows writing style and, best of all, Duke knows how to be a gentle but firm critic. For my 19th century baseball trilogy, the late historian Frederick Ivor-Campbell helped me in a very similar fashion, and I have been extremely fortunate to have two such kind and talented friends in one lifetime.

I would also like to thank each one of the interview subjects, who graciously agreed to spend time reminiscing about their baseball careers and that of Stuart. I like to think that the pleasure wasn't totally one-sided, for most of them seemed genuinely enthused about the opportunity to talk baseball.

Thanks to Jan Finkel for sharing his thoughts on Stuart, John Horne of the Hall of Fame for assistance with most of the photos, and once again to the folks at McFarland. We have done ten solo efforts and two collaborations over a 28-year relationship and they, like the others mentioned above, have the made the book a better product.

Finally, I want to thank each of you. Works of this nature are never best-sellers; most casual baseball fans haven't a clue who Dick Stuart was or why he might be an interesting biographical subject. I like exploring areas where few have gone, and thankfully there are enough of you out there with an interest in baseball history to make it worthwhile for someone to publish those more obscure but fascinating stories. I hope you enjoy it.

Introduction:
On the Brink of Greatness

It was late afternoon, Thursday, October 13, 1960; the hands on the giant 14-foot clock beyond the left field fence at Forbes Field showed about 25 minutes before four o'clock. The strangest game of one of the strangest World Series ever played hung in the balance; after six games and eight and a half innings of the seventh, the Pittsburgh Pirates and New York Yankees were as even as they had been before the first pitch was thrown. It was hard to believe, for the Yankees had obliterated the Pirates in three of the games by a combined score of 38–3. Pittsburgh, a gritty club that made a habit of coming from behind to win, took three close games to keep the Series even. The seventh game was a roller coaster affair in which the Pirates took an early lead, the Yankees came back, the Pirates rebounded a second time, and the Yankees rallied in the ninth to tie the score 9–9.

Twenty-four-year-old second baseman Bill Mazeroski was the first Pirate batter in the bottom of the ninth. "When we walked off the field for our turn at bat in the ninth," Mazeroski said later, "I was thinking, 'I'd like to hit a home run and win it all.'"[1] During the first six games of the Series, the Yankees hit eight home runs and the Pirates managed only one—by Bill Mazeroski. That was a bit surprising, for the slick-fielding infielder was not one of the Pirates' big power threats. First baseman Dick Stuart led the club with 23 homers but thus far Stuart had been a flop in the Series. He'd started five games, made just three singles in 20 at bats and had not driven in a single run. His fielding had also been a bit shaky and for the final game he had been replaced by Rocky Nelson. Spending the biggest game of his career on the bench was a bitter pill for a man with an ego the size of Dick Stuart's. Further, when the Pirates needed a right-handed pinch hitter in the eighth inning, manager Danny Murtaugh called on Gino Cimoli rather than Stuart. But now, in what might be the final inning of a miraculous Pirate season, he had a chance to redeem himself.

Pitcher Harvey Haddix, who'd stemmed a Yankee rally in the top of the ninth, was scheduled to bat after Mazeroski. Murtaugh told Stuart to bat for Haddix and the tall, lanky Californian pulled his bat out of the rack and sauntered to the on-deck circle. A home run would win the game and home runs were Stuart's specialty. He'd burst into national prominence in 1956 when he hit 66 of them for Lincoln, Nebraska, of the Class A Western League. It was not only the number of Stuart's home runs that attracted attention. He hit them farther than anyone else, majestic tape measure shots that people watched in awe.

Dick Stuart dreamed of people watching him in awe. In 1961, Roger Maris broke Babe Ruth's home run record and nearly lost his sanity in the process. Maris, who dreaded the spotlight, hid in the trainer's room to avoid reporters; during the summer of

1956 Stuart stood in front of Lincoln's Hotel Cornhusker hoping someone would walk by and recognize him. He said outrageous things and his brash, boastful personality made him the most famous minor leaguer of the mid–1950s.

Being a big man in Lincoln was nothing compared to what would await Dick Stuart if he won the World Series with a ninth inning home run. He stood in the on-deck circle swinging a couple of bats, loosening up his powerful forearms and waiting for his chance at glory. It didn't really matter whether Mazeroski reached base or made an out, because Dick Stuart was going to hit the ball over the wall and end the World Series then and there.

On the mound was 24-year-old right-hander Ralph Terry, the Yankees' fifth pitcher of the game. He'd warmed up several times during the long afternoon and by the time Terry entered the game he was arm-weary. He was also having trouble with the mound, which was much flatter than the one in the bullpen; his rhythm was all fouled up and his pitches were sailing high. Terry delivered his first pitch high, exactly where the Yankee scouting reports said Mazeroski liked it. Catcher Johnny Blanchard ran to the mound and Terry assured him he would get the ball down. At the plate, Mazeroski was saying to himself, "Don't overswing. Just meet the ball."[2]

While Blanchard and Terry huddled on the mound and Mazeroski waited anxiously at home plate, singer Bing Crosby, a minority owner of the Pirates, listened in the Paris apartment of his friend Charlie de Limur, where he had somehow contrived to pick up the Armed Forces Radio Network feed of the Pirate-Yankee game. Crosby was trying to open a bottle of brandy and was having as much trouble with the cap as Terry was having with the Forbes Field mound.

As Crosby rapped the top of the bottle against the fireplace, Terry's next pitch came in at almost the same location as the first, a high, hanging slider that Mazeroski hit over the left field fence becoming, in a split second, one of the greatest heroes in Pittsburgh's long sporting history. The euphoric Crosby smashed the bottle against the side of the fireplace and the brandy splashed into the fire, sending flames leaping out onto the carpet.

Mazeroski danced and leaped around the bases while Dick Stuart was left standing in the on-deck circle, his chance for glory dashed forever. The Pirates' dramatic victory meant that Stuart received a winning World Series share of $8,417.94, which was nice, for Stuart always craved money, but he craved attention even more. Reserve catcher Bob Oldis still recalls what Stuart said to Mazeroski afterward. "The people came to see me hit the home run, not you, Bill."[3] He was joking, but Stuart would have given anything to be in Mazeroski's shoes.

The near-miss was symbolic of Stuart's career. He hit 228 home runs, including 42 in one year, and once led the American League in runs batted in. He was the first man to hit 30 home runs and the first to drive in 100 runs in both leagues, but the big first baseman never achieved the greatness he predicted for himself. He did not fulfill his prediction that he would break Babe Ruth's record of 60 home runs in a season. He didn't come close to matching the performance of his idol Ted Williams. There were times it seemed Stuart was closing in on greatness, but he always fell short, just as he did in the final game of the 1960 World Series.

One of Stuart's problems was that he was born too soon. He was a power hitter who couldn't field in the era of the two-way player. He was an unabashed self-promoter in an era where humility was admired and expected. He struck out an average of 117 times a year at a time when strikeouts were considered a serious failing.

Stuart would be very much at home in today's game, where the American League has the designated hitter, social media has propelled the art of self-promotion to new heights, and no one worries about strikeouts. In 2019 there were 91 major leaguers, including many of the game's greatest stars, who fanned more than 117 times.

Even Stuart's swing was ahead of its time. "Now they call it a launch angle," said former teammate Dick Schofield. "When I played, they said you had an uppercut swing and you couldn't hit."[4] Batting coaches preached the crisp level swing designed to produce line drives, not the long sweeping upward stroke Stuart employed to launch fly balls over outfield fences.

Even in today's game, however, Dick Stuart would have his faults. Perhaps his greatest shortcoming was the lack of effort that kept him from getting the most out of his talent. Stuart was booed in every city he played in and left a trail of frustrated managers in his wake, frustrated that Stuart, with all his natural talent for swinging a bat, didn't seem to care about anything else. "The kid had so much ability," said Larry Shepard, who managed him at Lincoln, "but it was half effort. A great hitter. It was a shame that he didn't use some ability to try to learn how to play."[5]

In 1963, Robert Creamer wrote, "The inclination to boo him for his bad fielding is helped along by Stuart's appearance, which on the field is one of nonchalance bordering on indolence. He wears his cap rather forward on his head, so that the visor seems to function like a pair of sunglasses. He appears startled when a ground ball is hit in his direction. His general attitude gives the impression that the idea of sudden and obvious effort is distasteful."[6]

It was his horrible fielding that created Stuart's lasting legacy. He led his league's first basemen in errors his first seven seasons,[7] earned the nickname Dr. Strangeglove, and gave birth to classic stories that were repeated over and over through the years. Like the time he was cheered for snagging a hot dog wrapper blowing through the infield or the time Pirate manager Danny Murtaugh heard the standard stadium announcement that no one was to interfere with balls in play and said he hoped Stuart didn't think it applied to him. "He's a Williams type player," one writer quipped. "He bats like Ted and fields like (swimmer and actress) Esther."[8]

Stuart wasn't the only bad fielder in the history of the major leagues. What made him unique was that he embraced the idea and treated the entire concept of defense with disdain. "I get paid to hit," he said as a rookie. "Anybody can field. But few guys really hit a ball like me."[9] Most players who were criticized for their defense either insisted they weren't that bad or vowed to improve. Stu did neither. He admitted he was a bad fielder and joked about it.

One of his favorite lines was saying, after one of the rare occasions he made a nice play of a hard-hit ball, "I must be slowing down. A couple of years ago I could have gotten out of the way of that." Stuart got a lot of miles out of that joke, changing the name of the batter but always using the same punch line.

The one thing that interested Stuart was home runs. He never tired of talking about his magical year in Lincoln and afterward added the inscription "66" to his autograph. He hung two "6's" on the wall of every residence he inhabited. What Stuart loved most about his 1956 season was not the inner satisfaction of achievement but the fact that those achievements brought him national attention. He'd led the Pioneer League in home runs a couple of times, but it wasn't until he passed the magic number of 60 that reporters from around the country became interested in Dick Stuart.

When the media trooped to Lincoln to meet the young slugger, they liked what they found, for Stuart was a bottomless font of outrageous quotes. He was brash; he was boastful; he was funny, and nothing seemed to faze him. In early June he told reporters, "I'll break the Western League record. I don't care what the record is…. I'll break it and you can quote me."[10] Someone asked him if he thought he could break the all-time professional record of 72 homers. "Of course," he replied, "I've got the feeling I'll do it by a good margin—say 76 or so."[11] There weren't many minor leaguers—or even major leaguers—who talked like that.

For the rest of his career, reporters in every city he played in loved Dick Stuart. And he loved them. He loved attending banquets in the off-season and could always be counted on for a colorful remark or two. Although Stuart was a man of modest intelligence whose education ended with high school, he was clever and had a quick wit.

It's often said that in some previous, imaginary golden age, major leaguers played for the love of the game. Professional ballplayers haven't played for the love of the game since the 1860s, and Dick Stuart was no exception. From the time he was a minor leaguer, he talked about how much money he would make as a major league star. When asked if he'd like to be able to hit like Ted Williams, Stuart replied that he'd settle for Williams' salary, or even half of it. When he eventually made almost half of what Williams earned, he didn't hesitate to let people know about it. In fact, Stuart always seemed to equate his self-worth and importance with his salary.

Stuart was egotistical and boastful, but as he got a bit older and matured, he became likeable. Teammates who disliked him at first sight usually grew fond of him, or at least found him harmless and entertaining. "I liked him very, very much," said Pirate shortstop and captain Dick Groat, "and I think if you go back and talk to the Pirates, ninety percent of them would tell you the same thing—he was just a good guy. He loved to tease you, but he took it well when we teased him."[12] Even Red Sox manager Johnny Pesky, who was practically run out of Boston by Stuart and Carl Yastrzemski, said, "Don't ask me why, but I like the guy. There isn't a mean bone in his body."[13]

But even though Stuart's teammates liked him, he was never one of the guys and rarely went out with them after a game. He was a loner who had his own social life, and it wasn't always an admirable one. Married three times (twice to the same woman), he joked about his divorces and alimony and by all accounts wasn't a very attentive father.

Stuart loved to talk about himself, but despite all the words that flowed from his mouth, finding the real Dick Stuart is a challenge. He tried very hard to create the image of a talented, jovial, wise-cracking *bon vivant* who didn't worry about anything. Was the freewheeling public image anything like the real Stuart?

Jan Finkel, who wrote a biographical sketch of the former first baseman, sensed an emptiness behind the facade. "I've noticed," he wrote, "that Dick Stuart, Lou Gehrig, Abraham Lincoln and a few others have eyes that don't smile. Their mouths may show a smile, but their eyes have a sad, faraway look."[14] Finkel, a retired English professor, called on William Faulker for further description. "Doomed and knew it, accepted the doom without either seeking or fleeing it."[15]

Faulkner didn't know Dick Stuart, but longtime major league manager Birdie Tebbetts did, and Tebbetts said, "Stuart's a fellow who has a faculty for making people mad at him. He wants to do well, but doesn't show it. He gives just the opposite impression. He makes it look as though he doesn't care, but he does. He cares a lot. If he'd only throw his glove when he'd missed one, people would love him."[16] But caring isn't cool, and a man with an ego like Dick Stuart's couldn't admit to trying really hard to be a good fielder and failing. He therefore insisted it wasn't important enough to try.

When Stuart left baseball in 1969, he realized his greatest fear—people stopped paying attention to him. Hitting home runs and talking were his greatest talents. The first is irrelevant if one isn't a baseball player, and Stuart was never able to parlay his gift of gab into a career. He held a number of sales jobs in which he tried to capitalize on his fading name recognition, but he was as interested in learning about business as he was in mastering first base play. During his playing career, he'd worked for a brokerage firm, but his primary activity was taking customers on golf outings. He didn't learn much about the stock market and when he stopped playing baseball his value as a golfing partner diminished. Stuart's lack of dedication to baseball prevented him from being a star and a similar lack of industry prevented him from succeeding in business.

Dick Stuart isn't a Hall of Famer and doesn't deserve to be. But he is a fascinating subject because he *was* ahead of his time and although he wasn't a truly great player, Stuart was *fun*. "[Y]ou are watching a ball player," Myron Cope wrote in 1960, "who has color, who resembles nobody but himself—a ball player you will remember long after he is retired and gone."[17]

How is Stuart remembered today? He was a larger than life character in his prime and in some ways one of those unusual players who, despite a long major league career, reached the height of his fame as a minor leaguer. Stuart made news in Pittsburgh and Boston, but was never quite as uniquely popular as he was in Lincoln and Hollywood in 1956 and 1957. In 1960, Bill Bryson called Stuart "still the most talked-about player in Lincoln, Nebraska, and not merely because he hoisted 66 home runs for that club in 1956."[18]

Stuart's fame was not just a matter of statistics. There were other players who hit a lot of home runs, but they were just ballplayers, not celebrities. Jayne Mansfield didn't tell them she was jealous because they got more publicity than she did. In 1957, Stuart was featured in *Life* magazine—along with some of the most famous people in the world. It was fast company for a minor league first baseman, but Stuart was no ordinary minor leaguer.

Stuart wanted to be admired and went to great lengths, especially early in his career, to make sure others were aware of his accomplishments. His greatest renown, however, was as a comic figure, known for his bad fielding and rakish personality. In his later years, when the baseball glory was gone, he had little to fall back on. He was divorced, alone, and not even admired by his own family, who he rarely saw. A touch of the old jauntiness remained, but it was forced and hollow. He became secretive, hiding his whereabouts because he said his ex-wives were looking for him. Maybe he didn't want to admit that no one was looking for him.

Stuart's baseball career had high moments, low moments, exciting heroic moments, embarrassing moments, and times when he was just a puzzling enigma. But there were very few dull moments. There was always a big home run, a disastrous error, a conflict with his manager, or an outrageous quote that reminded the world that Dick Stuart was one of a kind.

1

Stuart Might as Well Not Even Take a Bat to the Plate: 1932–1951

San Carlos, California, is located on the San Francisco Peninsula, about a half hour drive from the city. It was not incorporated until 1925 and in 1930, two years before Dick Stuart was born, the population was only 1,132. The little town grew rapidly over the next two decades, until it had 14,371 residents in 1950. At the time Stuart was born, the city was mostly rural, known for agriculture. It was almost exclusively white, with just eight African-Americans living there in 1950. Unlike most towns in Southern California, San Carlos, despite its Spanish name, had just a handful of Hispanics.

Although Stuart grew up in San Carlos, he was actually born in San Francisco on November 7, 1932. At the time of his birth, Stuart's father Roy was an electrical engineer for Pacific Utility and his mother, the former Phyllis Dickerson, was a grocery clerk. When Dick was a boy, Roy Stuart opened a dry cleaning establishment named Stuart Cleaners; Phyllis was also active in the business.

The Stuarts' second son, Daryl, was born six years after Dick. "They had a typical sibling relationship," said Daryl's wife Laurel, "with older brother Dick picking on Daryl, who idolized Dick, particularly because he was so good at baseball. All he cared about was baseball. He dominated all of the neighborhood games."[1]

As a boy, Stuart spent hour after hour at a recreation complex where he, Daryl and their friends hit baseballs. Stuart hit them much farther than anyone else. "After he'd hit the ball out of the park," said Daryl, "and all of the balls were lost ... he was done, and he was going home. He was kind of one-way about that. He wanted to get his at-bats, and who cared about the rest of us."[2]

In the fall of 1947, Stuart began his freshman year at Sequoia High

Dick and younger brother Daryl circa 1939.

School in nearby Redwood City; the school was a large brick building that acquired its name from the fact that it was surrounded by sequoia trees.[3] The institution was founded in 1895 as a prep school for Stanford University, moved to the El Camino campus in 1924 and has been there ever since.

One of Stuart's classmates was Ray Dolby, founder of Dolby Laboratories, whose audio technology is perhaps the most famous in the film world, but Ray Dolby couldn't hit a baseball as far as Dick Stuart. Stuart's high school yearbook indicated that he liked all sports, played on the baseball and basketball teams, and planned to attend either Santa Clara University or the University of San Francisco. He also played baseball for local amateur teams and was a scoring star for the Stuart Cleaners basketball team sponsored by his father's business. Although he was quite good-looking, Dick was more interested in sports than girls, and had only one girlfriend, pretty, petite Diane Mellen, who also attended Sequoia.

Stuart wasn't interested in school and he didn't care for much for manual labor. He delivered newspapers as a boy, and when he needed $3.75 to buy a baseball bat, he worked in the artichoke fields for 35 cents an hour, but only until he had $3.75. Then he quit.

Dick Stuart didn't need to pick artichokes because he was going to become a professional athlete. No one had ever become famous in the artichoke fields and Dick Stuart wanted to be famous. In the late 1940s, professional basketball and football were secondary to the college game, and the athletic path to fame and fortune was in baseball.

Dick grew up in San Carlos, California, and was a good-looking young man who always had an eye for the ladies. At this point in his life, however, he was mostly interested in baseball. Courtesy Daryl and Laurel Stuart.

In the early days of professional baseball, most players came from large eastern cities and later they came from small, rural southern towns. It was not until the 1930s that California natives began to make a mark in major league baseball. Italian-Americans from the Bay Area like Joe DiMaggio, Frank Crosetti, and Tony Lazzeri starred with the championship Yankee teams of the 1920s, '30s, and '40s, and once Californian players began coming east, they never stopped. Of the 16,940 men who played in the major leagues through 2019, 2,304 were born in California, a number far greater than that of any other state. Pennsylvania is a distant second with 1,408. Bobby Bonds and his son Barry came from San Carlos, as did a number of other major league players who followed Stuart. California boys can play all year long, and by the time Dick Stuart was growing up, many young, athletic Californians, especially those who could hit a ball as far as he could, dreamed of baseball stardom.

In 1950, during his junior year, Stuart hit .400 and was named to the Peninsula Athletic League All Star team. His

1. Stuart Might as Well Not Even Take a Bat ... 1932–1951

Stuart's yearbook photograph for his graduation from Sequoia High School in 1951. Courtesy Daryl and Laurel Stuart.

batting skill came as no surprise, but what will astonish those who followed his professional career was a *San Mateo Times* report that, "His play in right field for the Cherokees was nearly flawless."[4] In his senior season, Stuart led Sequoia High with a .442 average, hit 14 homers in 22 games and later said that he once hit five triples in a game.

Stuart claimed he received a couple of college scholarship offers, but college meant classes and study, which wasn't for him. "I never brought a book home in my life," he said later. "They graduated me because of my .450 average."[5]

Sequoia was eliminated in three games in the first round of the 1951 Peninsula Athletic League playoffs by Jefferson High School, after which Stuart played for the San Carlos Gray Juniors, batting .469 with five home runs during his brief stint. He had five hits in five at bats in his last game as an amateur.

Professional scouts had been following Stuart during his high school days and shortly after his graduation, he and three other local boys were signed by Pirate scout Bob Fontaine. Stuart reportedly received a $10,000 bonus. For someone as publicity-conscious as he was, the article in the local *San Mateo Times* reporting his signing must have been crushing. Not only did he have to share a three-sentence dispatch with three other youngsters, the paper misspelled his surname as "Stewart."[6]

By late June, Stuart was in Modesto, California, to begin his professional baseball career. The city, located less than 100 miles west of Redwood City, was home to the Modesto Reds, the Pirates' affiliate in the Class C California League. That was somewhat fast company for an 18 year old; recent high school grads were more often found at the bottom of the ladder in Class D. The Pirates had 14 farm teams in 1951, five in the Class D category and three in Class C. Modesto was the only C or D team located in California, and perhaps that is why Stuart was assigned there.

Modesto, whose official motto is "Water, Wealth, Contentment, Health," was primarily an agricultural town. Although today it has a population of more than 200,000, in 1951 it was a small town with just over 17,000 residents. Modesto was established in 1870 as a stop on the rail line between Los Angeles and Sacramento and was originally intended to be named after its founder, financier William C. Ralston. Ralston demurred, and the name Modesto (Spanish for modest) was selected to commemorate his humility. A city whose name originated in modesty was an unlikely place for Dick Stuart to begin his career, for if anyone ever suggested naming a city after him, he would have been delighted to accept.[7]

The modern version of the California League played its first season in 1941, shut down for three years during the war, and resumed operations in 1946. The Reds had been in the league since it was rejuvenated and the 1951 club was managed by 43-year-old Tony Freitas, who was also the team's star pitcher. Freitas had been playing professionally since 1928 and pitched for the Philadelphia Athletics and Cincinnati Reds from 1932 through 1936.[8] When his days in the big leagues came to an end, he did what very few ex-major leaguers do today; he began a lengthy career in the minor leagues.

Other than during his service in the Army Air Corps during World War II, Freitas toiled on minor league mounds from 1936 through 1953. He spent several years in his home town of Sacramento, where he won 176 games, including six 20-win seasons in a row. By the time he took over the Reds, he was a grandfather.

In the 21st century, lower classification minor league teams are utilized solely for developing first and second year players for big league organizations. In 1951, the goal of every minor league club was to win the pennant, and it was not uncommon for a Class C or D team to feature several veterans. In addition to Freitas, the Modesto roster included 28-year-old Dick Wilson, who'd been the MVP of the California League in 1950. For batting .319, hitting 30 home runs, and driving in 154 runs, Wilson was rewarded with another season in Modesto. In 1948 at Mexicali, he'd hit 42 homers, which earned him a short trial in the Pacific Coast League. After about a month in the PCL, he was demoted to the California League, where he'd been ever since.

Modesto was a well-seasoned Class C club. Of the 26 players for whom ages are available, Freitas and one other pitcher were over 30, three players were between 25 and 30, 13 were between 20 and 25, and six, including Stuart, were teenagers. The only player younger than Stuart was future major leaguer Lee Walls.

Youngsters like Stuart and Walls needed coaching, but there was not a lot of it in the 1951 California League. Operating a team in the low minors was a precarious proposition, and expending a salary for a non-playing coach or manager was the exception. Most managers were also active players, and with Frietas taking a regular pitching turn, he didn't have a lot of time for instruction. Occasionally a rookie would get advice from a veteran, but mostly they were on their own; veterans weren't about to help rookies take their jobs.

After joining the Reds, Stuart made one unsuccessful pinch-hitting appearance and then got his first start on June 24, playing both games of a doubleheader. He was hitless in three trips in the opener but got his first two professional hits in the second game. On July 5, he did for the first time as a professional what he was to do 448 more times: he hit a home run.

By the time Stuart arrived, the Reds had established themselves as the best offensive team in the California League, due primarily to the triumvirate of Wilson, Jim Warner, and Walls. The latter, unlike Wilson and Warner, was a genuine major league prospect. A bonus boy like Stuart, he'd gotten $12,000 from the Pirates after showing a strong bat and pitching four no-hitters in high school. Walls could hit, he had power, he had speed, and the Pirates had their eye on him.

The three "W's" were tearing the league apart. Wilson was batting .370 with 20 home runs and 73 RBI, Warner was hitting .336 with 14 homers and 57 RBI, and Walls had a .376 average, 7 homers, and 53 RBI. Dick Stuart was not going to be the star of this team and he didn't get much notice in the local press, which was mostly focused on Wilson, Warner and Walls, plus Freitas, who was on his way to winning 25 games. By the end of the season, Modesto would set a California League single season home run mark with 126 and a record for most total bases in a season. They led the league in batting average, runs, hits, walks, and runs batted in.

While Stuart was overshadowed by the exploits of Modesto's big three, he was still a hero in his hometown. When the Reds visited San Jose, a large contingent from San Carlos made the short trek to see the local boy play. The night was a disaster for the Reds, who lost 20–4, but Stuart, as he was to do so often, rose to the occasion with his second homer of the season. His overall performance was no more than adequate, however, and by July 25 he had 21 hits in 88 times at bat for a .239 average, with his two homers and 11 RBI.

Modesto was going nowhere in the California League race; despite their offensive heroics, they were in the middle of the pack, with no chance at the league title and just an outside shot at making the playoffs. The heavy hitting attracted the fans, however, and by the end of the season attendance would reach 106,722, within 2,000 of the all-time record set the previous season with a much better team. Creative promotions were a key to minor league attendance, and the Reds had several special nights. On the last day of August, the team held a bathing beauty contest, which probably engaged Stuart's rapt attention.

Stuart started in the outfield on a semi-regular basis, and when he didn't start, he frequently pinch hit. Although he didn't generate a lot of heroics, he did manage to literally knock San Jose pitcher Al Curtis out of the box one night when he hit him on the knee with a line drive. Curtis had to be carried from the field on a stretcher.[9]

Stuart's final statistics were 66 games played, 201 official at bats, and a sorry .229 average with only four home runs. His final circuit clout of the year came on September 7 against San Jose in a losing cause. In a foreshadowing of what was to become Stuart's trademark, he was criticized for his defensive play. At the end of August, a *Modesto Bee* reader named Bob Buell wrote a letter to the paper about the team's disappointing fifth place finish.

Buell placed the blame squarely on the front office. "I believe the Reds pulled a real boner," he wrote, "when they released outfielder Don Hinchberger. Dick Stuart, his replacement, is hitting about his own weight." Then he laced into another acquisition, Jim Clark, "who, like Stuart, might as well not even take a bat to the plate."[10]

Even if he wasn't as bad as Buell indicated, Stuart's first professional season was not particularly impressive. The heroes of the Modesto Reds were Walls, Warner and especially Wilson, who set California League records with 40 home runs, 55 doubles, 205 hits, and 387 total bases. He also scored 144 runs and drove in 151.[11] The 18-year-old Walls was called up to the Pirates when Modesto's season ended, but did not play in any games. He made his Pittsburgh debut the following season and would catch up with Stuart a few years later in spring training.

Stuart was not summoned anywhere; he just went home. He had not shown the Pirates anything to indicate that he was a hot prospect, but he was young, he had good size, he had potential, and the Pirates were willing to stick with him. The next season, in Billings, Montana, Stuart would take his first step toward the major leagues.

2

He Has Power, He Has a Good Arm and He Will Give You a Million Laughs: 1952–1954

After his mediocre year at Modesto, Stuart was assigned to the Billings Mustangs of the Class C Pioneer League for the 1952 season. When he received his contract, the brash Stuart wrote back, "Your contract isn't much but I'm signing it. Your .229 hitter in 1951 is your .339 hitter in 1952."[1] Not many 19 year olds coming off a .229 year in the low minors were that boastful, but the baseball world would soon learn that Richard Lee Stuart was not shy.

Billings is located in the southern portion of Montana, not far from the Wyoming border. In 1950, it had less than 32,000 inhabitants, but it was in the midst of a growth spurt that saw its population grow from 16,000 in 1930 to 62,000 in 1970. While it was a small town by national standards, Billings was a big fish in the small pond of Montana, a sparsely populated state that in 1950 had only 593,000 residents. Great Falls, with 39,000, was the state's largest city, and only Great Falls and Idaho Falls were more populous than Billings.

Like most western towns, Billings wasn't settled until the late 19th century; its first homesteaders arrived in 1877. By 1952, it was a typical small town. Its two newspapers featured national news and local tidbits like the names of people visiting relatives in town, the activities of the city's civic organizations, and lists of students being honored by local schools. Billings would not, at first glance, seem like Dick Stuart's kind of town.

Without much of a population base, maintaining a professional baseball team in the far-flung territory covered by the Pioneer League was a challenge, but Billings was up to it. The Mustangs had been members of the Pioneer League since 1948 and would have a professional team through 1963. After a brief hiatus, Billings returned to organized baseball in 1969 and fielded a team each year through 2007. Wikipedia notes that many future major leaguers played in Billings, including Hall of Famers George Brett and Trevor Hoffman, current Yankee manager Aaron Boone, and former Yankee stars Danny Tartabull and Paul O'Neill. There was no mention of former Mustang Dick Stuart.

The Mustangs, who were alternately referred to by various equine appellations such as Ponies and Broncos, played at Cobb Field, named after Bob Cobb, owner of the Hollywood Stars of the Pacific Coast League and the Brown Derby Restaurant and the originator of the Cobb Salad. A Billings resident, Cobb was instrumental in getting the city back into the minor leagues in 1948. Cobb Field, first known as Athletic Park, was built in 1932 but was substantially renovated, at a cost of $100,000, prior to the Mustangs' entry to the

2. He Has Power, He Has a Good Arm ... 1952–1954

Pioneer League. It was a fair park for home run hitters, with distances of 335 feet to the left field foul pole, 405 feet in dead center, and 327 feet in right.

The 1952 Pioneer League was an eight-team circuit,[2] consisting of:

> Pocatello, Idaho (St. Louis Browns)
> Idaho Falls, Idaho (Independent)
> Billings, Montana (Pittsburgh)
> Great Falls, Montana (Brooklyn)
> Boise, Idaho (New York Yankees)
> Salt Lake City, Utah (Philadelphia Phillies)
> Magic Valley, Idaho (Independent)
> Ogden, Utah (Cincinnati)

Billings had been affiliated with the Brooklyn Dodgers for its first four years in the Pioneer League, but after Dodger part-owner Branch Rickey became the Pirates general manager in 1951, the team changed its affiliation to the Pirates.

Following the end of World War II, there had been a minor league baseball boom, but after reaching a peak of 449 teams in 54 leagues in 1949, the number of teams declined to 287 in 38 leagues by 1953. The shrinkage wasn't necessarily bad, for there weren't many major league prospects at the lower levels. "It is a farce to call Class D teams 'professionals'" wrote Gerry Hern. "They are ordinary high school players."[3]

One reason for the decline of the minor leagues was the advent of television. Not all Americans had sets, but many did, and when major league games were broadcast in minor league markets, many fans found it more comfortable to sit in their living rooms and watch the best brand of baseball rather than venture out to places like Cobb Field to watch the Mustangs, especially during Montana's chilly springs. It was difficult to make money in minor league baseball and the Mustangs, like many lower classification teams, were community-owned.

Running a minor league team wasn't glamorous. Longtime manager Frank Oceak once joked, "You've heard the standard gag about the fellow walking into the park and asking for the board of directors of the team. We always tell 'em, wait for the next foul ball. The men who get up and chase it, those are the board of directors."[4]

Billings, like most Pioneer League teams, had a playing manager, catcher Cliff Dapper, a 32 year old who had two unusual achievements in his past. The first was his career major league average of .471, achieved during eight games with the Dodgers during the war year of 1942.

Dapper's second claim to fame was being traded for a Hall of Famer. In 1948, he was playing for Brooklyn's Montreal farm club, and with young Roy Campanella catching for the Dodgers, Brooklyn didn't need another backstop. When broadcaster Red Barber became ill, however, the Dodgers needed someone to team with Connie Desmond in the booth, and traded Dapper for Ernie Harwell, who was calling the games of the minor league Atlanta club.

In 1951, Dapper batted .383 while serving as player-manager in Eugene. Had he been just a player, he would probably have been in a Triple-A league, and he was expected to dominate the teen-aged pitchers in the Pioneer League.

Dapper's club was very inexperienced, with seven rookies among the 19 players who left the San Bernardino, California, training camp. Pioneer League teams were required to carry a minimum of four rookies, but the Mustangs, with seven, had an average age of just 19, young even for a class C club. With nine pitchers, there was virtually no bench, for no major league organization wanted to pay its farmhands for sitting around. By May 24, rosters had to be trimmed to 16.

There wasn't a lot of talent on the Billings roster. Only Stuart and infielder Dick Barone, who got into three games with the Pirates in 1960, reached the majors. That didn't mean there weren't any prospects. First baseman Frank (Dutch) Van Burkleo supposedly received a $40,000 bonus and the Pirates had high expectations for him, but Van Burkleo would have a very disappointing season.

Stuart was the Broncos starting left fielder. He didn't look good early in camp, but just before spring training ended his bat came to life. After he hit three singles in a practice game, the *Billings Gazette* reported that "Two of the Bronco outfielders who have been sluggish as the plate also showed signs of life Wednesday."[5]

Stuart stayed hot the next two days as the Mustangs played exhibitions against a pair of military teams. His home run in the first game cleared the center field fence 445 feet from home plate and earned him a *Gazette* headline. He also hit an inside-the-park home run and had a single to close out camp on a very high note. "Stuart is the new 'sensation' here after his four-bagger over the center field barrier the other day,"[6] the *Gazette* said. "Stuart has blossomed into a strong slugger of late and if he continues to power the ball as he did in the final exhibition games, it will give the team a potent 1–2–3 punch" [Stuart, Dapper, and Van Burkleo].[7]

The Mustangs traveled from San Bernardino to Billings by bus, spending nights in Cedar City, Utah, and Idaho Falls. Upon their arrival, the citizens of Billings greeted their heroes as all good minor league fans did, with a welcome home dinner at the Shrine Auditorium, a parade to the ballpark on opening night, and a serenade by the Billings High School Band. More importantly, a capacity crowd of 5,985 showed up on opening night, an all-time record for Billings and the second-best attendance in Pioneer League history. An additional 1,000 fans were turned away.

The Mustangs were issued new uniforms before the opening game, which Dapper reminded them could not be altered. Fifteen minutes later, Stuart walked in with his sleeves cut in the bare arm style of Reds slugger Ted Kluszewski. Dapper fined him $35 and made him re-do the sleeves. Even in Class C ball, Dick Stuart cared about his appearance.

The Mustangs gave their fans an exciting show, winning their opener for the first time in their five years in the league. Manager Dapper coaxed a walk-off walk in the 11th inning to defeat Great Falls 7–6. Stuart played left field, had one hit in three at bats, and did not make an error.[8]

Billings won its first four games and moved into first place on May 1, paced by a Stuart homer. But that was one of his rare good early moments. League statistics were published each Sunday, and for the first few weeks of the season, even though the list included everyone batting over .200, Stuart's name did not appear.

Baseball in the Pioneer League wasn't always pretty. On April 30, Billings defeated Pocatello 15–8 in a game that featured 24 walks and 12 errors. The game took two hours and 47 minutes, about average today but an extraordinary length for 1952. On May 6, Billings committed eight errors and drew nine walks. On May 10, eight Billings and Magic Valley pitchers issued a combined total of 24 walks. That was why they were in Class C.

Attendance at Cobb Field was good, helped by relatively mild weather. Under the leadership of business manager Maury Enright, the Mustangs staged a number of crowd-pleasing promotions. They brought in entertainers like Max Patkin, who spent decades working the minor league circuit, and Jackie Price, an ex-major leaguer and lesser-remembered baseball clown.

Patkin's routine was mostly pantomime. He shadowed and mocked coaches, players, and especially umpires. One of his favorite tricks was filling his mouth with water and expelling it in a geyser, often at an umpire. The umpire feigned anger while parents in the stands cringed, knowing their young sons would be trying to duplicate the feat for days to come. Price had a number of stunts, including hitting pitches while suspended upside down and catching fly balls while riding in a car. You couldn't get that kind of entertainment sitting home watching the Yankees and Indians on television.

One of Enright's other ideas was a competition among nearby towns to see which could show the greatest support for the Mustangs. Each town had its designated night, and the number of fans from that town was multiplied by the miles they had driven, to determine which town could generate the highest number of fan/miles. The town of Powell captured the prize with 455 fans that traveled a total of 43,680 miles to Cobb Field. For good measure, they brought the 85-piece high school band. The poorest showing was by Roundup, whose 108 attendees included the female mayor, Mrs. Lillian Giltroy. The Roundup folks traveled just 5,615 miles and arrived without a band.

In mid–May, Stuart's bat started coming to life. On the 12th, he contributed a home run and another hit to a 7–0 win than featured a no-hit game by 20-year-old pitcher Wally Sinner. On May 18, Stuart demonstrated the inconsistency that was to mark his big league career. He had a triple and two singles in four at bats, but dropped a fly ball in the ninth inning that allowed Salt Lake City to tie the game. In the bottom of the ninth, he started the winning rally with a single; the Mustangs 7–6 win returned them to first place.

A couple of days later, Stuart scored the winning run by beating a throw to the plate on a grounder to shortstop with the bases loaded. The next night he hit a home run as Billings improved its record to 15–9 and built up a 3½ game lead.

After falling briefly to second place, the Mustangs took the lead again when Sinner pitched a one-hitter and Stuart hit a two-run homer to beat Great Falls at Cobb Field. Cab driver Leo Shipp was dropping off a passenger on North 27th Street when Stuart's drive cleared the left field fence and bounced through the open left rear window of Shipp's taxi. It was a great story, but even with his recent surge, Stuart was batting just .206.

Although Dick hit three home runs during the next week, the Mustangs were in the midst of a terrible 11-game road trip that dropped them from first to sixth place. "The road trip was just plain disastrous," said Dapper. "We just aren't hitting—especially with men on base."[9] But Stuart *was* starting to hit, with or without men on base. By mid–June, he'd raised his average to .242, with eight home runs and 26 RBI, not terrific but a vast improvement from his awful start.

On June 11, the *Gazette* reported two items about Dick Stuart that seem unbelievable in light of the image he would develop in later years. First, he stole a base, something he did just twice during his major league career. Second, Stuart, along with several teammates, attended a local luncheon and the paper did report a single quote from him. Stolen bases and silence were rarely seen from Stuart in subsequent seasons.

Beginning May 22, Pioneer League fans were allowed to vote for the league all-star team, through ballots available at league parks and in newspapers. The polling started slowly, and after a month no player had more than 25 votes. But then a flood of ballots began to arrive, many of them from Billings, and many of those listed the name of Dick Stuart for all-star outfielder.

By early July, Stuart's 412 votes were second among outfielders to Pocatello's Willie Tasby (a future major leaguer), who had 437.[10] In the final tally, Stuart placed third with 1,341 votes, which earned him a spot in the starting lineup. Player-managers were not eligible as players, but Dapper led the balloting for manager. Due to the enthusiasm of Billings' fans, several Mustang players, even those who weren't having very good seasons, ranked high in the voting.

The Pioneer League All-Stars played first place Pocatello and lost 2–1 in 14 innings.[11] Stuart started in left field, batted third. and did not have a good night. He was hitless in five at bats and dropped a fly ball in the 14th inning. It was a modest beginning to Stuart's all-star career.

As the weather got warmer, Stuart's bat heated up, which was to become characteristic of his career. On July 7, he hit two home runs and a triple in a 21–1 win over Ogden, driving in seven runs. That gave the big outfielder 13 home runs and tied him for the league lead with Dapper. His average, which had been below .200 in the season's early weeks, was .303 and climbing rapidly.

With the Mustangs in contention for the pennant, fans were coming out to Cobb Field in greater numbers than in previous years. By year's end attendance would reach 142,208, the most of any Class C franchise.[12] One of the main attractions was Stuart's home runs—by July 14 he was leading the league with 16. He was not only hitting home runs—he was hitting very long home runs. That was Dick Stuart's obsession—to hit longer home runs than anyone else.

Stuart had a big day July 31, hitting a two-run homer and a three-run homer in a 6–4 win over first place Pocatello. On August 4, Billings cut Pocatello's lead to 1½ games by defeating them 9–6. Stuart had an RBI double as the Mustangs welcomed their 100,000th fan of 1952, a local resident named Douglas Wallin who, like many fans of that era, attended the game wearing a sports coat and dress hat. He was given a free pass to all 1953 games.

The next day, Stuart hit one of the longest home runs in the history of Cobb Field, a towering drive far over the scoreboard beyond the left field fence. It was only the second time a ball had cleared the scoreboard and Stuart was rewarded with $110 from Cobb Field advertisers. On the 6th, the Mustangs moved into first place by a half-game with their third straight win over Pocatello. The crowd of 4,607 was the largest since opening day and included comedian Jack Benny.

The winning pitcher that night was Larry Manier, a 28-year-old veteran right-hander who'd won 26 games for Great Falls in 1951 and had most recently been pitching for Class A Denver. For their stretch run, Billings picked up Manier and 33-year-old outfielder–first baseman Buck Elliott. Today there are no 33-year-old veterans in the low minors, but in 1952, winning was as important as player development, and the Mustangs wanted a pennant.[13]

A 5–4 road trip dropped the Mustangs behind Pocatello, but Stuart continued to shine. He hit six home runs during the first two weeks of August, increasing his total to a league-leading 26. He also led the league in runs scored.

Billings wasn't able to catch Pocatello, but it had been an exciting season nonetheless, and Mustang fans showed manager Dapper how much they appreciated his efforts. September 3 was Cliff Dapper Night at Cobb Field, and fans presented the manager with a 1952 Ford pickup truck and other gifts with a total value of about $3,000. The club flew his wife and daughter in from California for the occasion. Dapper said that in his fourteen seasons of professional baseball he had never experienced anything like Cliff Dapper Night. "I will play ball in this town as long as you want me to play," he said.[14]

Three nights later came Player Appreciation Night. Billings beat Boise 10–1, as Stuart hit his 30th homer, but that was only part of the entertainment. There was a home run hitting contest in which Stuart participated, and there was a foot race between Stuart and Dapper, the culmination of a season of teasing between the two as to which was the slowest. Unfortunately, the *Gazette* did not identify the winner.

Branch Rickey was in the stands that evening. By 1952 he was a legend, and when he gave his opinion on any subject, it was dutifully recorded. When asked about the top Billings prospects, he said of Stuart, "He has power, he has a good arm—and he will give you a million laughs." Not much had been written about Stuart's personality to that point, but apparently it had caught Rickey's attention. The old man was amused at the way Stuart protested umpires' decision with silence. "The greatest silent protestor I have ever seen," Rickey said. "The boy says nothing, but that look of contempt is really something."[15]

On September 9, Stuart hit his 31st home run of the season, breaking the Billings record of 30 set by Bill Pinckard in 1950. Pinckard, like Stuart, was a slugger with serious defensive problems. He was on his way to hitting a combined 40 home runs for three different teams in 1952, but the *Gazette* noted, "In the vernacular of the trade, he's called a butcher in the field."[16] Pinckard never made it to the major leagues, and breaking his Billings record was certainly no guarantee that Stuart would become a major leaguer.[17] The bushes were filled with minor league record holders.

The Pioneer League used the Shaughnessy playoff system,[18] in which the teams with the four best regular season records staged a playoff for the championship. Billings faced Pocatello in a best-of-three series in the semi-finals and dropped the decisive third game 7–6 before the home crowd at Cobb Field.[19]

When signing his 1952 contract, Stuart had said that the .229 hitter of 1951 would hit .339 in 1952, and he came close. He batted .313, sixth among Pioneer Leaguers with 400 or more at bats. Stuart led the league with 31 home runs, 115 runs scored, 121 runs batted in, and 292 total bases, and tied for the lead with 161 hits. He struck out 99 times, but that was a minor distraction. Stuart was now a prospect. At Modesto he had scarcely been noticed, but after the 1952 season, people in the top echelons of the Pirate organization knew about Dick Stuart and his prodigious power, and being noticed was what Stuart craved most.

When the Billings team left for home, the *Gazette* noted, "some will work, some will play winter ball—and some will feel the long arm of Uncle Sam." Dick Stuart was one of those who would feel Uncle Sam's long arm on his shoulder and it would be three years before he would play professional baseball again.

On November 2, 1952, Stuart, just short of his 20th birthday, married Diane Mellon, who was also 19, at San Carlos Community Church in San Mateo, followed by a reception at the American Legion Hall.[20] Diane grew up in San Carlos, was a classmate of Stuart's at San Carlos Central and Sequoia High School, and had been working as a secretary in San Francisco.

During the winter, Stuart played ball in California, with teams like Pomona Tile and the Monterey Merchants, and by April 1953 he was a soldier and a member of the Fort Ord Braves, who played in California's Mission League.

The quality of military baseball in the mid–1950s was amazingly good. There was a universal military draft, which meant that virtually all healthy young males, including professional athletes, were required to serve. Major league stars like Willie Mays and Whitey Ford lost a couple of years to military service and they, along with most drafted athletes, spent most of their time on the athletic field.

By the time Stuart entered the service, the Korean War was winding down; an armistice was signed in July 1953, so there was little chance of an overseas deployment. Fort Ord was located on Monterey Bay on the California coast, which had a much nicer climate and view than the army posts in South Korea.

For people like Stuart, life in the peacetime army was pretty good. Their days consisted mainly of playing for the base team, and since commanding officers took great pride in the performance of their unit's teams, they made sure the athletes had plenty of time to practice and that their military duties weren't so strenuous that they would be too tired to play.

The 1953 Fort Ord Braves were a formidable combination, and the talent was so abundant that there was a second Fort Ord team called the Warriors. It was so good that Don Larsen, who later pitched a perfect game in the World Series, wasn't good enough to make the starting lineup when he played there in 1950.

The Braves' manager, 21-year-old Mike Donahue, was a catcher for the San Francisco Seals of the Pacific Coast League when he was called into service. Wally Sinner, Stuart's Billings teammate, was one of the pitchers. Nearly every member of the team had professional experience.

The Braves opened the 1953 season in Salinas against the local Merchants and won 9–0 in a game ended prematurely by rain. Pete Wilson allowed the Merchants just one hit and Stuart hit two homers. The second was one of the longest blasts ever hit at the Salinas park, bouncing off the top of a 20-foot high scoreboard that was 400 feet from home plate.

On the last day of May, Stuart again hit two homers against Salinas, each with two Braves on base. On August 8, he did it again, and this time one of them was a grand slam. Near the end of June, the *Humboldt Standard,* promoting an upcoming game with the Humboldt Crabs, featured a large photo of Stuart with the caption, "Spearhead of the Fort Ord Braves offensive is compactly constructed Dick Stuart."[21] He was described as a "fleet outfielder" who was batting .376 with 12 home runs. In September, the Braves won the Mission League championship by defeating Watsonville 9–5. Stuart finished the season with 24 homers, several of them the tape measure blasts he coveted.

During the winter of 1953–54 Stuart again played with Pomona Tile. By the time the 1954 baseball season rolled around, he was stationed at Fort Lewis, located about nine miles southwest of Tacoma, Washington. Like the team at Fort Ord, the Fort Lewis Explorers' roster was composed almost exclusively of professional players. The star pitcher was Connie Grob, who later pitched for the Washington Senators. John McNamara, a major league manager from 1969 to 1996, was one of the catchers. Another catcher was Charley Lau, who played in the majors for several years and then became a renowned batting coach. Sammy Esposito, a utility infielder for ten years with the Chicago White Sox, played the infield.

The Explorers played in the Timber League, although, as *The Daily Chronicle* of Centralia, Washington, pointed out, "Reading down the Fort Lewis roster gives the idea that the nine probably should be entered in the Western International League, if the rules permitted."[22] In addition to playing in the Timber League, the Explorers competed against other military nines, and on September 3 they had a 62-game winning streak snapped and lost the Sixth Army championship to the Fort Ord Warriors, despite a Stuart home run, his 26th of the season.

Bob Nold was a young Army reporter at Fort Lewis who later became a professional journalist. In 1967, he wrote an article in *The Akron Beacon Journal* reminiscing about his days covering Dick Stuart in 1954. "[H]e was a character from the beginning," Nold wrote, "full of himself and boasting continually of his masterful exploits with Billings, Montana.... To say he drove his Fort Lewis teammates to distraction is putting it mildly.... My job with the public information office consisted in part of reporting their deeds. Stuart was by far the best copy."[23]

Nold recounted the story of a game in which Stuart hit a pair of home runs. "After the second one, the players refused to greet him and shake his hand. Undaunted, he continued to the far end of the dugout and then walked down it, shaking hands with each of them."

On another occasion, the team was scheduled to play Yakima Junior College, but before they could leave for the game, they had to perform a reconnaissance mission, a large portion of which was spent crouching in foxholes. They left for Yakima with a full equipment load of steel pots, ponchos, cartridge belts, canteens, and weapons. "This is the first league I ever played in," Stuart said, "where we had to do this."[24]

Pro basketball player "Jungle Jim" Loscutoff grew up with Stuart in California and played against him on many occasions. He was a catcher on the Fort Lewis team and claimed that during a game at Camp Roberts, California, Stuart hit a home run that travelled 650 feet. It's hard to believe anyone could hit a baseball 650 feet without a couple of hundred feet of bounce and roll, but Loscutoff insisted that the center field fence was 650 feet away and Stuart cleared it. Although the story is highly unlikely, it added to the legend of Dick Stuart as a clouter of record distance home runs.

Stuart did not have the personality of the obedient, conforming soldier. But he could be a ball-playing soldier, and that is how he served his country for two years. By the time the 1955 baseball season began, he had been discharged from the service and was ready to return to professional baseball.

3

Potentially, He Is the Best Hitter in the Pittsburgh Organization: 1955

Stuart's big season at Billings and two years of hitting home runs in the Army made him one of the Pirates' prize prospects. He was included in a group of select farmhands invited to the team's early instructional camp at Fort Myers that preceded spring training. "The most highly recommended prospect," wrote Jack Hernon after the early session, "is a lad just out of service, Dick Stuart, an outfielder by trade. Stuart was the only player able to clear the fences at Terry Park ... rapping the ball over the 360-foot sign.... Stuart has a good arm and better than average speed."[1]

Branch Rickey, Jr., the Pirates' farm director, added, "Potentially, he is the best hitter in the Pittsburgh organization. He hit the ball hard all over the country when he was in the service. Bob Fontaine, our West Coast scout (and the man who had signed Stuart), made a glowing report on him this winter."[2] Left unsaid were the Pirates' doubts about Stuart's defensive skills. They'd seen his desultory play in the outfield, and in Fort Myers the Pirates tried him at first and third base.

Stuart was assigned to train with the New Orleans Pelicans of the Southern Association. A jump to the Southern Association would be a challenge for someone who'd last played in Class C. There was a lot more talent at that level, and life in the South was much different than it was in Stuart's native California.

The SA was a white man's league, like nearly every southern-based professional baseball circuit in the 1950s. *Times-Picayune* columnist Bill Keefe explained that the league's informal ban on blacks was designed not to punish the Negro but to avoid uncomfortable and potentially dangerous situations.

The owners firmly believed it was also good economics. Keefe cited an example from the 1954 season, when Nashville had a chance to get Frank Robinson, who was tearing up the South Atlantic League. Nashville owner Larry Gilbert declined because, Keefe explained, he was "mindful of the disastrous effects that the presence of a Negro in Atlanta's lineup made on Mobile's financial condition last spring.... After Atlanta opened the season in Mobile with a Negro player more than 50 per cent of the citizens who had subscribed to stock or bought season tickets to the Mobile games expressed resentment; many of them demanded their money back.... Gilbert had no wish to embarrass any other club owners or some of the white fans in Nashville; further than that he always has contended that one Negro playing on a Southern team would have such a hardship making good that it would be grossly unfair to him. He wouldn't be able to stop at the same hotel with his teammates or eat with them and his lonesome life very likely would lower his morale and affect his performances."[3]

It was for their own good, Keefe explained, that blacks were kept out of the Southern League. He pointed out that they couldn't play in Birmingham, which had a law prohibiting the mixing of races in sporting contests, and related the sad story of Sam Hill, who attended the Pirates' minor league camp in Huntsville, Texas, in 1954. Keefe said that while the white players interacted well with Hill on the ball field, he always ate alone in the dining hall. He asked one player why no one sat with Hill. "Mister," the player replied, "you can sit there if you want. There ain't nothin' holdin' you."

"Not 20 Supreme Court rulings," Keefe wrote, "can make a man sit at a table at which he doesn't want to sit." He said he wished southern hotels would integrate and that things would change, but, as the heading of his column read, "Customs [Are] Hard to Break Down."[4]

Besides, blacks didn't really mind. "Negro fans," Keefe wrote a month later when the Giants and Indians played an exhibition game in New Orleans, "who ever have been the most loyal Pelican supporters and who have always shown fine sportsmanship in refraining from boos, throwing back baseballs, forgiving errors by the home team and applauding good play or fine sportsmanship by visitors as well as Pelicans, good naturedly took the discomfort of standing in the hot sun, packed like sardines."[5] As if they had a choice.

The Pirate minor leaguers, including the Pelicans, trained at the Country Campus of Sam Houston State University in Huntsville, Texas. Throughout the spring, minor league clubs dickered for players they wanted on their rosters, often lobbying to get them sent down from a higher classification. New Orleans, like Billings, wanted a championship and President Jake Nowak and manager Andy Cohen's most fervent desire that spring was to convince Pirate GM Branch Rickey to send players with major league ability to New Orleans. To make his case, Nowak spent a week with Rickey in Fort Myers chewing on the old man's ear.

Of the players already in the New Orleans camp, one of Cohen's favorites was someone who did not have major league ability, twenty-four-year-old second baseman Earl Weaver. Weaver was invariably described as a "pepper pot," and most praise directed toward him was somewhat defensive. A *Denver Post* reporter wrote, "The dumpy little second baseman can't run, can't throw, can't hit. But he can field everything he gets to; he can bait umpires with the best of them [a talent he honed over the years]; he can out-think ball players with twice his ability, and he has that priceless facility of getting the vital base hit or walk when it means the ball game."[6] Weaver would spend the entire 1955 season in New Orleans and bat .278 in 119 games.

No one ever described Dick Stuart as a "pepper pot," but he impressed Cohen by hitting a few long balls in camp. However, when the season started and players were sent down from higher classifications, Stuart was relegated to part-time duty. John Powers, a left-handed hitter who wound up playing parts of six seasons in the big leagues, started most of the games in right field.

Stuart played in just 13 games for the Pelicans, some as a pinch hitter, and managed six hits in 30 at bats with no home runs. He also had a couple of misadventures in the outfield. Cut-down day was 30 days after the start of the Southern Association season, and when it appeared that another outfielder was going to be sent down to New Orleans, Stuart was the likely candidate to go. Sure enough, on May 5, he was sent to the Mexico City Azuls, a Pirate affiliate in the Mexican League.

Paul Pettit, another Pirate farmhand, had joined the Mexico City club a couple of weeks earlier. "My first recollection of Stuart," he said, "was when he showed up for batting practice the first day he got there. He walks up carrying a bag with a bat sticking out of it and said, 'What's the home run record in this league?' If you didn't know Dick, you'd think he was just curious. If you did, you knew he intended to break the record."[7]

Stuart wasn't in Mexico City very long, appearing in only seven games and nearly ruining his intestinal tract with Mexican food. "We were on a train headed for Monterey," Pettit recalled, "and there were three or four of us, including me and Dick, in a compartment. During the night he woke up sick and tossed his cookies and we had to wallow around in that slop all night long. Dick wasn't particular enough about where he ate. I was and I never got sick, but my whole family did and I had to send them home."[8]

"I lost 8 pounds in 12 days," Stuart said. "I told them send me somewhere else before I vomit my life away."[9] The Pirates sent him back to Billings, which was desperate for talent.

After winning their opener, the Mustangs lost nine games in a row, leading their fans to call on the Pirate organization to send better players and eventually to petition for an end to the Pittsburgh affiliation.[10] Branch Rickey sent scout and troubleshooter George Sisler to Billings to determine what was wrong, but it didn't take a Hall of Famer to determine that the Mustangs needed better players.

Some help would arrive, Rickey promised, when clubs in higher classifications made their final roster cuts. "Help is on the way as fast as we can get it there," he said.

The biggest need was for anyone who could hit a baseball; on May 3 the Mustangs stood at the foot of the Pioneer League with a .193 average. Jack Paepke, a veteran catcher who'd taken over from Cliff Dapper as manager, was leading the way at the plate, but none of his players were following. With little support, Paepke tried to do it all himself. Late in one game, with the score tied at 6–6, he removed his catching gear and trudged to the mound to take over the pitching chores. The first two batters he faced hit home runs and the Mustangs lost again.

As promised, help began to arrive, and soon the Mustangs had an almost completely new roster. Only three players who started the season were on the team when it ended. First baseman Tex Taylor, who had refused to accept a demotion to Billings at the end of spring training, changed his mind. The club received two pitchers, thin right hander Charley Beene from Hollywood and diminutive William (Red) Dunn from Waco. Dunn was a known quantity in Billings, having won 15 games for the Mustangs in 1954 before coming down with arm trouble.

It didn't take long for the changes to have a positive effect. Dunn won his first start on May 19 and Taylor was soon batting over .400. The Mustangs began winning some games, and the Pirates continued to send help. On May 25, two outfielders joined the Mustangs from Mexico City. One was Bob Ryan and the other was Richard Lee Stuart, returning to the city in which he played three years earlier and to the league he'd led in home runs.

Stuart, who always had a knack for the dramatic entrance, hit a home run in his first time at bat to spark a victory that improved the Mustangs' record to 9–21. Although the team was still in last place, the recent spurt had given Business Manager Maury Enright pennant fever. While trying to find housing for Stuart, Enright rejected one potential rental because it would have to be vacated when school started. He said Stuart would need to be there through September 15, which was when the Pioneer League playoffs ended.

Dunn won his first five decisions and soon the Mustangs had a five-game winning streak. That didn't mean they were playing sparkling baseball. On June 6 at Great Falls, Billings struggled to an 11–10 win despite the fact that their pitchers gave up 20 walks. The Mustangs went into the ninth inning with an 11–3 lead, but eight walks by four different pitchers yielded seven runs before they managed to get the final out. The winning pitcher, Merlin Jorgenson, gave up 15 walks in 8⅓ innings. Two days later, he retired and went home to Centerville, South Dakota, to help his father on the family farm. The following day, Billings' pitchers were wild again, walking 12 and losing 3–1 despite a Stuart home run. Stuart hit another home run the next day in a losing cause.

On June 17, Branch Rickey came to Billings to meet with the Mustang directors and hook up with his old buddy Bob Cobb, the Billings native who was one of Rickey's favorite fishing partners. Now that he had provided the Mustangs with some assistance, it was safe for Rickey to show his face in Montana.

Shortly after Rickey left, the Mustangs received another pitcher, Bennie Daniels, a promising right-hander who'd split eight decisions at Class A Lincoln. Daniels would join outfielder Carl Long as the only black players on the Billings roster. While the Pioneer League was not the Southern Association, living in Montana, where even today less than one percent of the residents are African-American, wasn't easy for a black man.

In mid–June, Long was ejected from a game against Idaho Falls when he started a fight in reaction to some "bench-jockeying" from the opposing dugout. One can only guess the nature of the remarks emanating from the Idaho Falls bench.

In early July, Long was fined $25 and suspended for five days for pushing umpire Dick Kent while disputing a call. While being a black man in the Pioneer League was a tough life, the lot of the league's umpires wasn't much better. Only one of them, Augie Donatelli, who worked the circuit in 1946 and 1947, ever made it to the major leagues. The umpires were young (the average age in 1955 was about 26), they worked in two-man crews, spent their days driving the desolate western prairies from one isolated Pioneer League city to another, absorbed abuse at every stop, and often became discouraged. In early July, two umpires quit and two others were released.

Umpire Moran Freeman was suspended for five days for unprofessional conduct during a game at Billings. Once, an umpire was accidentally locked in Cobb Field and had to be freed by the police. The officer who rescued him said he should have locked him out of the park, not in.

In Daniels' first start for Billings, Stuart hit a single, double, and homer and drove in five runs to help the Mustangs to a 12–8 win. Daniels not only had the arm of a major league prospect; he could swing the bat, and was often used as a pinch hitter. Later in the season, when injuries crippled the Billings outfield, Daniels started several games in right field.

During the second half of June, Stuart got red-hot, getting 16 hits, including five home runs, in 32 at bats over a nine-game stretch. That gave him 11 home runs for the season and hiked his batting average to .354. He finished June with a flourish, hitting his 12th home run on the final day of the month. It was a titanic blast that hit a clock just beyond the center field wall, an estimated 390 feet from home plate. It was the first time any batter had hit the clock and the jeweler who sponsored it gave Stuart a $500 diamond ring. The next day the *Gazette* featured a photo of Stuart holding the ball, accompanied by his wife and daughter Debra.

July started as well as June had ended. On the first day of the month, Stuart hit a triple and his 13th home run, which went over the scoreboard. A few days later, he even sparkled on defense, grabbing a fly ball off the left field wall. But despite Stuart's heroics, the Mustangs were still in 7th place, with a record well below .500. But now they had the pitching they lacked early in the season and were getting consistently strong performances from Daniels, Beene, and Dunn.

In late July, Billings made a managerial change. Paepke went to Salinas and Buck Elliot, who'd played with Billings in 1952, became the new Mustang manager. It made no difference to Stuart, who continued with his hot hitting, smacking homers 20 and 21 on back-to-back nights. Number 20 was a towering drive over the left field fence and #21 a 400-foot shot over the center field fence with two Mustangs aboard. That put him in the Pioneer League home run lead and his average was a robust .340.

On August 9, Stuart homered as a pinch hitter and the following night he blasted two home runs. The next evening, he made it four in three nights, giving him a total of 25 for the year. Two days later #26 helped Dunn, who struck out seven batters in a row at one point, to his 13th win. In his next start, Dunn was even better, striking out 17, three short of the league record. By season's end he had a 15–7 mark and led the league in winning percentage and ERA and tied for the lead with five shutouts.

Meanwhile, Stuart continued with his powerful hitting. A poll of Pioneer League managers unanimously voted him the league's most powerful man at the plate, not much of a surprise, since he was the home run leader, but he was not selected as the one with the most major league potential. That honor went to Buddy Gilbert, whose major league career consisted of seven games with the Reds in 1959.

Stuart was named to the Pioneer League all-star team but lost out on the MVP Award to Don LeJohn. LeJohn, who played a few games with the Dodgers in 1965, was rated the second-best major league prospect. But Stuart had his advocates. Hall of Famer Paul Waner, a singles hitter in his day, watched Stuart in a late-season game and said, "He hits 'em like I couldn't. He has real good power."[11]

Doomed by their horrible start, the Mustangs finished fifth with a 64–68 mark, 13½ games out of first place and out of the playoffs. Attendance was a disappointing 82,000.

Although he didn't arrive in Billings until May, Stuart played in 101 of Mustangs' 132 games, batting .309 with a league-leading 32 home runs (breaking the team record of 31 he'd set three years earlier) and 104 RBI, which placed him sixth. His 1.064 OPS was second in the league, but he struck out 109 times.

At the end of the season, Stuart was assigned to Hollywood, the Pirates top farm team. He had established himself as one of the organization's leading prospects, not just because of his number of home runs, but because of their majestic distances. Still, not many outside of the Pirates organization and the Pioneer League had ever heard of Dick Stuart. That would change in 1956.

4

The Most Sensational Individual Player in the Capital City's Diamond Memory: 1956

Nineteen fifty-six was the greatest year of Dick Stuart's life. He entered the national stage for the first time and for the rest of his career he would refer to the events of that year with a fondness he had for no other year, not even 1960, when the Pirates were World Champions. Winning the World Series was nice, but it was in Lincoln, Nebraska, in 1956 that Dick Stuart became forever known as the man who hit 66 home runs in a single season.

Lincoln was a lot different than Billings. For one thing, it was bigger; with a population[1] of over 100,000 in 1956 it was the second largest city in the state behind Omaha. As the state capital and home to the University of Nebraska, government and higher education were two of its leading employers. Both tend to be growth industries and Lincoln was therefore a city on the move, its population increasing 19 percent from 1950 to 1960.

Lincoln's minor league history dated back to the 1886 Western League, and since 1947 the city had been a member of a reconstituted Class A Western League. The Chiefs played their home games at Sherman Field, which had been constructed in the post war boom of 1947 in anticipation of the Chiefs' entry into the new league. "It was a typical, old-timey park," recalled Bob Wirz, a former MLB executive who was a University of Nebraska undergraduate in 1956. "There were railroad tracks not very far beyond the left field fence and during the game freight trains would rumble by."[2] Sherman was a relatively cozy park, with distances of 330 feet to the left and right field foul poles and 380 feet in dead center field. In addition, the wind generally blew toward left field, making the park even more attractive for right-handed power hitters—like Dick Stuart.

Although the Chiefs finished last in 1955, they were still big news in Lincoln. Since the arrival of legendary coach Bob Devaney in 1962, Nebraska Cornhusker football has been the center of the city's sporting life, but in 1956 and 1957, when Stuart played for the Chiefs, the Nebraska football team was a combined 5–15. "The Chiefs," said Wirz, "were the biggest thing they had going on in town."[3]

For the 1956 campaign, Pittsburgh assigned Larry Shepard to manage the Chiefs. Shepard, 37, had piloted Williamsport of the Eastern League the previous two seasons and was the team's best pitcher in 1955, posting a record of 16–7 with a 3.14 ERA. Although Williamsport's record hadn't been spectacular, Shepard acquired a reputation as a respected, level-headed leader of men and was marked for bigger things.[4]

Lincoln's general manager was Dick Wagner,[5] who at 28 was in his tenth season in professional baseball. He'd taken his first job in 1947 in the Class D Georgia-Florida League and over the next few years rose steadily through the ranks. Like Shepard, Wagner was a prospect. In the 1970s, he would become the General Manager of the Cincinnati Reds and eventually took a job in the commissioners' office under Peter Ueberroth.

But in 1956 Wagner was just another minor league executive trying to make ends meet and scrambling to sell tickets. Before the start of the season, Lincoln civic organizations conducted a competition to see which could sell the most tickets. The 1955 campaign had resulted in 40,000 sales and the goal for 1956 was 50,000 tickets in three days. The drive was a disappointment, as a total of only 31,418 tickets were sold, with the Rotary Club winning the competition by selling 5,335. Wagner needed to find a way to sell more tickets and by the end of the summer he was fortunate enough to have the biggest gate attraction in the minor leagues.

Meanwhile, Shepard prepared his team for the season at the Pirates' minor league camp in Huntsville, Texas. When the players were distributed throughout the organization, Shepard found himself with a very competitive roster. Perhaps his best pitcher was hard-throwing Bennie Daniels (described as a "big Negro right-hander"[6]), who'd played most of the previous season with Stuart at Billings. Left hander Don Rowe[7] was brought up from Waco and left-hander Andy Olson, who later became a National League umpire, from Burlington. At 37 and nursing a tender arm, Shepard would pitch when needed.

One of the best prospects among the hitters was twenty-one-year-old second baseman Kenny Toothman, who attended the 1955 prospects camp with Stuart. Toothman had a fantastic 1954 season at Phoenix, leading the league with 46 stolen bases, driving in 123 runs, and hitting .355. He hadn't done quite as well in 1955. Sam Miley, who could hit but not field, would play somewhere and Reggie Grenald, who'd had an injury-plagued season under Shepard at Williamsport, would man an outfield position.

Stuart began the spring with Hollywood of the Pacific Coast League, where manager Clay Hopper said he was such a bad fielder he would have to hit three home runs a game to help his team, a remark that would come back to haunt him. When camp broke, Stuart was assigned to Lincoln, where he would play left field, right field, or first base.

Dick's competition for the first base job in Lincoln was veteran Bill Jackson. The *Lincoln Star* pointed out that "neither Stuart nor Jackson is polished defensively,"[8] but both had power; Jackson hit 28 homers in 1955. In order to get both of their bats in the lineup, Shepard wound up putting Jackson at first and Stuart in the outfield.

When Stuart arrived in Lincoln, he and several teammates rented rooms on the 70-acre spread of Mrs. Wesley Small, who took in more than a hundred Lincoln Chiefs over the years. Life in the lower minors was tough and it wasn't easy to live on the low salaries and meager meal money. "They'll sleep late," said minor league manager Frank Oceak, "and miss breakfast. They eat heavy at noon, light before a game and eat heavy after a game if they have any meal money left. Some buy meal tickets. Many have baked goods sent to them by their mothers. They usually do their own laundry and they're good customers of the laundromats. At home, the boys live two or three in a room for $5 a week. On the road we put two or three in a room and sometimes have to use a rollaway cot."[9]

Apparently, Mrs. Small's cooking agreed with her boarders, for the team got off to a flying start, winning their first five games. The fourth win featured a game-tying Stuart home run over the Hotel Cornhusker sign on the center field fence, for which the hotel awarded him a $100 bond.

Dick Stuart did not arrive quietly in any town, and Lincoln was no exception. While most Class A minor leaguers lived on a shoestring, Stuart drove a large Cadillac and dressed like a Hollywood movie star. Larry Gerlach, who later became a well-known baseball historian, was a Lincoln teenager who in the summer of 1956 was getting ready to enter high school. He and his friend Kenny Fox were rabid Chiefs fans who attended just about every game, sneaking in for free if possible.

"Kenny and I would go out to Sherman Field before the games," Gerlach recalled, "to watch the players arrive. Sherman was a wooden stadium with a gravel parking lot. We're standing there when this black Cadillac with California plates comes screeching in, throwing up gravel. Out stepped this guy in a lime-green short-sleeved shirt, tan slacks, brown loafers with no socks, shades, and a black ducktail haircut. God, he was handsome. He looked like somebody we'd never seen before. We idolized him from that moment on."[10]

Stuart's appearance and his wardrobe were very important to him. He favored monogrammed apparel, and when he played with the Pirates, he carried garment bags containing four or five different suits on road trips. At times Stuart added a long thin cigar as a prop, and Gerlach recalled that he often ducked out of the dugout in mid-game to sneak a cigarette beneath the stands.

Stu was known for spending inordinate amounts of time combing his hair in front of the clubhouse mirror. In the early days, he relied on local barbers but when he became an established major leaguer, he could afford to have top-flight professionals working on the Stuart coiffure. In 1965, he was paying $15 for a styling session at a time when the average haircut cost around $2 and many major leaguers wore crew cuts. Stuart got his money's worth, since the process took about two-and-a-half hours. "This fellow cuts your hair wet," Stu explained, "because wet hair tends to follow the contour of the head. He gives you two shampoos also and cutting the hair alone takes almost an hour."[11]

As styles changed, Stuart's hairstyle evolved from his 1950s ducktail and after his retirement he wore his hair stylishly long. He always had one of the largest hat sizes on his team, and longer hair made his head even bigger. At one Old Timers game he had to wear a different style of hat because the one the other players wore didn't fit over his hair.

The Lincoln club was plagued by horrible weather early in the season; in 1955, the Chiefs had just two rainouts all season but by May 1, 1956, they already had six. No one realized it at the time, but the postponements would eventually play a critical role in the pennant race.

Stuart batted .343 in his first 35 at bats but had just one home run, and since he lived for the home run, he was disappointed. He didn't hit his second home run until May 9, but he added two more the next day. One was a three-run blast well above the light towers in left field, one of the longest balls ever hit at Sherman Field. Still, with four homers, he was well in arrears of league leader Art Ciutti of Amarillo, who had nine.

By mid–May, the Chiefs were in first place by a half game with a 14–6 record. Stuart had six homers and the Lincoln *Star* said, "Stuart, incidentally, may be on his way to being the most popular player at Sherman Field…. The big fellow loves to swing a bat … granted, he's no Pavlova with a glove, but Dick creates a thrill when he steps up to the plate. He's swinging for the fences and gives out with the thrills when he misses, but when he connects—well, it's a sight to behold."[12]

On May 16, Stuart created a lot of excitement in Amarillo, which was one of his favorite parks that year. The Chiefs beat the Gold Sox 22–10, hitting seven home runs, including three by Stuart. It was the 13th time that a Western League player homered three times in a game. Stuart had a total of five homers during the three-game series, during which Lincoln scored 47 runs. He hit another the next night against Colorado Springs, which gave him 10 for the season in just 80 at bats.

The Chiefs had a tough road trip in May, going 6–7–1 and losing five games in a row, despite a .304 team batting average and 31 home runs in the 14 games. Lincoln had a hard-hitting team in a hard-hitting league. Stuart was batting .328 with 15 homers and 42 RBI, Miley was batting .360, Grenald .355, and Toothman .330 with seven home runs. The problem was pitching. Shepard won his first three decisions, but was at the end of the line as a pitcher; every time he took the mound, he was doing so against his doctor's orders. Daniels and Rowe were pitching well, but the rest of the staff was inconsistent.

In addition to the seven road defeats, the Chiefs suffered a monetary loss in Topeka when a burglar broke into their locker room, pried open the valuables trunk and made off with 8 rings, 12 watches, and 18 billfolds (apparently one man on the 19-man roster did not carry a billfold), with a total take of $736. Fortunately, the loss was covered by Topeka's insurance.

Umpires in the Class A Western League weren't much better off than those in the Pioneer League; apparently their pay was so low that some turned to crime, as three Western League umps were fired for stealing baseballs.

Umpire Max Stone was a particular villain in Lincoln. Stone was an actor during the off-season, sometimes performing Shakespeare, and he transferred his knack for drama from the stage to minor league ballparks. During one game, Stone tossed peanuts to Stuart, who ate them between pitches. His antics agitated fans, managers, and players; he once got into a fight with a Sioux City player.[13] Fans loved to heckle him and Stone reveled in the abuse. One creative Des Moines critic shouted, "We know you've got a good eye, Stone. Now why don't you take it out of your pocket and use it."[14]

On May 30, after ejecting Shepard over a balk call, Stone began arguing with fans in the right field stands. He demanded that Dick Wagner eject them and when Wagner refused, the two got into an argument.

Stone found himself in trouble again on June 18 when he ordered the lights turned on although there appeared to be sufficient sunlight to play without them. Shepard said he was crazy and protested so vehemently that he got himself ejected again. Wagner said he would bill the Western League for the electricity.

A few weeks later, Stone ejected Toothman and Rowe for yakking at him from the bench and told four other Chiefs to repair to the clubhouse until they were needed. "Plate Umpire Max Stone was at his crowd-baiting best," wrote *Star* sports editor Don Bryant. Stone, he added, "revels in glaring at players and fans."[15] It was all part of the show, as entertaining as the antics of Max Patkin and Jackie Price.

There was more entertainment on June 8, when Shepard was delivered to the field by helicopter. Stuart hit his 22nd homer that night and was on a pace to challenge several records, the first being the Lincoln mark of 29 set by Lou Limmer in 1949. On June 10, Stuart belted two more home runs as Daniels won his fifth game without a loss. Stuart's home runs were getting attention, and for the first time, people around the country were learning about the brash personality of Dick Stuart. Bryant called him "Mr. Confidence."[16] "You'd have to look a long ways," he wrote, "to find a more confident young man than Dick Stuart."[17] After Stuart hit two homers against Pueblo, Bryant greeted him with, "Hi, lucky." Most youngsters would have ducked their heads sheepishly, but not Dick Stuart. "Lucky I didn't hit three, you mean," he countered.[18]

Bryant was a friendly, outgoing man, very skilled at generating publicity, who later parlayed his newspaper career into a job as Sports Information Director at the University of Nebraska. He realized he had a gold mine in Dick Stuart and cultivated him all season. Stuart called him his good luck charm and throughout that glorious summer Bryant gave his readers insight into the thoughts that coursed through the brain of Dick Stuart and the many words that emerged from his mouth.

In June, the Western League learned that its Sioux City franchise was in trouble. The team was in last place with a 12–46 record and hemorrhaging money. Owner Adam Pratt, who'd run the team since its inception, said he would withdraw from the league unless Western League President O'Neal Hobbs agreed to institute a split season and local boosters sold 12,000 tickets. He also said that the parent St. Louis Cardinals were not providing enough talent and asked the league to send him some decent players. Hobbs agreed to call a league meeting at Lincoln's Hotel Cornhusker to discuss the situation.

Pratt was in a difficult situation. He'd been losing money for years and was the only man who owned a Western League team individually; Des Moines was owned by the Cubs and the other six teams were community-owned. Pratt was one of the founders of the Western League and well-liked by the other owners, who wanted to find a way to help him out of his dilemma. One possibility was for the league to operate the team and have them play all their games on the road. Other possibilities included finding a new owner or moving the team to another city.

On June 15, the Western League agreed to a split season, which would give Sioux City a fresh start, and the local business community pledged to generate $15,000 in ticket sales and take over the team in 1957. Pratt, who owned the stadium, agreed to sell it to the new owners at a nominal price.[19]

The Chiefs, who were running neck and neck in a battle with Topeka for first place, were not happy with the prospect of a split season. Shepard called it "ridiculous." "I've never heard of a league doing a thing like that," he said, "for one team at the expense of the others. From now on it looks like any team that gets ten games out of first place will just ask everyone else to cancel the record and start over."[20]

The situation was further complicated by President Hobbs' ruling that makeup games of prior rainouts would count in the first half standings. The Chiefs had four games to make up and Topeka had one, which meant that the first half standings would not be determined until well into the second half. Most games were made up as part of doubleheaders, and Hobbs ruled that the first game would be the makeup and the second the regularly scheduled contest.

Meanwhile, Stuart continued to hit home runs. On June 17 he hit two to tie Limmer's Lincoln record with the season not even half over. The next night he broke the record with #30, a shot that was one of the longest home runs ever hit in Pueblo,[21] a three-run blast over the left field fence. It was at that point, Stuart said later, that Branch Rickey, Jr., sent him the ten dollars he had bet that Stuart wouldn't hit 20 home runs at Lincoln.[22]

Stuart hit three homers (35, 36, and 37) on June 24 in a 13–2 win against Albuquerque, giving him eleven in the past six games. The Chiefs set a league record with eight homers in all and had already broken the Lincoln record for homers in a season, besting the 103 hit by the 1949 team.

With one game left in the season's first half, Lincoln was in second place, 1½ games behind Topeka, pending the completion of the four postponements. The situation was further confused when the *Star* indicated that the top four teams in the overall standings would make the playoffs, which would render the first half title meaningless.

On the final day of the first half, the Chiefs defeated Albuquerque 11–5 to move past Topeka into first place by percentage points. Stuart hit his 40th home run, a majestic shot that exited the park over the 420 foot sign. The next night, with Branch Rickey, Sr., in the stands, he didn't hit any homers but slapped four hard singles in four at bats. "My boy, that was quite an authoritative display of hitting," Rickey said afterward. "Naw," Stuart replied, "no homers."[23]

"From what I've seen," Rickey told reporters, "Stuart could be in Pittsburgh any day.... He convinced me that all this home run hitting hasn't gone to his head.... He swings with definite authority and has a fine arm."[24] "Why, it's absolutely amazing.... The boy is definitely an eccentric fellow, but he has great confidence and that's important."[25]

Rickey was disappointed in the progress of Lincoln outfielder Howie Goss, who he thought had great ability but lacked confidence. "It's too bad," wrote Bryant, "there isn't some way for Howie, who has speed and power to burn, to confiscate some of Dick Stuart's confidence."[26]

It was not Stuart's confidence but his home runs that were attracting national attention. Bryant said that if Lincoln fans went to Sherman Field "they'll be viewing the most sensational individual player in the Capital City's diamond memory."[27] Wagner was overwhelmed with requests for interviews and photos.

After hitting 23 home runs in June, Stuart had a total of 40 and was batting .339 with 95 RBI. Miley was also at .339 while Toothman was hitting .319. Bill Jackson was hitting with power. Even the Chiefs' pitchers were a threat at the plate; Rowe was hitting .317 and Daniels .311. Although Goss had 10 home runs, he was batting a disappointing .238. The first half standings, after Topeka lost its makeup game, were:

	Wins	*Losses*	*Pct.*	*GB*
Lincoln	42	25	.627	—
Topeka	44	27	.620	—

On July 2, Stuart hit three home runs in a game for the third time, giving him a total of 43 and inching him to within one of the "modern" Western League record of 44 set by Pat Seery of Colorado Springs in 1950. The all-time mark was 49 by Guy Sturdy in 1926. Stuart tied Seery's record on July 3 and broke it a day later.

On July 6, the *Star* ran a long feature article on Stuart. "My next step," he said, "is breaking the all-time Western League record (49), which shouldn't take too long. And after that I might as well shoot for the moon—the all-time minor league record [72]. I'll keep my fingers crossed and hope the Good Lord is on my side."

He was asked about his prospects for a major league career. "If I can improve my fielding," he replied, "and correct some flaws in my batting, I believe I stand a good chance to make the majors. Defensively, I think I have improved over my previous years [the night before he had leaped against the right field fence to rob Topeka's Al Weygandt of a home run], but I still have a great deal of work to do in this department before being of major league caliber. I hope that my hitting will carry me to the big leagues. And if I ever do play up there I will be there to stay." He said he was looking forward to a visit from his wife and daughter, who were arriving for Dick Stuart Night that evening; he hoped to hit a few home runs for them.

Stuart told Bryant his hero was Ted Williams. "If I could only become half the hitter he is," Stuart said, "I would be well-satisfied. Also, I would be well-satisfied to be making half his salary."[28] Bryant ended the article by saying that Stuart's main goal was for Lincoln to win the Western League title, which one would never have guessed from Big Stu's remarks.

The following evening, 4,027 fans, the largest crowd since 1949, turned out for Dick Stuart Night. The Chiefs beat Topeka for their fifth straight win, giving them a 9–1 mark for the second half. Stuart was given a golf cart, a Polaroid camera, approximately $800 in cash, and various other gifts. As he looked over the gifts, Stuart joked, "Where's the car?"[29] a remark that was later used unfairly to illustrate his selfishness and ungratefulness. Nebraska governor Vic Anderson named Stuart an Admiral in the Nebraska Navy. Although Stuart didn't reward his fans with a home run, he did drive in his 108th run of the season.

Stuart's home runs had drawn attention to the Nebraska city. "Dick Stuart's hot bat," Bryant wrote, "has put Lincoln on the baseball map this summer. You can't pick up a newspaper anywhere without finding a story about the big slugger—datelined Lincoln, Nebraska…. Guys like Nellie Fox, Bobby Shantz [former Chiefs who'd become major league stars], Dick Stuart and the 1956 Chiefs have given the capital city of Nebraska tremendous amounts of advertising that money couldn't buy."[30] "Seldom, if ever, has a Class A club been able to field such an array of power."[31]

Stuart was Bryant's favorite subject. "Dick is good copy," he wrote. "He likes to talk and modesty isn't one of his obvious virtues. If you want to write about him or his home runs, he'll supply plenty of material."[32] Bryant wrote a long article about Stuart for *The Sporting News* in mid–July from which readers learned about Stuart's home runs, his role as a movie extra, and his background in sports. After lauding his power hitting, Bryant added, "His defensive ability is not on a par with his offense, but he has improved somewhat since last spring when, while training with Hollywood (Pacific Coast) he was told, 'You'll have to hit three homers a game to help the Stars.'"[33]

That remark, of course, had been made by Hollywood manager Clay Hopper, and when Stuart began receiving massive amounts of press coverage, he clipped out the articles and mailed them to Hopper as a reminder.[34]

Stuart also kept his parents up to date on his accomplishments. "He sent a lot of (newspaper) clippings to my parents," said his younger brother Daryl. "Every time he hit a home run, he would send a clipping and write, 'N. 10, No. 11….'"[35]

On July 9, the Chiefs won a makeup from Sioux City 19–3, and two wins in the three remaining makeup games would give them the first half title. They were running two races at once, and on the 13th, they increased their second half lead to 3½ games. Daniels won his 10th decision without a loss and Stuart accomplished a feat far rarer for him than a home run when he was part of a double steal. The following night the Chiefs lost and were held to just one hit, but it was Stuart's 48th homer, which brought him to within one of the all-time WL record.

The record was tied and broken four days later, as Stuart hit his 49th and 50th against Albuquerque at home. There was nothing cheap about either homer, a 450-foot two-run shot in the 4th followed by a grand slam an inning later. After rounding the bases, Stuart jumped on home plate with both feet as the crowd went berserk. Not only had the big

Lincoln outfielder broken the league record, he did it with 49 games left in the season, giving him a good shot at the all-time minor league record of 72, set by Roswell's Joe Bauman just two years earlier. It had taken Guy Sturdy 161 games to hit 49, while Stuart hit his 50th in his 93rd game. "I sure picked a good time to break the record, huh?" Stuart told a reporter. "With the bases loaded. Boy, that makes it an even greater thrill."[36] Stuart was also thrilled by the distance, which he thought made his homers even more special.

In Stuart's era, home run distance was estimated, usually with a bias toward longer, and very few tape measure home runs actually featured a tape measure. Many years later, Bob Wirz was involved with the IBM project to measure distances to various points in major league ballparks and report home run distances more accurately. "The number of 500 foot home runs dropped markedly after they started that project," Wirz said.[37] But in Stuart's era, if someone said a home run went 500 or even 600 feet (his longest reported blast was 650 feet in Pueblo), that was what went in the books.

The following night, the Chiefs won another makeup game, clinching a tie for the first half title, as Stuart wasted no time hitting #51. On July 20, he hit three more home runs against Pueblo, giving him a total of 54 and 131 RBI, two RBI short of the mark established by Ken Landenberger of Colorado Springs in 1952. The record had not done much for Landenberger, who was still in the Western League with Sioux City.

Each of Stuart's three homers, in front of a Sherman Field Elk's Night crowd of 2,540, came after Reg Grenald drew a walk. The first barely made it over the left field wall ("A rather weak shot for him"[38]). By the time he hit #53, the Chiefs were trailing 7–2, and Stuart's blast made in 7–4. A two-run homer by Marcos Cobos made it 7–6 when Stuart came to bat with Grenald on first in the eighth. "It couldn't happen again," Bryant wrote. But it did, as Stuart's towering fly ball landed near the railroad embankment beyond the left field wall to give the Chiefs an 8–7 lead. After Pueblo tied the game, Sam Miley won it with a homer in the 11th. Stuart said the homers were a going away present for his wife and daughter.

Stuart wasn't the only Chief hitting home runs. Cobos, filling in for the injured Chiefs catcher, hit five homers in seven days. Bill Jackson won a game with a ninth-inning homer. By the 24th of July, when Stuart hit his 55th, Lincoln was within one of the modern Western League mark of 164 home runs in a season, set by Sioux City in 1950.

The next day, the Chiefs clinched the first half title, despite Hobbs' quirky ruling, by winning another makeup game. Stuart hit #56, the thirteenth homer he'd hit at Amarillo. "Stuart … just another night," read the caption under his photo.[39] Unfortunately for Amarillo manager Chuck Stevens, it was just another night of watching balls sail over the outfield walls. "It's just murder there," he said, "because so many routine outs sail over the short fences."[40]

On the first day of August, Stuart hit #58. The 59th came two days later, the same day that pitcher Bennie Daniels hit his eighth homer and won his 12th game against just one loss.[41] With about a month left in the season, Stuart needed 13 homers to tie the all-time record, and it seemed possible. After all, he'd hit 23 homers in June and 17 in July.

Home run #60, which matched Babe Ruth's 1927 total, came on August 5. It wasn't the titanic blast Sherman Field fans were accustomed to; it barely cleared the left field fence and appeared to be aided by a last second gust of wind. The 2,001 fans burst into mad applause, and Stuart tipped his cap as he crossed home plate. He hit #61 on August 6 and Bauman's record seemed well within reach.

It was not to be. Stuart, bothered by a bone bruise on his hand, soon encountered his first home run drought since the early days of the season. It was August 17 before he hit another homer, a line drive, three-run shot against Pueblo.

Four days later, against Colorado Springs, Stuart went 0 for 8 in a doubleheader, striking out five times. That made him 0 for 13 for the series; he was in the midst of as slump that would eventually extend to two hits in 57 at bats. Even worse, in the second game of the doubleheader Stuart, who'd been moved to first base after Bill Jackson broke his wrist, dropped a throw with the bases loaded to let in the winning run.

Shepard said he decided first base was the position for Stuart after the fleet Goss was injured. "As soon as I had to replace Goss with an ordinary center fielder," he said, "balls started dropping in right-center for doubles and triples. Then it hit me. I realized that while Goss was out there Stu had been jogging toward flies, yelling 'Go get it, Goss!' Goss had been getting them but the new man couldn't. I decided Stu had to be a first baseman."[42]

Despite his slump, Stuart remained big news around the Western League. When the Chiefs visited Albuquerque, Dukes general manager William (Perk) Purnage posted about a thousand wanted posters with pictures of Stuart around town. They said he was sought for "losing more than 60 baseballs" and "embarrassing Western League pitchers." The reward for his capture was three good games of baseball. Stuart managed just a single in 12 at bats during the three-game series and struck out seven times, but he loved the attention. Even if his picture was on a genuine wanted poster, as least everyone would see it.

Stuart finally hit #63 on August 24 against Des Moines, but the big story that day was a brawl started by Lincoln left hander Don Rowe. "I had a pretty good reputation as a guy who would fight," Rowe said.[43] When he was knocked out of the box, he shouted at Marty Garber on the Des Moines bench. After the game, Rowe went after Garber, who wound up being punched by Lincoln catcher Joe Zavatarro. Stuart plowed into the melee and lifted up a Des Moines player and pulled him out of the fray. The fight was the only thing the Chiefs won that evening, their loss dropping them seven games behind with 11 to play.

The next day, Pirate general manager Joe Brown spoke at a luncheon honoring the Chiefs. "We feel there are several players on your team," he told the audience, "that are slated for major league careers. I honestly feel there are several players on your team that will be in Pirate uniforms before too long"[44] He noted, however, that the most important thing he looked for in a player was determination, which did not bode well for Dick Stuart. Governor Anderson made Brown an admiral in the Nebraska Navy, giving the state more admirals than any other landlocked state.

Brown and Branch Rickey, Jr., then went out to watch the doubleheader with Des Moines and didn't like what they saw of Dick Stuart. He made two errors, then hit a grounder to short, took about three steps to first, flipped the bat away in disgust and headed for the dugout. "Thank the Lord my father never saw that," Rickey said. "They would have had to take him away in an ambulance."[45]

The next time up, Stuart hit a fly ball to left field and stood at the plate and watched it. After the game, Rickey went to the Lincoln clubhouse and told Stuart, "I wouldn't have you on a major league team. I wouldn't have you within a thousand miles. You don't know what this game is about. Why, if you pulled that stuff in the major leagues, why a manager would…."

Stuart interrupted him. "Well," he said, "I still hit 63 home runs." "Hit 63 again," Rickey thundered. "Stay here and hit 63 every year. Have a wonderful time. Enjoy it.

You'll be here all your life." As he started to leave, Stuart asked, "How much am I going to get when you bring me up to Pittsburgh?"[46]

On the 28th of August Stuart hit what looked to be #64, but as it was leaving Sherman Field, it struck a light tower and bounced back for a double. It was the second time Stuart had hit the tower and lost a home run, for which he blamed Shepard, who set the ground rules prior to the season. It looked as though Stuart's quest for 72 or 73 home runs, which looked quite possible a few weeks earlier, was doomed and he thought he knew the reason. Don Bryant was on vacation. "I wish Bryant would get back," Stuart said. "I can't hit them out when he's gone."[47]

The next night, Stuart, even in Bryant's absence, managed to hit #64. He hit two more before the season ended, giving him Western League records for home runs (66), RBI (158), total bases (385), and strikeouts (171). On four occasions he hit three homers in a game. Thanks in large part to Stuart, the Chiefs set a Western League record with 208 homers, breaking not only the modern record but also the all-time mark of 202 set by Tulsa in 1929.

"At the end of 12 games that season," he later told journalist Jimmy Breslin, "I had just one home run. At the end of 65 I had 40. And at the end of 103 games I had 60. Isn't that something? I could stand flat-footed and left-handed in batting practice and still hit it out of the park.... The pitching here is bad. If the pitching was good I would have hit 90 home runs. I had to chase a lot of bad pitches to get those home runs."[48]

The friendly dimensions of Sherman Field had not been the only reason for Stuart's remarkable feats, as 34 of his homers came on the road. The disquieting feature of his play, in addition to the strikeouts, was his fielding, as he posted a .920 average in the outfield and .945 at first base.

After all the machinations regarding the split season and the plan to have the top four teams in the playoffs, the league decided Lincoln and Amarillo (which won the second half title) would play a best-of-seven series for the Western League championship. The winning team would split $1,500 while the losers would divide $1,000. It was the first time Lincoln had been in the playoffs since 1949.

The series, matching two powerful teams in a couple of cozy ballparks, promised to be a high-scoring one. Amarillo's 29-year-old veteran Art Ciutti led the league with a .364 average (the highest mark since the Western League had been re-established in 1947) and added 46 home runs. Even though Bill Jackson, who'd hit 24 homers, missed the series with his broken wrist, Lincoln had Stuart, Toothman, who hit .327 with 23 homers, and Goss (23 homers). It also promised to be a competitive series, since the two teams had split 20 games evenly during the season.

Daniels (14–3) started the first game against Amarillo's Hugh Blanton. It was a chilly and windy 58 degrees, with the wind blowing in from left field. Stuart hit a tremendous homer that cut right through the wind, but the Chiefs were defeated 4–2. Daniels pitched a complete game but was victimized by a couple of bad hops on the rough Amarillo infield.

The next day, the Chiefs evened the series with an 8–2 win. John Mungo (Jackie) Brown, a 23-year-old right hander obtained from Williamsport late in the season, struck out 21 Amarillo batters, breaking the league record of 18 set by Dodger phenom Karl Spooner in 1953. He gave up four hits and walked eight, and undoubtedly threw a remarkably high number of pitches.[49] But that was 1956 and as long as he continued to pile up strikeouts, Shepard left him in.

The Chiefs took a 2–1 game lead with a 9–5 win on September 7, on two Goss home runs. That ended the Amarillo portion of the series, and the Chiefs took a train to Newton, Kansas, and then a bus to Lincoln for the final games.

Don Rowe, who'd pitched a no-hitter during the regular season, won Game 4, 6–0 with a two-hit, 11-strikeout performance, as Stuart homered for the 68th time. The Chiefs won the title the next day as Daniels pitched a four-hitter. Goss was the batting hero once more, singling in the winning runs in a 5–2 victory. For the first time, the Lincoln Chiefs were champions of the Western League.

It had been quite a season for Dick Stuart and the Chiefs. Stuart was unanimously selected as the right fielder on the Western League all-star team. Toothman and Daniels also made the first team and Miley and Manager Shepard were picked for the second team. Although Lincoln won the league title, they drew a disappointing total of 92,554 fans, partly attributable to the terrible early season weather, and didn't come close to selling out the playoff games. Wagner said the team made a small profit, however, due to the fact that they had controlled expenses.

At the end of the season, Bryant gave his choices for the top performers in various categories. Miley, Toothman, and Goss were named the best major league prospects (Stuart was not included); Umpire Max Stone was "Most Aggravating" and Stuart was named the "Biggest Loafer" and "Loudest." In a poll of Western League managers to determine the best major league prospects, Stuart and Toothman were the only unanimous choices.[50]

Just about every baseball fan in America knew about Stuart and his 66 home runs (he always reminded people he actually hit 68, including his two during the playoffs), and for the first time people cared what he said. For many years afterward, he signed his autograph with a star over the "i" in Dick and the number "66" above his name and carried the numerals "66" with him to hang in every place he lived. He placed a sticker reading "66" on his suitcase. It was his defining moment.

But the goal of any minor leaguer is not just to excel in Class A ball; they want to make it to the major leagues, and hitting more than 60 home runs was no guarantee of a spot on a big league roster. Several minor league players had hit more than 60 home runs in a season, but only one of them, Tony Lazzeri, went on to have a meaningful major league career.

In 1995, researcher Ernest J. Green analyzed the records of the men who hit more than 60 home runs. Their average age was 28, much older than the typical major league prospect. At 23, Stuart was the youngest. He had the fourth best ratio of home runs per at bat (7.92), which was better than the ratios of Babe Ruth in 1927 (9.0) and Roger Maris in 1961 (9.67).[51]

A major factor in home run production, Green concluded, was altitude. Most of the big home run seasons took place in parks with an average altitude of 1,884 feet above sea level. Balls hit through the thin air of high altitudes, of course, travel farther than those hit at sea level and the thinner air makes it more difficult to throw a good curve ball. Roswell, New Mexico, where Bauman stroked his record 72, had an altitude of 3,573 feet. Lincoln, at 1,176 feet above sea level, was lower than most.[52] Prior to 1954, 37 men had hit more than 50 home runs in a minor league season. Seven of them played in the West Texas–New Mexico League or the Longhorn League, which had a number of parks at relatively high altitudes.[53]

Lazzeri was the first to break the magic barrier, hitting 60 for Salt Lake City in 1925.

Salt Lake was a member of the Pacific Coast League, which had a 197-game schedule that year; Lazzeri played in 192 of them, batting 710 times. Despite the 60 homers, major league scouts were skeptical. They wondered whether the light air of the Utah mountains had contributed to the second baseman's power and they worried about Lazzeri's epilepsy. The Yankees took a chance and were rewarded, for he played through the 1939 season, hit 169 homers, and was an integral part of New York's Murderers' Row. Still, he never hit more than 18 homers in a major league season.

Of the others, only first baseman Joe Hauser logged any significant time in the majors, and that came before he hit 63 homers for Baltimore in 1930 and 69 for Minneapolis in 1933. Hauser had three good seasons for Connie Mack's Athletics in 1922–24 before breaking his leg at the age of 25. After that, he was never the same. By the time he was setting home run marks in the minors, he was old and damaged and major league clubs weren't interested. Further, home runs in Minneapolis were suspect due to the fact that the right field fence was only 279 feet from home plate.

Bob Lennon, who hit 64 homers in 1954, might have had a better major league career if he hadn't been plagued by injuries. He could field, run, and had a good arm before he hurt it. Prior to 1954, Lennon had never been a prodigious slugger; in his best season he'd hit 24 homers. Two things happened to change his luck. First, he altered his stance, assuming more of a crouch, and second, he joined the Nashville Vols, who played in Sulphur Dell Park, where the right field fence was just 262 feet from home plate. "We couldn't pitch sidearm," Lefty Gomez once said, "because we scraped our knuckles on the right field screen."[54] Forty-two of Lennon's 64 homers were hit at Sulphur Dell. During the 61 years of the Southern Association's existence, all eight men who hit 40 or more home runs were left-handed hitters who player their home games in Nashville.

The other 60-homer men, Moose Clabaugh, Bob Crues, and Joe Bauman, were never really serious prospects. Their feats were achieved in the low minors and there were extenuating circumstances. Clabaugh, who hit 62 in the Class D East Texas League in 1926, was a terrible fielder who hit nearly two-thirds of his round trippers at home, where the right field fence was just 250 feet from home plate.

Crues hit 69 in 1948 and lost one when an umpire mistakenly ruled a blast off the scoreboard in play. His 254 RBI were an all-time record. Like Clabaugh, Crues played in the low minors, the Class C West Texas–New Mexico League. He benefited not only from a cozy ballpark, but one that had favorable prevailing winds.

Bauman, an imposing 6'5" and 245 pounds, was the all-time minor league leader with 72. He played his entire career in the low minors so he could be near his business interests and spent three of his prime years playing semi-pro ball. Bauman was 32 when he set his record in Roswell, New Mexico, where he played first base, drove the team bus, and worked at his Texaco station when the team was at home. The Class C Longhorn League had short fences, thin air, and prevailing winds.

When it became apparent that Bauman had a chance at Crues' record of 69 homers, *Sports Illustrated* and *Life* Magazine sent camera crews to record the quest. Bauman didn't disappoint them. He hit 13 home runs in his last 14 games, including three in a season-ending doubleheader. The 72 homers came in just 138 games.

Hitting 60 home runs in the minors was not a sure ticket to the majors. Would Stuart be another Tony Lazzeri or just another Joe Bauman or Bob Crues, an interesting story of fleeting baseball fame? *Sports Illustrated* thought Stuart was different from the other sluggers. "At 23," it opined, "Stuart is on the way up.... [Ken] Guettler (the other

60-homer man of 1956) on the other hand, describes himself as a 29-year-old outfielder with a crooked right arm, poor vision and 11 years of minor league baseball behind him. He doesn't expect to make the majors ever."[55]

Despite his 66 homers, many people didn't expect Stuart to make the majors. "I don't think he's a big league prospect," said Pueblo manager Ray Hathaway. "But I will say he can hit a ball a long, long way." Others thought he had a lot of holes in his swing and that good pitching would neutralize him. Manager Lou Klein of Des Moines added, "I don't think he'll ever hit the big league fastball." Nearly all opposing Western League managers said he'd need to improve both his attitude and his fielding.

Back then, people didn't talk about Stuart's fielding that much, although the home runs had called some attention to it. *Sports Illustrated* referred to Stuart's portrayal of a dead soldier in a movie called *D-Day, The Sixth of June,* and said that several of Stuart's teammates thought he played the outfield the same way. But he wasn't known as Dr. Strangeglove or celebrated as one of the worst fielders in baseball. That legend would begin the following spring.

5

Jesus, There Goes Dick Stuart: 1957

Dick Stuart was on top of the world in 1956, but in 1957, he hit bottom. It didn't appear he was headed there in the fall of 1956 when, following his historic season at Lincoln, the Pirates promoted Stuart to Hollywood of the Pacific Coast League and invited him to the Pittsburgh training camp in Fort Myers, Florida. Not many players jumped from Lincoln to the National League, but Stuart, fresh off his 66 homers, was as supremely confident as ever. Before he arrived in camp, he said, "If I can play regularly, I'll hit anywhere. I always have and always will. My dream for the future is to break Babe Ruth's record and you can quote me, some day I will."[1]

Major league scouts didn't share Stuart's lofty opinion of himself. A scouting report published before the start of the 1957 season read, "Big, powerfully built fellow whose only interest is home runs. Tries to hit every ball out of sight and succeeds occasionally. Has terrific power but can be pitched to. Murders low pitches, but high ball usually makes him look silly. Adequate arm and average runner. Stubborn about exploiting his raw ability in other departments. Won't work to improve his shoddy fielding. Not very good team man. Could help big league club with his bat but not as a regular."[2]

Before the Pirates' first exhibition game, Stuart was holding court in the locker room, boasting about his hitting, when outfielder Lee Walls, who played with Stuart at Modesto, walked by and said, "You have to learn to use the glove up here, too, you know. If you could field like me, you'd have it made. We'll be reading about you in Columbus or Hollywood this summer."

After Walls walked away Stuart told the reporter, "If Walls could hit like me and I could field like him, this game would be a cinch. The way he can field, if he could handle a bat like me, he'd be making $30,000 a year right now."[3] Later reports modified the exchange to quote Stuart saying, "If you had my color, Mouse, you'd be making $30,000 a year." "Well, I hope the people in Hollywood like your color, Mouth," Walls supposedly replied, "cuz that's where you'll wind up."[4]

Stuart's first appearance on the major league scene received mixed reviews. While he was a bit too brash for Lee Walls, Les Biederman of the *Pittsburgh Press* found Stuart "a most refreshing young man. He has oodles of confidence in his ability to swing a bat.... The only shake of the head comes when they think of his fielding ... yet, there are those who say the kid isn't that bad and he's getting a bum rap."[5]

David Condon was also in Stuart's corner. "The stories about Stuart," he wrote, "make one anticipate a Ring Lardner character suddenly come to life.... But when you

5. Jesus, There Goes Dick Stuart: 1957

meet Stuart, you find him a pleasant young man. Cocksure and confident, yes. Brash, yes. But he's no busher."

Then Condon presented Stuart's thoughts, mostly, of course, about himself. When asked about his 66 home runs, Stuart reminded Condon it was actually 68. Could he break Babe Ruth's single season home run record? Possibly, although he'd have to hit a lot on the road, since Forbes Field was a difficult park for home runs. Could he hit 30 home runs for the Pirates in 1957? Sure, since pitchers at higher levels had good control and would give him better pitches to hit. Would the Pirates bring him north? "If they don't, it's not my fault." If they did, he was certain he would hit more home runs than Pittsburgh slugger Frank Thomas or anyone else on the team.

What about his fielding? "[I]'m not much of a fielder," Stuart admitted. "Fly balls some fielders'd get in their pockets I have to take on a bounce." What about a movie career? "I've quit. Not enough money." Would he go back to the movies if he became famous? "Sure, if the price was right." Did he regret not going to college? "They couldn't pay me to go to college."[6] While Condon said Stuart was no busher, there were many baseball men who, after reading Condon's quotes, thought that was exactly what he was.

Stuart always had a great appreciation for a dollar, and when a Fort Myers merchant offered five dollars for the first Pirate homer of the spring, he took notice.[7] When he was the first to homer, Stuart returned to the dugout, took off his spikes and made his way to the press box in his stocking feet to collect his money. Pulling his leg, someone (Abrams suspected Dick Groat) told him that Al Abrams of the *Pittsburgh Post-Gazette* was the man to see. "A tall, handsome youngster," Abrams recalled, "still in uniform, sweaty and out of breath from a dash up two flights of stairs to the press box, shouted at me, 'Where do I go to get my five bucks?'"

To show that the first homer was no fluke, Stuart hit five in his first four exhibitions, including one off White Sox lefty Billy Pierce, one of the American League's best pitchers. When Stuart hit his home run off Pierce, his teammates shook his hand when he returned to the bench. After the next one they gave him the silent treatment. When Stuart realized what was happening, he said, "Don't worry boys, there's plenty more where that came from."[8] Then he walked the length of the bench, shaking hands with everyone.

It was an auspicious beginning, but it wasn't long before Stuart and manager Bobby Bragan were at loggerheads. Bragan, known as Bad Boy Bragan or Bobby Braggin, was typical of major league managers of the 1950s. Men like Leo Durocher, Eddie Stanky, and Chuck Dressen made it clear that they were the boss; players were expected to bow to their authority and tolerate whatever insults they threw at them. They were small, mouthy men with large egos who battled with umpires, opposing players, and often their own players. It was inevitable that two men with egos like Bragan and Stuart would clash.

Bragan, like many managers, had been a player of limited ability who was willing to do whatever it took to stay in the big leagues.[9] He started his major league career as a shortstop with some sorry Philadelphia Phillies teams, but soon realized he didn't have the skills to be a top-flight defensive infielder. Bragan therefore donned a mask and mitt and learned to catch in order to prolong his career.

After Bragan was traded to the Dodgers in 1943, he met Branch Rickey and Leo Durocher, each of whom would have a profound influence on his career. He listened to Rickey's famous "skull sessions" and studied Durocher carefully, for he knew that when the top players returned after the war, his big league career would probably be over. He wanted to remain in baseball, and hoped to learn enough and make sufficient connections to get a job coaching or managing in the minor leagues.

Bragan spent two years in the Army and when he returned to the Dodgers in 1947, he found a rookie named Jackie Robinson in the Brooklyn training camp. As a southerner, Bragan didn't like the idea of playing with a black man, and asked to be traded. The Dodgers declined and Bragan came to like and respect Robinson.

When his major league playing career ended in 1948, Bragan took a job managing in the Dodger farm system. When Rickey left Brooklyn for Pittsburgh, he made him manager of the Pirates' top farm club in Hollywood. In three years in the Pacific Coast League, Bragan finished first, second, and third and in 1956 he replaced Fred Haney as manager of the Pirates.

Bragan was a disciplinarian who often fined Pirate players for mental errors, once docking outfielder Bob Skinner $10 for failing to slide and on another occasion fining catcher Danny Kravitz $20 for ignoring a sign. The Pirates had a young team and Bragan's irritable carping and annoying fines got under their tender skins. His 1956 Pirates won six more games that they had in 1955, but the additional wins came at the price of a number of disgruntled players. If he didn't show more improvement in 1957, Bragan would be on the hot seat.

The pairing of the intense Bragan and the boastful, nonchalant Stuart had the potential for fireworks. Of course, Stuart was not a good match for most baseball lifers, who considered baseball the most important thing in the world and winning the most important thing in baseball. If players wanted the manager to like them, they at least had to pay lip service to winning and not focus on their personal accomplishments. In 1957, that was not in the nature of Dick Stuart.

Although he'd been moved to first base late in the 1956 season, Stuart spent most of the spring in the outfield, and after watching him for a few days, Bragan shuddered at the thought of Stuart trying to cover Forbes Field's spacious outer garden. Stuart could run, Bragan admitted, and he had a good arm. But he didn't seem to get to many fly balls and didn't appear concerned when he didn't. "If Stuart wants to catch the ball, okay," Bragan said. "If he doesn't, he takes it on the first bounce."[10] He called Stuart "the goshawfulest fielder I've ever seen."[11]

"I took him aside the other day and talked to him like a father," Bragan added.[12] He told Stuart he had an opportunity to make the team because of his hitting, but was killing his chances with his lackadaisical attitude toward defense. "He drives me nuts when he goes after a fly ball or plays it nonchalantly," Bragan said.[13] "If he'd concentrate, he could get good enough to be just bad."[14]

Fielding drills didn't seem to help. "I tried to hit to him before the game," Bragan said in exasperation, "but he says he prefers to conserve his strength for the game itself.... So I decided to hit to him after games but he catches one or two, then tries to take a rest."[15] Not only was Bragan exasperated; he was perplexed. Most rookies would do anything to make a major league team, but this rookie didn't seem to care.

One area in which Stuart was not lackadaisical was self-promotion. Columnist Oscar Ruhl wrote, "[Stuart] makes a big hit with writers visiting the Pirate dugout. The California kid is a refreshing personality and holds nothing back. The other day he picked up a copy of the *Pittsburgh Press* in which Les Biederman had written a column about Stuart. Dick was disappointed when he discovered a picture of Mickey Mantle above his own photo. So, folding the paper to hide the Yankee star's pic, he proceeded to read about his favorite subject, Dick Stuart."[16]

On another occasion, Stuart asked his teammates what number was on his back. It was 5, which he pointed out was also Joe DiMaggio's number, and said he hoped to be as good as DiMaggio one day. At least he didn't say he was already as good as DiMaggio.

In 1957, rookies were supposed to be deferential, say "yes, sir," and "no, sir," and speak when spoken to. Stuart spoke all the time—generally on the same subject: Dick Stuart and his great hitting ability. A few veterans found him amusing, but most found him irritating. He irritated them when he spent three hours on the beach and came down with a minor case of sun poisoning. Or when he left the batting cage and disdained fielding practice. Stuart further ingratiated himself with his teammates when, every time the team bus passed a Phillips 66 gasoline station, he announced loudly, "There you are fellows. They knew Old Dick was coming and hung out his sign."[17]

It came as no surprise when, near the end of spring training, the Pirates assigned Stuart to Hollywood. He acted nonchalant when he left Fort Myers, saying he told Bragan he would come back and lead the National League in home runs. Years later, Stuart said that after hitting his five quick home runs, Bragan told him he wasn't going to play anymore. "He said he didn't want me on the club and if I did well it would look bad for him."[18]

"It took [Bragan] an hour and a half to explain why he was sending me down," Stuart told reporters. "Then he must have developed a stutter," one of them wrote, "because it only took him five words to explain it to us."[19] When a reporter asked Bragan if he demoted Stuart because of his strikeouts, he replied, "No, I sent him out so he'd learn when the ball is hit to left center, he's supposed to chase it, not yell to Virdon, 'Go get it, Bill.'"[20] He said he told Stuart that if he brought him to Pittsburgh, he knew he would continue to hit, but that he would embarrass himself, Bragan, and the entire team with his sorry fielding. "There's a lot more to baseball than hitting home runs," he told Stuart as he packed him off to Hollywood.[21]

Stuart headed for California looking for a more understanding manager. "I just hope Clyde King here at Hollywood," he said, "will go along with my moody moments, because nothing helps a club like home runs. The reason I get moody is because I want to be a great ball player, and if I don't do good all the time it upsets me."[22]

King, a 32-year-old former pitcher, was a protégé of Branch Rickey, a "Rickey man," who was well-respected by his players. "Clyde King was a very religious guy," said Hollywood outfielder Paul Pettit, "a good person, a very fine person. He didn't cuss, he didn't get on anyone, and he was very straightforward."[23] King said he thought Stuart would do just fine.[24]

The Pacific Coast League had once been considered by Westerners to be the equivalent of the NL and AL, and there was a time when many PCL players could have been playing in the major leagues. In the early 1950s it aspired to be a third major league. "The major leagues didn't mean a damn thing to me," said long-time big league infielder Ed Bressoud, who grew up in California. "The Coast League was the thing. If you talk to people who live on the West Coast, we have names that are embedded in our memories that you don't even think about in New York or Boston."[25]

In past years, some PCL players earned more than major leaguers, but that was no longer the case. "In 1957," said PCL historian Dick Beverage, "Steve Bilko was the biggest star in the league, and he made just over the major league minimum."[26]

Playing in the Coast League had a number of benefits. One was the climate.

California weather in April and May was much better than that in Boston or Chicago, and in the summer it was better than it was in oppressively humid St. Louis. Another attraction was the lifestyle. "We used to fly everywhere," said Pettit. "The hotels were good. The eating was good. The towns were great. And we had a day and a half off every week. There was a doubleheader on Sunday afternoon and you didn't play again until Tuesday night."[27]

The Giants were in New York, the Dodgers in Brooklyn, and the nearest major league franchise was in St. Louis. But by the mid–1950s Californians could watch big league baseball on television, and PCL attendance had been declining. "Midway through the 1957 season," Beverage said, "it became widely known that the Giants and Dodgers were coming to California, and interest just sort of petered out."[28] By 1969, there would be five major league franchises on the Coast, and the PCL would be pushed out of four major cities.

The decline of the PCL began in the early 1950s. For years, the league had played a longer schedule than the majors, usually around 200 games. By the early '50s, that was too many and the schedule was cut back. Fewer games meant lower attendance, and in 1951 league attendance declined from 3.2 million to 2.3 million. "In a span of three years," wrote Bill Conlin in 1954, "the Coast League has run the course from solid entrenchment to disaster's brink." He pointed particularly to Hollywood as being troubled by an unfavorable stadium and economic situation.[29]

But in 1957, the PCL was still the only game in a big media market, and Hollywood was the league's most glamorous city. Over the years, the Marx Brothers had been regulars at Stars games, as were Jack Benny, Ronald Reagan, and Jimmy Durante. One night, Durante was settling down with a hotdog when a foul ball sent the dog flying and spewed mustard over his shirt, a unique and unscripted moment that could only take place in Hollywood.

When Stuart arrived, he found a bevy of reporters eager to hear what he had to say. He had a lot to say, and newspaper readers could be forgiven if they thought Dick Stuart was the only player in the Hollywood training camp. The papers were filled with Stuart stories because Dick Stuart was good press.

On one occasion, Stuart visited the 20th Century–Fox studios and met actress Jayne Mansfield. "Hey," Mansfield asked him, "how come you're getting your name in the papers more than me?" "You're just not hitting the home runs," Stuart replied.[30]

Stuart had done a little acting himself, as an extra in a film about the Normandy invasion. After he became a major leaguer, he hinted that an acting career had been a possibility, but the only role anyone was sure Stuart played was that of a dead soldier on D-Day. "How'd they ever keep him quiet that long?" wondered a friend.[31]

Columnist Hank Hollingsworth of the Long Beach *Press-Telegram* said that PCL owners hoped Stuart stayed in the league all season rather than get called up to Pittsburgh. "He's got color and a chesty attitude. These pay off in ticket sales.... A refreshing character, Stuart is bound to enliven things in the staid PCL."[32] "This guy's got more color than anyone this league's ever seen, and that includes some of San Diego's great sluggers like Luke Easter, Minnie Minoso, Jack Graham, Max West, and Al Rosen. Get your bleacher tickets now! Mr. Stuart's in town."[33]

If you bought bleacher tickets, you might end up having a conversation with Mr. Stuart. Hollingsworth loved the way he jawed back and forth with the fans and blamed some of his fielding problems on the fact that he got distracted. "[H]e starts yakking with the bleacherites and forgets about the ballgame. Then—whammo—a ball comes winging his way and the kid's in hot water."[34]

One day Stuart was engaged in a debate with the folks in the right field stands when a ball hit by Los Angeles' Steve Bilko fell in front of him for a single. The fans started razzing him, but a home run brought them back on his side. That's the way it went with Stuart.

Other PCL players and managers, at least for publication, spoke well of Stuart. Bob Darnell of the Angels said, "I'll let Stuart play on my club, make one error per game and strike out three times for just one of his homers." Angels' manager Clay Bryant added, "I'll put up with a lot from a poor fielder if he can win a game with one blow." King said, "I don't mind if he strikes out 150 times if he hits 50 homers."[35]

Privately, many players had a different opinion. "He wasn't very well liked because he was so egotistical," said Pettit. "He didn't care how the team did. He only cared about how he did and that kind of galled some of the guys. But I never had any words with him, even though we were fighting for the same position. He was just a big kid who never grew up. His mentality was like that of a 15 year old, or maybe a 12 year old. I don't think he knew who was president of the United States. He was all about himself, baseball, and hitting home runs."[36]

Stuart predicted that Hollywood would win the PCL pennant, he would win the home run title, and he would be recalled to the Pirates after which he would lead the National League in home runs. He didn't explain how the Stars would manage to win without him, or how he could lead both leagues in homers.

Things went well at first, as Stuart hit a couple of long home runs in exhibition games. More surprisingly, he wasn't the butcher in the field that PCL fans had been led to expect, even making a great catch against San Diego. "[H]e doesn't do a bad job there at all," King said.[37] "Anyone who has watched the last few Hollywood Stars exhibition games," Hollingsworth wrote, "must be wondering how word got around that outfield slugger Dick Stuart was such a clown in the fielding department."[38]

Apparently, news of Stuart's new-found wizardry with the glove hadn't reached New York. "Hitting homers is this quaint lad's only interest in life," wrote veteran columnist Arthur Daley of the *New York Times*. "Unfortunately for his future in the sport, that isn't sufficient. Stuart is an outfielder with the same approximate skills of Smead Jolley, Buzz Arlett and some of the sport's most tanglefooted operatives. In comparison to Stuart, Babe Herman was a Joe DiMaggio."[39] Some young players might have been offended, but Stuart was probably thrilled to be mentioned by the great Arthur Daley, who usually wrote about Mickey Mantle and Ted Williams, not minor leaguers.

Stuart started the regular season with a bang, hitting two homers on April 11 against San Diego and a third the next day, a titanic 450-foot blast over the scoreboard in left-center field. "The wind blew to right field in San Diego," said Pettit, "and to hit one into the left field stands was almost unheard of."[40] The *Press-Telegram* pointed out that Stuart was on a pace to hit 168 homers for the season.

Stuart got publicity even when he didn't do anything. After he went hitless and struck out six times in a doubleheader, the *Press-Telegram* headline read, "Stars Win Pair but Stuart Fails."[41] Unfortunately, Stuart began to fail more often than he succeeded. His main problem wasn't his fielding, but his inability to make contact. Current day SABR-metricians have adopted Stuart's theory that an out is an out, but in 1957, making contact was important, and he wasn't doing it very often.

The top slugger in the PCL was big Steve Bilko of the Los Angeles Angels, who'd hit 55 home runs in 1956 and was named Minor League Player of the Year by *The Sporting News*. Bilko was a terror in the PCL but never established himself as a major league slugger. "Wrigley Field (where the Angels played their home games) was very conducive to Steve's batting style," said Pettit. "He hit the ball to right center a lot and not only was the fence relatively close, the prevailing winds blew in that direction. But we didn't have a lot of trouble with Steve because we had good pitching. Good pitching could really tie Steve up."

Stuart made the first series with the Angels a personal battle between him and the LA slugger, who was as quiet and modest as Stuart was loquacious and boastful. The *Press-Telegram* headline read, "Bilko-Stuart Series Opens Today at Gilmore Field."[42] Stuart predicted he would hit four or five homers and the Stars would win every game.

The publicity drew 7,707 fans to Gilmore Field for the first game of the series, but neither Bilko nor Stuart cleared the fences. Stuart had an RBI single but struck out with two outs and two men on as the Stars lost 5–3. Neither slugger hit a homer in the second game. The Angels swept the five-game series, as Stuart hit just one homer while Bilko hit three. When it was over, the *Press-Telegram* referred to Stuart, who had just one hit in his last 18 at bats, as a "deflated young man."[43]

Stuart was pressing. Pitchers were throwing him curve balls outside the strike zone and he was chasing them. "He was swinging at everything," said Pettit. "He would swing at balls in the dirt and over his head. He was going through a divorce and he just kind of fell apart."[44] Once, when he was removed for a pinch hitter, Stuart infuriated King by returning to the bench and flipping his bat end over end into the bat rack.

Although he had six homers, Stuart was batting just .238 and had struck out 22 times in 42 at bats. He'd also begun living up to his reputation as an atrocious fielder. Just two weeks into the season, Stuart found himself on the bench, replaced by Pettit, who was only 25 years old, but who'd already had two careers. In 1950, at the age of 18, he signed with the Pirates as a pitcher for a total of $100,000 (payable over ten years), to become baseball's first six-figure bonus baby. The left-handed flame thrower had become the most coveted young player in America by hurling six no-hitters in high school (three in succession) and striking out 390 in 140 innings.[45] The Pirates thought he couldn't miss. "There hasn't been a schoolboy pitcher around like this for a long, long time," said Branch Rickey.[46]

Pettit missed, for the same reason so many fabulous teen pitchers never make it; he hurt his elbow in his first professional start for the New Orleans Pelicans. Today, a rookie who was the highest paid player of all time would be treated with kid gloves and held out of action until the team was certain his arm was sound. But in 1955 they looked at things differently. Pettit was a hot gate attraction and the Pelicans ran him out to the mound as soon as he could function. "While favoring my elbow," Pettit related, "I hurt my shoulder. The elbow recovered. The shoulder never did."[47]

Pettit won just one major league game, and in 1954 he was converted to the outfield in the hope that the Pirates could salvage something from their $100,000 investment. By 1957, he was the fourth outfielder on the Hollywood Stars and when Stuart began striking out too often, King put Pettit in right field.

If the intent of sitting Stuart on the bench was to teach him a little humility, it was unsuccessful. He said he would soon be back in the lineup and would make everyone forget Paul Pettit. Stuart attributed his batting troubles to excessive bowling. "No more bowling for me," he said.[48] Perhaps, one might surmise, he had confused the fact that while a strike is good for bowlers, it is bad for batters.

In his first few games, it looked like Pettit was going to make people forget Dick Stuart. He hit three home runs in short order, while Stuart languished on the bench, save for an occasional pinch-hitting appearance. When Stuart did play, he was booed.

After two weeks on the bench, during which the Stars won seven in a row, Stuart returned to the starting lineup. In the second inning of his first game back, he struck out with men on base, giving him 28 in 59 at bats. That's a lot of strikeouts in any era, but a phenomenal total for 1957. For the season, the Stars struck out only 757 times in 5,628 at bats (13.4 percent).

With the cut-down date looming, there was speculation that Stuart would be axed, since the Stars had six outfielders and would probably carry just four. Pettit was staying, and the final roster spot appeared to be a contest between Stuart and 25-year-old Joe Duhem, a hustling ballplayer who'd been a regular in 1956, could also play the infield, and had hit well in limited opportunities. King said that Stuart would probably be cut unless he unleashed a sudden barrage of home runs.

That would be hard to do from the bench, and although Stuart started a few games, he didn't hit any homers and continued to strike out a lot. Stuart's final record with Hollywood was a .236 average, six home runs, 17 runs batted in and 32 strikeouts in 72 at bats. In the field, he made three errors in just 32 chances for a .906 percentage.[49]

On May 11, Stu's contract was transferred to the Atlanta Crackers of the Southern Association. "Although he must have known the axe was going to fall," reported the *Lincoln Sunday Journal and Star*, "Stuart seemed shocked when given the bad news."[50]

Although Atlanta was not a Pittsburgh farm team, Stuart remained under a Pirate option. King, who'd managed the Crackers the previous season, said he pleaded with Atlanta to take him so he didn't have to go back to Lincoln. He added that Stuart was a fine prospect but not ready for the PCL.

At first Stuart said he wouldn't report to Atlanta, threatening to go to Canada and play semi-pro ball. "If this is a fair shake," he said, "then I'm a Chinaman." But as expected, after delaying for a few days, Stuart agreed to go to Atlanta, a decision Cracker manager Buddy Bates undoubtedly received with mixed emotions.[51] He'd managed Wichita of the Western League the previous season and was well aware of Stuart's reputation.

One benefit of having Stuart in Atlanta was that he drew crowds. "Stuart Real Tonic for Southern Loop," read a headline in the *Albuquerque Journal*.[52] The *Lima News* called him "the most talked about player the Southern Association has seen in many a season."[53] When the Crackers visited Nashville, Stuart said he'd make the fans forget Bob Lennon, who'd hit 64 homers there the year before. When he managed just one single in nine trips to the plate, the fans let him hear about it.

When Stuart arrived in Atlanta, he said he anticipated no trouble with Southern Association pitching but doubted he could break the league record of 64 home runs, since he'd started late. He was disappointed Hollywood had given up on him so quickly, "But I'm not discouraged. I believe I'll do okay with Atlanta."[54] He remembered Bates from the Western League and thought he was a fine manager.

Stuart, always concerned with money, was disappointed to learn that Atlanta no longer gave out cash awards for home runs. "Oh, well," he sighed, "I'm ready to play anyway." But he closed his initial interview with the wistful comment, "And you say they don't give away money for home runs anymore?"[55]

"He showed up with a chauffeur," recalled Atlanta pitcher Ken MacKenzie. "We thought maybe he was gay and that was his boyfriend, but he was just the guy who drove him down there. When we asked him how he got there, he said, 'Route 66.'"[56]

Some players would have been chastened by a demotion, but not Dick Stuart. When he received his uniform, he complained to trainer Jim Bernhardt that it didn't fit well. "Five people told me I don't look good in this uniform," he told Bernhardt. "What's the chance of getting it tailored to fit?"[57]

Bates couldn't find a fit for Stuart either. He said that after watching him play the outfield and first base at Lincoln he thought third base was the place for him. It wasn't, and after five errors in ten games, Bates moved him back to the outfield.[58] "They tried him at third," said MacKenzie. "They tried him at first and they tried him in the outfield. He didn't care whether he caught the ball or not. He'd go to touch first base and do this little twinkle-toes routine—just barely touch the bag with his toe. One day he missed the bag and Buddy Bates went through the roof."[59]

In Stuart's first game in Atlanta, he went 0 for 4 with two strikeouts. On the 21st of May, after four straight strikeouts, he lined his first Atlanta home run over the left field fence. As Stuart approached home plate, he jumped up and landed on it with a giant leap.

Stuart's sixth home run was estimated at 450 feet, one of the longest ever hit at Sulphur Dell. A few days later, however, he struck out three times and made an error that let in two unearned runs. It wasn't long before he ended up on Buddy Bates' bench.

And it wasn't long after that that Stuart was asked to leave Atlanta. His experience in the Southern Association was similar to what he experienced in Hollywood. He hit with power, with eight home runs in 90 at bats, his fielding was very shaky, and although he didn't strike out as frequently as he had in Hollywood, he batted just .211. And Stuart didn't get along with Bates.

"[W]e're going for the pennant," the manager said, "and he's going for the whole world."[60] "He's a man without a position. His value is strictly in his bat, and his bat wasn't enough value to us at the moment."[61]

When reporter Jesse Outlar caught up with Stuart in a Mobile restaurant after he'd been benched, he said he wished he was back in the PCL. After his brief stint with New Orleans in 1955, he hadn't wanted to return to the Southern Association. "But I thought I was going good.... I don't think I got a fair chance.... I think it was another one of Bates' baffling moves. I just don't understand it. You know, I wish I had hit six home runs instead of 66. I think I would get more of a chance."[62]

Outlar said Stuart's presence was fueling attendance and that fans were unhappy he was leaving. Reporter Paul Atkinson spent some time in the stands gathering opinions, and nearly everyone he spoke with was sorry to see Stuart go. They liked his home runs and his moxie and weren't that worried about his fielding.

"I've heard more fans discussing the big man," Outlar wrote, "than the rest of the club combined.... Writers traveling with the club have reported that Stuart was the big attraction wherever the Crackers stopped.... Stuart has received more national publicity than any Southern Assn. player in at least a decade.... [H]e was dern interesting to watch, even more interesting to hear."[63]

The only negative comment came from Cracker fan Roy Johnson, who said, "The morale will be better. I know there are some guys on this club that don't go for Stuart's popping off."[64] Was that true? One player said, "He talks all of the time. But he doesn't hurt anyone, because he's always talking about himself."[65]

"I didn't have any trouble with the other players," Stuart said. "They're a nice bunch, and the fellows out at Hollywood were nice. I don't associate too much with the players during the season, but I liked them."[66]

MacKenzie got a kick out of Stuart. A Yale graduate who later became famous as the only pitcher on the 1962 New York Mets to post a winning record, he was 23 years old and in his first year of professional baseball. One day he asked Stuart, "Slam, what's the farthest you ever hit a ball? He said, '806 feet.' I said you can't count the roll. He said, 'Roll, your ass, MacKenzie. It landed in the mud on a river bank and it didn't roll at all.'"[67]

The reporters loved Stuart, the fans loved him, and the players didn't care. Apparently, Buddy Bates was the only one who wanted Stuart gone, but he was the one who counted, and the Crackers returned Stuart to the Pittsburgh organization in mid–June.

The Pirates wanted to teach Stuart a lesson and assigned him to Lincoln, his third demotion in a season that was only a couple of months old. Again, Stuart said he wouldn't report. This time, instead of going to Canada, he was going back to Hollywood to work in the movies. "America's #1 sport may lose one of its zaniest characters," proclaimed a wire service report.[68]

Stuart departed with a final, gratuitous shot at the Stars. "When I left Hollywood," he said, "they were in first place. Now they're about seven games out. Draw your own conclusion." The *Constitution's* conclusion was, "The young man had confidence, huh?"[69]

Others drew different conclusions. When *The Sporting News* published a photo of Stuart with the caption, "Complete Cycle," a Southern Association player quipped that it should read, "Complete Psycho."[70]

Stuart said he wouldn't report to Lincoln unless they gave him a big bonus. When he'd been dispatched to Atlanta, he'd said, "I don't think any club has enough money to pay what I think I'm worth today."[71] Stuart said that if the Pirates didn't want him he wished they'd trade or release him. "I think my father hit the situation on the head," he reflected. "He said since I hit 66 home runs for Lincoln, people would expect twice as much from me as other players."[72]

Pirate General Manager Joe Brown called Stuart, advised him to report to Lincoln, and said if he didn't play there, he wasn't playing anywhere. He told reporters he didn't know what his AWOL slugger would do, but Lincoln General Manager Dick Wagner said he thought Stuart would report for duty. The most he could offer was $6,000 per year, and found it difficult to believe that Stuart could ask for a bonus after failing in Hollywood and Atlanta.

As expected, Stuart capitulated and went to Lincoln, driving for 24 hours straight from Atlanta. "[I]f I wasn't making $900 a month," he said, "I wouldn't stay here five seconds. I don't see that I can prove anything here."[73] Then he lapsed into self-pity. "Nobody wants me, I guess. I've got 14 home runs and I've played pretty good, but here I am…. Pittsburgh didn't want me, Hollywood didn't want me, Atlanta didn't want me—and my wife didn't want me. She divorced me when I got back to California from spring training."[74] Diane's divorce suit had been granted in May, while Stuart was in Atlanta.

When Stuart arrived in Lincoln, Don Bryant, his favorite sportswriter, looked him up. "Maybe we'll try making some less noise," Stuart told him. "If that's what they want, then that's what they'll get. I'll be a whole new man."[75] But that was just talk from a momentarily chastened athlete. There would be no new Dick Stuart.

Stuart broke in with his usual bang on June 17, hitting a grand slam in his first game. The Southern Association and Pacific Coast League's loss was the Western League's gain, and its cities lost no time promoting Stuart's arrival. After all, he was the man who had hit

66 home runs in the same city a year earlier. Stuart soon hit his second home run, which rated a photo in the *Amarillo Globe Times* and a description of Stuart as "one of the most discussed players in baseball."[76] A crowd of 1,716 turned out for Stuart's first home game, the second largest crowd of the season at Sherman Field.

Joe Brown watched Stuart in action against Amarillo and said, "He has the ability. But he must learn there is more to baseball than home runs. He could be a passable major league outfielder, but it's up to him. He has a good arm. He can run, but he doesn't run."[77]

The next day Stuart blasted three home runs in a Lincoln doubleheader sweep. He hit six homers in his first eight games, and nine in his first fifteen. The Chiefs were hot and it looked as though they had an even better team than the 1956 champions. In addition to Stuart, they had returnees Sam Miley (who hit .374) and Reg Grenald, and had added future major leaguers Joe Christopher and Ken Hamlin.

But where Lincoln really excelled was on the pitching mound. Nineteen-year-old George Perez was 15–6. Jack Lamabe, who pitched several seasons in the majors, was 13–7. The Chiefs also had future major leaguers Joe Gibbon, Jim Duffalo, Al Jackson, and Dave Wickersham and former Pirate Bill Bell.[78]

Gibbon was sent to Lincoln with instructions to use him only in the outfield. He wasn't hitting very well when Shepard used him to mop up a couple of lost causes. When Gibbon continued to pitch much better than he hit, Shepard, despite objections from the Pirate front office, kept him on the mound. Gibbon was in the major leagues by 1960 and stayed there for 13 years.

Bell was as famous as Stuart. When he signed as a bonus player with the Pirates, Branch Rickey said, "He's a major leaguer if ever one was born."[79] Bell's problem was that he could throw very hard, but not very straight. In 1951, his first minor league season, he struck out 124 men in 104 innings, but walked 106.

The next season, in Class D Bristol, Tennessee, Bell was paired with Ron Neccai, another phenom who pitched a no-hitter in which he struck out 27. Bell pitched consecutive no-hitters; in the first he walked 11 and struck out 17. In the second he struck out 20. After suffering some arm trouble, he came back in August and pitched a third no-hitter. For the season, Bell struck out 194 in 112 innings.

"I would say," recalled Harry Dunlop, who caught all three of Bell's no-hitters, "that he could probably throw in the low to mid 90s. We didn't have radar guns in those days. But he had a natural sinker and threw a real heavy ball. It was like catching an 8-pound shot put. After catching him for nine innings, you really felt it. He was an outstanding competitor and I thought he was going to be a great major league pitcher. On that Lincoln staff we had Joe Gibbon and some other great pitchers, but if I had to pick one guy who was going to be an outstanding pitcher, it was Bill Bell."[80]

At the end of the 1952 season, Bell was called up to the Pirates and pitched 16 undistinguished innings before being drafted into the Army. After serving his two-year hitch, Bell returned to the minor leagues with a mysterious injury. His arm didn't really hurt; he just didn't have any velocity. In 1957, Bell made a comeback with the Chiefs, posting an 11–4 record, but he continued to have trouble with his control.[81]

For Stuart, 1957 in Lincoln was almost as good as 1956 in Lincoln. He was hitting home runs and after a few weeks was batting .382. He'd said, perhaps facetiously, he was focusing on winning the batting title, since his 66 home runs hadn't gotten him to the majors.[82]

For a while, things went smoothly, but in mid–July, Stuart got in trouble again.

5. Jesus, There Goes Dick Stuart: 1957

Manager Larry Shepard was a patient man who carried rosary beads in his pocket and liked to pray. Carrying a rosary was probably a good idea for anyone managing Dick Stuart, but one night in Topeka, Shepard saw something that saying the rosary couldn't cure.

Early in the game, Stuart struck out and hurled his bat against the screen. Then he made an error. Then came the straw that broke Shepard's back. Backup catcher Dunlop was in the Lincoln bullpen watching the action. "There was a ground ball to shortstop," he recalled. "The throw to first bounced off the palm of Stuart's glove and dropped at his feet. He just sort of looked at it, didn't pick it up right away, the runner got to first and another runner scored. The dugouts in Topeka had a real low ceiling, only about six feet high. I looked down to the dugout and saw that Shepard had jumped up and hit his head on the roof. He yelled down to the bullpen, 'Dunlop, get down here.' He asked me if I'd ever played first base. I said I did, in high school. He said, 'Then get in there.' I didn't have a first baseman's glove, so Dick said, 'Here, take mine. Have a great game, Harry.'"[83]

"He's going to stay benched," Shepard said, "maybe permanently. It just doesn't work—eight guys playing their hearts out for a pennant, and one guy loafing."[84] That sounded like Buddy Bates. The Lincoln fans, who'd cheered Stuart so lustily the previous year, started booing him, even though at the time he was taken out of the lineup he'd hit 13 homers in 25 games, giving him 27 for his peripatetic season. When Dunlop was announced as his replacement, the fans cheered.

Stuart's stay on the bench lasted just five days. "I played first for a couple of days," Dunlop said, "and then Larry told me he was putting Stuart back in. 'They told me to put the big donkey back in there,' he told me."

Ten years and many disputes later, Stuart, when asked about his numerous managers, said Shepard had the greatest influence on him. "Shepard knew how to handle me," he recalled. "He knew what to say and what to do to get the most out of me."[85]

In 1957 Shepard wasn't so sure. "Maybe the benching's what he needed," he said. "This I'll say with no reservations.... Stuart rates as one of the five best hitters in baseball in my book ... potentially. But I said potentially.... I've tried to get through to him like Bob Bragan, Clyde King and Buddy Bates at Atlanta. You say all Stuart needs is a little humility and you're right. But I'll ask you. How in samhill do you INJECT humility?"[86]

Stuart returned to the lineup in Albuquerque and hit two home runs during a doubleheader, but committed an error that let in seven unearned runs. He hit another homer the next night and then drove in eight runs against Colorado Springs.

Joe Brown, always a big Stuart supporter, saw the games in Albuquerque and said, "Dick Stuart could be a great ballplayer if he wasn't continuously going for the home run."[87] "One of these days he will wake up and be a good, if not great player."[88]

Scouting reports on Stuart generally read more like psychological evaluations. Brown said Stuart had "average major league speed ... if he wants to run ... above average major league arm ... when he really wants to throw."[89] Despite Shepard's hopeful comment that his benching had lit a fire under Stuart, Brown hadn't noticed any improvement in his attitude. He reminded Stuart that despite his high opinion of himself, he had yet to prove himself at any level above A ball.

Stuart continued to try Shepard's patience on a daily basis. "I have the fabulous Stuart back," he said. "He sure draws the fans ... and drives me to ulcers."[90] One day, Shepard warned his players against sunbathing at the local lake, lest they get sunburned and be unable to play. "The very next day," Dunlop recalled, "Dick came into the locker room— he was usually one of the last ones there. He takes off his shirt and he looks like a lobster.

I saw him and said, 'Cover up!' In the Lincoln locker room, the manager didn't have an office. Shepard dressed right across from me and Stuart. He heard me and looked around and saw Dick. He was so mad. He said, 'I thought I told you guys not to get sunburned!' Dick said, 'You never said not to go swimming.' Then he went out and had a good night."[91]

Shepard said, "[W]e'd be on the bench ... and Stuart would say, 'What will they pay me up at Pittsburgh if I hit 70 home runs this season?'"[92] Despite the ulcers, Shepard was glad to have Stuart back. He hit 21 homers in his first six weeks in Lincoln, while no one else had more than nine for the entire season.

If Shepard and Brown were looking for a little fire, they saw it on August 5. When Stuart was called out on strikes, he threw his bat in the air, piled dirt on home plate, and threw a towel at the umpire's feet, earning his first professional ejection. A few days later, Stuart came to the aid of the umpires, wading into a brawl to grab teammate Dave Brennan and drag him away before he had a chance to slug that old Lincoln nemesis, Max Stone.

Stuart continued to hit well for the rest of the season. Although it had been a frustrating and disappointing year for him, his overall statistics were very good. It was his behavior that had landed him back in A ball. On August 23, he hit his 40th home run of the season (his 26th for Lincoln) as the Chiefs won to pull to within two games of league-leading Amarillo.

Despite the series of demotions, Stuart was still good copy, such good copy that well-known writer Mark Harris was assigned to do a story on him for *Life* magazine.[93] Being featured in *Life* was a big deal. In its heyday the magazine had a weekly circulation of more than four million copies and was one of the most popular periodicals in the United States. The September 2 issue in which Stuart appeared also featured articles on labor leader Jimmy Hoffa, future heavyweight boxing champion Floyd Patterson and actor Jimmy Cagney. Earlier that year, Prince Juan Carlos and evangelist Billy Graham were portrayed on *Life's* cover. That was pretty fast company for a Class A first baseman who couldn't field.

Dick Kranz of the *Globe Times* caught up with Stuart shortly after the article appeared. "Dick," he wrote, "wearing sunglasses, stretched his long legs out on the coffee table and began looking at the advance copy of this week's *Life* magazine which has six pages devoted to Stuart." He looked at the pictures and thought they were a little small. Then he saw a picture of him flubbing a grounder. "They had to have a pitcher (picture) of me missing a ball," he complained, although not very vehemently. Finally, Stuart decided he liked the article. After all, it was about him.[94]

As Stuart admired the article, a few other players, including future major league manager John McNamara, came along. "Hi, Fabulous Richard," said Amarillo's Frank Murray, who pointed to McNamara and told Kranz, "John and I are the only two remaining members of the Dick Stuart Fan Club." When Shepard was asked if he'd read the article, he replied, "No, not yet. But I live it every day."

One of the lines in the *Life* article claimed that Stuart wanted to walk down the street and have people say of him, like they said of Ted Williams, "J[esus], there goes Ted Williams." Therefore, when Stuart walked into the Lincoln dressing room one night after the article appeared, the players shouted in chorus, "J[esus], there goes Dick Stuart."[95]

Against all odds, Stuart was popular with his teammates, and one can't help wondering how such a self-centered egotist could avoid antagonizing them. "He was just a fun-loving guy," said Dunlop. "He knew he was good and he ate up the attention. He'd say,

'Wouldn't you like to be able to hit the ball like me, Harry?' I never saw him get mad, and he was fun to be around. He never," Dunlap said with a laugh, "bothered anybody but the manager. We laughed at the things he did. We were busting our tails trying to advance while he just seemed like he didn't care. Whether he actually believed that or not, I don't know, but that's the way he always acted. If any of us had been taken out of a game in the middle of an inning like he was, we would have been embarrassed. But Dick just handed me his glove and said, 'Have a good game, Harry.'"[96]

For the second year in a row, Lincoln won the Western League title, defeating Topeka 3–2 to win the crown on September 15. The Chiefs were leading 1–0 in the fifth when Stuart led off with a double and scored on a homer by Willie Melendez, which proved to be the winning runs.

Stuart finished his Lincoln season with 31 home runs, giving him an overall total of 45 with three teams. That wasn't 66, but it was pretty impressive, particularly given all his tribulations. It was certainly impressive to the Pirates, whose players hit just 91 home runs all year. Only two, Frank Thomas with 23 and Bob Skinner with 13, reached double figures. Due in part to their lack of power, the Pirates finished last, and were in dire need of a long ball hitter. When the Western League season ended, they brought Stuart to Pittsburgh. He didn't play in any games; the reason for the summons was so that he could become the special project of Pirate coach and Hall of Fame first baseman George Sisler.

Sisler, 64, was one of the greatest hitters of the early 20th century and was considered the best fielding first baseman of his era. He batted over .400 on two occasions and had a career average of .340. Moreover, Sisler was not just an old timer who'd been a great hitter. He was a student of batting, and in addition to the mechanics of hitting, was particularly interested in the mental aspects.

Sisler, who averaged less than 10 homers a season, had been a spray hitter, but he was not one of those coaches who insisted that his pupils hit the way he did. When he worked with Roberto Clemente, he didn't, as many coaches would have, tell him to stop swinging at pitches outside the strike zone. Sisler merely got Clemente to keep his head still and stay back on the ball, which made him a better hitter.

For two weeks, Sisler worked with Stuart every day. On the first day, Stu hit ten balls into the stands. Once, Sisler placed a ball on a batting tee and Stuart hit it over the left field fence, which was very hard to do. "He's a very fine hitter," Sisler said. "There were two or three things I thought he did wrong and I corrected him. This boy has so much power he doesn't have to aim for the fences."[97]

One thing Sisler taught Stuart was a slightly difference stance that would help him lay off high pitches and another was not to cock the bat toward the pitcher.[98] He also worked with Stuart on first base play, but even George Sisler couldn't perform miracles. He thought Stuart was too nonchalant in the field but added, "I think he could be an acceptable first baseman.... The future is strictly up to him. He can make of himself what he wants to."[99]

Sisler confirmed that Stuart had great potential as a hitter and couldn't field, but the thing that caught everyone's attention during Stuart's time in Pittsburgh was his new attitude. Apparently, being kicked around the minors all season had put a small dent in his ego. "I tried it my way," he told Brown, "and it got me back where I started—in Lincoln. Now I'm ready to try it your way."[100]

On that hopeful note, Dick left for the Dominican Republic to play for Aguilas Cibenas in the Dominican Winter League under the management of Pirate coach Frank

Oceak. He took along a list, drafted by Sisler, of things he was supposed to concentrate on.

Aguilas Cibenas lost its first eight games, but couldn't blame Stuart, who hit five homers in his first five games. After 17 games (of which his team lost 15), he led the league in batting average (.357), home runs (7) and RBI (15). On December 4, he tied the league record of nine home runs set by Willie Kirkland two years earlier.[101] On December 28 and 29, with tutor Sisler watching from the stands, he hit his 12th and 13th. Although Stuart left before the season was over, he ended the year with 14 homers, the most ever hit in the league, even in the years before it was part of organized baseball. He also led the Dominican League in RBI, but on the negative side of the ledger he set a league record with 48 strikeouts. Branch Rickey, Jr., came down to watch the Pirate prospects and said he thought Stuart's attitude was much better and that he had shown some improvement in the field.[102]

Oceak reported moderate success. He said it was hard to get Stuart to maintain his concentration, for he tended to talk to umpires, base runners, coaches, and anyone else who strayed in the vicinity of first base. "He is very sociable," Oceak said. Still, Oceak thought Stuart had made progress in the field. "He learned to play first base adequately. Not well but adequately."[103]

During the winter, Stuart's contract was assigned from Lincoln to Hollywood, where he would receive a second chance. All reports indicated he had "turned over a new leaf" and a new, mature Dick Stuart would appear in the spring of 1958. The world breathlessly awaited.

6

Shepard Has a Problem—
So Had Miller Huggins with
Babe Ruth: 1958—Part 1

The Dick Stuart who arrived in Fort Myers in the spring of 1958 appeared to be a different man than the one who'd sparred with Lee Walls the previous year. This Dick Stuart was no longer going to make predictions. "I've learned my lesson last year after telling people what I thought I would do," he told the *Pittsburgh Press*, but then said he expected to hit 20–25 home runs for the Pirates.

"I've changed in a great many ways," Stuart told another reporter. "In the first place, I'm minding my own business. I want to be more of a team man and I've found out that you can't talk your way onto a ball club."[1] "Every time I'd say something, which was usually all the time, I'd be quoted. Reporters from magazines and newspapers would call me at all hours of the day or night because they knew I'd sound off about something. I learned some kind of lesson from that."[2]

Stuart even appeared to be making progress at first base. Frank Oceak, who'd managed Stuart in the Dominican, said, "He fooled me. On what he showed me, he could play first base in the major leagues."[3] It baffled the imagination. Dick Stuart with a new attitude and a slick glove? Should the press be worried?

Not really. The new Stuart arrived at camp owing $80 in excess luggage charges for his flight and seemed to most observers a lot like the old Stuart. His chances of making the Pittsburgh roster depended on the condition of first baseman Ted Kluszewski's aching back. Ted, a powerful 33-year-old veteran with massive arms and shoulders, had been one of the National League's premier sluggers in the mid-1950s. Robin Roberts once said that Klu was so strong that if he missed the ball with his bat but hit it with his arm, it would still leave the park.[4]

Between 1953 and 1956, Ted hit 171 home runs for the Cincinnati Reds, including 49 in 1954 and 47 in 1955. He drove in 464 runs during those four years and in 1954 led the National League in homers and RBI. "If he played in New York," said his manager Birdie Tebbetts, "they would say he was better than Mays and Snider put together."[5] Sluggers Ralph Kiner and Johnny Mize said Klu had the best chance of any ballplayer to beat Babe Ruth's record of 60 home runs in a season.

Then Klu's back started hurting. His troubles began in 1956 when he bent over to field a ball on the second day of spring training and felt a pain in his right hip. He took a week off but the pain wouldn't go away. The Reds sent Kluszewski to a series of doctors, but none could identify the precise nature of the injury.

Although Kluszewski hit 35 homers in 1956, his back bothered him all season, and he didn't start a game the final two weeks. His doctor advised him to lose weight, and he reported to training camp in 1957 at 235 pounds, about five to ten pounds less than usual. Klu seemed to be improved and more agile but then, he said, "We headed north and ran into cold, damp weather. That did it. The next day I couldn't move."[6]

Finally, doctors were able to determine the problem—a slipped disc. They advised against an operation, which they said might end Ted's career. They told him to build himself up with exercises and learn to live with the pain. When Kluszewski returned to the active roster he was used mostly as a pinch hitter, playing just 23 games at first base. He appeared in only 69 games overall, and while he hit .269, the one-time slugger managed just six homers and 21 RBI. The Reds thought he was finished and during the winter they traded him to the Pirates for first baseman Dee Fondy.

Kluszewski was what the Pirates hoped Stuart would become, absent the bad back. Like Stuart, Ted had been a crude, unpolished fielder when he began playing professionally. Like Stuart, he'd started as an outfielder, but was moved to first after the day he ran over centerfielder Mike McCormick. "Get that big guy out of my outfield," said Reds manager Bill McKechnie, "before he runs over any more centerfielders."[7] Klu worked hard at becoming a good first baseman, and while he wasn't graceful and didn't have much range, he handled what he reached and was considered competent in the field.

Kluszewski was determined to prove the Reds had made a mistake and showed up in Fort Myers a week early at his own expense. He swam and exercised daily, but said he wouldn't know how his back would respond until he started playing ball.

Big Klu was one of the keys to the Pirates hopes for 1958, for if his back was better, he would provide the power the Pirates sorely lacked. "His presence pervades the camp," wrote *Sports Illustrated*, "and one reason the reporter cannot stop watching him is that everyone in the camp is watching him too…. The first day Klu walked into the batting cage, everything stopped dead. The pepper games behind the cage stopped. The pitchers running in the outfield stopped. The coaches hitting fungoes, they stopped. Everybody just stood there watching Klu hit."[8] After practice, Kluszewski was hooked up to a contraption with rubber cords and a lamp that was applied to his back. Meanwhile Joe Brown and manager Danny Murtaugh prayed and hoped for the best.

In addition to Kluszewski and Stuart, the Pirates had 23-year-old rookie first baseman R.C. Stevens in camp.[9] Stevens had divided the 1957 season between the Pirates' top two farm clubs, Hollywood and Columbus, and batted a combined .256 with 19 home runs. If Kluszewski couldn't play regularly, Stuart and Stevens would compete for the starting job.

Stuart didn't have the spectacular start he'd had in 1957, but he hit well in the spring. Unfortunately, he didn't field very well. On March 16 he committed two errors and the next day he made another. And as always, he took a lot of kidding from the Pirate veterans. One day, after pitcher Bob Friend got into a long bantering session with Stuart in the middle of the clubhouse, he was asked by beat writer Les Beiderman, "Would you rather have Johnny O'Brien or Dick Stuart as a pinch hitter this season?" "Why, Stuart of course," Friend answered. "You're going to get O'Brien," Biederman replied. "Stuart is a cinch to be sent to the minors. You're ridiculing him too much."[10]

Kluszewski showed enough mobility to convince Murtaugh he could play at least semi-regularly, and therefore Stuart was sent to the minor league camp on March 28. Stevens stayed with the Pirates to back up Big Klu.

6. Shepard Has a Problem ... 1958—Part 1

The Pirates' Hollywood franchise had been relocated to Salt Lake City, to get away from the Dodgers in Los Angeles, and it appeared that Stuart would be assigned there, especially since Larry Shepard was the Bees' new manager. During Stuart's minor league career, Shepard had been the manager who'd gotten the most out of him.

"The main trouble," Shepard said, "was finding a position for him. He'd fall asleep in the outfield while trying to figure out why he popped up. Bringing him closer to the batter kept him awake. He might get hit on the head with a batted ball if he dozed off at first. That woke him up."[11] "I'm convinced Stuart has the potential of greatness," he said. "He just needs to be watched."[12]

The *Salt Lake City Tribune's* John Mooney wrote, "If Shepard, by some miracle, could get Stuart accustomed to living in the same world with his fellow men, instead of orbiting in space, Larry might be 'made' in the Pittsburgh organization."[13] Stuart must have loved Mooney's next comment. "Shepard has a problem. So had Miller Huggins with Babe Ruth."[14]

The Pacific Coast League had a different look in 1958. The Dodgers and Giants were about to begin their first season on the West Coast, and the PCL replaced them with Phoenix and Spokane. The league still retained its semi–Major League look, however, by employing many veteran players. The average age of 1958 PCL players was 27.9 while that of National Leaguers was an almost identical 28.2.

Bob Clements, the western farm director of the Pirates, had an optimistic view of the new situation. "Look at it this way," he said, "both Los Angeles and San Francisco had outgrown their usefulness in the PCL, just as Salt Lake may have worn out its value in the Pioneer League. The fans in each city had come to view the league competition in a jaded light. The new enthusiasm in Phoenix, Salt Lake and Spokane will make the Pacific Coast League stronger than ever."[15]

That sounded like whistling in the dark, but for a league in transition, if not in trouble, a controversial figure like Dick Stuart would generate interest. Salt Lake fans remembered Stuart from his Pioneer League days and were eager to see him join the Bees, who were locally owned, with the number of individual owners reported at various times between 5,000 and 10,000.

The Bees played at Derks Field, which was opened in 1915 and rebuilt in 1947 after a fire. When the city stepped up from the Pioneer League to the PCL, the stadium was renovated and expanded. After the work was completed, Derks would seat about 12,000 fans.[16] For power hitters, the most appealing part of Derks was not the distances to the outfield fences but the fact that it was 4,230 feet above sea level.

Dr. Alan M. Nathan, in his article, *The Physics of Baseball,* explained that the atmospheric theories affecting the flight of a baseball are drag and Magnus forces, both of which are greatly reduced at higher altitudes. Less drag results in longer fly balls while lower Magnus forces reduce the effective distance. The reduced drag had a greater impact than the difference in Magnus forces, and Dr. Nathan predicted that a baseball hit a mile above sea level will travel about 5 percent farther than a ball hit at sea level, making a 380-foot fly ball a 400-footer. The Colorado Rockies claim the impact is actually 9 percent, which would make the same ball travel about 415 feet.[17] In 1923, the Salt Lake City team set a league record with 204 home runs in a 199-game season. Two years later, when Tony Lazzeri set the PCL record of 60 homers in a season, 37 of them sailed through the thin air at Derks Field.

The dimensions of Derks were not that cozy. The left field fence was 350 feet away, center field 400 and right field 365. A five percent altitude discount from 350 is 333, which made the distance roughly equivalent to the barrier at Sherman Field in Lincoln, which Stuart cleared 34 times in 1956.

There were a number of power hitters in the 1958 PCL who were capable of clearing the Derks fences. Phoenix, a Giants farm club, featured Willie McCovey, Leon Wagner, Willie Kirkland, and Felipe Alou, four young sluggers on their way up, and Dusty Rhodes, a former World Series hero on his way down. One could expect fireworks when the Giants visited Salt Lake, or when the Bees went to Phoenix, which was an equally inviting home run haven.

In early April, Stuart began playing exhibition games with the Bees, even though he had not been formally assigned there. As always, he quickly became the center of attention. The headline after one game, in which Stuart hit two home runs in a losing cause, read, "Wichita Nine Defeats Stuart, Buzzers."[18] Two days later, he connected for another pair of homers in a game in which the Bees hit seven in total. And they weren't even at high altitude yet.

As expected, Stuart was assigned to the Bees. He arrived in style, riding in the welcome home parade seated in a car between two beautiful young ladies. When Stuart didn't hit a home run in his first few games, the *Tribune* puckishly noted, "Note to Bobby Bragan: You'd hardly recognize Dick Stuart these days. He's the slick-fielding, light-hitting first baseman of the Pacific Coast League's Salt Lake City Bees."[19] The "slick-fielding" description was a bit of an exaggeration, but thus far Stuart hadn't hurt the Bees with his defense.

It wasn't long before the home runs and errors started coming. Stuart hit two homers in Seattle before the Bees returned to Salt Lake for the home opener. The city's first PCL opening day should have been a big deal, but it turned out to be a series of minor disasters. First, the crowd of 4,849 was nowhere near a sellout, partly due to the fact that the game had to be played during the day, since the new light towers were not yet installed. Second, Mayor Adiel Stewart's toss of the ceremonial first pitch was wild. Finally, the rope on the flagpole broke as the banner was being raised, and therefore the National Anthem had to be played twice. Public address announcer Jim Grebe glibly covered up the flub by attributing the incident to the difference between the Pioneer League and the PCL. "In the PCL we play it twice," he said.[20] After all the snafus, the game itself wasn't all that satisfying for the home folks. The Bees lost to Vancouver 8–4 and Stuart managed just a ninth-inning single.

Stuart had a good first home stand, with 14 hits in 30 at bats, which gave him an overall .398 batting average for 20 games. It wasn't long before the home runs started flying off his bat, and with Stuart they always seemed to come in bunches. And when he hit home runs, Stuart ate well. John Rossetto and Phillip Anton, proprietors of a local steak house, gave a complimentary T-bone steak dinner to any Bee hitting a home run. By May 12, Stuart had earned eight T-bones.[21]

By that time, slick-fielding, light-hitting Dick Stuart had become the power hitting, distracted Dick Stuart who drove his manager batty. One night, the bases were loaded, with Stuart on third and a 3 and 1 count on the batter. Shepard, who was coaching at third, told Stuart there was no sign and the batter was hitting away. When the pitcher started to wind up, Shepard yelled, "There he goes," to try to distract him. Stuart took off for the plate and was caught easily. "I thought you might have changed your mind," he told Shepard afterward.[22]

Once Stuart got started, it was like 1956. Paul Pettit, who had followed Stuart to Salt Lake City, said, "In 1957 he was vulnerable to the high fastball. In 1958, he learned to lay off the high fastball. He made them throw strikes and he could hit those."[23]

By late May, reporters were tracking Stuart's progress against Tony Lazzeri's PCL home run record of 60. If Stuart threatened the mark, the PCL would face the opposite of the Roger Maris problem Ford Frick solved with an asterisk in 1961. The 1925 PCL season was nearly 200 games, and on September 7, the date the 1958 season would end, Lazzeri had 42 homers. Would Stuart break his record if he hit 43 in a shorter season? Would Lazzeri get a posthumous asterisk?

When Stuart hit his 14th homer on May 20, he was 25 days ahead of Lazzeri's pace. When he hit his 18th, he was about a month ahead. On June 9, the *Tribune* published a homer-by-homer chart comparing Stuart, Lazzeri, and Steve Bilko, who hit 57 home runs in 1957.[24] Eventually the *Tribune* added Babe Ruth to the chart, which must have pleased Stuart to no end. With 26 homers through June 22, Stuart was behind the 31 Bilko hit through the end of June 1957, but ahead of Ruth's 25 and Lazzeri's 24. And Stuart had eight more days to go. It was estimated that his 1958 hits had already covered 3.6 miles, based on estimated distances for singles, doubles, triples, and home runs.

The 3.6 mile trip had been an exciting one. On May 16, Stuart hit three home runs (11, 12, and 13) in an 11-inning game against Spokane. On the 27th, he hit his 16th and 17th, also against Spokane. In the first inning, the Bees loaded the bases and, as described floridly by the *Tribune*, "[T]hat crowd shook the new concrete stands as Stuart, mighty Stuart, strode masterfully to the plate in the first inning.... [D]auntless Dick did not disappoint. Like Ben Hogan connecting with all his power, Stuart caught the ball and sent it screaming. It cleared the center field fence before the fleet Tom Taffell took more than a couple of steps."[25]

Home run number 28 was the third of three consecutive Bee round-trippers, as Carlos Bernier, Jim McDaniel, and Stuart connected in sequence. During that same game, Bernier[26] extended his hitting streak to 34 games. There were many players in the PCL of the 1950s who would have been in the majors if they'd played during the post-expansion era, and Bernier was one of them. He'd been the first black Pirate player but lasted just one season (1953) and at age 31 was in his fifth consecutive year with Pittsburgh's PCL farm club. Bernier had an excellent 1958 season in Salt Lake, batting .332 with 15 homers and 34 steals, but he would never see the majors again.

Bernier was a good hitter with some power, but his outstanding attribute was his speed. He stole 15 bases in his one season with the Pirates and as many as 94 in the PCL, at a time when the stolen base was in hibernation. In 1952, a year in which Bernier stole 65, Minnie Minoso led the American League with 22.

While his feet were fleet, Bernier's Achilles heel was at the opposite end of his body. "Carlos Bernier had a temper as big as his chaw of tobacco," wrote John Schulian.[27] Bernier was one of very few black players in organized baseball in the late 1940s and, unlike Jackie Robinson, he did not turn the other cheek when confronted by racial slurs. Nor did he walk away from any confrontation with umpires, opposing players, or his own manager. In August 1954 Bernier was suspended for the remainder of the season for slapping an umpire after being called out on strikes. Lest one think his troubles were solely due to racism, Bernier was also involved in several brawls with black players during Winter League games in the Caribbean.

Although he had virtually no temper at all, Dick Stuart was similar to Bernier in that he was a very talented player who was being held back by his personality. But while Bernier never changed, it appeared to many observers that the big slugger was a new man. "Remember Richard Lee Stuart," said *Sports Illustrated,* "the big, old boy with the strong back and the ego the size of a mushmelon who believed his singular mission in life was to hit home runs? … Dick Stuart seems to have undergone a metamorphosis."[28] They noted Stuart's prodigious offensive output at Salt Lake City and pointed out that he had become a smarter hitter. He didn't get upset when he hit singles and he didn't chase as many bad pitches. And perhaps most astonishing at all, they pointed out that his fielding was much improved.

"I used to sulk," Stuart told *SI*. "If I wasn't hitting, I'd sulk real bad. I'd be so mad I wouldn't even want to go back to the outfield. When I'd get there, I'd be cussing myself out so hard that when somebody hit the ball out near me, I wasn't ready for it. But I like it better and I work harder at first base."[29]

Shepard said, "I say without any hesitancy that Stuart is a better-fielding first baseman right now than several regulars in the major leagues."[30] He also noted that when Stuart had two strikes, he was trying to meet the ball rather than swinging wildly for home runs.

All was not as rosy as it sounded, but the home runs were making people forget about the times Stuart failed to run out a ground ball or made a bad error in the field. And he certainly hadn't become a modest shrinking violet. "The guy who breaks Babe Ruth's home run record," he said, "will make a million bucks. Maybe he'll make that much on endorsements alone. You know how old Ruth was when he got his 60? Thirty-three [Ruth was actually 32]. Just hitting his stride. I'm working on it. I've got time."[31]

It was a good year for Stuart in many ways. He was threatening the PCL home run record. He seemed to have tempered his personality, and on the personal front, he got married again on May 31. Stuart, who'd been divorced for about a year, met the former Lois Murano, a National Airlines stewardess from Greenwich, Connecticut, during training camp in Fort Myers. After a brief courtship, they were married in a ceremony held at the home of Bees president Nick Morgan. Shepard was the best man.

On June 30, Stuart played first

Larry Shepard, pictured here when he was pitching coach for the Cincinnati Reds, managed Stuart at Lincoln, Nebraska, when Stuart achieved national fame by hitting 66 home runs in 1956, and at Salt Lake City in 1958. Stuart later said Shepard was one of the best managers he ever played for, and Shepard was best man at Stuart's second marriage ceremony. National Baseball Hall of Fame.

After breaking home run records in the Pittsburgh minor league system, Stuart was called up midway through the 1958 season and had an excellent rookie year, helping the Pirates to a second-place finish, their best season since the 1940s. National Baseball Hall of Fame.

base for the Southern Division in the PCL All-Star game at Vancouver. He hit a home run estimated at more than 400 feet, a single, and drove in two runs. He was tearing the league apart, but it didn't appear that Stuart was going to break Lazzeri's record, because it seemed impossible that the power-starved Pirates would let him spend the entire season in Salt Lake. Joe Brown made a scouting trip to the West Coast and when he returned, he indicated that Stuart might soon be called up to Pittsburgh.

The Pirates needed Stuart's power. Kluszewski had just four home runs. R.C. Stevens had seven homers, but hadn't hit one in nearly a month and had just two hits in his last 21 at bats. It therefore came as no surprise when Stuart was recalled on the Fourth of July, the day he hit his 31st home run. It was as if the fireworks displays were honoring his promotion. The Pirates sent Stevens to Salt Lake in his place.

Stuart claimed to be surprised by the summons, saying, "I really thought they had forgotten all about me," but no one took him seriously. Stuart could believe that people loved him, they hated him, or that they were persecuting him. But he could never bring himself to believe that anyone had forgotten him.

The *Tribune* gave a lot of credit for Stuart's success to Shepard. "It was Larry, it may be recalled, who wouldn't give up on Dick Stuart, who convinced the big guy he had outgrown his childish antics and was ready to make his bid for the big time ... until he made good this summer with the Pirates [this was written in September] Stuart seemed unable to produce for any other manager but Shepard."[32]

Salt Lake City wasn't happy to see Stuart leave, nor were the other teams in the PCL. "For Salt Lake," wrote John Mooney, "the blow is staggering. Stuart's loss may hurt the gate, because the big boy had most of the color on the Salt Lake club."[33] "This is a blow not only in Salt Lake City," said San Diego general manager Ralph Kiner, "but also to the entire Coast League. Stuart is responsible for the crowds we have been getting this week. He is the only draw in the league."[34]

Six years later, Mooney was still writing about Stuart's appeal. "Maybe it's comedy relief," he said, "but the casual fans will go to see a Stuart in preference to the assembly-line perfectionists that modern baseball fosters. If for no other reason, Stuart is an asset to baseball because he is controversial. All sports need men who can create a reaction of intense loyalty or hate among the paying customers."[35]

Despite being informed of his recall on the 4th, Stuart was told to play out the weekend series for the Bees before reporting to Pittsburgh. The Major League All-Star break was coming up, and the Pirates wouldn't resume their schedule until the 10th. Stuart didn't mind, for he was in no hurry to get to Pittsburgh. He was confident that when he got there, he would stay for a long time.

7

I'm Living in a Dream World at the Moment: 1958—Part 2

Stuart, accompanied by his new wife Lois, spent three days driving from Salt Lake City to Chicago to join the Pirates. It was a grueling trip of about 1,400 miles (Stuart, with his penchant for exaggeration, always described it as 2,000 miles), begun just after Stuart finished playing a doubleheader in Salt Lake.

Stuart had come a long way not only geographically but also in status. He'd begun the season as an unmarried minor leaguer and was now a major league rookie with a new wife. Lois was a looker, and *The Sporting News* published a photo of her smiling and hanging the numerals "66" on the wall of the new Stuart residence in Pittsburgh.

The call-up of a youngster to the major leagues wasn't usually a big story. The last rookie to make his major league debut prior to Stuart was Boston lefty Duane Wilson, who rated a one-sentence mention in *TSN*. But Stuart was no ordinary rookie. He was the most publicized minor leaguer of the past three years, and the July 23 issue of *The Sporting News* not only featured Lois and Stuart's beloved "66" but a large head shot of Stuart, a full-length article, and two sidebar articles.

Pittsburgh, like all large American cities in the 1950s, had a number of daily newspapers, including *The Pittsburgh Press,* the *Sun-Telegraph,* and the *Post-Gazette.* Each weighed in with its opinion on the new Pirates' first baseman. Davis J. Walsh of the *Sun-Telegraph* noted Stuart's massive ego and his questionable fielding skills, stating he "could do practically anything around first base except take throws, field ground balls and handle the bunt sacrifice."[1]

Chester Smith, sports editor of *The Pittsburgh Press*, noted the arrival of "Richard Controversy, alias Dick Stuart," and wondered, "Is he a phenomenal minor leaguer who will never make it up here or merely a guy who has had to lick a frightfully bad approach to the game of baseball?"[2]

Throughout Stuart's tenure in Pittsburgh, the *Press* had a schizophrenic relationship with the controversial first baseman. Smith, a World War I vet, tended to have little patience with Stuart's foibles and bobbles but Les Biederman found Stuart amusing and loved to tease him in his column. He noted once that Stuart had borrowed his typewriter during a team flight to compose a letter to his parents, and that afterwards the "I" key was worn down.

All of the Pittsburgh writers wondered how Stuart would get along with his teammates, many of whom he had alienated during the previous two spring training camps. Stuart, wrote Jack Hernon of the *Post-Gazette,* "hasn't as yet become the most popular Pirate. Because of his popoffish attitude of the past, he will have to win friends on the club." One way to win friends was to hit a few home runs and Hernon quoted one Pirate who said, "I have no love for the guy, but if he can give us a lift, I don't care what he does or says."[3]

Before he put on a Pirate uniform, Stuart had a heart-to-heart talk with Joe Brown, who said he was impressed by the fact that Stuart had played hard in Salt Lake. "We brought you back with the Pirates," Brown told him, "not for the gate but because we feel you can help us.... You were always fighting the organization and fighting yourself.... It's a shame to see a fellow like you waste all your ability and this move shows we have confidence in you and that we feel you're ready. Now you have a more serious approach to your work and it's paying off."[4] In other words, keep your mouth shut. Stuart assured the GM he was a changed man and said Brown wouldn't be sorry he'd called him up.

When he stepped into the batting cage for the first time at Wrigley Field, players on both clubs stopped to watch him hit. Cub catcher Sammy Taylor, a teammate in Atlanta the year before, sidled up to him and told him, "I can see a change in your attitude. In the minors, you felt you were the only big shot around and maybe you were right. But in the majors, the field is full of big shots and you're just one of many."[5]

The Pirates were a rising team. After landing in the basement in 1950, they hired the legendary Branch Rickey as general manager under a five-year $500,000 contract. Rickey began a slow, methodical, painful rebuilding process, doubling the number of minor league affiliates, spending a lot of bonus money on prospects, trading veterans for youngsters, and convincing the club to get rid of beloved but fading slugger Ralph Kiner.[6] Rickey once said that if he signed 300 players and got one major leaguer out of the batch, he was happy. "Out of quantity we get quality," he said.[7]

When he was hired, Rickey said the Pirates would contend for the pennant within three years, but results were slow in coming. The Pirates moved up to seventh place in 1951, but other than another seventh-place finish in 1956, they finished last every year through 1957. "Ridiculing the Pittsburgh Pirates," wrote David Maraniss, "was one of the simple pleasures of the national pastime in the first half of the 1950s."[8] Former Pirate catcher Joe Garagiola built a broadcast career on Yogi Berra jokes and making fun of his Pittsburgh teams of the early '50s.

Losing games led to losing money, and from 1952 through 1956, the Pirates dropped a total of almost two million dollars.[9] Fortunately, the club's principal owner was John Galbreath, a self-made man with thriving real estate and construction businesses. In addition to his own money, Galbreath had married well; his second wife was a member of the Firestone family.

In addition to owning the Pirates, Galbreath had another expensive hobby—his Darby Dan Farm, where he bred and trained race horses. Thus far, his horses had been much more successful than the bi-peds who worked for him at Forbes Field. "It's possible that Mr. Galbreath," wrote Gordon Cobbledick, "may yet win a Kentucky Derby with a Darby Dan colt. As to winning a pennant with the Pittsburgh Pirates, he should live so long."[10]

The Pirate owner played high school and college baseball, was a big fan and loved associating with the players. That and the notoriety that came to the owner of a major league team constituted a large portion of the return on his investment. Entertainer Bing Crosby owned 15 percent of the Pirate stock and he, like Galbreath, was more interested in winning ballgames than making money.

Galbreath and Crosby had experienced success in every other area of their lives and were frustrated to see the Pirates in last place every year. Galbreath said he considered the Pirates his one failure and kept pouring money into the team in order to build a winner.

While the club was losing, Rickey was signing and grooming an army of young players. "Mr. Rickey said," recalled pitcher Bob Friend, "If we're going to lose, we're going to lose with young guys."[11] Rickey liked youngsters for two reasons. First, they had a chance to develop into stars and; second, he didn't have to pay them very much. While Rickey's enduring baseball legacy was his signing of Jackie Robinson, he was best known among the players for his parsimonious approach to salaries. When someone teased former star pitcher Dizzy Dean about his weight gain and how thin he'd been as a player, he replied, "Yeah, but in those days I was being paid by Branch Rickey."[12] During one game in 1955, the Pirates fielded a team on which only two players made more than the minimum salary of $6,000.

At first the young Pirates got their brains beaten out, but eventually they learned how to play the game and some of them got better. Two of them, right-handed pitchers Vernon Law and Bob Friend, developed into solid major league starters. Law was just 20 when he became a Pirate in 1950, and Friend was the same age when he joined Law in the rotation a year later.

Law was rough around the edges when the Pirates signed him. "I had no instruction whatsoever growing up," he said. "In high school we had a coach who didn't know anything about the game. I didn't even know how to wind up."[13]

When the Pirates wanted to sign Law, Bing Crosby was sent to close the deal, and to Rickey's delight, convinced Law's mother that he should not get a bonus, since that would require him to spend two years on a major league roster. He said her son needed to go to the minor leagues and learn how to pitch, which was true. When Law reported to the Pirates Class D club, his manager asked him how he threw his changeup. "What's a changeup?" Law replied. Eventually, Law came under the tutelage of former big league hurler Bill Burwell, who taught him the rudiments of pitching. Law was 40–57 through the end of the 1956 season, but in 1957 he posted a 10–8 record and a fine 2.87 ERA.

Friend was a bright, industrious youngster who completed a bachelor's degree in economics at Purdue during the off season and then spent his winters as a stockbroker. Backed by terrible teams, he was 28–50 in his first four seasons but 45–44 the next three with teams that weren't much better. "In 1951," he recalled, "I was 20 years old and shut out Ewell Blackwell 3–0 (the score was actually 4–1). I thought I was on my way, but I wasn't ready to pitch in the big leagues."[14] By 1958, Friend was ready.

In 1952, Rickey signed shortstop Dick Groat off the Duke University campus for a $30,000 bonus. Groat was a two-time All-American basketball player who was named UPI National Player of the Year after averaging more than 25 points a game as a senior. Professional basketball was a hard way to earn a living in the early 1950s and Groat, a Pittsburgh native, opted to sign with the Pirates. He went from a Duke undergraduate to the Pirates regular shortstop without playing a single game in the minor leagues.

Groat batted .284 in 95 games his first year and was named to *The Sporting News* All-Rookie team. After the season, he played with the NBA's Fort Wayne Pistons[15] before being inducted into the Army for two years. He rejoined the Pirates in 1955, gave up basketball, and had been the shortstop ever since.

Although Groat was a basketball and baseball star, he didn't look like either. He had a pale complexion, didn't have an impressive physique and lost his hair at a young age, which made him look older. In the field, Groat was slow afoot, had limited range, and didn't have much of an arm. At the plate, he had no power. "I always thought that Dick got more out of his talent than anyone who ever lived," said teammate Bill Virdon. "He didn't have any exciting physical talent but he always got the job done. It was his mind. His mind just led him all the way."[16]

Groat studied the hitters and knew where to play them. He admired veteran shortstop Alvin Dark and went to Dark for help. He took every aspect of the game seriously. "Groat," Smoky Burgess once said, "is one of the few hitters around today who gets some benefit from batting practice."[17] He excelled at the hit-and-run play, using his natural stroke to hit the ball to right field.

When Bobby Bragan managed the Pirates, he made Groat keenly aware of his physical shortcomings. "Bragan could be abrasive," Groat recalled. "I used to read in the newspapers that he said he couldn't win because he had a Triple-A infield except for Mazeroski. I went into his office and confronted him. I said, 'You're telling me I'm a Triple-A player, but every morning I see myself in the top five hitters in the National League.' He said, 'I didn't say you weren't a major leaguer. I said you weren't a shortstop.'"[18]

The same year Groat returned from the Army, the Pirates drafted outfielder Roberto Clemente from the Dodger organization. Clemente, in his only minor league season, batted just .257 in 87 games, but anyone who saw him play couldn't miss his quick bat, his speed, his fielding ability and, most of all, his throwing arm, which was one of the most powerful in baseball.[19] By 1958, Clemente was a fixture in right field.

In 1956, Joe L. Brown, son of the famous comedian Joe E. Brown, succeeded Rickey as GM. Brown continued the building process, adding players through trades and being more generous with salaries than Rickey had been. In his first year, Brown brought up 19-year-old second baseman Bill Mazeroski and obtained center fielder Bill Virdon in a trade with the Cardinals.

The Pirates got off to a great start in 1956, winning 30 of their first 50 games, but then lost 36 of the next 50, and ended up seventh. In the spring of 1957, *Baseball Digest* predicted, "Bobby Bragan has survived his freshman year as manager and should handle the club even better."[20] Yet, despite all their talented youngsters, the Pirates finished last again. They were the youngest team in baseball and their inexperience showed in close games; the Pirates always seemed to find a way to lose in the late innings. Their biggest shortcoming was a lack of power.

When the Pirates continued to lose, Bragan blamed Brown for not getting better players. Brown, on the other hand, thought the Pirates needed a better manager, or at least one who was less disruptive. Bragan was Rickey's boy, not Brown's, and the manager didn't help his cause with his sideshow antics. He battled with umpires, feuded with opposing managers, was sometimes short with the press, and his constant carping was alienating the Pirate players. "A winnin' ball club's got to be a *mad* ball club," Bragan once said.[21] The Pirates were indeed mad, but at their manager rather than the opposition.

The final "straw" came during a game against the Milwaukee Braves on July 31, 1957. Bragan, who as a minor league manager had pulled stunts like using eight pinch hitters for each other to make a farce of the game and pretending to faint after a bad call, had a running feud with that day's umpiring team of Frank Dascoli, Frank Secory, Stan Landes, and Bill Baker. "I ain't had trouble with many umpires," he said. "Just a few egomaniacs—guys that thought they was God in a blue suit."[22] That would be the volatile Frank Dascoli.

In the fourth inning, a Braves runner was called safe on a close play at second. Bragan stood in the dugout ostentatiously holding his nose, which caused Landes to eject him from the game. Bragan strolled casually out of the dugout, walked up to Landes and said he wanted to discuss the play, but first he needed a drink. He returned to the dugout, where coach Danny Murtaugh handed him a cardboard container of orange juice with two straws. When Bragan walked onto the field with his juice, Dascoli started screaming and waving his arms, telling Bragan to get off the field or he would forfeit the game.

Bragan offered a straw to Dascoli, then to Secory. "You want a little sip, Frank?" he asked. Secory told him in no uncertain terms that he didn't. "Maybe it would be better if I threw it in your face," Bragan replied. Secory dared him to do that, but Bragan, smiling, walked off the field sipping his orange juice.[23]

Joe Brown denied that he fired Bragan because of the orange juice incident, but it wasn't long after that that he replaced him with Murtaugh, a swarthy-looking, craggy-faced Irishman and former journeyman infielder who spent the last four years of his major league career with the Pirates. After batting just .199 in 1951, Murtaugh realized his days as a major league player were over and asked Rickey for a job in the Pittsburgh organization.

Rickey appointed Murtaugh manager of the Pirates' AA farm club in New Orleans, where he worked with Pelicans' GM Joe Brown. After three years, Murtaugh decided he'd had enough of traveling and left baseball to be closer to his family. His resolution was short-lived, however, and in 1955 he wound up managing the Charleston, West Virginia, team for the Senators. When the club experienced financial problems, Murtaugh was dismissed in mid-season.

Brown offered Danny a job as manager of the Williamsport club, which was closer to his home, and he accepted. But before the 1956 season began, Tommy Tatum, who'd been named a Pirate coach, decided to stay in Oklahoma City, where he was in the radio business. That left an opening on the Pirate staff and Murtaugh was selected to fill it. Therefore, when Bragan was fired in August 1957, Murtaugh was nearby and available. Brown first offered the job to coach Clyde McCullough, but when McCullough declined he turned to the 39-year-old Murtaugh.

The team that had been 36–67 under Bragan finished 26–25 under Murtaugh. Moreover, the new manager had been a breath of fresh air to the players. Murtaugh was calm and supportive, with a dry sense of humor, something the maturing young players needed more than petty fines and tantrums. When Murtaugh got angry, he just chewed more feverishly on his huge wad of tobacco. If he had something to say to a player, he did so in private. When Murtaugh took over, Bill Mazeroski said he felt as if an elephant

Pirate manager Danny Murtaugh reaches for his chewing tobacco during the dramatic 1960 World Series. The low-key Murtaugh replaced fiery Bobby Bragan as Pirate manager in 1957 and led the team to the 1960 championship. His patient nature allowed him to get along with Stuart and bring out the best in the moody slugger. National Baseball Hall of Fame.

had just climbed down from his shoulder.[24] "If Bragan was still managing," Stuart said after being called up to the Pirates, "I know I never would have gotten the chance to play here."[25]

In 1958, Murtaugh's first full year at the helm, the Pirates suddenly jumped off like pennant contenders. Their play surprised everyone, for in a preseason poll of its staff, *Sports Illustrated* picked the Pirates for seventh; of the 36 people polled, none selected them higher than fifth.[26]

After beginning the season with a 17–9 burst, the Bucs went into a slump. But the 1958 slump was not like the horrific slumps of previous years, and when Stuart joined the Pirates, they were in seventh place with a record of 36–41. Although that wasn't great for most teams, it put the Pirates on a pace for their most wins in ten years. Further, in the tightly packed NL race, they were just 5½ games out of first.

Sports Illustrated wasn't sure what to make of the Pittsburgh club. "Curious team," they noted at mid-season, "composed of unknowns a year or so ago, is laced with stars now (same people, mostly, grown up) but is still fiddling near bottom of league. No real reason for it, either, except pitching went sour in June…. But club has bad habit of making mistakes, losing games it should win."[27]

That was the team Dick Stuart joined after the All Star break. Although he arrived in Chicago at two o'clock in the morning of July 10 after a three-day journey, Murtaugh wrote his name on the lineup card for the first game of a doubleheader.

Stuart uncharacteristically admitted to nervousness. "I tried to act nonchalant but I don't think I succeeded."[28] Batting third against lefty Taylor Phillips, Stuart grounded to third in his first at bat. After a strikeout, a popup, and a fly ball, he came up against Chicago relief ace Don Elston in the ninth with two outs, Virdon on second, and the Pirates trailing 8–5. He described what happened next in a ghost-written newspaper article. "The Cubs had been pitching me on the outside of the plate and I was foolishly trying to pull the ball. But on the fifth turn at the plate I decided to swing where the ball was pitched. This one came in high and outside and I swung and it landed in the right-field stands. I'm living in a dream world at the moment, so please forgive me if I say some things now that may not sound just right."[29]

It was a great debut. The champion home run hitter of the minor leagues had burst upon the major league scene with a home run in his first game. The next day, Stuart did it again, hitting a grand slam off Moe Drabowsky, giving him two homers and six runs batted in for his first two major league games. It was just the way he'd imagined it.

Not everyone was convinced Stuart was the real thing. Crusty Davis J. Walsh of the *Sun-Telegraph* asked, "whether Stuart was the answer to a Pittsburgh prayer or just another bumstead who happened to get off to a rousing start … the woods are full of ballfield bric-a-brac that wowed everybody for two days, or two weeks, and were never heard of again."[30]

It would be wonderful for Walsh and his press box colleagues if Stuart was the real thing. As Al Abrams of the *Post-Gazette* put it, "No one is rooting harder for him to make good than the baseball writers who are ever on the hunt for good copy. Stuart can become the city's most exciting sports figure since Ralph Kiner if he continues to boom for distance."[31]

One "journalist" who joined the Stuart rooting section was Ted Kluszewski, the man Stuart replaced at first base. Kluszewski, one of the most likeable men in baseball, had a ghosted column in *The Pittsburgh Press,* where he wrote that he would be "the happiest benchwarmer in the league" if Stuart continued to hit.[32] Klu asked Pirate fans to be patient with Stuart's inevitable strikeouts and said he was a better fielder than they had been led to believe.

Stuart's burst of power was just what the Pirates needed, and they won five of the first seven games he played. Although still hovering near the basement, they were creeping toward the .500 mark, a level they hadn't seen for a full season in a decade.

Ted Kluszewski was one of the great sluggers of the 1950s until a back injury robbed him of his power. He loved to cut off his uniform sleeves to show off his powerful arms. In 1958, Stuart replaced Kluszewski as the Pirate first baseman. National Baseball Hall of Fame.

The second half of July consisted of home-and-home series with the Giants and Dodgers, in which the Pirates were successful both on the field and at the box office. They won 8 of 13 games, taking the season series from the Dodgers for the first time since 1951. It was a long trip from Pittsburgh to California but well worth it, for the Pirates drew a total of 388,657 for their 22 games on the West Coast, compared to 157,995 for the games they'd played against the two clubs in New York and Brooklyn in 1957.

Stuart hit two homers in California, one over the friendly screen at the Los Angeles Coliseum and the second at San Francisco's Seals Stadium.[33] Stuart's parents and several other relatives came down from San Carlos to see his home run in San Francisco.

The Coliseum's left field fence, although protected by a 42-foot-high screen, was just 250 feet from home plate, by far the shortest home run distance in the major leagues. "When we went to play the Dodgers in the Coliseum," said Vern Law, "it felt like you could reach around and touch the left field fence with your hand."[34]

The Coliseum was built for football, and the only way it could be adapted to baseball was to have a very short left field fence and an almost unreachable one in right. In the first nine games in the Dodgers' new park, there were 28 home runs, all to left field. For a right-handed power hitter like Stuart, the Coliseum was the most welcome sight west of Fenway Park. Pirate catcher Hal Smith hit seven of his eleven 1960 homers at the Coliseum and in his three-and-a-half seasons playing there, Stuart had ten.

The only negative note during Stuart's first two weeks in the big leagues was his old bugaboo, the strikeout. At one point he fanned nine times in three games and his batting average was just .170. Still, four home runs in less than three weeks were enough to put Kluszewski permanently on the bench; his only 12 appearances during the next month were as a pinch hitter. It wasn't his back that was keeping Klu on the bench, Joe Brown told reporters. It was the hitting of Dick Stuart.

Sam Balter of the *Los Angeles Herald & Express*, who remembered Stuart from his Hollywood days, warned Pirate fans about getting too excited over Stuart's hot start. "[T]hat city now has Stuart fever," Balter wrote. "Whether the fever persists or subsides, however, will depend on a perusal of other familiar phases of the Stuart box-score: errors, mental lapses, and strikeouts. Pittsburgh fans may be blissfully ignorant of these bits of trivia, but witnesses for the prosecution may be found aplenty in such geographical centers as Lincoln, Hollywood, Atlanta, and Salt Lake."[35]

Davis Walsh decided Stuart was not just a two-day wonder, for he said Stuart was a new man, much different than he'd been a year earlier. "It's a period in my career I'm trying to live down," Stuart told Walsh. "There I was, a small town boy from San Carlos, Cal., surrounded every day by big town reporters asking a lot of questions because I'd hit 66 home runs at Lincoln, Neb. the year before. Maybe I gave the wrong kind of answers to the right questions.... All I can say is I wound up looking pretty flip in the newspapers...."

Stuart also realized he had rubbed some of his teammates the wrong way. "The Pirates have a lot of ribbers," he said, "who kept kidding me every day in the dressing room and I thought it was up to me to hold up my end, only I guess I didn't handle it right."

Finally, Stuart displayed his new modest persona while predicting his personal accomplishments. He didn't say he was going to break Babe Ruth's record or be as good as Ted Williams; he just said he hoped to do well. "I say 'hope' because that's all a sensible man can do after being in the league for only seven or eight days." "By all accounts," Davis concluded, "he's a greatly changed man who now speaks mostly when spoken to, and then with becoming brevity."[36]

What caused this miraculous transformation? Later in the season, Stuart said that marriage had settled him down. "Lois helped me understand myself," he told writer Rudy Cernkovic. "She is sympathetic and determined and helped me change my attitude…. Lois has been the inspiration I needed." "A woman's touch," Cernkovic wrote, "has transformed Pirate first baseman Dick Stuart from baseball's 'bad boy' to an obedient player who wants to make his mark as a major leaguer."[37]

There was still a touch of the old Dick Stuart in the new, however, and when he'd been in Pittsburgh less than a month he told a friend that he might send a cable to Spokane, Washington, where Bobby Bragan was managing the Pacific Coast League team "and tell him I see he is where he belongs and I'm up here where I belong."[38]

During his minor league career, Stuart had been his own press agent—and a damn good one—but now that he was a big leaguer, he decided to hire a professional. Almost immediately after arriving in Pittsburgh, he signed up with agent Frank Scott, who'd recently been engaged by fellow Pirates Bill Mazeroski and Bob Skinner.

Scott was not like today's agents in that he did not handle his clients' salary negotiations. His job was to connect them with promotional opportunities. Scott served as the Yankees' traveling secretary for four years, got to know many of the players and gained their trust. When he hung out his shingle, Yankee stars flocked to him. Yogi Berra was the first, and Mickey Mantle and Phil Rizzuto followed shortly thereafter.

Scott made his reputation by lining up appearances and endorsements for Mantle that earned him $50,000 after his 1956 Triple Crown season, far more than the $30,000 salary Mickey received from the Yankees. "All the players don't cash in," Scott explained. "I'd say about one-fourth are the big moneymakers, picking up at least $5,000 for outside activities. The others may average about $1,000 apiece."[39]

With four home runs under his belt, Stuart prepared for his home debut. He'd seen Forbes Field when he worked with George Sisler late in the 1957 season and knew it wouldn't be a good park for him. It was too big. The stadium, located in the Oakland section of the city, adjacent to the University of Pittsburgh, opened in 1909. Named after John Forbes, a British general who fought in the French and Indian War, Forbes Field was built for the deadball era. The Pirates had the best team in their history in 1909, winning 110 games, but they hit just 25 home runs all season and gave up just 12 to their opponents. Only 10 of the 25 Pirate homers were hit in Pittsburgh.[40]

Barney Dreyfuss, the owner of the Pirates when Forbes Field was built, didn't like "cheap" home runs and vowed there wouldn't be any in his new stadium. The original distances were 360 feet in left field, 462 feet in center and 376 feet to the right field foul pole.[41] In addition to the distance, high fences and extensive foul territory worked to the hitters' disadvantage. The probability of anyone hitting the ball to the center field fence was so slim that, after batting practice, the batting cage was folded up, wheeled out to deep left center field, and left there during the game.

The baseball had been juiced up since 1909, but home runs were still hard to come by at Forbes Field. The 1957 Pirates hit just 20 homers there; Frank Thomas was the leader with eight and no other Pirate hit more than three. No other NL team hit less than 60 home runs in their home park.

In 1947, when slugger Hank Greenberg joined the Pirates, they decided to shorten the fences for him, creating a new configuration in left field called Greenberg Gardens. When Greenberg retired, another right-handed slugger, Ralph Kiner, came along, and the area was rechristened Kiner's Korner.

Built in 1909, Forbes Field had a distant left field fence that was the bane of Stuart's existence during his time in Pittsburgh. He claimed could never break any home run records as long as he played his home games at Forbes. National Baseball Hall of Fame.

When Kiner was traded prior to the 1954 season, Forbes Field was restored to its original dimensions, and stayed that way until the Pirates departed in 1970. Stuart had to aim at the post–Greenberg and Kiner fences, which were much farther away than those at Sherman Field and much closer to sea level than those at Derks Field. Further, the Forbes Field infield was rock-hard and produced bad hops with troubling regularity. Stuart had trouble on a well-manicured field, and Forbes would present him with a real challenge. "If you can field a ball at Forbes Field," Cincinnati manager Fred Hutchinson once said, "you should be awarded a Distinguished Service Cross. I've seen better brickyards than that infield, and I feel sorry for the Pirates, who must play 77 games there."[42]

One day, Bob Friend hit a high chop off the hard infield that went for a single. Bill Virdon, the next batter, hit a towering fly ball to center field. Cubs public relations man Don Biebel, who was sitting in the press box, joked, "I didn't see it, fellows. Was it a fly ball or did it bounce?"[43]

Some players thrived in the old stadium. "It was a *great* park for me to play in," said Groat. "I was a line drive hitter who hit the ball from line to line, so I loved Forbes Field."[44] As a pitcher, Vern Law also loved it. "It was perfect to pitch in when you have an outfield like we had," he said. "Clemente, Virdon, and Skinner could all cover a lot of ground for you, and with that kind of outfield behind me, I loved pitching there."[45]

The Pirates had built a defensive outfield that was very well suited for their home park. "We always played a little deeper there," Virdon said. "You had to go both ways. Fortunately, Clemente had some of the best hands in the game. We played side-by-side for about ten years and I think we only ran together one time. And not too many fell between us."[46] For pitchers, line drive hitters, and fleet outfielders, Forbes Field was ideal. For lumbering power hitters who had difficulty in the field, it was another matter.

Stuart's first game at Forbes Field, however, was a success, even more spectacular than his major league debut. The Dodgers were in town for a mid-week doubleheader, and young right-hander Stan Williams started the first game for them. In the second inning, Stuart singled. In the third, he tripled to drive in Clemente, tying the game 3–3. Then he scored the go-ahead run. Stuart singled and scored in the seventh and in the eighth he tripled in another run. Four hits, two triples, and two runs batted in added up to quite an afternoon. The only thing missing was a home run, and that came the next day off Williams who, after being knocked out after two innings, started again the following day.

Hitting triples seemed out of character for a lumbering slugger like Stuart but, during his five years in cavernous, triples-friendly Forbes Field, he hit 30 of them, including 8 in 1961. Forbes was a great place to watch a game if you liked triples; Pittsburgh's Chief Wilson set the major league single season record with 36 of them in 1912, 24 coming in his home park. Wilson was not unusually fast, but one did not need great speed to hit a triple in Pittsburgh.

Stuart had always compared himself to Ted Williams and Mickey Mantle, but after three weeks in the big leagues he found himself being compared to Dino Restelli. Dino Restelli? Stuart must have shuddered when he read the articles, and he unfailingly read every article about himself.

Eccentric minor league veteran Rocky Nelson made the Pirates roster in 1959 and alternated with Stuart at first base for the next two years. He had an odd stance, an outgoing personality and in 1959 and 1960 had the two best years of his major league career. National Baseball Hall of Fame.

Restelli had been summoned to the Pirates in 1949 after a great half season in the Pacific Coast League—like Stuart. Restelli hit seven home runs in his first 12 games with the Pirates—even better than Stuart. Then he crashed suddenly down to earth. By the end of the season, Restelli had 12 home runs and a .250 batting average. He played in 21 more big league games before going back to the minor leagues and eventually the San Francisco Police Department. Was Stuart destined to be a star or would he be pounding a police beat in a few years?

The Pirates had a great homestand in late July and early August, winning 12 of 14 games. The team arrived in Pittsburgh with a 41–47 record and left with a 53–49 mark. Law, Friend, and Ron Kline pitched consecutive shutouts. The 14 games drew more than 220,000 fans, including two crowds of more than 30,000. The Pirates' reawakening was bringing fans out to Forbes Field in numbers not seen in several seasons.

It was only August 3 and the Pirates already had more wins than they achieved during the entire 1952 and 1953 seasons, and they'd equaled their win total of 1954. What happened? "Very simple," said Groat. "We learned how to play the game. When you played for Bobby Bragan and Danny Murtaugh you knew how to play the game. Guys were advancing runners, moving people along, playing good defense, hitting the relay man, doing the little things that winning clubs do."[47] "I became a better pitcher," said Friend. "Vern Law became a better pitcher."[48]

The young Pirates had seemingly come of age all at once. Stuart and Thomas were hitting home runs, Groat, Virdon, and Clemente were playing like mature major leaguers, and Friend and Law had developed into solid major league starters. Friend would end the season with 22 wins and Law finished with 14. Two young pitchers, Curt Raydon and George (Red) Witt, came out of nowhere. Witt was 9–2 with a 1.61 ERA and threw three shutouts in 15 starts. Raydon was 8–4 in 20 starts and 11 relief appearances.

The remainder of the 1958 season was a happy time for both Stuart and the Pirates. On the 29th of July, Stuart hit what was believed to be the longest triple in the history of Forbes Field, sending a waist high fastball from John Briggs of the Cubs to the flagpole in deep center field. The ball hit the 457-foot mark on one bounce, scoring three runs. That gave Stuart four triples in his first 19 games.

Murtaugh was not with the team that day; he had gone back to Chester, Pennsylvania, for his mother's funeral. By the time the Pirates played, the funeral was over and Murtaugh was driving his family back to Pittsburgh, listening to Bob Prince and Jim Woods' radio broadcast. As Briggs wound up to pitch to Stuart, the Murtaughs entered a tunnel and Prince went silent. Murtaugh pressed hard on the accelerator, and when he came out the other side, he heard that at one time there were three Pirates between second and third. Did they score? Was there a triple play? Finally, he learned that the Pirates had scored three runs and all was well.

When reporters came around after the game, Stuart had a story for them. "I've hit longer ones," he said, "but this is the longest I ever hit that I could still see. I hit one in Pueblo, Colo., two years ago and it stuck in a river bank beyond the center field fence. They couldn't find it until the next day and it was almost buried. Measured 600 feet, or so they said. Next night I hit one almost to the same spot. This one was 550 feet. Of course, the air is light and the ball takes off."[49]

In his first 20 major league games, Stuart hit five homers and drove home 22 runs, exactly what Brown was hoping for when he summoned him from Salt Lake. There were even favorable comments about his defense; he had such a horrible reputation that people were amazed when he executed routine plays.

On August 15, the Pirates arrived in Cincinnati for a weekend series with the Reds. They were in second place with a 59–52 record, six games behind the Milwaukee Braves. On Friday night, Bob Purkey beat the Pirates 6–1, but the Bucs turned the tables the next day behind three homers by Thomas and a monstrous blast by Stuart that landed in the street beyond the center field fence. The ball was hit so hard that Reds center fielder Frank Robinson didn't even move.

Stuart hit two more long homers on Sunday, but the Pirates dropped both games of a doubleheader when the Pittsburgh bullpen collapsed. The 1950s were an era of complete games and most pitching staffs consisted of ten men, the best of whom were starters.

Bullpens were thin, and the heart and soul of the Pirate relief crew was little Roy Face, a 5'8", 155-pound fork-baller who looked more like the carpenter he was during the off-season than a major league pitcher.

Face had been used seven times in the past ten games and the little fellow was running out of steam. Murtaugh kept him out of the first game and watched lefty Don Gross surrender the winning run in the bottom of the ninth. In the second game, the Pirates rallied to tie the game 5–5 in the top of the eighth. In the bottom half of the inning, after Gross loaded the bases with one out, Murtaugh summoned the over-worked Face from the bullpen. He gave up a single and a walk to the first two batters he faced and the Pirate ship was sunk. They left Cincinnati in third place, nine long games behind the Braves.

But the Pirates weren't dead yet. Stuart hit home runs in his next two games, giving him five in four games, and the Pirates won both days. Despite the debacle in Cincinnati, they won 21 of 33 August games and went into a September 7 doubleheader with the Braves back in second place, 7½ games out.

Warren Spahn and Ron Kline were locked in a 1–1 duel in the eighth inning of the first game when the Braves mounted a rally. With Johnny Logan on second, Hank Aaron singled to right. Clemente came up throwing and Logan was out at the plate on Clemente's 21st assist of the year. That left two men on, two out, the score still tied, and left-handed slugger Wes Covington at bat.

Covington lofted a high pop foul outside the first base line. Stuart came in and, predictably, hollered for catcher Hank Foiles to take it. But the wind caught the ball and carried it toward Stuart, who backed off and then ducked. Foiles lunged for the ball but it blew away from him and fell harmlessly to the ground. Give a second chance, Covington blasted a two-run double and the Pirates lost.

Many considered the play the turning point of the season. "You know," Murtaugh said several months later, "it's barely possible we might have overtaken the Braves if someone had caught a little foul fly."[50] Everyone knew who "someone" was. Murtaugh said he'd only blown his stack twice during the year, once when he went after Giants' pitcher Ruben Gomez during a brawl and then when he chewed Stuart out in the locker room for missing Covington's popup.

In addition to his fielding misplays, Stuart had streaks where he had trouble making contact. At the beginning of September, he struck out six times in two games. Roger Craig of the Dodgers fanned him four straight times. In September he tied the major league mark by striking out six times in a row. "If I'd have known seven was the record, I'd have gone for it," he said. "I'm out to get my name in the record books."[51]

The strikeouts and errors brought on the booing that would define Stuart's relationship with Pirate fans over the next five years. When fans got on Stuart, his supporters wrote to the newspapers urging them not to boo. Stuart's most ardent defenders tended to be women, who took fans and columnists to task for picking on poor, handsome Dick. Letter writers pointed out that Pittsburgh fans had abused former Pirate Bob Elliot and hinted that it had driven Elliot out of town. His teammates also came to Stuart's defense. "He carried us on the Western trip," one player said. "They could ruin a kid like Stuart with their booing."[52]

It was assumed that fan abuse would bother most players, but no one was certain how it affected Stuart. It seemed to roll off his back, or at least he pretended it did. He always said it didn't bother him but it did bother his wife. When the fans ignored him, Stuart said, he would start to worry.

The mess-up on Covington's pop foul wasn't Stuart's only fielding blunder. Although everyone, when he first came up, said he wasn't as bad as they'd heard he was, he wasn't good. He led the league's first baseman in errors, even though he didn't join the Pirates until after the All-Star break. His fielding percentage of .973 was by far the worst of any National League first baseman. Stan Musial was next on the list with .989.

Although the Pirates were effectively out of the race after the loss in Milwaukee, there were still individual honors to be gained. On September 10, Bob Friend went to the mound against the Giants trying to reach the 20-win mark for the first time in his career. He'd been knocked out of the box on his first try and, although it seemed he had plenty of time to get to 20, Friend was nervous. Of course, Friend was always nervous.

Stuart, who loved lucky numbers, posted the number 20 over Friend's locker, which made Friend even more nervous. "Don't worry," Stuart said, "I'm gonna hit a couple for you tonight."[53] He didn't hit a couple, and for nine innings Big Stu didn't do much to help Friend. He was hitless in four at bats and committed an error. The game went to the tenth with the score tied 4–4 and Friend was still in there. Stuart sidled up to him in the dugout and said, "Hang on and I'll win it for you. You've waited too long."[54] In the bottom of the 10th, with two outs and Clemente on first, Stuart hit a two-run homer off Marv Grissom that cleared the left-center field wall and gave Friend his coveted 20th win.

Stuart, who was rounding first base when he saw the ball leave the park, jumped up and clapped his hands. When he was about six feet from home plate, he leapt in the air and landed on the plate with both feet. Friend was standing there to embrace him and, in the stands, Pat Friend, Bob's wife, burst into tears.

The Pirates didn't win the pennant, but they came in second, with an 84–70 record, their highest finish and most wins since 1944 and an amazing leap from last place in 1957. It was only the fourth time in major league history that a team ascended from eighth place to second. At one point, they won 32 of 45 games and, like so many overachieving teams, won a lot of close ones, going 30–19 in games decided by one run. The Pirates clinched second place on September 20 with a 4–3 win over the Phillies as Stuart hit his 16th and final home run of the season. The win was Pittsburgh's sixth straight and the 11th in 12 games.

After such a long wait, Pittsburgh fans were ready to celebrate as if their team *had* won the pennant. When they clinched second, the Pirates were welcomed home with a parade that attracted an estimated 75,000–100,000 people. The players rode in cars that had their names plastered on the side, with Murtaugh and Pittsburgh mayor David Lawrence in the lead car. A police band marched with them and played "Take Me Out to the Ballgame." A large delegation of Polish-Americans came to cheer Ted Kluszewski. The parade ended with a luncheon at the Webster Hall Hotel sponsored by the Chamber of Commerce. "We didn't lose the pennant," Murtaugh said. "The Braves won it."[55] Murtaugh was also a winner; he was the Associated Press Manager of the Year while *The Sporting News* named Joe Brown its Executive of the Year.

The exciting revival led to the third best attendance in Pittsburgh history, as the club drew 1,311,988 fans, trailing only the 1948 and 1949 postwar teams. The fans who came to Forbes Field saw good baseball, as their club won 49 and lost just 28 at home, including 30 wins in their last 39 games.

"The climb of the Pirates," reported *Sports Illustrated,* "has made Pittsburgh as happy a city as you can find in America just now. For the last two weeks, while many a major league team has been playing to crowds of only 5,000 to 6,000, euphoric gatherings of 20,000 and 30,000 have been turning up at Forbes Field.... Business ground to a halt when the Pirates played day games; cab drivers neglected passengers to listen to their radios...."[56]

There were many individual heroes. Friend's 22 wins were the most by a Pirate pitcher since Burleigh Grimes won 25 in 1928. But one of the most valuable players on the '58 Pirates, the man whose recall helped spark the sterling stretch run, was rookie Dick Stuart, who finished with a .268 average, 16 home runs and 48 RBI in just 67 games. His home run total was third on the team behind Frank Thomas's 35 and Bill Mazeroski's 19. Thirteen of his 16 homers had been hit on the road, at least one in every park.[57] Combined with his 31 homers at Salt Lake, Stuart had a total of 47 for the season, exactly the same number of circuit clouts with which Ernie Banks led all of major league baseball. He finished second to Orlando Cepeda (who played 148 games) for the all-rookie team.

Everyone agreed the Pirates wouldn't have finished second without Stuart. Before he arrived, the Pirates were 36–41. For the rest of the season, with him at first base nearly every day, they were 48–29.

"Some of the Pirates," speculated Biederman, "were wondering, as they went down the stretch with the hottest team in the league, what might have happened had Dick Stuart been with the club all season."[58]

The top four clubs in each league received a share of the World Series pool, and each Pirate full share for their second place finish was $1,507.04. His teammates voted Stuart a half-share, the same as they gave the bat boy. Why? "Stuart isn't the most popular member of the team," wrote Biederman, "yet he's highly regarded when he walks to the plate with a bat in his hands. He's one of the boys and I doubt if popularity had anything to do with it."[59] He said that slighting Stuart made him more popular with the fans, most of whom thought he'd been treated unfairly.[60]

They even thought so in Europe. Don Reabe, son of the Braddock Chief of Police, wrote from his military post in Germany that he and many of his fellow soldiers thought Stuart had gotten a raw deal. "[A]t the rate public sentiment is piling up," wrote Myron Cope, "[Stuart] might do well to ask his teammates to cut him to a quarter share before the season starts, so that the public will make opening day Dick Stuart Day and give him a Cadillac."[61]

Player representative Bob Friend insisted that the decision was made on the length of time each player had been with the team and denied that it was due to the fact that the players didn't like Stuart. That wasn't exactly true, since they voted a full share to Dick Schofield, who joined the team in June, and a half-share to Jim Pendleton, who'd been with the Pirates only a few weeks. In 1959 they gave a full share to Harry (Suitcase) Simpson, who only spent about five weeks with the team.

In fairness to the Pirates, they hadn't had a lot of experience splitting up World Series money, since there was no reward for finishing last. Friend said at the time, "We feel we were fair with Stuart and Stuart feels the same way."[62] He added recently that he believed the shares had been adjusted after Biederman criticized the split. "We took care of it,"[63] he said, but that does not appear to have been the case.

For the second straight season, Stuart left for the Dominican Republic to play in the winter league, which had some pretty good young ballplayers that year, including Willie McCovey, Felipe Alou, Juan Marichal, and Bill White.[64] They were minor league prospects, as Stuart had been the previous year. Now he was a bona fide major leaguer.

As always, Stuart's announced goal was to work on his defense and curtail his strikeouts. But wherever he went, Dick Stuart's main goal was to hit long home runs. He thought he'd hit a few in the Dominican and a lot the next summer in Pittsburgh. The Pirates thought he might become one of the leading power hitters in the National League. Maybe he wouldn't hit 66 home runs, but who knew?

8

You Can't Blame It All on Stuart: 1959

On January 30, 1959, Pirate GM Joe Brown took a huge gamble. He traded slugger Frank Thomas, who'd led the club with 35 homers and been the National League starting All Star third baseman, along with three other players, to Cincinnati for pitcher Harvey Haddix, third baseman Don Hoak, and catcher Smoky Burgess. From a team that was starved for power, Brown gave up his biggest home run threat for three players who, while they had attributes, also had noticeable weaknesses.

Haddix was a former 20-game winner, but that was six years ago. He was 33 years old and had a reputation for not being able to finish games. Hoak was 31 and had only one solid season under his belt. He batted .293 for the Reds in 1957, but the previous year with the Cubs he'd hit just .215, the lowest average of any National Leaguer with enough at bats to qualify for the batting title.

Brown had reason to believe the Pirates were getting the 1957 Hoak rather than the 1956 version. For some time, Hoak suffered from persistent headaches. Before the 1957 season, doctors operated on his sinuses and removed 26 bone splinters and cartilage from his nose, sinus, and eye areas, which put an end to the headaches. He changed his batting stance and hiked his average by 78 points.

Burgess was a catcher with a big waist, small feet, and a weak arm. While serving in the Army in Germany in 1946, he'd been involved in a jeep accident that badly damaged his shoulder and hindered his throwing for the next several years. By 1959, the shoulder was a little better, but Burgess had other problems. For most of his career, he suffered from painful ulcers that forced him to adhere to a restricted but apparently not abstemious diet. Despite his physical condition, however, Smoky had always been able to hit, and boasted the highest batting average of any active major league catcher.

Burgess consistently batted over .280 and in 1954 hit .368 for the Phillies. Power wasn't his forte but in 1955 he knocked out 21 home runs. There was no question that Burgess could hit, but he was 32 and not getting any thinner or more agile behind the plate. "I'm no Roy Campanella," he once said. "Campy can do things I can't. He was always able to keep the ball in front of him…. When pitchers throw the ball in the dirt to me, it always seems to carom off my shins to the left or right. But I'll tell you one thing. I'm not as bad a catcher as most people think."[1]

That sounded like the faint praise given to Dick Stuart. Murtaugh planned to platoon the left-handed Burgess with the right-handed Foiles. "Oh, how I wish Smoky Burgess could catch like Hank Foiles," said one of the Pirates, "and Foiles could hit like Burgess."[2]

The Pirates had traded their biggest slugger for three players on the far side of 30, none of whom had a record of consistent success. In the 1950s, players in their early 30s, unless they were Warren Spahn or Stan Musial, were usually in the twilight of their big league careers. No one claimed any of the new Pirates was a Spahn or a Musial.

There was another angle. Met manager Wes Westrum once told broadcaster Lindsay Nelson that 80 percent of trades were made because of personalities.[3] Few major leaguers had more controversial personalities than Frank Thomas.

On the positive side, Thomas, who grew up in Pittsburgh, was very good with fans. He signed autographs, visited hospitals, was cooperative with the press, and never neglected a youngster.

In the clubhouse, Thomas never neglected an opportunity to razz a teammate. "We liked Frank," said Vern Law, "but Frank was a needler. He could get under your skin and he could get you mad. There were times that he would get some of the guys upset. It's alright to have fun, but there's a time when you should cut it off. Frank didn't know the 'off' button. If he could see you getting agitated, he'd stay with it."[4] Teammates called Thomas "The Big Donkey" and later "Lurch" after the odd giant in the Addams Family television show.[5]

"He's a real needler," Bob Friend said in 1958, "but I don't think he means anything by it. He's not mean. He's just having fun. But you have to admit that he has a real talent for saying the wrong thing at the wrong time. I know that he sometimes makes me so mad I could shoot him."[6]

"I used to tease [Friend] a lot," Thomas admitted. "I used to go in the clubhouse and he'd be pacing back and forth. I'd agitate him no end and when I knew I had him, I'd walk away from him. He'd take it out on the opposition. It would take the nervousness out of him and that's why I did it."[7]

"[I]t is extremely doubtful," wrote Roy Terrell in *Sports Illustrated,* "that [Thomas] will ever be voted the most popular player in the league among opposing players or even those on his own team. Very few of them really know him, and no one completely understands him. This is partially because he is somewhat of a loner, without any really close friends in the game...."[8] Thomas alienated Brown with some unpleasant salary battles, and he had been very critical of Rickey after the old gentleman left the Pirates.

Thomas played the outfield, third base, and first base but was not a particularly proficient fielder at any position. Brown was also aware that of Thomas's 35 home runs, 19 were hit in Los Angeles, San Francisco, and Chicago, very cozy parks for right-handed hitters. Only nine came at Forbes Field. The Dodgers and Giants would soon move into new stadiums, which were much less conducive to power hitters, especially right-handed pull hitters, and perhaps the Pirate GM thought he was getting rid of Thomas at the peak of his value.

The trade turned out to be one of the best Brown ever made. None of the three players who went to Cincinnati with Thomas made much of a contribution to the Reds, and during his first year in Cincinnati Thomas, who'd been expected to blossom once he was out of spacious Forbes Field, slumped to a .225 average with just 12 homers and 47 RBI.

For the Pirates, Haddix was 12–12 with a 3.13 ERA and on May 26 pitched one of the most remarkable games in the history of major league baseball. Hoak started all 155 games at third base and batted .294, while Burgess batted .297, hit 11 homers, and drove in 59 runs.

The trade of Thomas left Stuart as Pittsburgh's principal power threat. "When the Pirates traded Thomas and his 35 homers, they just about settled on the fact that I would have to be the home-run man," he said. "That's all right with me. I need the Pirates and the Pirates can use me." Dick predicted he would double his 1958 home run output. "Some people have confidence and don't show it," he said. "I have confidence in my ability and I simply wear it on my sleeve. Is that bad? ... I'm not cocky or anything like that. I'm confident."[9]

Sports Illustrated wasn't quite as confident, describing Stuart as "the controversial kid with the large bat and mouth ... who has tempered slightly his admiration for Dick Stuart. Good pitching still fools him sometimes—and so does any kind of pitching—but his strength and power dredge up a daily gleam in Murtaugh's eye." They predicted he might hit 30 homers if he played regularly.[10]

Stuart negotiated a bit with Brown before signing a contract estimated at $12,000, a nice raise from the $7,500 he'd gotten in 1958. When he heard the estimate of his salary, Stuart said, "[Y]ou should give me credit for being a better negotiator than that."[11] He said he was getting $15,000.

After the garrison finish of 1958, the Pirates went to Fort Myers with high hopes. "Bucco Staff Shapes Up as New N.L. Dynasty," trumpeted a headline in *The Sporting News*.[12] With Friend and Law leading, supported by third starter Ron Kline, who'd been a hard-luck 13–16 in 1958, and youngsters George Witt and Curt Raydon, the Pirates felt their rotation was as good as any in the National League. And there was always little Roy Face in the bullpen in the event the starters should falter. With their strong pitching, the Pirates thought they could dislodge the champion Braves. "Most fans," wrote *Sports Illustrated*, "hope to see someone other than the Braves and the Yankees in the World Series next fall. Pittsburgh is their best bet."[13]

A dissenting opinion came from the Cincinnati training camp, where Frank Thomas said, "I can't see Pittsburgh going all the way. I'd say that even if I were still with them. Look, in 1958 there were seven of us who had good years and we didn't have a single injury. Yet we couldn't make it. Now if someone gets hurt it'll be tough on them. They just don't have enough power and their bench is weak. They'll never make it."[14]

Ted Kluszewski reported for spring training with a waistline four inches smaller than a year ago, although he still weighed 240 pounds. He discarded the corset he wore in 1958 and said he intended to play 100 games. Perhaps to light a fire under the sometimes lackadaisical Stuart, Joe Brown said that if he was healthy, Kluszewski would be a contender for the regular job at first. "[W]hoever gets the first base job will have to work for it,"[15] Brown said.

In addition to Kluszewski, the Pirates had drafted first baseman Glenn (Rocky) Nelson, who'd batted .326 with 43 homers and 120 RBI for Toronto in 1958, winning the International League MVP and Triple Crown. Nelson was a 34-year-old left-handed hitter, a longtime minor league star with a balding head and a very strange batting stance. He stood at the plate as if he was sitting down, except there was no chair.

Jim Murray of the *Los Angeles Times* said Nelson's stance was "right out of a lithograph from the archives of baseball—right foot at right angles to the left foot, knees bent. It was so archaic that a magazine once devoted a whole, fascinated story to it on the notion it was obscene to have this kind of a stance without a handlebar mustache to go with it."[16] Bill Conlin called it "a lover's stance. I told him he looked like he was going to sit down on the catcher's lap."[17]

Nelson, who was not particularly big at 5'10" and 175 pounds, had twice been the MVP of the International League, but in six major league seasons with five different clubs, he'd never had as many as 250 at bats in a year. Anyone whose given name is not Rocco and who is nicknamed Rocky is usually a little eccentric, and Nelson clearly was. He was a self-proclaimed expert on a myriad of topics and loved to talk almost as much as he liked to hit, keeping up a constant stream of chatter at the plate and always having a reason (which many called alibis) for anything that went wrong in his life. And a lot had gone wrong in Nelson's baseball life, which was why he'd spent most of his career in the minors.[18]

"I've never been able to hit in the spring," he said, "and nobody had been willing to stay with me until the Pirates did." When he first came up with the Cardinals, Nelson said, they didn't need left-handed hitters and decided to go with right-handers Steve Bilko and Nippy Jones. The next year, Stan Musial was moved to first and that took care of any chance Nelson may have had.

The lasting legacy of Nelson's time with the Cardinals was his nickname. During batting practice one day in spring training, he was hit on the head with a line drive off the bat of catcher Del Rice. When he was unhurt, Whitey Kurowski said that if a line drive didn't faze him, Nelson's head must be made of rocks.

After his stint with the Cardinals, Nelson went to Pittsburgh and the White Sox, where all he did was pinch hit. "You know that most batters can't get their timing down," he said, "unless they're playing regular, and that's the way I am."[19] Then he went to the Dodgers and broke his leg. After a great season with Montreal in 1953, Nelson got a shot with Cleveland the next spring. "That was a funny deal,"[20] he said. Nelson thought he should have been judged on his 1953 season rather than what he did in spring training, but manager Al Lopez thought otherwise and he ended up back in the minors.

Many people thought Nelson was so anxious whenever he got a big league trial that his nerves destroyed him. "He was tighter than a drum," said Indian coach Red Kress about Nelson's time in the Cleveland camp. "Just plain nervous. He looked terrible. He couldn't even catch the ball."[21]

In June of 1956, Nelson got a shot in Brooklyn. "Most hitters get tired in August or September," he said. "Well, I get tired in June. After that, I'm alright."[22] His biggest accomplishment in Ebbets Field was hitting a plethora of foul homers. "If they had just moved the foul pole over about ten feet," said one writer, "Rocky would have broken Ruth's record in a breeze."[23]

The Cardinals claimed Nelson on waivers from the Dodgers, and the following spring the Cards sent him to Toronto, where he had two outstanding seasons. Dixie Walker, who managed Nelson at Toronto, was a booster, but thought that Nelson damaged his big league chances with his loquacious manner. "You never have to wonder where Rocky is," Walker said. "You can always hear him. He does talk a lot. In fact, he spouts off."[24]

By 1958 Nelson had almost resigned himself to the fact that he might never get another major league opportunity. He was making as much in Toronto as many big league players, but he needed just two more months to qualify for a pension. "If he hadn't been up so many times before," said Reds' scout Dutch Dotterer, "the way he is hitting right now there would be 16 major league teams after him with big money. As it is, I guess no one is interested. It's a funny case."[25]

In 1959, for the first time, Nelson was able to hit well in a major league camp, earning a roster spot as one of three Pirate first basemen, along with Stuart and Kluszewski.[26] "Three long knockers," Stuart mused. "I wish the other two were outfielders."[27] Nelson was a pretty good fielder, and had, one writer pointed out, the "ability to do a superb defensive job in late-inning relief of the tangle-footed Stuart."[28]

Stuart told everyone in the spring of 1959 he wouldn't need a late inning caddy because his fielding was much improved. In a March 9 exhibition against the White Sox, he proved otherwise, making four errors, including three in one inning that led to five unearned runs. After dropping a throw from shortstop Dick Groat, he compounded his error by making a wild throw to the plate. He did the same thing later in the inning. He also had two doubles and a single, which typified the saga of Dick Stuart. Drive them in, let them in, and hopefully drive in more than he let in. As Les Biederman noted, he batted .750 for the day and fielded .250.[29]

The Pirates were an odd defensive team, excelling in some positions while being woefully inadequate in others. Virdon and Clemente were outstanding in the outfield, while left fielder Bob Skinner had improved to barely adequate. Bill Mazeroski was one of the best second baseman in the game, Hoak was good at third and Groat, while not physically gifted, got the job done at short. Then there was Stuart, the worst first baseman in baseball. Behind the plate, it depended. When Hank Foiles caught, the defense was sound; when Burgess caught, it was not and the Pirates had three holes in their defense.

Amidst the leisurely routine of spring training, renowned columnist Red Smith found the subject of Stuart worthy of an entire column, titled "Dick Stuart, 1959 Model."[30] It began, "No male animal ever looked more like a big league ball player than Richard Lee Stuart and no character out of Ring Lardner ever sounded more like a busher than the same Dick Stuart...." He recalled Stuart's first appearance in a major league camp in 1957 when "his gift for reticence was as undeveloped as his skill in the outfield." But now, Smith reported, there was a new Stuart. "I guess I used to say some pretty funny things," he told the columnist. "I settled down. I got married again and we're having a baby in May and that sort of thing makes anybody serious."

Stuart claimed that some of the things he said had been misconstrued and writers, particularly those from New York, tailored his quotes to their preconceived notions. He told Smith of the heartache of 1957, when he'd been bounced all the way back to Lincoln. "It's been a long, hard road," he said. "I never wanted to be anything but a ball player in the big leagues—not with Pittsburgh especially, with any team in the majors."[31]

Another New York writer, Milton Gross, produced a long article that was far from complimentary. Stuart, he wrote, "might break his arm patting himself on the back." Then Gross reported a string of boastful quotes, such as Stuart saying he might reach 50 home runs in 1959 and if his home park was anywhere but Forbes Field, he might hit 60. Perhaps the most arrogant statement was when Stuart supposedly said, "I'd just love to hit against (Lew) Burdette and (Warren) Spahn every day." Burdette and Spahn were the Braves best two pitchers and two of the best in the National League, and for a man with a half year in the big leagues to say he owned them was not in the script of 1959 ballplayers.

Gross followed that quote with Stuart saying, "I know now when to keep my mouth shut." "Oddly," Gross wrote, "Stuart says all of this without so much as a grin wrinkling his mouth. The 26 year old doesn't consider himself a braggart." Once during their conversation, Gross inadvertently referred to Stuart as "Ted," which he said Stu took to mean that he was comparing him to Ted Williams. "That's wonderful," Gross reported Stuart as saying. "Put that down in your notes."[32]

After the Gross story appeared, Stuart was asked about the quote regarding Burdette and Spahn. "I didn't say that," he responded. He said Gross invited him and Lois to New

York for lunch and asked how he'd fared against the Braves. "I said that the only hits I had against the Braves came off Spahn and Burdette. That's all I said…. So it comes out in his column that I would like to hit against those two every day…. The people read stuff like that and it isn't going to help me at all."[33]

When Stuart reported to Fort Myers he said he thought the first base job belonged to him and it was up to Kluszewski, Nelson, or R.C. Stevens[34] to take it away from him. Kluszewski thought otherwise, saying that for the first time in two years he had hardly any pain in his back and was swinging freely once more. Pie Traynor, the Pirate legend who visited the Pittsburgh camp for two weeks, thought the team would win the pennant if they put Klu at first.

For most of the spring, writers, especially those who didn't care for the brash Stuart, speculated on the identity of the Pirate starting first baseman. But the Pirates were a relatively young, maturing team, and Murtaugh believed that Stuart was his first baseman until he played himself out of the lineup. That was fortunate, for Stuart had a desultory spring. His fielding was shaky and he didn't hit that well.

The biggest news Stuart made all spring was when Murtaugh fined him $200 for missing a bus to an exhibition game. It was Stuart's second missed bus of the spring, but on the first occasion Stu told Murtaugh he'd been ill and was excused, even though someone had seen him later that day on a golf course. The second time the Pirate manager was not as understanding and levied the first fine he'd imposed since taking over the team in 1957. Stuart understood and said Murtaugh should have fined him $500.

Part of the magic of Dick Stuart was his ability to get back in people's good graces after he'd driven them to the brink. The day after he was fined for missing the bus, he had three hits, including a home run, and all was forgiven.

On April 8, the day before the Pirates' opening game, Stuart became a father for the second time, as Lois presented him with his first son, a seven pound youngster they named Richard Lee, Jr. The daughter from Stuart's first marriage was pretty much out of his life, and Lois and Richard, Jr., gave him a second chance to be a family man.

Thanks to the efforts of Frank Scott, both Dick and Lois appeared in numerous advertising campaigns, pitching products like Stauffer's "magic cradle" in which Dick was shown rocking his new son. The magic cradle, which featured its own lullaby music, was designed for those "who can't find the time or energy to rock the cradle." Stuart, who rarely found time to rock the cradle, was an appropriate spokesperson.

Lois was shown lying down using Stauffer's magic "trimmer," one of many devices from that era which were supposed to get rid of fat by jiggling it. Trimmers were the lazy person's dream—a way to lose weight while just sitting there strapped to a vibrating belt. They didn't work, of course, and the already trim Lois didn't need to lose any weight in the first place.

In addition to being featured in advertisements, Stuart made appearances at shopping centers and events, such as assisting "Big Boy" Professor Frank Marvin, "a nationally known authority on barbecuing."[35] He also enhanced his image with visits to hospitals and orphanages.

The Pirates entered the season with high hopes, but in its pre-season prognostications, *The Sporting News* sounded a cautionary note, saying, "Was their strong finish in 1958 a flash in the pan or was it a long overdue project finally taking shape?"[36] Pittsburghers clearly thought it was the latter, and in the days before the season opener, local newspapers were crammed with coverage of every aspect of the Pirate nine. Sports seasons didn't overlap by much in those days, and in any event Pittsburgh did not have a major league basketball or hockey team. The Pirates were the only game in town in April and fans who subscribed to the *Press, Post-Gazette,* or *Post-Telegram* could spend hours reading about their heroes.

The season got off to a bad start as the Pirates lost their first five games. Although Kluszewski had a terrific spring, Stuart started nearly every game once the season began. By May 12, Klu was hitting .405, but most of his appearances were as a pinch hitter. When the Pirates got off slowly, however, Murtaugh began using Klu against right-handed pitching. Regular play didn't agree with him and the cold weather caused Klu's balky back to act up again, putting him on the sidelines and solidifying Stuart's hold on first base.[37] Nelson's activity was mainly limited to pinch-hitting.

The pitching, which appeared to be such a strength in the spring, turned sour when the season started. Friend, who won 22 games in 1958, gained weight during the off season, reported to camp at 210 pounds, and lost his first seven decisions. "I wouldn't listen to anybody," Friend said. "I was on the banquet tour that winter and I learned a lesson."[38] Friend eventually started winning, but he finished the year with an 8–19 record, a far cry from his 22 wins of 1958.

Red Witt, who'd been 9–2 as a rookie, came up with a sore elbow and pitched just 51 innings all year, finishing 0–7 with a horrible 6.93 ERA. He had some soreness in spring training, but when Dr. Joseph Finegold examined him the day before the opener, he said Witt would have no more pain than he had in 1958. The headline of the article in The *Post-Gazette,* "Witt's Elbow Not Serious, Says Doctor," wouldn't stand the test of time. Witt went on the disabled list in May and would never again be the pitcher he was in 1958.[39] The other 1958 rookie sensation, Curt Raydon, came up with a sore arm and never pitched another game in the major leagues. Friend, Witt and Raydon, who'd combined for a 39–20 mark in 1958, were 8–26 in 1959.

A series with the Cardinals at Forbes Field in early May produced a Stuart tape measure homer and a riot. The home run, Stuart's third of the year, came in the ninth inning of the opening game off Jim Brosnan, who would become one of his favorite targets.[40] The ball appeared to still be rising when it went over the left field scoreboard and it eventually landed in a parking lot in Schenley Park. The distance was estimated at about 500 feet and manager Solly Hemus and several other Cardinals said it was the longest ball they'd ever seen hit at Forbes Field. Announcers Joe Garagiola, Harry Caray, and Bob Prince all said it was the longest home run they'd ever seen anywhere. Unfortunately, the Pirates were trailing 7–4 and Stuart's blast left them a run short.

The riot occurred during the Sunday doubleheader. Pitcher Bennie Daniels, who'd played with Stuart in Billings and Lincoln, made the Pittsburgh squad in 1959 and was pressed into duty as a starter in the second game. A close 4–3 loss in the first game had put pepper pot little manager Hemus in a foul mood and when Solly got upset, he could be volatile, for he was cut from the Leo Durocher/Eddie Stanky mold.

Hemus, who was a playing manager, put himself in the lineup at second base for the second game, and came to bat with one out in the first inning. Daniels hit him with a pitch, which didn't improve his disposition. He shouted at Daniels and started toward him, but Stuart moved in from first base and intercepted him. Both benches emptied, but peace was maintained and Hemus and Daniels repaired to neutral corners, Hemus to first base and Daniels to the mound.

In the top of the sixth, with the Cards holding a 2–1 lead, Hemus came to bat for the third time. Daniels' first delivery brushed him back from the plate. On the next pitch, Hemus swung and let go of the bat, which flew in the direction of the mound but didn't come close to hitting Daniels. The intent was obvious, however, and when Hemus followed with a racial epithet, the battle was on. Daniels went after Hemus, players from both teams joined the fray, Pittsburgh fans pelted the field with debris, and the police charged out to restore order.

It was a fairly typical baseball fight, with the main participants becoming most belligerent when they were being safely restrained, but a few punches were landed. Hemus wound up with a little blood on his face and said he'd been punched a couple of times. Pirate coach Len Levy said he was the one who hit him. Danny Murtaugh also tried to get at Hemus but was restrained. Remarkably, no one was ejected. Hemus went back to the plate, grounded out to shortstop and then took himself out of the game.

Stuart's average soared well over the .300 mark in early May and by the 15th he had six home runs. But the big story of the early season was Stuart's apparent maturation. When the Pirates went to the West Coast, the writers who'd covered him at Hollywood were amazed.

The change in Stuart had also been noted in the Pirate yearbook, which read, "The 'New Stuart' is no longer the talkative, brash and cocky youngster. This Stuart is just as sure of his own ability, but lets others do most of the talking."[41]

Not everyone liked the transformation. Al Abrams, writing in the *Post-Gazette*, described an interview Bob Prince did with Stuart. "Prince had introduced him," Abrams wrote, "as Dick Stuart, slugging first baseman of the Pirates. He must have been mistaken. That wasn't Dick Stuart. He looked like Dick Stuart, but he didn't talk like Dick Stuart. He spoke articulately, but in a carefully modulated voice, and when Prince went into raptures over the homer Stuart had hit over the center field wall at Forbes Field (on June 5) this imposter grinned shyly and looked down at the table."

"The Dick Stuart I know—and admire—," Abrams continued, "is a guy who does not say, 'Thank you very much for having me on your show.' He is a guy who says, 'Some day I may let you write my life story.' … This is my kind of ball player.… I have never considered Dick Stuart offensive—perhaps maddening at times, but not offensive.… [I]t will be a shame if he starts acting nicey-nicey.… There are enough ball players making nice impressions on TV nowadays, so many that the color is disappearing from the game.… As soon as the Pirates get back to town, I'm going to look up Dick Stuart and ask him if he knows that guy who posed as him. And if he does, I'll ask him to get rid of the guy."[42]

Several of Abrams' readers agreed with him. Mrs. R.J. Renk wrote, "I like sweet Golden Boy, I really do.… I sure get tired of these good, clean-cut, yes-I-ate-my-Wheaties boys. Please tell Dick the girls in my neighborhood go to see him on Ladies Day."[43]

The ladies of Pittsburgh liked just about any version of the Pirate first baseman. "Stuart's popularity is tremendous," wrote one Pittsburgh reporter while describing the Pirates victory parade after they clinched the 1960 pennant, "especially with the teenage girls. They squealed and moaned at the sight of big Stu. Some of them tore at his clothes. At least three reached over to kiss him."[44] "Dare put down something nasty about Stu," wrote another reporter, "…and the fems start sending letters to the editor."[45]

By the end of May, the Pirates were in third place with a 24–21 record, 4½ games behind the Braves, who were seeking their third straight pennant, and two behind the Giants. Starting pitching continued to be a problem, but Elroy Face was racking up wins out of the bullpen. By May 31, he was 7–0 and had saved three other games, accounting for 10 of the 24 Pittsburgh wins.

In today's game, Face might never have made it to the major leagues because of his diminutive size and his lack of an overpowering fastball. He dropped out of high school and when he signed a Class D contract for $150 per month, the scout who signed him said, "You ought to be able to win in Class D. But whether you'll ever go higher—well, you're going to need a lot of luck."[46]

Face had a little luck and, more importantly, a devastating fork ball that he'd supposedly learned from old Yankee relief star Joe Page when the two were playing in New Orleans. Although Face began his career as a starter, he was switched to the bullpen because he could pitch almost every day and his forkball induced double play grounders. Like most good relievers, Face could get ready in a hurry, and when Murtaugh went to the mound to summon him, he held his hand waist-high, palm down, to indicate he wanted the little man.

In order to accumulate a substantial number of victories in relief, a pitcher needs to be both good and lucky, and in 1959 Roy Face was both. In some of his wins he wasn't even good, which became somewhat of a joke among the Pirate starters, who teasingly accused him of stealing their wins. "Face," *The Sporting News* said, "...makes a specialty of giving up the tying run, then winning later on."[47]

Face's first victory came on April 22, when he entered a tie game, gave up the go-ahead run and got the win when his team rallied. His second victory came after he'd squandered a lead for reliever Bob Smith. On May 13, Face inherited a 6–3 lead from Vernon Law, allowed the Dodgers to tie the score and was the winning pitcher when Stuart homered in the ninth.

Stuart became a key factor in Face's winning streak. He sometimes made a fielding misplay that allowed the opponent to tie the score and then delivered the hit that gave Face the victory. Bob Prince claimed that Stuart shifted five victories from Haddix and Law to Face.[48]

The Pirates weren't staging as many miraculous rallies as they had in 1958 or would do in 1960, but they always seemed to happen when Face was the pitcher of record. By September 10, he was a remarkable 17–0, with 22 straight wins overall, before his luck ran out. That day, Face came into the game in the eighth inning to protect a 4–3 lead for Friend at the Coliseum. The Dodgers scored twice in the ninth to win the game and saddle Face with his first loss. He got one more win to finish 18–1 but, unlike today's closers, Face had just 10 saves.

The Dodger series in mid–May was a good one for Stuart. "I guess the Dodgers'll be glad to get me out of town," he said afterward. "I really hit them up for a lot of passes to the games for friends." It wasn't just the 53 free tickets he requested for the two games, which set an unofficial Pittsburgh record.[49] On the 13th, Stuart's two-run homer off Don Drysdale led to a 6–4 Pirate win. The next night was Lois's birthday and Dick promised her a home run. His ninth inning blast off reliever Clem Labine gave Face his second win in two nights.

On May 26, newcomer Harvey Haddix took the mound against Milwaukee with a mediocre 3–2 mark. He'd pitched better than his record indicated and would have had a few additional wins if he'd gotten more support. Haddix had a bad cold that night and didn't feel well when he warmed up, but once he started pitching, it was the Braves who didn't feel too well. Over the first 12 innings, Haddix retired 36 straight hitters, something that had never been done before in the long history of major league baseball. In fact, the only two perfect games in National League history took place prior to the 60'6" pitching distance. No one had thrown even nine perfect innings at that distance, let alone twelve. Unfortunately, the Pirates, although they knocked out 12 hits off Lew Burdette during the course of the evening, hadn't been able to cross home plate.

Roy Face was a little man with a devastating forkball who was one of the top relievers in the National League for more than a decade. In 1959, aided by a little luck, he fashioned an amazing 18–1 record. National Baseball Hall of Fame.

Stuart, pinch hitting, nearly won the game in the 10th, hitting a long fly ball that Andy Pafko caught against the center field fence. The 11th and 12th were scoreless and the game moved into the 13th inning with Haddix's perfect game still intact. Felix Mantilla, the 37th man to face him, hit a ground ball to Hoak. He threw wildly to first, the ball hit Nelson on the foot and Mantilla was safe. After a sacrifice and an intentional walk to Hank Aaron, Joe Adcock hit a Haddix pitch over the right field fence to end the game. He passed Aaron, who'd peeled off after touching second, and was credited with a single, resulting in a final score of 1–0.

As Haddix walked dejectedly off the field, Murtaugh came out of the dugout and hugged him. The heroic effort had turned tragic, but it remains one of the great pitching performances in major league history, unlikely to be equaled unless modern pitching patterns change dramatically.[50]

Although Stuart was known primarily as a home run hitter, people were getting the impression that he was becoming a better all-around player. "So far my fielding has amazed a lot of people (Stuart's fielding had always amazed people), including myself.... I believe I'm improving all the time."[51] In addition to apparently becoming an adequate fielder, Stuart was hitting for a high average. In June, he batted .427 with 10 home runs and 22 RBI and finished second to Face in the Player of the Month balloting.

Some thought Stuart was the most improved player on the Pirate team and Dodger coach Pee Wee Reese said he was the most improved hitter in the National League. When Ty Cobb saw Stuart at the Hall of Fame game, he said, "You are really hitting those balls, son. My, what big muscles you've got."[52]

One of Stuart's June homers had a historical footnote. On the 27th, Carl Erskine, one of Brooklyn's star pitchers in the early 1950s, started for the Dodgers at Forbes Field. In the first inning, Stuart touched him for a two-run homer, and three batters later Erskine was out of the game. When manager Walter Alston came to the mound, he said, "Bad day." "Don't worry," Erskine replied, "That's the last time you'll have to take me out."[53] It was his final appearance in the major leagues and Stuart was the last man to take him over the wall.

By July 22, Stuart was batting .310 with 18 home runs, half of them in Forbes Field. "A lot of people told me," he said, "I don't have to swing hard to get those home runs and I guess they're right.... I was sitting on the bench one day, hitting .240. I figured I'd better start swinging for base hits."[54]

That didn't mean Stuart wasn't hitting the occasional tape measure blast, including a stupendous clout on June 5. "Everybody's Talking About Stu's Homer," blared the headline above Dick Groat's ghostwritten column in the *Pittsburgh Press*.[55] With the Pirates trailing the Cubs 3–0, Stuart came to bat in the bottom of the first with Smoky Burgess on base. After pitcher Glen Hobbie delivered, he said, "I saw the bat 'bend.' And the ball went out straight as a string. I'm glad he didn't hit it lower through the box. I might not have been here to tell this story."[56]

The ball sailed over the center field fence and landed about 500 feet away, the first time in the fifty-year history of Forbes Field that anyone had ever homered to center field. Not even Ralph Kiner or Hank Greenberg had done it.

"The reaction of the fellows on the Pirate bench," Groat reported, "was sort of a numb feeling. We couldn't conceive of anybody hitting a ball that far here and we jumped up immediately when Stuart connected, then sat down and shook our heads in bewilderment."[57] Stuart, who was running toward second when the ball cleared the barrier, jumped up and clapped his hands. His only disappointment was that his wife didn't arrive at the game until the second inning and missed the historic blast.

On July 10, the one year anniversary of his major league debut, Stuart beat the Cubs with a three-run home run in the bottom of the 11th. He was leading the Pirates in average, home runs, and runs batted in. Despite the team's slow start, Pirate fans were hopeful, noting at the all-star break that the 1959 club was in better position than the 1958 team had been. Face was in the midst of his long winning streak, Law was pitching well, and Friend was beginning to turn his season around. The second half would commence with a long homestand at Forbes Field, where the '58 Pirates had played so well. Perhaps history would repeat itself.

By the end of July, however, both Stuart and Pirate fans were less sanguine. Stuart's problems began when his ex-wife Diane claimed that his batting average in child support payments was about the same as his baseball batting average. On the 28th, he was served with a warrant giving him ten days to appear at a hearing in Santa Ana, where Diane resided. Accompanied by his attorney, Max Gillan, Stuart surrendered at the Los Angeles Hall of Justice and posted a $1,000 bond. He said the entire incident was a misunderstanding and that he was sending two payments that would put him a month ahead of schedule.

The Pirates also hit hard times, hindered by their age-old problem, a lack of power. During one ten-game stretch they hit just two home runs, both by Stuart. That led to a long losing streak and an August 5 headline in *The Sporting News* that read, "Murtaugh Tries All Hands at Pump on Leaking Buc Craft."[58]

Part of the reason the Buc craft was leaking was that Stuart encountered a slump that at one point reached 18 hitless at bats and dropped his average well below .300. Even worse, Stu wasn't hitting the home runs the Pirates needed from him. "This is the worst month I've ever had," he admitted in early August. "I don't know what's wrong. I know where I used to be ahead of the pitchers, they're ahead of me. I guess maybe I'm just not a .300 hitter."[59]

The Pirates lost nine in a row and 12 of 13, dropping them below .500 at 50–56. "You can't blame it all on Stuart," said coach George Detore. "We've all stopped hitting at once."[60] Dick Groat and Bob Skinner, who'd hit .321 and .300, respectively, in 1958, finished the season at .280 and .275. Bill Mazeroski, who hit .275 with 19 home runs in 1958, plummeted to .241 with just seven homers. He missed over 20 games with a leg injury and, like Friend, was criticized for having gained weight during the winter. Although Face had a phenomenal won-lost record, he too hit the skids late in the season, suffering through a 19-inning stretch in which he surrendered 33 hits and 16 runs.

Although many Pirate players were having off-seasons, the fans chose Stuart as their primary target. The main cause of their discontent was his fielding lapses. "He is at once a hero and a bum with Pirate fans," declared *The Sporting News*. "Dick knocks them out of their seats with his mighty home run smashes but is their despair with his fielding at first base. He makes spectacular plays on hard smashes and goofs on easy ones, such as having the ball hit past him or letting it trickle out of his glove. Dick makes no pretense of being a good fielder, but he is working at it and is improving."[61]

As the Pirates' pennant hopes faded, Murtaugh began giving Nelson more time at first base. The club won 14 of 20 games and Nelson had 22 hits in 62 at bats, driving in 14 runs and boosting his average from .233 to .295. It may have been coincidence, but the Pirates had a far superior record when Nelson started. With Rocky playing well,

Kluszewski became expendable and on August 26 the Bucs traded him to the Chicago White Sox, who were fighting for the American League pennant, receiving well-travelled veteran Harry (Suitcase) Simpson in return.

One of the keys to the success of the 1958 Pirates, as Frank Thomas pointed out before the season, was their remarkably good fortune in avoiding injuries. The 1959 club was as unlucky as their predecessors had been fortunate; almost every regular fell victim to at least some minor malady. Stuart missed a few games with an inflamed left eye and during the latter part of the season wore a special pad to protect his bruised right thumb. The most serious casualty was Clemente, who went on the disabled list in May with a sore right elbow. The injury took a long time to heal and he wound up playing just 105 games and in many of those he was below par. Although he batted .296, Clemente had just four home runs and 50 RBI, and his sore elbow reduced his outfield assists from a league-leading 22 to 10. He also made 13 errors, most of them on bad throws. Clemente's replacement, Joe Christopher, was rendered *hors de combat* after just 12 at bats.

The Pirates also committed mental blunders that drove Murtaugh mad. The usually reliable Bill Virdon was the culprit on two occasions. On June 17, with the Pirates and Cubs tied 2–2 in the eighth inning and Chicago runners on first and second, slow-footed catcher Cal Neeman lined a hit to left field. Bob Skinner tried to scoop the ball up on the short hop and it got by him. Virdon, who should have been backing up the play, thought it was the ninth inning and the hit had ended the game. He headed for the dugout. Shortstop Dick Groat raced into left field, but when he saw Virdon running in, he became confused and took his eye off the ball to check the scoreboard. By the time he located the ball, Neeman had plodded around the bases for an inside-the-park home run.

A few days later, with the bases full of Giants and the score tied in the bottom of the ninth, San Francisco's Leon Wagner hit a pop fly behind second base. The umpire invoked the infield fly rule, making Wagner automatically out. Virdon came charging in from center field, knocked the ball loose from Mazeroski and then threw late to the plate as the winning run scored.

Mental blunders would always be Dick Stuart's signature play. On one occasion, he was thrown out trying to stretch a double into a triple when the Pirates were trailing by five runs. But it was in the field that he most often fell asleep. "At first base," said catcher Bob Oldis, "he'd be talking to the runner and forget about what was going on in the field sometimes."[62]

On September 9, Stuart's lack of attention cost the Pirates a game. With the bases loaded, the Giants' Orlando Cepeda hit a ground ball to Groat. The Pirates attempted to turn a double play but, on a close decision, Cepeda was ruled safe at first as a run scored. While Stuart argued the call in vain with umpire Frank Dascoli, Willie Mays scored a second run. Cepeda went to second and scored when Mazeroski dropped a pop fly. The 1958 Pirates had played smart baseball. In 1959, they often played careless baseball.

Somehow, despite all their tribulations, the Pirates managed to stay in the National League race. At the end of August, during which they won 20 of 29 games, the Pirates were in fourth place, just 3½ games behind the league-leading Giants.

An 8–14 September sealed the Pirates' fate. They wound up in fourth place with a 78–76 record, nine games behind the Dodgers, who beat the Braves in a playoff. *Sports Illustrated* called Pittsburgh the most disappointing team of 1959. An anonymous Pirate said, "Apparently we played over our heads in 1958 and had no pressure of any kind, with the Braves always holding a commanding lead. We couldn't stand the pressure when we had three teams to battle."[63]

A couple of years earlier, Pirate fans would have been ecstatic with a 78–76 record, but after the promise of 1958, they were disappointed and began to find fault with the players and the front office. Joe Brown had been a genius a year earlier, but he came under fire when Kluszewski had a big World Series for the White Sox, hitting three homers and tying Yogi Berra's all-time Series record with 10 RBI. When the Pirates sent Simpson back to the White Sox after the season, it appeared they had given Kluszewski away for nothing.

The most puzzling aspect of the Pirates' season was a 47–30 mark at home and a 31–46 record on the road. The Bucs lost 29 of their last 38 road games, bringing up the familiar criticism that the team had been assembled for the unique contours of Forbes Field and couldn't succeed elsewhere. A Pirate player, who wouldn't allow his name to be used, said, "We have a team built for Forbes Field and it plays accordingly, trying to hit singles and stretch 'em. The players know they don't have the power to hit 'em out and they don't make any attempt at home. But when they get on the road and see some of these shorter parks, they try to become muscle men and their swing is all fouled up."[64]

The breakdown of individual Pirate averages told a grim story.

	Average at Home	*Average on the Road*
Virdon	.266	.242
Burgess	.306	.289
Groat	.308	.243
Nelson	.319	.259
Clemente	.319	.275
Hoak	.269	.318
Mazeroski	.249	.235
Skinner	.270	.289
Stuart	.317	.277

With Nelson getting more time late in the season, Stuart wound up playing just 118 games, but batted .297 with 27 homers (15 on the road) and 78 RBI. He matched Burgess for the team lead in average and led in home runs and RBI by a large margin. His home run total was more than twice that of any teammate, despite ranking only seventh in at bats and he tied a Pirate record with three pinch-hit home runs.[65]

During the final week of the season, Stuart was involved in a fight, a rare occurrence for the easy-going first baseman, and just as unlikely for the other party, mild-mannered Braves infielder Felix Mantilla. "He's the only guy I ever fought in the major leagues," Mantilla said. "We had a little misunderstanding and we went at it pretty good."[66]

Stuart was on first when Hoak singled to center. As Stuart rounded second, he somehow collided with Mantilla. Murtaugh ran on the field claiming interference as Stuart and Mantilla began jawing at each other. Each threw one punch that failed to connect before Stuart wrestled the 160-pound Mantilla to the ground. As they got up, massive Pirate coach Sam Narron went after Mantilla, but the altercation was quickly ended. No one was injured and the game resumed without ejections.

In September, Stuart was the subject of a long article in *True* magazine, written by

New York journalist Jimmy Breslin. It was ironic that Breslin, known to twist the facts in the interest of a good story, wrote for a publication called "True," but he was an entertaining writer with a big following.

Breslin followed the Pirate first baseman through a typical day, focusing on Stuart's monumental ego and his obsession with his appearance. "Stuart had on a crisp white short-sleeved sports shirt," Breslin wrote, "and he carefully knotted a black tie in front of the mirror." He barely noticed teammate Rocky Nelson because "Dick was too busy looking at himself in the mirror. This is a major occupation for Stuart. In all of sport, nobody ever looked at himself in the mirror as hard as Stuart.... Stuart was looking at his wavy brown hair, complete with Elvis Presley sideburns. Then he began to comb it. Next to looking hard at his reflection in a mirror, the best thing Stuart does is comb his hair."[67]

Stuart and Breslin went to a club called "The Clock" where the Pirate first baseman regaled the writer with stories of his home runs and compared himself to Mickey Mantle. Stuart liked going to places like The Clock because people recognized him.

Despite Stuart's preening and boasting, Breslin decided that he liked the big guy. "Stuart leaves some people, his own teammates included, cold," he wrote. "But once you get over the idea that this isn't one of those 'I-can't-tell-you-how-lucky-I-am' dullards and accept the fact that this is a character, a good one, too, you forget about the ego. There isn't a thing in the world wrong with him. This is a big, engaging kid who hits the ball a mile and loves to talk about it. Get 25 more like him and you could bring back baseball."[68] Al Abrams couldn't have put it better.

When they were talking, Stuart apologized to Breslin for not introducing him to a man who approached them. "[F]or the life of me," Stuart told him, "I couldn't think of his name. I know him real well. He's a close personal friend." Then he told Breslin about his 61st home run in Lincoln, hit off a pitcher who was also a very good friend, but whose name likewise escaped him. All in all, Breslin was delighted to find someone who gave him such interesting quotes. Stuart was a good antidote, he believed, for the sterile baseball of the 1950s.

Following the season, Stuart participated in a new television series called *Home Run Derby*,[69] a creation of producer Lou Breslow and a 45-year-old sportscaster named Mark Scott. Scott managed to convince nearly all of the major leagues' biggest sluggers to enter weekly competitions for cash prizes. Two men were paired against each other, with the winner returning the following week to defend his title and get a shot at winning more money.

Home Run Derby was packaged by Ziv Television Productions and distributed to local independent stations around the country. Each episode was filmed at Wrigley Field in Los Angeles, which was described each week by Scott but never identified. In addition to Scott and the two contestants, the cast included a pitcher, catcher, a couple of outfielders, and umpires. Under Home Run Derby rules, any pitch over the plate that was not hit out of the park was an out. There were three outs per inning and nine innings per batter, just as in a regular game of baseball, and the player with the most homers was the winner. Each week's winner got $2,000, the loser got $1,000, and there was a $500 bonus for three home runs in a row, plus an additional $500 for each consecutive homer after three.

Scott gave a play-by-play commentary and talked with the player who was not batting. The conversation was antiseptic and not very scintillating, consisting of snippets like, "The pressure's really on now, Dick." "Yes, it is." The player would describe the pitches they hit out, the ones they failed to hit out, and the difficulty of hitting home runs.

8. You Can't Blame It All on Stuart: 1959

Stuart first appeared in episode #14, facing Phillies slugger Wally Post. The previous week, Post had deposed six-time winner Hank Aaron, who walked away with $13,500 for his seven weeks on the show. Stuart beat Post 11 homers to 9. He hit five in an inning, the most ever to that point, and his 11 homers in nine innings was also the best performance to date.[70]

The next week, Stuart successfully defended his title, beating Orioles' catcher Gus Triandos rather easily, hitting seven home runs to only one for Triandos. Each inning, as Stuart batted, Triandos sat with Scott and lamented his inability to hit the ball over the fence. He changed his bat and removed his batting glove, but nothing helped.

Late in the broadcast, while Triandos was batting, Scott said to Stuart, "You had a reputation as a pop-off guy," and stated how good it was for the fans to see that he was a regular guy rather than a braggart. "A few years ago," Stuart admitted, "I did say a few off-beat things," but added that he had learned his lesson. "You're a fine gentleman," Scott replied, "and a great credit to the game of baseball."[71]

The following week, Stuart was beaten by Frank Robinson of the Reds and his time on *Home Run Derby* came to an end. Scott injected some rare humor into the repartee during Stuart's final appearance, jokingly asking if he was going to protect him if there were any foul balls in their vicinity. Stuart said he didn't have his glove with him as he'd been told to leave it at home. In three weeks, Stuart earned $6,000, not bad for someone who made $12,000 for a 154-game season.[72]

For the third straight year, Stuart went to the Dominican Republic, where he would face off against 23-year-old giant Frank Howard of the Escogido Lions. In two minor league seasons, Dodger farmhand Howard had hit 80 home runs, and the upcoming Dominican duel with Stuart was touted like the Bilko-Stuart matchup in the Pacific Coast League.

On October 25, a crowd of 11,000 gathered for the opening game of the winter season at a brand new stadium in San Pedro de Macoris. Stuart's former Atlanta teammate Ken MacKenzie was on the opposing team and Stuart told him, "MacKenzie, have you seen the ballpark they built for me? It's only 385 feet in left center. You're going to love it." Then he asked if MacKenzie was pitching. Without waiting for an answer, he said, "You must be. My bats were jumping up and down in the rack."[73]

Generalissimo Rafael Trujillo threw the switch that turned on the stadium's lights, and Stuart provided the fireworks with the new park's first homer. That was one of the few high moments of Big Stu's winter season. He had trouble with the food, as he had in Mexico, and lost almost 20 pounds, making him so weak he could barely play. His wife and son also got sick. After hitting just .221 with only five home runs in 39 games, Stuart was released on December 22 and returned to the States, where he played golf and rested up for spring training. He and the Pirates had a big season ahead of them in 1960.

9

The People Came to See Me Hit the Home Run, Not You, Bill: 1960

The 1960 Pirates more than made up for the disappointment of 1959, ending the longest pennant drought of any major league team and giving Pittsburgh its first World Series title since 1925, with essentially the same team that had fallen on its collective face the previous year. Before the 1960 season began, someone asked Danny Murtaugh why a team that finished fourth had not made any significant moves during the winter. "We don't expect guys like Friend, Skinner, Mazeroski and Groat to have two bad years in a row," he replied.[1] If Skinner didn't run into any fences and Friend and Mazeroski learned to push themselves away from the dinner table, Murtaugh thought his Pirates could win the pennant. After all, even with all their 1959 problems, they'd been within 3½ games of first at the end of August.

Murtaugh's sole regret was that he had not been able to acquire a second power hitter to support Stuart. The only meaningful transactions between the 1959 and 1960 seasons were one that sent pitcher Ron Kline to the Cardinals for outfielder Gino Cimoli and young pitcher Tom Cheney and a second that dispatched Hank Foiles and two other players to the Athletics for catcher Hal Smith. Smith, a better hitter than Foiles, would share catching duties with Burgess, who contemplated retirement over the winter but decided against it.[2]

When Stuart went in to talk contract, he got his annual lecture on attitude. Nelson had finished strong in 1959, he was reminded, and might be the starter if Stuart didn't bear down. Negotiations weren't terribly contentious, and Stuart was one of the first Pirates to sign, agreeing to a contract estimated at $18,000 in early January.

Since he had left the Dominican Republic earlier than expected, Stuart had some time to kill before the start of spring training. He stayed in Connecticut with Lois's family for a while and then returned to California. One advantage of spending the winter in California was that Stuart could play golf. Throughout his life, he played frequently and was pretty good at it. He usually finished near the top in ballplayer tournaments, played in numerous charity events, and one of his main tasks during his career in the finance business was to entertain his firm's clients on the golf course.

As one might expect, Stuart was known to use a little "gamesmanship" on the course. Dick Groat, who at the time I interviewed him in 2018 was still active as the operator of a Pittsburgh-area course, played many rounds with Stuart when they were teammates. "You had to watch him," Groat cautioned, sharing a few stories of miraculously found lost balls, improved lies, and uncounted strokes.[3]

When he signed his Pirate contract, Stuart made his annual pledge to improve his fielding, although his expectations were modest. "At least," he said, "I won't be the worst in the league."[4] "The only hole in our defense," he said, "is when I play first base.... I'm trying to get more agile around the bag. George Sisler helps me some and Rocky Nelson gave me some tips last year.... The trouble with me is I boot the easy plays. I can make the hard ones. Anything I can do easy I seem to mess up. Like the little dribbler coming right at me or the short throw to the pitcher covering the bag.... Once you get the rep of being a bad glove man, it's hard to shake it."[5]

In spring training, Mickey Vernon, a former All-Star first baseman starting his first year as a Pirate coach said, "He doesn't want to field. He doesn't want to do anything but hit."[6] "Many times last year," Murtaugh added, "he was not a real good first baseman."

No matter what Murtaugh thought about Stuart's fielding, he needed him in the lineup because he was the Pirates' only power threat. "Home runs pervade his talk and his thoughts," wrote one scribe. "He fights with Pittsburgh teammates to get in the batting cage for extra licks.... All the players stop to watch, for no one swings a bat with more grace and power. The feeling persists that it could be this season when the rangy Californian, now 27, reaches maturity as a player and generates the type of excitement commanded only by a Ted Williams."[7]

Stuart was very self-centered and throughout his career many reporters indicated that his teammates didn't like him. Les Biederman said that Joe Brown was "a bit disturbed by the way the Pirates fail to accept Dick Stuart. He admits he's called several players into the front office regarding their attitude toward Stuart." "I tried to impress on them," Brown told Biederman, "that Stuart could carry this team with his home run bat, and if they downgraded him on and off the field, they were only hurting themselves."[8]

Brown said he had gotten on well with Stuart. "Frankly," he told writer Myron Cope, "I pride myself that my method of handling him has been successful. I've been his friend as well as his boss. I got something out of him that nobody else could."[9]

Today, Stuart's Pirate teammates insist that they liked him. It's possible that attitudes have softened with time, or that some people don't like to speak poorly of others for publication, but the consistency of their comments is convincing.

"Believe it or not," said Dick Groat, "Dick Stuart was loved by everyone on that Pirate club. I don't care what anybody says [I had mentioned media comments regarding the players' dislike of Stuart]. Everybody on the Pirates loved him. Why it went the other way when he went to Boston and Philadelphia I don't know, but we all thought the world of him. You knew what he was like and we enjoyed him, even when he made fun of us. I liked him very, very much and I think if you go back and talk to the Pirates, ninety percent of them would tell you the same thing—he was just a good guy. He loved to tease you, but he took it well when we teased him."[10]

"I don't know who said he was disliked on that Pirate team, but I can't believe that, and I had a pretty good feeling for that whole team [Groat was the captain]. Dick Stuart was something special for us and you couldn't help but like him. You accepted the way he was."

"As many teammates have put it," Myron Cope wrote in 1962, "he doesn't have a mean bone in his body. His spoken tributes to himself used to infuriate Pirate players, but they have learned to laugh at them, and today they regard Stu as a giant among baseball wits."[11]

"He got along good with all his teammates," said catcher Bob Oldis. "We used to kid him a lot about his fielding, but he could hit. He was a funny guy to be around."[12] "He was a good guy," added Dick Schofield, "a very nice guy."[13]

"I liked him from the get-go," said Bob Friend, who was in the midst of the controversy over the 1958 post-season money. When told of the newspaper reports that Stuart was disliked by his teammates, Friend said, "Oh, that's not true. That's not true."[14]

Friend appreciated Stuart's humor. "I remember one time I had a runner on first," he recalled, "I made a pickoff throw, and Stuart came over to the mound and said, 'You're throwing it into the ground. Throw that kind of stuff to the hitters and maybe you'll get someone out.' He's a guy who could get on you, and we'd kid him about a lot of things, but everybody liked him."[15]

Vern Law was more expansive. Law, a devout Mormon, had a philosophy of life that was dramatically different from that of the carefree Stuart. He thought Stuart could have been a better family man, wished he'd worked a little harder, and got frustrated when Stuart's fielding blunders cost him a run or a game, but even the serious Vern Law liked Stuart—for the most part.

"He was a different individual," Law said. "One time in LA we had a night game and then a day game. The day game was getaway day and I was pitching. I was usually one of the first ones to hit the sack, and the next morning I got up early to have breakfast. Then I went back upstairs to watch a little TV before we had to catch the bus to the park. When I got in the elevator, the operator said, 'Do you know what time your big boy got in last night?' I said no. He said, 'I just took him upstairs.' That day he made two errors and almost cost me the game. How are you supposed to feel toward a guy when he doesn't take care of himself? When he's out chasing around all night and having a good time and then trying to go out and play a ballgame when he's half awake? But you still liked the guy. He was fun to be around. He made some crazy statements but he was fun to be around and everybody liked him." Law laughed. "But I would have liked him a heck of a lot more if he'd taken care of himself and really worked on his fielding so he'd be more of a help to our team."

Law recalled another game against the Dodgers in 1960 when he was trying for his 20th win. Champion base stealer Maury Wills was on first and Law picked him off, catching him so far off the bag that Wills had no choice but to break for second. "He runs," Law said, "and Stuart ran after him faking like he was going to throw to get him to stop. He was giving the old arm movements and chased him all the way to second base and didn't even throw the ball. My wife was in the stands and she stood up and yelled, 'You big dumb lunkhead!'" [Apparently "lunkhead" was the Mormon equivalent of an F-Bomb.][16]

For some reason, Stuart seemed to have a lot of trouble in Los Angeles, as evidenced by another incident related by both Groat and Law. "At the Coliseum," Law said, "the Dodger dugout was close to first base and the guys would get on Stuart all the time. He would argue with them and they would banter back and forth between pitches."

Groat picked up the story from there. "Gil Hodges hit a ball in the hole. It got by Don Hoak but I was playing Hodges to pull and backhanded the ball. Stuart [whose attention was on the Dodger dugout] assumed the ball had gone through into left field and turned his back. I didn't notice that and just cranked up and let it fly. If he had been standing directly in line, the ball would have hit him right on the '7.' Elroy Face came in and got us out of the inning, and the first thing Stuart said when he got to the dugout was, 'Two-base error—E-6.' Everybody laughed and so did I, because that was Dick Stuart."[17]

It's very possible that the Pirate players disliked the arrogant youngster who first came to the major leagues and the likeable fellow they described in their interviews came along a couple of years later. When Stuart was a minor leaguer, and during his early days in the majors, he loved to boast about himself and predict future greatness. That Stuart was probably not popular with his teammates. In the spring of 1959 he said, "There's always one player the others ride in any baseball camp and here it's me."[18]

After a couple of years, however, Stuart grew on his teammates. He was a great kidder, loved to joust back and forth with the other players, and his humor was either self-deprecating or so outlandish that no one took him seriously.

As he matured, Stuart learned to get laughs by poking fun at himself. One day, when he walked to start a game-winning rally, he told former teammate Ron Kline, "That's what happens when you walk a .240 hitter."[19] After the Pirates won the World Series in 1960, some of his teammates were teasing him about his fielding. "All right, wise guys," he replied. "Where do you think the Pirates would have finished without me? Well, I'll tell you. They'd have finished fifteen games out in front instead of seven."[20] A remark like that was not in Stuart's repertoire a couple of years earlier.

Stu loved teasing other players and they liked giving it back to him. "How can a big bum like you who weighs 200 pounds," he asked former roommate Gino Cimoli, "not even hit one home run in a season?" After Cimoli hit a long home run in an exhibition game, he told Stuart, "Any time you want a lesson on how to hit the long ball, just call on Uncle Gino." "He hits one home run in two years," Stuart retorted. "Now he wants to give lessons."[21] Later, when he played with the Red Sox, reserve Dick Williams hit three home runs in a game. "Well," Stuart said afterwards, "this kind of cheapens the home run to see Williams do this."[22]

When Stuart saw teammate Dick Groat and the Yankees' Roger Maris being interviewed together before an exhibition game, he quipped, "Now there's a fine picture for you. A couple of real long ball hitters." Groat replied in kind.[23]

Willie Mays was a favorite sparring partner. After Mays hit four homers in a game in May 1961, he was asked to appear on *The Ed Sullivan Show* in New York. Stuart, always interested in finances, asked Mays how much he was paid. When Mays told him he got $750, Stuart said that when he was asked to be on television after hitting his 66 home runs, he got $1,000. "Yes," Mays replied, "but your name is Dick Stuart. I'm ONLY Willie Mays."[24]

Later that season, Stuart asked Mays how much he was asking for his home in New Rochelle, which was for sale. When he told him, Stuart said Mays was asking too much. Mays said Stuart didn't make enough money to worry about buying it. Stuart ended the conversation with, "So you hit three homers against the Phils, eh? Well, you earn your $9,000 a year. Aren't you going to congratulate me for making the All Star team?"[25]

In 1964, Stuart sidled up to Mays before an exhibition game. "I guess I had a better season than you did, Willie," he said. "I didn't see anything about your getting more money, but I got a $10,000 raise."[26] Mays was in the second year of a two-year contract that called for $100,000 a season.

Vern Law said he thought Stuart could have been a better family man. That was a recurring theme with those who knew him. They said that when he returned from a road trip, he had Lois send the boys to stay with relatives or neighbors so they wouldn't disturb him. A teammate recalled that Stuart once brought his family to New York on a road trip and when the players walked down the hallway, they saw a crib outside the Stuarts' door. One of Stuart's sons was there so his father could get his sleep. That was somewhat ironic, for when Stuart traveled without his family, he was rarely in his room resting up for the next game.

Pirate traveling secretary Bob Rice chose Stuart's road roommates carefully, realizing Stuart was a loquacious egotist who could dominate a quiet roommate. "You put a rabbit in a cage with a lion," Rice said, "and the lion will eat the rabbit. So you put two lions together."

Rice first paired Stuart with college-educated George Witt, who he thought could match him word for word. In one of their first conversations, Witt listened to Stuart ramble on interminably about himself, then interrupted and, without pausing for breath, told him his life story, in great detail. "Finally he fell asleep," Witt said.[27]

Regardless of what Stuart's teammates thought of him, he had some diehard supporters among Pirate fans. Perhaps the most enthusiastic was a shoe salesman named Bill Spears. When Spears contacted Les Biederman in early 1960, he told the writer he was Stuart's biggest fan, although he'd never met him. Spears' sales territory encompassed six states, and wherever he went he promoted the virtues of his favorite Pirate. When a customer saw him come in, Spears told Biederman, they always said, "Here comes Dick Stuart's rooter."

One of Spears' biggest concerns was that the other Pirates didn't like Stuart. "[I]f I had anything to do with the Pirates," he said, "I'd call a meeting and lay down the law. The players simply must accept Stuart as one of the 25 men on the team and not treat him as an outsider."[28]

Spears also believed it was unsettling for Stuart to have Nelson and Stevens waiting in the wings in the event he should falter. He compared it to his company assigning two other salesmen to his territory. Spears wanted Joe Brown to show his confidence in Stuart and asked the fans to encourage him rather than boo him. He promised to donate five dollars to the Children's Hospital for every Stuart home run.

When Biederman wrote a column about Spears and Stuart, it precipitated a stream of letters agreeing with what Spears had said. "Dick Stuart does have some friends after all," Biederman began before quoting from letters from readers who thought the Pirates needed to be more accepting of Stuart and that fans needed to get behind him as well.[29]

In February 1960, Stuart rolled into Fort Myers in his powder blue Caddy (which he purchased with his winnings from *Home Run Derby*) with his entire family, prepared to contest with Nelson for the starting job at first. The best news from training camp was that Friend, who worked out all winter, reported at 195 pounds and appeared to have regained his 1958 form. Mazeroski was also trimmer. Still, a poll of 11 writers picked the Giants as slight favorites over the defending champion Dodgers for the National League flag. Four picked the Pirates for fourth, five for fifth, and two for sixth.

Dick Young, who apparently was not part of that poll, thought otherwise. "A year ago at this time," he wrote, "many of the BBWA (Baseball Writers of America) boys were giving the Pirates a good shot at the N.L. flag. Now, nobody gives them a tumble. Why not? Pitt is pretty much the same team. It went through a tough season, just as the Dodgers of '58 had done the year before.... [W]ith a share of the breaks, the Pirates can bounce back this time—because the same talent that excited everybody a year ago is pretty much there to begin with. The Bucs definitely are the overlay of the league. As a long-shot stabber from way back, I pick them."[30] *Sports Illustrated* also thought the Pirates had a chance. "This is a team with unusual balance, no glaring weaknesses, just enough of everything to be dangerous."[31]

The 1959 Pirates had been damned by their inability to win away from home, and in the spring of 1960 they were 10–3 at Fort Myers and 4–7 on the road. Stuart tied Skinner for the team lead in homers with three, one of which was a shot of more than 450 feet against the Tigers, but didn't hit for much of an average. But then, as he always reminded everyone, he never hit in the spring.

Stuart continued his slump when the regular season began, failing to hit a home run until mid–May and striking out frequently. On the other hand, he was hitting for a fairly respectable average and his fielding was a little better. Biederman headlined one of his paragraphs, "Stuart Gazelle in Field."[32] "So far his fielding has been adequate," he wrote on another occasion, and for Stuart adequate was a vast improvement. "He's no longer waving at balls whizzing past him or dropping easy throws. His attitude has changed and he is on his way to becoming a complete player."[33]

When a New York writer asked about his lack of hitting, Stuart replied, "They told me this spring to forget about hitting and concentrate on fielding. That's exactly what I've done. I'm fielding fine but can't hit a lick."[34] "Hey, Skinner," he yelled on another occasion, "did you see me out there? I've been practicing what I'm best at this year, fielding."[35]

Dick Young joined the chorus in writing about the "new Stuart," and the change was not just in his defense. "He realizes," Young wrote, "that Dick Stuart is a part of the Pittsburgh Pirate baseball club, not that the Pittsburgh club was created for Dick Stuart. He speaks freely about his past attitudes and the small, isolated world of Dick Stuart that he had made for himself—and how wrong he was."

Stuart told Young that he used to be happy if he did well and the team lost and despondent if the team won but he did poorly. All that had all changed, he said, and now he was mainly concerned with winning. But, Stuart admitted, he was a little worried about not having a home run. Ralph Kiner had coined the phrase about home run hitters driving Cadillacs and Stuart said, "I guess I'll have to turn in my Caddy. I'm not getting the ball up in the air.... I guess I'm pressing a little, too. I want to get that first home run so bad I can taste it—so I'm swinging at bad balls."[36]

Stuart's frustration was beginning to show, and during the first week in May he earned his first and only major league ejection. Stuart wasn't playing that day, but when Don Hoak was called out on strikes leading off the ninth inning, he started yelling at umpire Tony Venzon. Venzon told Stuart to leave the premises and he did, but he took his time, strolling slowly across the infield and outfield grass on his way to the clubhouse. His estimated travel time was a leisurely three minutes.

Stuart finally hit his first home run on May 13 but during the first week in June, Al Abrams pointed out that the Pirates biggest power threat had two home runs in 151 at bats, while pitcher Fred Green had two in four at bats.

The Pirates began the season with 12 wins in their first 15 games, their best start since 1938. A nine-game winning streak between April 20 and May 1 was the club's longest since 1944. Between them, Friend and Law posted seven wins and had yet to lose and Law completed each of his first four starting assignments. Murtaugh, summoning the Spahn and Sain analogy, said, "We have Law and Friend and that's the end."[37] None of the other starters were consistent, and everyone agreed that the Pirates biggest need was a reliable third starting pitcher.

After winning nine of ten games, the Pirates found themselves in first place with a 22–10 record, 1½ games ahead of the Giants. Perhaps the most encouraging aspect of the early season success was that the Pirates went 10–7 on their first extended road trip and were beginning to oust the road demons that plagued them in 1959.

While Stuart was not hitting home runs, Roberto Clemente was; he hit six in the season's first month and was battling Willie Mays for the batting title with a .378 average. Clemente had always had talent, but 1960 was the year he blossomed as a full-fledged major league star. Until then he'd never hit more than seven home runs in a season or driven in more than 60 runs. In 1960, he hit 16 homers and drove home 94.

On May 28, Joe Brown got his third starter, acquiring veteran left-hander Wilmer (Vinegar Bend) Mizell and utility infielder Dick Gray for promising second baseman Julian Javier and Cuban relief pitcher Ed Bauta. The two players who mattered were Mizell and Javier and it was a good move for both teams, a classic case of a contender giving up a prospect for a solid veteran. Javier became a star with the Cardinals, but he wasn't about to move Mazeroski off second base in Pittsburgh.

Mizell was a colorful character who didn't really come from the town of Vinegar Bend, Alabama (he lived just across the Mississippi line). Cardinal scout Buddy Lewis fetched him out of a swimming hole where Wilmer, according to the story, was skinny dipping, in order to sign him. When Mizell first came up to St. Louis, he threw so hard they called him the next Dizzy Dean.

By 1960 Vinegar Bend was only 29, but he didn't have a lot of vinegar left in his tank. That was all right, for the Pirates only needed him for a sprint, not the Indy 500. Mizell had become a finesse pitcher, combining an assortment of pitches with an odd, deceptive motion. He kicked his right foot high in the air and nearly scraped the knuckles of his left hand on the ground when he rocked back. Cardinal third baseman Ken Boyer said, "The guy shows you his glove, his rear, and somebody tells you it's a strike."[38] Mizell once told Ken MacKenzie, "I just put my leg up in the air, let it go and look up to see what damage was done."[39] Mizell had a 14–7 career record against the Pirates and if he could pitch as well for them as he had against them, the Pirates would be delighted.

By June 15, the Pirates had a three-game lead over the Giants and five of their hitters (Clemente, Skinner, Burgess, Groat, and Smith) were hitting above .300. Clemente led the league with a .341 average and Groat was right behind at .336. Hoak and Skinner were first and second in runs scored, Groat and Clemente one and two in hits, and Groat led the league in doubles. He got six hits in one game and put together some remarkable hot streaks, including 27 hits in 56 at bats at one point.

Meanwhile, Law and Friend were carrying the pitching load. Law was tied with Larry Jackson of St. Louis for the league lead with nine wins and Friend was one behind. The two had completed 13 games, while no other Pirate hurler had finished even one.

Stuart led NL batters with 50 strikeouts, but after going homerless in his first 86 at bats, he hit seven in his next 78. Young, in his mid-season assessment of the Pirates, pointed out, "[I]t is reasonable to assume that Dick Stuart will break loose in the second half to pick up a falloff elsewhere."[40]

At the time Young wrote his column, Stuart had been benched in favor of Nelson. Eventually, Murtaugh rotated Stuart and Nelson, although not in a strict lefty-righty platoon. When Stuart slumped, Nelson played. And when Nelson played, he produced. In 200 at bats, he hit an even .300 with seven homers and 35 RBI.

Whenever a team wins a pennant, unlikely heroes have a knack for rising up and performing feats they'd never done before and would never equal again. In 1960, Nelson was one of those heroes. On July 5, the Pirates were playing Milwaukee, which had crept to within 3½ games of the lead. The Braves led 2–0 when Nelson led off the top of the ninth with a home run. Hoak's two-run homer put the Pirates in front but the Braves tied the game in the bottom of the ninth. In the 10th, Nelson hit his second homer in two innings, a two-run shot that gave the Pirates a 5–4 win.

The next day, the Pirates came from behind to beat the Reds on Bob Skinner's inside-the-park grand slam home run. A few days earlier, little-used outfielder Joe Christopher scored from second base on an infield hit to beat the Dodgers. And so it went all summer.

The Pirates weren't mashers and they didn't scare people, but they won. "The Pittsburgh Pirates," wrote Roy Terrell, "are a team that can wear you out just watching them. To play against them is torture. They protect the plate, they slice doubles into the opposite field, they bounce singles over your head off the hardest-packed infield in all baseball; they bunt, they walk, they hit and run. Almost never do they strike out. They are always standing in front of your line drives, they cut you down trying to stretch a single … and then along about the 27th inning they score a run somehow, and the ball game is over."[41] "We did everything right in 1960," recalled Bill Mazeroski. "We'd try to bunt, couldn't do it, then hit a double. We didn't have a great team, but we did all the little things right."[42]

Many people couldn't believe the Pirates were leading the league. A couple of years later, Warren Spahn was asked for his opinion of the upcoming 1962 pennant race. "We cannot have a succession of weird wins (like the Pirates and the 1961 Reds)," he said. "Now the National League pennant will come back in 1962 to the teams that have the material. I think Milwaukee heads the list with Los Angeles second and San Francisco third."[43]

Even the Pirates realized that 1960 was a miracle year. The following spring, Pittsburgh outfielder Gino Cimoli said, "We can't win the way we won last year. You can't win 30 games in the ninth inning."[44]

On June 14–18, the Pirates visited the West Coast and won five in a row from the Giants and Dodgers, giving them a four-game lead. On the 18th, the Pirates trailed 3–0 with two outs in the ninth and rallied to tie the game and won in the 10th. The streak ended on the 19th, despite Stuart's grand slam off Sandy Koufax.

Los Angeles columnist Braven Dyer wasn't talking about Stuart's hitting. He was raving about "The 'new' Stuart, [who] has become a defensive star and more of a team man than any of his admirers had ever believed possible…. Unbelievable but true. Dick has changed. Pittsburgh officials tell me that Stuart has developed into an expert at digging up balls thrown in the dirt. The big guy has turned out to be a better-than-adequate first baseman."[45]

There had been so many "new" Stuarts that you could populate an entire team with them, but even the new slick-fielding team player Dick Stuart couldn't avoid controversy. During a June 15 game at Candlestick Park, Stuart struck out and was returning to the dugout when a 36-year-old Giant fan named Willis Newman, owner of an Oakland restaurant who was sitting behind the Pirate dugout, started taunting him. Stuart responded in kind and, according to Newman, poked him in the knee. The poke and Stuart's harsh language caused Newman "much emotional distress and mental anguish, as well as bodily harm." He said he had been unable to work since the incident and sued for a total of $125,000, $75,000 from Stuart and $50,000 from the Pirates.[46]

Stuart was incredulous. "I remember this fellow riding me pretty hard after I struck out the second time against Billy O'Dell and he kept it up after I got to the bench. I tapped my bat against the high brick wall and told him to get the h--- out of there and go home," he said. "The wall is eight feet high, and I would have to be nine feet tall to reach his knee."[47]

The next year, Stu had a similar incident at Forbes Field that had a better ending. A Duquesne University student named Peter Mullen, who was seated behind the Pirate dugout, leaned over and started heckling Danny Murtaugh. Stuart thought the remarks were directed at him and threw a punch at Mullen. The blow landed on the young man's shirt pocket, shattering his glasses.

The Pirates paid for the glasses and gave Mullen four tickets to a Pirates game. When the young man went to the game, Stuart sought him out and apologized. "I'd always thought Stu was a big show-off," Mullen said, "but when I met him he was such a nice guy that now I'm converting all my friends to Stuart fans."[48]

Stuart had a very productive June. He hit nine home runs and took over the team lead with 11. Three came against the Giants in the second game of a Forbes Field doubleheader on the last day of the month, as Stuart drove in seven runs with four hits. Roberto Clemente gave Stuart one of his bats, which was a few ounces lighter than the model Stuart was using, and suggested he try it. In the first inning, using Clemente's bat, Stuart hit a three-run homer off lefty Mike McCormick to wipe out a 2–1 Giant lead. The Giants came back to take a 5–4 lead, but Stuart tied the game when he led off the third with a homer off Billy Loes. In his third at bat, facing Stu Miller in the fifth inning, Stuart hit a solo homer to give the Bucs a 6–5 lead.

Stuart's next at bat was against Bud Byerly in the seventh inning. Only a handful of major leaguers had ever hit four homers in a game, and Stuart wanted very badly to join the select group. He was overanxious and, while trying to check his swing, hit a weak grounder to third. He had one more chance in the eighth and added a two-run single as the Pirates won 11–6. That day, Les Biederman wrote, "Stuart actually heard strange noises at Forbes Field—cheers."[49] He even got a round of applause when he grounded out.[50]

Since 1958, the Pirates had a habit of coming behind to win in the late innings, and they were better than ever in 1960. The 1960 Bucs were 12–6 in extra inning affairs and won 23 games in their final at bat, including 12 times with two outs. "It started in our first series against the Cincinnati Reds," said Groat.[51] The Pirates were down five runs going into the ninth inning when a flurry of singles and homers by Hal Smith and Bob Skinner resulted in six runs and the Pirates' first walk-off win of the year. The victory set the tone for the season and sent hot-tempered Reds manager Fred Hutchinson into a rage, causing food and furniture to fly around the Cincinnati clubhouse.

"What I remember about that year," said infielder Dick Schofield, "is that we won games we were not supposed to win. They hadn't won [a pennant] in 33 years, so everybody was excited from opening day to the end of the season. That made it magical."[52] Bobby Bragan, now a coach with the Dodgers, called the Pirates a "team of destiny."[53] Legendary Pirate announcer Bob Prince had a favorite saying when the team pulled out a dramatic victory. "We had 'em all the way," he'd say, and he said it often in 1960.

Pirate fans, after so many years of suffering with their basement dwellers, were wildly enthusiastic about the 1960 team. They'd given the '58 team a parade for finishing second, and the prospect of a pennant set the city aflame with enthusiasm. "In Pittsburgh…," wrote Reds pitcher Jim Brosnan, "the professional baseball player became a celebrity."[54] The slogan "Beat 'em Bucs" could be found and heard all over town and Benny Benack's band, The Iron City Six, played "The Bucs are Going All the Way" so many times that everyone outside of Pittsburgh grew heartily sick of it. Pirate fans couldn't get enough of the song, which consisted mostly of the line "The Bucs are Going All the Way" repeated endlessly with a bit of screaming in the background.⁵⁵ "It's just Stephen Collins Foster's 'Camp Town Races,'" Benack said, "without the 'doo-dah.'"

Hall of Famer Fred Clarke, manager of the 1903 World Champion Pirates, said, "This is the year we are going to do it. I can feel it."⁵⁶ Unfortunately, Clarke died on August 14, missing one of the most dramatic World Series since his club won the first of the 20th century.

The rabid enthusiasm of Pirate fans did not keep them from booing their favorite target. Stuart still struck out, and despite the early enthusiasm about his fielding, he would once more lead NL first basemen in errors. As the abuse mounted, Stuart's loyal supporters peppered the newspapers with letters criticizing those who didn't appreciate their hero. "If we lost the pennant," wrote Joseph J. Balobeck, "it will, in my estimation, be the fault of the fans. Anybody who boos Stuart is not a loyal fan but a plain and simple lout...." As always, Stuart claimed to be unconcerned. "They've been booing me for three years," he told a broadcaster. "If they stopped now I think I'd miss it. Anyway, I'd rather be booed than unrecognized."⁵⁷

Sometimes Stuart deserved the abuse. In mid–August, he was utilized as a pinch runner for the only time in his career. It wasn't because of his speed. Murtaugh put him in when Nelson was hit by a pitch on the right elbow and had to leave the game. As he trotted to first base, someone hoisted a sign in the upper deck that read, "Don't Boo Stu—He'll Come Through."⁵⁸ A few seconds later, Stuart was picked off by catcher Clay Dalrymple. The boos rained down.

On one of the few occasions when Stuart was cheered in Pittsburgh, he wasn't there to hear it. On August 18, the Pirates played the Reds in Cincinnati while the Pittsburgh Steelers took on the Cleveland Browns in an exhibition game at Forbes Field. During the fourth quarter, as the Steelers went into their offensive huddle, a large roar erupted from the stands. Cleveland coach Paul Brown was puzzled, for nothing was happening on the field.

The reason for the cheer was that Steeler fans had transistor radios that were tuned to Bob Prince's broadcast of the Pirates-Reds game. When Prince called Stuart's three-run pinch hit homer off Cal McLish that wiped out the Reds' 1–0 eighth inning lead, the fans gave Stuart a bigger cheer than he generally received in person.

"The average citizen," wrote Myron Cope, "if booed ferociously by mobs of thousands as Pirate first baseman Dick Stuart has been soon would become cranky, withdrawn, belligerent, nervous, and perhaps neurotic." But, Cope informed his readers, Stuart wasn't any of those things. "Perhaps one reason Stuart is booed," Cope wrote, "is that he infuriates his detractors by refusing to give the slightest sign that they are succeeding in destroying him."⁵⁹

Stuart charmed Cope, as he had so many others. Stu could be infuriating, he could be self-centered and egotistical, but he was hard to dislike. "[O]nce you meet him," Cope wrote, "you have to grit your teeth for many weeks while listening to him say the wrong thing at the right time. Then, one day, you find suddenly that you are laughing and that you like the guy."⁶⁰

Cope described Stuart's routines, including getting ten hours of sleep per night (Vern Law could have told him otherwise), being the last Pirate to report to the clubhouse before a game, and sitting in front of his locker having his pre-game cigar. He talked about his fastidiousness about his clothes and his incessant teasing of his teammates and opposing players. All in all, Cope concluded, Stuart was a good fellow.

Always game to put on a show, Stuart helped comic performer Jackie Price with his act when the latter performed at Forbes Field in mid–August. Stuart operated a rocket launcher that fired baseballs high in the air while Price drove around in a jeep and caught them. Unfortunately, the mechanism jammed after only two shots.

On July 16, after two consecutive losses cut the Pirates' lead from five to three games, the Pirates were tied 5–5 with the Reds in the bottom of the ninth inning. Nelson had started at first base, but with one out, Murtaugh sent Stuart up to hit for pitcher Earl Francis. Jim Brosnan was on the mound for the Reds. His first pitch was a fastball that Stuart swung at and missed. He came back with another fastball and Stuart hit it over the scoreboard in left center field, giving the Pirates a dramatic 6–5 win. "It was all or nothing," Stuart said in the clubhouse. "He was throwing hard and I was swinging hard."[61]

July was a mediocre month. The Pirates won 15 and lost 14, but the second place Braves didn't play any better and cut just a game off the Pirates' lead. July was also a slow month for Stuart, who hit just one home run other than the game-winning blast against Brosnan.

Law and Friend hit a mid-summer dry spell and Clemente, who'd been spectacular, was merely good. The bullpen was thin behind Face, who by the end of the season appeared in 68 games (at that time, the Major League record for most appearances by a relief pitcher was 74 by the Phillies' Jim Konstanty). Although his record wasn't as gaudy, Face probably pitched better in 1960 than he had in 1959.

The best news in the pitching department was that Mizell, who'd been just 1–3 with the Cardinals, was turning out to be a life-saver, winning 13 of 18 decisions (including eight of his first ten) for the Pirates and reeling off 30 consecutive scoreless innings at one point. "If we don't have Mizell," said Schofield, "we probably don't win the pennant."[62] Still, by the end of July, the Braves were just two games in arrears, and the Dodgers and Giants were right behind them.

The Pirates regained their momentum in August, going 21–10, and by the end of the month they held a more comfortable 6½ game cushion over second place St. Louis. Stuart had four home runs during the month, three of them against the Reds. The future looked bright, for the Pirates were scheduled to play 18 of their last 26 games at friendly Forbes Field, where they'd always done well.

In early September, when it seemed like the Pirates had a clear path to the pennant, their fortunes suffered a cruel blow when Groat, who'd played every inning of every game, was hit on the wrist by an inside slider from Lew Burdette of the Braves. Groat insisted on staying in the game, but when his next turn at bat came around, he found he could not grip the bat.[63]

Groat, who would win both the batting title and MVP award, wasn't supposed to be with the Pirates in 1960. During the previous winter, Brown and Murtaugh had agreed to a trade with the Kansas City Athletics that would send Groat to Kansas City in exchange for Roger Maris. Before the deal was consummated, Murtaugh had second thoughts and told Brown to call it off. Soon afterward, Maris was traded to the Yankees.

Earlier in the season, Roy Terrell had written, "[I]f something should happen to Dick Groat, the Pirates would probably fall apart."[64] But they didn't, and the reason was that they had utility infielder Dick Schofield in reserve. Schofield was only 25, but he'd been in the major leagues since 1953. The Cardinals had given him a sizable bonus to sign, and under the rules, they were required to carry Schofield on their roster for two years. He sat on the bench, rarely getting into a game, was sent to the minors, and then was

Dick Groat was the National League MVP during the Pirates' world championship season in 1960. A man of modest physical ability, he made himself into a great player through his intelligence and hard work. National Baseball Hall of Fame.

traded to the Pirates in June 1958. For three years, he'd been backing up Groat, Mazeroski, and Hoak.

With all three enjoying strong seasons and good health, Schofield hadn't played much. In fact, before Groat was injured, he'd batted just 35 times all year. It wasn't easy staying in shape sitting on the bench and Schofield worked hard in practice to keep his edge. He wasn't expecting to play the day Groat was hit and put himself through a rigorous workout before the game. "It was real hot that day," he recalled, "and before the game I drank a couple of bottles of lemon and lime soda pop." When Groat realized he couldn't hit, Murtaugh sent Schofield up to bat for him in the third inning. Schofield singled and then had to sprint hard around the bases to score on Skinner's double. "I almost lost my lime soda pop," he recalled.[65]

Schofield started almost every game for the rest of the season, getting 27 hits in 67 at bats, a .403 average. That was typical of the 1960 Pirate season—replacing a batting champion with a .400 hitter. Schofield also fielded well, which was somewhat of a challenge when Stuart was playing first base. "If you played shortstop and let go of the ball," he said, "you looked back at the scoreboard to see if it was E-3 or E-6. He could take some routine throws and make them pretty exciting."[66]

Another valuable late season addition was veteran pitcher Clem Labine, the star reliever on the Brooklyn Dodgers' World Series teams of the '50s. By 1960, Labine was 34 years old and scuffling to stay in the big leagues. The Dodgers traded him to the Tigers, who released him in mid–August with an ERA of more than five runs a game. Joe Brown signed him to augment the Pirates' thin bullpen, and in 30 innings of relief Labine won three games, saved three more, and posted a 1.48 ERA.

"I got to Pittsburgh," Labine said, "and my god! We'd be six runs behind in the eighth and we'd score seven runs and win. This was a club like the Dodgers used to have because they could come from behind and win."[67]

As the Pirates kept winning, reporters tried to get a prediction from Murtaugh as to if and when the Pirates would clinch the pennant. He wouldn't give it to them. In frustration, one writer asked if he would go so far as to predict whether Easter would fall on a Sunday next year. "Well," he said, "it depends on who's selected President. Remember, one of those guys kept changing Thanksgiving around."[68]

The Pirates clinched the pennant September 25 when the Braves lost to the Cubs. The final margin was seven games, and team statistics showed why the Pirates won. Pittsburgh led the NL in batting with a .276 average, well above the league average of .255 and 11 points higher than the second place Braves. They also scored the most runs (734) and even managed to hit 51 homers at Forbes Field, the most they'd hit at home since 1953. The Pirates' 3.49 ERA was second to the Dodgers' 3.40 and their .979 fielding average was tied for the league lead.

Stuart hit six home runs in September, including one long tape measure shot off the Giants' Jack Sanford that traveled more than 450 feet into Shenley Park. He finished the season with a .260 average, 23 homers, and 88 RBI in 122 games. Coincidentally, when the season ended, he had exactly 66 career home runs, his lucky number.

Like so many championship teams, the Pirates had great camaraderie. "We would go out to have a beer after a game," said Groat, "and there might be 12 to 15 Pirates there. That was a very, very close-knit team. The friendships went from top to bottom. Believe it or not, I don't think anyone was enemies with anyone else. And the longer the season went on, the closer we became."[69]

While Stuart was not usually part of the Pirates' hijinks, he was involved on one memorable occasion. Pirate announcer Bob Prince, known as the Gunner, was a former college swimmer who, after he'd had a few drinks, thought he could dive as well as he ever had during his school days. One night when the Pirates were in St. Louis, Stuart bet Prince $20 (some said it was $200) that he couldn't dive into the hotel pool from his third floor room at the Chase Hotel. "It was 90 feet up and seven feet out," Prince recalled, and he made the dive successfully, landing in nine feet of water. He claimed Stuart never paid off the bet.[70]

Law gave third baseman Don Hoak a lot of credit for the Pirate spirit. Hoak, whose nickname was Tiger, was a former Navy man,[71] boxer, and all-around tough guy who never backed away from a fight. He was in a number of them during his baseball career, including one of the most memorable brawls in the history of professional baseball, a donnybrook involving Hoak's Fort Worth team that lasted 35 violent minutes. He was playing in the Dominican Republic one winter when the son-in-law of dictator Rafael Trujillo came out of the stands with a knife and went after one of the umpires. Before he could do any damage, Hoak knocked the knife out of his hand with a bat.

Hoak had a rough childhood that he didn't like to talk about. "The streets were his playground growing up," said Law. "Life was not good for him." Baseball was Hoak's escape from the streets and when he was on a baseball field, Hoak was in charge. "He was what I call the straw boss of the outfit," said Law. "If he felt a pitcher wasn't giving 100%, he'd go over and make the hair stand up on their head with the language he'd use. There are guys you have to get fired up, and Don had the ability to do that."[72]

Hoak was an angry man, and his anger touched everyone—opponents, teammates, umpires, and anyone else who irritated him. He was vulgar and abusive on the field, which resulted in eleven ejections during his major league career. Umpires got back at him by throwing him out and opponents got back at him by throwing at him and sliding into third with their spikes high.

When Hank Aaron said the Braves were going to pass the Pirates and take first place, Hoak replied, "The next time Aaron slides into third base, I might just tag him in the teeth so hard he'll think there's a crap game going on in his mouth."[73] Hoak once got punched by infielder Charley Neal during a brawl with the Dodgers and for more than a year he kept looking for an opportunity to repay Neal in kind. After he was traded to the Phillies, Hoak slid hard into second base and kicked the ball out of Groat's glove. "We're not teammates any more," he said.[74]

Stuart, with his lackadaisical attitude, was a particular target of Hoak, who couldn't understand how anyone could take baseball as casually as Stuart appeared to. "He really says some awful things to Stuart," said a Pirate teammate.[75] When Hoak found out that Stuart was writing letters in the clubhouse during a game, he was speechless. "I don't see how a guy…" he began, and then just shook his head sadly.[76] One day Stuart easily bested Hoak in arm-wrestling and Hoak, who hated to lose at anything, wanted a rematch. "He wouldn't lose, either," said Prince. "He might have to rabbit-punch Stuart, but he wouldn't lose."[77]

Although the Pirates were a close-knit group, some members were more aloof. Clemente tended to be suspicious of others, often felt he did not get the credit due him, and kept to himself. Stuart also went his own way. "I didn't hang around with Dick," said Schofield. "What I remember is that he was kind of a loner."[78] When his former Pirate teammates spoke of Stu, they described him as a nice guy, fun to be around in the locker room, but he was not part of their social circle. It is difficult to find any former Pirate teammates who knew Stuart well. They liked him, but when the game was over, he disappeared.

The Pirates, making their first World Series appearance in 33 years, faced the Yankees, playing in the Series for the 10th time in the past 12 years. The upstart Pirates were 13–10 underdogs, but statistically there was not much difference between the two teams. In particular, the 1960 Yankees were a bit weak in the pitching department. "[The pitching staff]," said veteran Yankee infielder Gil McDougald, "wasn't anywhere close to what we had in the early '50s."[79]

Position by position the players lined up relatively equally. "There were some pretty good players on the Pirates," said Schofield, "and there were some guys on the Yankees who couldn't have played on the Pirates. We had Clemente against Maris, and let's face it, Mantle was a better hitter, but Virdon was probably a better defensive player than Mantle was at that stage of his career."[80]

The main reason most experts favored the Yankees seemed to be simply because they were the *Yankees*, who'd dominated baseball for almost 40 years. The Bombers had a wealth of World Series experience on their roster while the Pirates had just four players (Hoak, Nelson, Labine, and Cimoli) who'd ever played in the Fall Classic. Only Labine had made more than a token appearance. But people who hadn't watched the Pirates all year didn't appreciate how formidable they were, despite a lack of experience and Yankee-like power.

The biggest statistical disparity was that while the Yankees hit an American League record 193 homers, the Bucs hit just 120. That was mostly due, however, to the difference in their home ballparks. Would the vastness of Forbes Field negate the Yankee power? In 1927, even Babe Ruth had been unable to reach the seats in Pittsburgh. Would the Pirates struggle in Yankee Stadium? In the two years prior to 1960, they'd played poorly on the road, and although they did much better in 1960, they were still nine games better at home than on the road.

Pittsburgh and the entire state of Pennsylvania were excited at the prospect of their team's first World Series since 1927 and during the first half of October the Pirates were all that mattered. Governor David Lawrence told Vice Presidential candidate Lyndon Johnson that if he came to the state during the Series, he would have to campaign without him. Johnson postponed the trip. Pittsburgh courts closed at noon when the World Series was in town.

The biggest question for Stuart was how often he would play. Murtaugh told reporters he might start him in every game, rather than alternate him with Nelson. "Stuart will play at first until he goofs off," he said.[81] Writer Joe Williams said, "Stuart could be the hero or the bum of the series. His protean gifts are such [that] apparently he can handle either role with facility."[82]

The biggest surprise of the Series came when the Yankees chose veteran right-hander Art Ditmar as their Game One starter rather than Whitey Ford. "I was a little surprised," said Law, who started for the Pirates. "As a matter of fact, I had my picture taken with Whitey Ford because they thought we were going to start against each other."[83]

Starting Ditmar turned out to be a bad decision, one of several Yankee Manager Casey Stengel made during the course of the Series, as he was routed after retiring just one man in the first inning. Despite the fact that Ditmar was right-handed, Murtaugh started Stuart at first. He had a single in four at bats as the Pirates won 6–4. Law, who'd suffered an ankle injury in some horseplay after the Pirates clinched the pennant, wasn't at his best, but he was good enough to win with help from Face.

Nelson started the second game against Yankee right-hander Bob Turley. "The wind … was blowing to right field," said Murtaugh, "and I was hoping Rocky would be able to get one in the stands."[84] A second reason for using Nelson was that Skinner had been injured in the first game and Murtaugh wanted another left-handed bat against Turley. Nelson got two hits in five at bats, but the Yankees evened the Series with a 16–3 laugher. When the scene shifted to Yankee Stadium for the third game, Ford made his first start and shut out the Pirates 10–0. Stuart again contributed a single in four at bats.

Stuart started the next three games, but had just one single, giving him three hits in 20 at bats, with no extra base hits and no runs batted in. With the Pirates holding a 3–2 lead in games, the Series moved back to Pittsburgh for Game Six, which pitted Ford against Friend. Friend held the Yankees scoreless in the top of the first and the Pirates got two singles off Ford in the bottom half. Then Stuart, described by *The Sporting News* as "a flop on offense in the Series" fanned to end the threat. The Pirates never mounted another, while the Yankees piled up 12 runs in support of Ford's second shutout.

Stuart hadn't hit at all in the first six games and he irritated Murtaugh during Game Six when he nonchalantly waved at a Roger Maris single as it bounced past him. That was the final straw, and Murtaugh decided that Nelson would start against Turley in Game Seven.

Throughout it all, Stuart retained his aplomb, kidding with reporters and pointing out that Mantle's tape measure blast at Forbes Field was not quite as long as the ball he hit off Glen Hobbie in 1959. He joked around during batting practice, providing dramatic commentary as he hit and surmised that perhaps a lack of booing was causing his slump. "Maybe if I'd been booed I'd have been more at home and hit more. The first time I came up and heard the applause I looked around to see who was being introduced."[85]

After six games, the two teams were tied, despite the fact that the Pirates had been outscored 46–17. The seventh game of the 1960 World Series was one of the greatest post-season battles of all time, with comebacks by both teams and an incredibly dramatic finish.[86] The story of that game has been told many times[87] and here we will only touch on those aspects that affected Dick Stuart. Since he didn't play, they were few.

For his entire baseball career—his entire life, Stuart had dreamed of being the hero on baseball's greatest stage, winning a World Series with a dramatic home run. But thus far, Mickey Mantle had smacked the tape measure clouts, while Stuart managed just three measly singles. "Mickey Mantle made Dick Stuart look like he was hitting with a newspaper," said Pirate pitcher George Witt.[88] Game Seven was Stuart's last chance, but it began with him on the bench and ended with him in the on-deck circle.

Nelson hit a two-run homer off Turley in the first inning to give the Pirates an early lead. The Yankees came back, but a three-run eighth inning homer by catcher Hal Smith gave the Pirates a 9–7 advantage going into the ninth inning.

The Yankees scored a run in the ninth, closing the margin to a single run, and had runners on first and third with Yogi Berra at the plate. Berra slapped a hard grounder to Nelson, who stepped on first for the second out and then had to decide what to do. Pinch runner Gil McDougald was streaking for the plate and Mantle was a couple of steps off first. When Nelson hesitated, Mantle, with the force play removed, dived back into first as McDougald scored the tying run.

"Rocky was asked after the game," said Groat, "if he thought about throwing to second. He said 'Groat didn't cover second.' I was playing Yogi to pull, so I was right in line with first base. I was right there. Then they asked if he thought about going home. He said Hal Smith didn't cover home. Then the reporter said, 'Why do you think they call him Rocky?'"[89] If the Pirates had lost, Nelson might have been the goat.

What if Stuart had been playing first? What might he have done? Would he have even been able to stop the ball? Many reporters thought not, as did Bob Friend. "That might have been too much for Dick," he said.[90]

In any event, the two teams entered the bottom of the ninth inning locked in a 9–9 tie, with Bill Mazeroski leading off against Ralph Terry, who'd been brought in to get the final out in the eighth. "I think we had them right where we wanted them," said Schofield. "It was the late innings and we were going to win. That's how we won games."[91]

Roy Terrell had been one of the few writers to pick the Pirates to win, and while he was correct, he was a bit off on the detail. "The 1960 World Series is going to be won," he predicted, "by singles hit to the opposite field and by tight pitching and the sacrifice bunt and sharp defense and the refusal to quit."[92] There had been a lot of opposite field singles, not much tight pitching, but the World Series was about to be decided by the last thing Terrell thought would provide the Pirate margin of victory.

Pitcher Harvey Haddix was due to bat second in the inning and Stuart went to the on-deck circle to pinch hit for him. It was the opportunity he'd dreamed of—a chance for a walk-off game winning homer that would make everyone forget about his miserable series, make him a national hero, and earn him the money he so dearly coveted.

Mazeroski never gave Stuart a chance. His home run made him a villain for many Yankee fans, in the way Bucky Dent was despised by the next generation of Red Sox fans, but Mazeroski was also a villain in the drama of Dick Stuart. Pirate catcher Bob Oldis remembered what Stuart said in the winning locker room. "With his dry humor," Oldis recalled, "he said, 'The people came to see me hit the home run, not you, Bill.'"[93] The next spring, when his Pirate teammates kidded Mazeroski about his wild leap around the bases, Stuart said, "You should have seen what I had planned."[94]

When Pittsburgh mayor Joseph Barr came into the Pirate clubhouse after the game, Stuart poured a cup of champagne over his head. When the mayor looked shocked, Stuart gave him a big grin and shouted, "Ya old so-and-so, ya shouldn't have come in here if you didn't want to get wet."[95] Les Biederman wrote, "It was the only good hit of the Series made by Stuart."[96]

Although Stuart was disappointed in his post-season performance (writer Neal Russo ranked him as the worst hitter in the Series), his sorrow was assuaged by his $8,417.94 share of the World Series loot. Financially, it was a good year for the Pirates, as attendance was a record 1,705,828, an increase of more than 350,000 over the previous year, and a dramatic climb from the 475,000 the last place Pirates drew in 1954. The planning of Branch Rickey and Joe Brown and the calm leadership of Danny Murtaugh had brought a championship and prosperity to Pittsburgh.[97] Although Dick Stuart got lost in the heroics of Mazeroski, Law, and Face, the Pirates probably wouldn't have won the pennant without his power. For the first time in his major league career, Dick Stuart was a champion, and he liked the way it felt.

Stu no longer played winter ball. He remained in Pittsburgh during the off-season working in a public relations capacity. He said he was earning $250 a week and the use of a new Caddy. It's not certain whether he had the car on October 26, when he had to drive Lois to the hospital to deliver their new son Robert, who weighed in at nine pounds and four ounces.

Coming off a world championship, expectations were high for the 1961 season. Pirate fans would be disappointed, but 1961 would be a banner season for Dick Stuart.

10

I Want This Club to Play Me Regularly or Trade Me: 1961

Although the 1960 season ended in glory for the Pirates, it finished on a down note for Stuart, due to his disappointing World Series. During the off season, there were several rumors that he might be traded, most likely to an American League team. Nelson, although he would be 36 in 1961, was coming off a very good year and perennial prospect R.C. Stevens had a terrific season at Salt Lake City, hitting .276 with 37 home runs and 109 RBI.

Although Stuart led the 1960 Pirates in home runs by a wide margin, many observers, including columnist Harry Keck, thought the Pirates might be better off with someone else at first base. "Stuart continues to be a problem defensively," Keck wrote, "and also in the matter of his strikeouts as against his leadership in home run hitting."[1]

Stevens was soon out of the picture, traded to the new Washington Senators, along with Bennie Daniels and utility man Harry Bright for veteran left-hander Bobby Shantz. Despite all the promise generated by his great minor league statistics, Stevens was a flop in Washington, playing just 33 games and batting a mere .129 with no home runs. With Stevens gone and no new first baseman on the scene, 1961 looked like a repeat of 1960, a platoon between Stuart and Nelson. That did not sit well with Big Stu.

Stuart was the last Pirate to sign a 1961 contract, joking that all he was asking for as a salary was the amount of Dick Groat's raise. He dickered with Joe Brown for a bit, and was miffed when Brown would not accept his collect calls. Stuart flew to Florida at his own expense to negotiate, and on the 25th of February, after an hour-long discussion, Brown gave Stuart his "final offer."

Stuart had a good spring, hitting much better than he had in previous training camps and again giving the promise of better fielding. Yet, there was more controversy, fueled once again by Milton Gross, who'd infuriated Stuart the previous spring by misquoting him.

Gross had a few more negative things to say about Stuart in the spring of 1961, including his observation that Stuart's enthusiasm during the locker room celebration the previous October had been resented by his teammates. Nobody cared, he said, when Hoak, Face, or Virdon sprayed champagne around the locker room, "but the resentment was almost a physical thing when Stuart's overzealousness in the aftermath of the victory far outdid his contribution to it."[2] Ironically, Gross was criticizing Stuart for doing what he'd always been accused of not doing—taking joy in team rather than personal success.

Gross said no one on the Pirates wanted to room with Stuart, and accused him of trying to live on the glory of his 66 homers in 1956. "It must seem so long ago to Dick,"

Gross wrote, "because now the bluster is only on the surface, where he is still playing a part. Beneath it is the solid appreciation that in the big leagues you fool nobody but yourself and in the quiet of the night you cannot even fool yourself."[3] He quoted Stuart as saying that he *was* growing up, but the overall tone of the article was that Dick Stuart was still an immature, self-centered jerk.

Just a few days after Gross's article appeared, Biederman came to Stuart's defense with a column that talked about his improved fielding and, more importantly, that he appeared to be getting along better with the other players. "There was a time," Biederman wrote, "when his teammates deeply resented him and even the youngest of the rookies cast slurs at him because it seemed to be the fashionable thing to do. But now Stuart is being accepted—or being accepted better than was the case a year or two ago. His teammates realized that he has a good sense of humor—oddball as it may seem at times—and they kid him and he kids back."[4]

Stuart, Biederman said later, was Stuart and you either liked him or you didn't. He quoted an anonymous teammate who said, "We simply try to measure him by the standards of the other players and it isn't fair. He doesn't have their ability. His job for the Pirates is to hit the long ball. That's why a lot of us don't get angry when Stu misses a ball or gets thrown out on the bases when another player would make it. If Stu had the ability to think fast and react fast and had speed, then maybe we'd get riled up."[5]

One of the chronic laments of the 1960s was that there was a dearth of "colorful" players like those of prior decades. *Baseball Digest* asked former star player and manager Frankie Frisch, who led the Gashouse Gang Cardinals of the 1930s, which current players he would name to a "1961 Gashouse Gang" team. Stuart was his first baseman. "Ring Lardner himself would have worshipped the boy," Frisch wrote. "Dick is big and strong, cocky as they come and he murders baseballs, as well as the English language." He loved Stuart's comments about Sisler trying to teach him to play first base. "They oughta let me hit and let George field," Stu had said. "The man who busts Babe Ruth's records will be a millionaire. They ain't paying me off on fielding ground balls."[6] Although Frisch said he thought Stuart was great for baseball, he might have loved him a bit less if he were his manager.

The Pirates' 1961 season began much like 1960 had ended; they defeated the Giants on a three-run ninth inning homer by Bill Virdon. But this season would turn out much differently. The National League was well-balanced, in the midst of a seven-year cycle of seven different pennant winners. Without a dominant team, the pennant winner was usually the one that pulled out a lot of close games and got miraculous seasons from unexpected sources. It was too much to expect a repeat of the magic of 1960 and many of the surprise stars of that year were unable to duplicate their amazing performances.

One of the main reasons for the Pirates' decline was the arm miseries of 1960 Cy Young Award winner Vern Law. During the '60 Series, Law had altered his pitching motion to compensate for his injured ankle and hurt his arm in the process. "I'd had to change my pitching style in order to try to get more velocity on the ball," he said. "I didn't know it but I had a torn rotor cuff."[7]

Law was hit hard in the spring of 1961, but insisted his arm was OK and he just needed more work. But when the season began he missed four starts and when he did pitch, it was obvious something was wrong. He continued to insist his arm was fine; he just couldn't get loose. But Law seemed to have nothing on the ball, and after one rough outing, Stuart teased him by asking if he would be interested in serving as a pitcher for the Home Run Derby show.

Right-hander Vernon Law won the 1960 Cy Young Award and was the ace of the Pirates staff. His severe arm injury ruined the Pirates 1961 hopes, but he came back to have several productive seasons. National Baseball Hall of Fame.

Law had experienced similar shoulder problems early in his career. "I tore my rotator cuff at the beginning of the 1951 season in Chicago," he said. "It was rainy, cold, and windy as only Chicago can be. They stopped the game in the seventh inning, and it was about an hour and a half before they started it again. It was still raining but they decided to finish. They put me back in there and that's when I tore it. I was done, and I struggled the whole year."

After the season, Law was drafted into the Army, which gave him two years to rest his arm. He played first base in the service, but didn't pitch. After he was discharged, Law started throwing to his brother and found that his arm still hurt. Then a miracle occurred. "You may not believe this," he said, "but it actually happened."

Law was a devout member of the Mormon Church, which believed in the laying on of hands. While at a speaking engagement in Salt Lake City, Law asked one of the church elders if he would give him a blessing. "They gave me the blessing," Law recalled, "and as soon as I got home I picked up a baseball and went out to throw to my brother. All of a sudden, I heard a little pop. I kept throwing and it felt better and better."[8]

By the time he got to spring training, Law was a new man. He pitched 162 innings for the Pirates in 1954, and although he wasn't great, he gradually became more effective and the pain disappeared.

Perhaps the Mormons had a limit of one healing per person, but there was no miracle cure in 1961, just a prescription of rest and the passage of time. Law pitched only 59 innings all year and won just three games, a precipitous drop from the 20 he'd won in 1960.

Other Pirate heroes also ran out of magic. Vinegar Bend Mizell was 7–10 with an ERA of more than five runs a game. His career would be over the following year. Dick Groat's batting average dropped 50 points to .275. Hal Smith's average dropped from .295 to .223 and his home run total from 11 to 3. Bob Friend was 14–19 and Roy Face was 6–12. Face's ERA soared from 2.90 to 3.82. The biggest star for the '61 Pirates was Roberto Clemente, who won his first of four batting titles with a .351 mark, hit 23 home runs, the best mark of his career to that point, and played as superlatively in the field as ever.

Meanwhile, Stuart, while hitting for a good average, did not hit his first home run until May 7, in the Pirates' 20th game. As always when Stuart didn't hit, the Pirate fans let him know of their displeasure. When the Reds came to Forbes Field on May 12, pitcher Jim Brosnan spotted a "Don't Boo Stu" banner in the upper grandstand. "They must really be on Stuart this year," Cincinnati reliever Bill Henry said.[9] Pirate fans had even booed Stuart when he was given his championship ring at the home opener.

In addition to being a pitcher, Brosnan was the author of a book on the 1959 season and was writing another on the current campaign. His books were fairly tame by today's standards, but they were among the very few baseball books to expose players as human beings and delve beyond superficial heroic attributes. That upset a lot of people, but not Stuart, who loved publicity of any kind. He had hit some monumental blasts off Brosnan in the past and gave him a warm greeting when the Reds came to Pittsburgh. He said he'd noted that Brosnan had written that the only way to get Stuart out was to throw behind him. "Broz, please don't hit me," Stuart said. "I wanna get in your next book."[10]

As seemed inevitable with Stuart, it wasn't long before he found himself embroiled in controversy. In mid–May, when the Pirates visited St. Louis, he was a guest on Cardinal broadcaster Harry Caray's pregame show. Caray loved a juicy story, and he got one when Stuart said that if he couldn't play every day with Pirates, he would just as soon be traded.

"I don't have any chip on my shoulder," he told Caray, "but I want to play regularly. If not here, maybe on some other team. I can't make any money sitting on the bench.... I'm not one of those play-me-or-trade-me fellows, but I just can't sit on the bench.... This isn't any ultimatum or anything like that. I simply feel I can play regularly in the majors, and I'd like to prove it.... I just can't come off the bench and hit."[11]

While Stuart insisted this was not a "play me or trade me" ultimatum, it certainly sounded like one. He was desperate to earn a large salary, and at 28 years of age, saw his window of opportunity closing before too many seasons passed. He was playing part time in an unfriendly park and thought something had to change if he was going to earn a superstar's salary.

Another manager might have taken great offense. Bobby Bragan would have blasted Stuart. Another general manager might have fulfilled Stuart's request to be traded. But Danny Murtaugh and Joe Brown were patient men who, while realizing Stuart's shortcomings, thought the Pirates were a better team with him on the roster. Murtaugh put a positive spin on Stuart's remarks, saying that he showed the spirit Murtaugh was looking for on his team. "You have a player on the bench who's contented," he said, "and he's no use to you. Waltz him."[12]

It wasn't long before Stuart tested Murtaugh's patience. On May 22, in the middle of a game with the Braves, Murtaugh went into the clubhouse to retrieve something and found Stuart sitting there writing a letter. Murtaugh thought that leaving the bench during a game was odd behavior for someone who insisted he had a burning desire to play and fined Stuart fifty dollars.

Stu got out of Murtaugh's doghouse the way he always did—by hitting home runs. By the end of May he had five, and the fifth, off Cardinal southpaw Ray Sadecki, traveled an estimated 450 feet into Busch Stadium's left center field stands. It was one of the longest home runs ever hit in St. Louis.

When the Pirates went to Los Angeles, Stuart made another plea. "I want this club to play me regularly or trade me," he said. "I don't go for this alternating with Rocky Nelson. I'd rather play every day with a club like the Phillies (who were in last place) than be an alternate with the World Champions."[13]

If Stuart wanted the regular job at first base, the best way to get it was to produce. A few days later, he had a big game against the first-place Reds, hitting a home run and driving in four runs, including the two game-winning tallies in the ninth. Once again, Brosnan was the victim, which ensured that Stuart would be in his next book. "If he pulls me tonight," Brosnan wrote, "he's gonna have to step across the plate. Everything away from him."[14] Brosnan did exactly what he wanted to do, but Stuart hit a slider just off the outside corner hard enough to send it high into the right field screen for a triple.

That was reminiscent of the 1960 magic, and it took the boo birds off Stuart's back for awhile, but the hustling Nelson was the fans' favorite and Stuart remained the villain. "There are many Pittsburgh partisans," wrote one reporter, "who go to Forbes Field for the two-fold purpose of seeing the Pirates lose and the privilege of booing Stu."[15]

The opening game of the 1961 season typified Stuart's relationship with the fans. He struck out in the first inning, which got the boo-birds going. In the fourth, he let a grounder go through his legs, which initiated another outburst. When he came to bat in the fifth with the score tied, two outs, and Clemente on second, he was greeted with a chorus of jeers. Stu leaned into a pitch from the Cub's Dick Ellsworth and lined it off the 416 foot marker in left center, driving in Clemente to give the Pirates the lead, and then he drove in another run in the seventh that iced the game. He was back to ground zero.

The 1961 Pirates never got back to ground zero. The miracle finishes of 1960 were missing and the team was so riddled by injuries that one day in late May, Murtaugh put Stuart in left field, the first time he'd been in the outfield since his minor league days. "Don't laugh," Biederman wrote when informing his readers of the move.[16]

Bad things kept happening to the Pirates. "Series of Boners, Mishaps, Injuries Add Up to Long Afternoon for Crowd," read a May 31 headline in *The Pittsburgh Press*. That was the day Stuart struck out with the bases loaded in a key situation. Shortly afterward, during a game against the Dodgers, a typical Stuart blunder led to a big rally. The Dodgers' Tommy Davis singled to right field, sending Wally Moon, who'd been on first, around to third base. Clemente, knowing he couldn't get Moon at third, fired a rifle shot to first, where he caught Davis well off the bag. Stuart tagged Davis, but when he whirled to check Moon at third, the ball popped out of his glove and umpire Mel Steiner called Davis safe. After the battery of Labine and Burgess was ejected for protesting the call, a wild pitch, a double, and a triple sealed the Pirates' fate.

That play was typical of Stuart's fielding problems. He often made difficult plays, and wasn't bad at completing the challenging 3–6–3 (first base to shortstop to first base) double play. But he dropped balls for no apparent reason, missed tags, and for some reason had trouble with slowly hit balls right at him. He also had an unfortunate tendency to be photographed in awkward fielding positions, falling, stumbling, or standing by seemingly unconcerned as a teammate valiantly tried to make a play.

Perhaps the low point of the Pirate season came on June 23, when they blew an 11–2 lead in the eighth inning to the last place Phillies. Murtaugh's two best relievers, Labine and Face, were routed. That dropped Pittsburgh's record to 32–28; they were in fourth place, seven games behind the league leading Reds.

When the Pirates kept losing, Murtaugh tried a number of different combinations but none worked. Joe Brown, to make it clear that he didn't think Murtaugh had gone from genius to dolt in a single year, did more than give him the dreaded vote of confidence. He gave him a contract for the 1962 season.

In mid-June, with the Pirates struggling, Murtaugh gave Stuart what he wanted— full time duty at first base. Although he had just eight home runs, he was batting a robust .307 and the Pirates thought the home runs would come, as they always had. Nelson, the only alternative, wasn't hitting for average or power, and would finish his final big league season with a .197 average.

Once he became a regular, Stuart kept his average at a high level, and though his home run output was relatively modest Murtaugh named him to the National League All-Star team as a reserve. Bill White of the Cardinals won the player ballot with 110 votes, while Stuart was second with 55, well ahead of the 24 given to third-place Joe Adcock of the Braves. It was the first and only time Stuart would make a major league all-star squad. He was ecstatic and commemorated the occasion by ordering a cigarette lighter inscribed, "Dick Stuart***1961 All Star Game, San Francisco and Boston."

Number One Fan Bill Spears was almost as pumped up as Stuart. "The election could be the making of him," Spears said excitedly. "This is sort of a vote of confidence and if there's anything Stuart needed, it was a good word from his opponents."[17]

There were two All-Star games in those days, and the first was held on July 11 at San Francisco's new Candlestick Park. Stuart pinch-hit for starting pitcher Warren Spahn in the third inning and doubled off Whitey Ford, something he hadn't been able to do in the World Series.

The second game took place in Boston, where Stuart grounded out as a pinch-hitter and got his first look at Fenway Park and its inviting left field wall. "Just give me a pay cut and I'll stay right here," he told broadcaster Joe Garagiola.[18] In batting practice he hit two balls over the wall and three off it.

As the summer went on, Stuart started hitting more homers. At the end of July, he had 15 and during August he hit seven more. With a strong September, he had a chance to beat his career best of 27.

Stuart had more than a strong month in September. He had a terrific month, the best of his career. Stu said things began to change for him on August 23, when he started using one of Dick Schofield's bats. The bat didn't produce any home runs for Schofield in 1961, but it was lighter than the one Stuart had been using and perhaps, nearing the end of a long season, that was just what he needed. Stuart had a single, a double, and a home run the first day, and kept using the new bat.

Stu began his epic month of September on the 2nd against the Cardinals, hitting two homers (#23 and #24) to lead the Pirates to a 5–4 win. He drove in all five Pittsburgh runs, but his winning hit was not either of the home runs. It was a broken bat single that barely cleared the pitchers' mound.

On the 5th, Stuart victimized the Cubs' Glen Hobbie, who'd surrendered his mammoth homer in 1959, for #25. Number 26 came in Milwaukee, just before the Pirates went to the West Coast to play the Giants and Dodgers.

Stuart hit four home runs in four games on the Coast, including three in two games at Candlestick Park and two in one game off lefty Mike McCormick. The homers accounted for all three runs in a 3–0 Pirate win and enabled Stuart to break the 100 RBI mark for the first time. Two homers in a game at Candlestick was a prodigious feat, for not only did Stuart hit them into the wind, which always blew toward right field, he hit them at night, when it was cold and the ball didn't carry as well.

It was a great road trip. In 14 games, Stuart had 20 hits in 57 times at bat, with eight homers and 19 RBI. From August 23 through September 18, over a 27-game stretch, he batted .388 with a remarkable 12 home runs and 34 RBI. He'd raised his average 22 points to .299 and was hotter than Roger Maris and Mickey Mantle, who were challenging Babe Ruth's home run record in New York.

Stuart returned from the West Coast with an even 30 homers, three better than his previous best, and he wasn't finished. He hit five more before the end of the season, all at Forbes Field. One came off Cardinal reliever Lindy McDaniel, one each against the Giants and Dodgers, and Stuart climaxed his season on September 30, in the Pirates' next-to-last game, when he hit two off the World Series bound Cincinnati Reds. The first, off 21-game winner Joey Jay, was the 100th of Stuart's major league career.

Stuart started all 29 games in September and batted .355 with 13 home runs and 33 RBI. It was a terrific finish to Stuart's best season as a Pirate and he was runner-up to Reds pitcher Jim O'Toole for Player of the Month honors. Nelson became a forgotten man; his only appearances were as a pinch hitter. Thirty-five homers weren't close to the 66 he'd hit in Lincoln, but this was the National League, not the Western League. Stuart had done what he'd always said he could do if he played every day. He could hit home runs in the big leagues.

Overall, Stuart ended the season with 35 homers, an all-time record for Pirate first basemen, 117 RBI, and a .301 average. It was the only time in his career he would best the .300 mark and the 117 RBI were the most for any Pirate since Kiner drove in 137 ten years earlier. Sixteen of Stuart's 35 home runs were hit at Forbes Field, where the entire Pirate team hit only 49. As he had in 1958, Stuart homered in each National League park, and he hit two homers in a game three times.[19] He even got one tenth place vote for MVP. Stuart also led the league and set a career high with 121 strikeouts, but that was mainly due to having more at bats.

Nineteen-sixty-one was the year of the home run, and the big story was Maris and Mantle's pursuit of Ruth. Stuart, with a mere 35, was relegated to the background. He was out-homered in his own league by Orlando Cepeda, Willie Mays, and Frank Robinson, while the Braves' Joe Adcock also hit 35.

When Maris and Mantle began to approach Ruth's record, reporters asked Stuart, the only man in the major leagues who'd ever hit more than 60 in a season, for his opinion of their chances. Stu thought at least one of them would make it, and said that the record should have to be set in 154 games, the number of games played in 1927. It wound up taking Maris 162 games, which Commissioner Ford Frick said was eight too many, but he did it. "I'm jealous as hell," Stuart said. "I wish it were me. I'd become a rich man."[20]

What made Stuart's record even more impressive was the fact that, due to his early season platooning, he played in just 138 games. He would have hit 50, he said, if he'd played every day. The three National Leaguers who hit more homers each played at least 151 games.

There was also the Forbes Field factor. A Pittsburgh dentist named Phillip E. Antonucci, who was also an amateur baseball statistician and a friend of Stuart's, calculated that Stuart hit 27 balls at Forbes Field that would have been home runs if the dimensions were the same as when Kiner and Greenburg played. Twenty-seven plus thirty-five would have given Stuart 62 home runs, conveniently one more than Maris hit. And since the National League played only 154 games, there would have been no question that he had surpassed Ruth. The extra homers would have raised his batting average to .352 and his RBI total close to 150. "Wow," Stuart said when told of Antonucci's findings, "I might have been a high-priced ball player in 1962."[21] As always, Stu reduced everything to dollars and cents.

By the end of the season, Stuart, after just three-and-a-half years, ranked fourth on the all-time Pirate home run list, behind Kiner, Frank Thomas, and Paul Waner. With 101, he was a long way from Kiner's 301, but Kiner hit his homers over seven and a half years in the reduced dimensions of the modified Forbes Field. Since Forbes opened in 1909, Kiner, Stuart, and Thomas were the only right-handed Pirate batters to hit 30 or more home runs in a season.

Stuart and Clemente were virtually the only bright spots in what was a miserable season for the Pirates. From World Champions, they fell to a sub-.500 75–79 record and a disappointing sixth place finish. A 75–79 record would have been a major triumph in the early 1950s but for a defending World Series champion, it was unacceptable, and attendance was down more than 500,000. "It seems everything the '60 Bucs did was right," Biederman wrote, "and most everything they did in '61 was wrong."[22]

The Pirates' record both at home and on the road was worse than it had been in 1960, but the biggest difference was the disappearance of the late inning magic. They had been 12–5 in extra inning games in 1960 but were 1–7 in 1961. The championship team had won 23 games in its final at bat, while the 1961 team pulled out just nine. They never won more than four games in a row.

After the season ended, Stuart took a job in public relations and securities sales for Frank Street and Company of Pittsburgh. By remaining in town, he hoped to cash in on speaking opportunities and make some public appearances. After his big season, Big Stu, who was never at a loss for words, was in demand on the banquet circuit.

Nineteen sixty-one was also the year Stuart gave up competitive arm wrestling. For years, he had been considered the champion of major league baseball and at times he ventured into other sports. In 1959, he pinned 260-pound Ram lineman George Strugar easily.

Stuart had been arm-wrestling since his minor league days. When he played in Mexico, he was riding in Paul Pettit's car one day with a couple of other players, heading for Mexico City. As always, Stuart was talking, and being stuck in a car for a long ride on a hot day with Dick Stuart could get on a man's nerves.

"Bob Ryan got mad at Dick," Pettit recalled, "and said 'stop the car.' He wanted to duke it out. Dick said, 'I don't want to fight. I want to arm wrestle.' He never fought anyone. He would stay away from challenges. I had never lost an arm-wrestling match to anyone until I wrestled with Dick. He put me down like nothing. He'd say, 'Are you ready? Are you ready?' Then, boom! You were down

Stuart's powerful forearms made him baseball's unofficial arm wrestling champ and gave him the power to hit some of the longest home runs of his day. The hands attached to those powerful arms were not quite as efficient, and he was also the worst fielder of his day. National Baseball Hall of Fame.

just like that—no struggle. He was ungodly strong in his forearms, not his upper arms, but his forearms, the part of the arm that swings the bat."[23]

A few years later, another first baseman with an outrageous personality named Ken (Hawk) Harrelson (referred to by *The Sporting News* as "the poor man's Dick Stuart"[24]) assumed the major league arm-wrestling title. At one point, Harrelson and Stuart were supposed to meet in a grand match in Miami, but Stuart begged out, claiming a bad back. With the money he was making, Stuart told Harrelson, there was no use risking injury.

At the end of the season, Nelson, who'd been drafted from Toronto in 1959, was sold back to the Maple Leafs. But while he and Stevens, Stuart's competitors for the first base job, were both gone, there was a new challenger. In September, the Pirates recalled young Donn Clendenon from Columbus, where he'd batted .290 with 22 home runs and 82 RBI.

Like Stuart, Clendenon struck out a lot (121 times) and made a lot of errors. But he also stole 25 bases, something Stuart didn't do. After he was called up, Clendenon played exclusively in the outfield, batting .314 in nine games, but his primary position was first base. He was young and very athletic (he had offers from the Cleveland Browns and Harlem Globetrotters) and the following season he would ease Dick Stuart out of Pittsburgh.

11

He's Too Good a Hitter to Be Kept in Check for a Long Time: 1962

The National League expanded to ten teams for the 1962 season with the addition of the New York Mets and Houston Colt 45s. Although the Pirates lost six men in the expansion draft, none were front line players and the core of the team remained intact. If most of them could play like they had in 1960, the club would be pennant contenders once more.

Expansion boded well for Dick Stuart, as the common wisdom was that thinned pitching staffs would yield more home runs. Presumably, 20 pitchers who would otherwise have been in the minor leagues would be on National League mounds in 1962. When the American League expanded in 1961, the average number of homers per team rose from 136 to 153. In 1960, Mickey Mantle led the AL with 40 homers, while in 1961 seven American Leaguers hit more than 40.

Although no National Leaguer had hit 50 home runs since Willie Mays in 1956, Stuart predicted that Mays, Orlando Cepeda, and Hank Aaron would each hit at least 50 in 1961, with Aaron's teammate Eddie Mathews a fourth possibility. Stuart was always making predictions, but what made this one unique was that he did not include himself as a potential 50 home run man. "Nobody playing in Forbes Field as it is," he explained, "can hit 50."[1]

A couple of weeks later, however, Pittsburgh writer Harry Keck predicted Stuart would lead the league in homers in 1962. He pointed to Stuart's torrid September as an indication that he was more serious about baseball, removing the last obstacle to his becoming one of the top sluggers in the game. Keck pointed out that Mantle and Maris had combined for just 15 homers in September (although Mantle was injured much of the month) and that Babe Ruth, in one of the best Septembers on record, hit 17, just four more than Stuart. He believed that Stuart might have a chance to beat Maris's record.[2]

Surprisingly, in light of Stuart's league-leading error total, Keck said that his fielding had greatly improved, for which he credited the coaching of George Sisler. "I had to become accustomed to playing first base," Stuart said. "As I became more familiar with it, the hard plays became routine. I learned the feel of the bag, to step off and take the high throw and tag the runner."[3]

Hitting 35 home runs also made Stuart more likeable. When he was a part-time, fumble-fingered first basemen, Stuart had been arrogant and boastful. Now that he was a 35-home run man, he was colorful and charismatic. "[I]t is consoling and refreshing," wrote *The Sporting News*, "that there is a player of the stature of Dick Stuart. He is a throwback to the days of the Ring Lardner player. Stuart is the first to admit he is a good hitter, discusses his own prowess without being abashed in the least. His fielding problems have kept things a bit frantic in Pittsburgh [apparently the editor had not read Keck's earlier column] and Manager Danny Murtaugh at times has been less than enchanted by Richard's antics. Like the fans, though, we believe that baseball needs a few characters like Dick Stuart. Let them talk. Let them admit they are good. The fans love it."[4]

Al Abrams of the *Pittsburgh Post-Gazette* had been gradually warming up to Stuart and the latter's 1961 performance "converted me into a Stuart fan—hitting wise. This was something I didn't believe would happen. Dick has it made as a hitter.... There's no question but that Stuart has made himself into one of the most feared sluggers in the game today." Abrams closed with a tribute to Stuart's maturation, noting his off-season job and the fact that he was now a family man.[5]

Stuart was eager to pass on the lessons he'd learned. "Young players should always listen to their manager, coaches and teammates," he told another writer. "Don't be as hard-headed as I was. It took me a few years longer to reach the majors because I wouldn't listen or take advice."[6]

It had been an active and pleasant winter for Stuart, basking in the glory of his finest major league season. He attended the wedding of third baseman Don Hoak and singer Jill Corey, participated in charity basketball games, appeared on television in Junior Celebrity Bowling, and won a golf trophy in a Lake Tahoe tournament.

Stuart worked for Frank and Street, a Pittsburgh brokerage firm, but his duties weren't that rigorous and after the Christmas holidays he found time to work out with Pirate trainer Danny Whelan and some of his teammates at the local YMHA and then to repair to Florida for two weeks of golfing before spring training began.

Joe Brown had a reputation as a relatively fair man in contract negotiations, generous by the standard of the times. Stuart was coming off a good year and didn't have any trouble with his contract, signing in early February for what was believed to be a 50 percent increase to $30,000.

At the beginning of the season, Stuart was the subject of a long article in *The Saturday Evening Post* by Myron Cope, a 33-year-old journalist who in 1968 would join the Pittsburgh Steelers broadcast team and become a fixture for the next 35 years. He was a loyal Pittsburgher, and the article, though titled "Irrepressible Egotist," was generally favorable.

Cope opened with a dramatic description of Stuart stepping up to the plate. "His fans applaud vigorously—a hopeless effort to drown out the booing of the anti–Stuarts. Stuart's small but resolute chin is thrust forward. The visor of his batting helmet hovers low over his eyes. He chews a wad of gum as though trying to destroy it. As he reaches the plate he invariably bites off a piece of the gum and throws it away. He then fondles the crown of his helmet, perhaps to reassure himself that the twelve-ounce Fiberglass headpiece has not blown off. Now he is ready to bat."[7]

"Stu grinned as he spoke," Cope wrote, "and he was impossible to dislike. He has none of the braggart's nastiness."[8] In past years, Cope said, the Pirates had tried to tone Stuart down, but abandoned the effort. Farm director Bob Clements said, "Nobody can change him. Time may change him, but that would be a loss rather than a gain. He may mellow, but tell me, what's the use of his mellowing?"[9]

Cope conducted the interview at the office at Frank and Street. Stuart interrupted the conversation several times to make phone calls, announcing each with, "This is Dick Stuart. I'm in my office at the Carlton House and I'm being interviewed by *The Saturday Evening Post*."[10]

What about Dick's family, Cope asked? There was his younger brother Daryl, a journalism student at The University of Washington. "He writes fiction stories," Stuart said, "—or is it nonfiction? Which kind is true? Oh, nonfiction—that's right."[11]

Stuart loved the article, but it turned out to be about the best thing that happened to him in 1962, which was as disappointing as 1961 had been exhilarating. He had a mediocre exhibition season, batting .250 with four home runs, a couple of them mammoth tape-measure blasts. He'd always gotten off to slow starts and no one was terribly worried when he didn't hit the cover off the ball in the spring. After his great 1961 season, there was no question he was the Pirates regular first baseman.

Part of the annual new Stuart was the hope that he had finally learned how to play defense. In early May, Biederman wrote a favorable article about his play at first, noting that Murtaugh no longer removed him for defensive purposes. At a luncheon, Murtaugh urged the fans to come see the Pirates play by saying, "You might be in for some surprises. Dick Stuart has been making some unusual fielding plays. Come on out and maybe I can have him steal a base."[12]

"I feel more relaxed at first base," Stuart said.[13] "People keep telling me my fielding has improved. They didn't say anything like that before I hit 35 home runs."[14] "It's wonderful," he said on another occasion. "You hit .301 and suddenly people begin to call you a good fielder."[15] That wasn't exactly true, for after publishing the latter quote, *Sports Illustrated* added, "It is true that Stuart is no longer the defensive catastrophe he used to be, but he isn't ready to give lessons either."

That didn't mean that there were no adventures in the field. The Mets were a comical team during their maiden season and perhaps it was contagious. During the first win in Met history, Stuart let in a run when he launched a throw into right field. In another game against the Mets, one that was fortunately rained and snowed out before it was official, the Pirates managed to play worse than the Mets.

The comic sequence began with a bunt fielded by Harvey Haddix with a runner on first. Haddix threw too late to second and Mazeroski's relay to first skipped past Stuart and bounced off the wall behind first base. One run scored before Stuart retrieved the ball and threw to third trying to get the batter. His throw was wild and the runner headed for home. Haddix, backing up third, threw the ball way over catcher Don Leppert's head. Hoak, backing up home, slipped and fell down in the mud.

It soon became evident that Stuart was not fielding noticeably better than he had in past seasons, which wouldn't have been a big issue if he was hitting like he did in past seasons. But he wasn't.[16] Stu had always gotten off to slow starts and Pirate fans assumed that he would heat up with the weather, as he had in previous years. But when the weather got warmer, Stuart stayed cold.

That didn't seem to matter when the Pirates got off to a 10–0 start against the soft underbelly of the expanded NL, but when the Bucs lost 14 of their next 20 games, people started to notice that Stuart still wasn't hitting. By mid–May, the club's hot start was history, the Pirates were in fifth place, and Stuart was batting .206 with just two home runs. He was striking out as much as ever and didn't know what was wrong. "It's not because I'm not in shape. I'm in excellent condition…. Perhaps it's psychological. I don't know. I do know it's irritating."[17]

At a fan club luncheon, Murtaugh was handed a package containing a foot-long tablespoon and a gallon jug with the following directions: "One tablespoon before each game for each Pirate; four tablespoons before each game for Dick Stuart."[18] A joke making the rounds in Pittsburgh involved asking whether someone knew that Stuart was in the hospital. "What for?" "He's having the bat taken off his shoulder."[19]

Murtaugh asked the fans to encourage Stuart rather than boo him. "If ever a fellow needed a friend," he said, "Stu needs one now.... He's really a confused young man right now. And we aren't going to get anywhere unless he starts hitting and dropping some home runs."[20] Despite his slump, Stuart was still leading the team in homers. "I know Stuart will find the groove for keeps real soon," said Murtaugh. "He's too good a hitter to be kept in check for a long time."[21]

With Stuart's bat cold and Nelson gone, the Pirates acquired left-handed hitting veteran Jim Marshall from the Mets for Vinegar Bend Mizell, who had lost the magic of 1960 and would soon be out of baseball, headed for a career in the U.S. Congress. Rookie Donn Clendenon, who began the season in the outfield, began playing first more often.

By the end of May, Stuart was batting .219 with just four homers and 18 RBI. Over a 17-game stretch, he hit at a .174 clip. When his family came to see him play a series in San Francisco, he went hitless in 15 at bats and managed to get just two balls out of the infield.

His fellow players offered advice. Joe Christopher told him he was swinging too hard. Sammy Taylor said he was gripping the bat too tightly. Stuart was baffled. "My timing and selection of pitches and everything else is all messed up," he said.[22] He was swinging at bad pitches, he was trying to pull the ball, and he was intimidated by Forbes Field. Everything was wrong.

Despite what Murtaugh thought, Stuart *was* kept in check—for the rest of the season. He never emerged from his slump, which brought the boo birds out in full force. When Bob Skinner incurred the wrath of the Pittsburgh faithful by dropping a fly ball, Stuart shook his hand and said, "Thanks for taking my customers."[23]

The fans soon forgave Skinner and returned to booing Stuart. The *Pittsburgh Press* thought it had little to do with Stuart doing poorly, because Pirate fans had booed him even when he was going well. One reason, the *Press* said, was that when Stuart first came to the Pirates, he alienated the players with his arrogance, and the fans took their cue.

A second reason was inherent in the character of Pittsburgh. "At no time in its history has Pittsburgh known what to do with a genius. Pittsburgh hasn't had many geniuses, as far as the record shows, and the reason is that we have throttled them or driven them out. Look, for instance, at the fate of Stephen Foster. All the way along, Pittsburgh has had no use for a genius unless it could make him a drudge.... It's just the way we're built."[24] It was the only time Stuart was ever compared to Stephen Foster and the analysis ignored the fact that Pirate fans generally cheered geniuses like Clemente.

Stuart had a few bright moments, like the three-run homer in the bottom of the 9th off the Dodgers' Larry Sherry that gave the Pirates a 3–2 win ("Gosh, was I overdue for winning a game," he said),[25] and on June 11, when he hit two homers against the Cubs at Wrigley Field, the only time all year he would hit more than one in a game. Stu prided himself on his tape measure clouts, but his first home run that day was the shortest of his career. It was no more than a ground ball past third base into the Chicago bullpen in left field. The problem was that Cub outfielder Billy Williams couldn't find it and as Williams frantically scrambled under the bullpen bench looking for the ball, assisted by the Cubs' relievers, Stuart lumbered around the bases.

Williams finally found the ball lodged inside a fold of tarpaulin, but his throw wasn't even close to getting Stuart, who scored standing up. "Funniest thing I ever saw," Stuart said. "I was ready to stop at second and settle for a double. I thought Williams was giving me the decoy ... then I realized he was having trouble and I could make it to third.... When I reached third base I saw [third base coach] Frank Oceak telling me to go all the way and that's when I turned on the gas. ... I could've beaten anybody, including Willie Davis or Vada Pinson or any of those Olympic sprinters that final 90 feet."[26] The second homer was more Stuart-like, a 400-foot blast into the bleachers.

Meanwhile, the errors piled up. In a mid–July game against the Giants, Stuart let a ground ball get by him for a single, and a Willie Mays home run followed. Then he missed a low throw from Earl Francis that let in two runs. He struck out in all three official at bats. "The final score," he said, "should have read: Stuart 6 Pirates 3."[27]

There were also physical problems, including a couple of tooth extractions and gum surgery. When Stu returned to the lineup, he suffered a pulled leg muscle that prevented him from swinging properly. By that time, his season was virtually a lost cause.

The Pirates had high expectations for 1962. In late May and early June, they won seven in a row and 12 of 14 to boost their record to 28–18. Unfortunately, the Giants and Dodgers were off to hotter starts and the Pirates were in fourth place, 6½ games behind.

In its preseason predictions, *Sports Illustrated* said, "Assuming Law is back in form, the Pirates should have a role in the National League pennant race. Without Law, Pittsburgh will be an also-ran again." Although Law's arm still hurt, he was able to pitch effectively with extended rest between starts. In 1962, pitchers were not "shut down" when they felt a twinge. They were supposed to go out and pitch if they could get hitters out, no matter how much their arm was throbbing. Once, when Murtaugh came to the mound to ask him how his arm felt, Law replied, "No worse now than it was when I started."[28] Murtaugh left him in. Battery mate Smoky Burgess said, "I can see the pain in his face when he starts warming up.... The first four or five warm-up pitches each inning seem like torture, then the pain lessens, although it's evident the pain is still there."[29]

In spite of the pain, Law managed to pitch 139 innings and win 10 games while losing seven. Bob Friend also rebounded from a lackluster 1961 campaign and posted an 18–14 mark. Rookie Al McBean got off to a hot start and won 15 games.

One of the greatest strengths of the Pittsburgh team was its bullpen, led by Face and 43-year-old rookie Dominican lefthander Diomedes Olivo, who Stuart had recommended to the Pirates three years earlier.[30] Olivo had been pitching summers and winters in Mexico and the Caribbean since 1947, but was reluctant to play in the U.S. because he didn't speak English, didn't like the segregated atmosphere in the United States and didn't like the low minor league salaries. He owned a large cattle and dairy ranch in the Dominican, was relatively well-off and was happy just to play near home in the winters.

In 1959, Stuart, who'd had little success hitting Olivo in winter ball, encouraged the Pirates to sign him. He told Myron Cope, "'I told them, 'Sign this guy!' But you know how it is with me. Anything Stuart says around here, they say forget it.'"[31] A year later, when Pirate scout Howie Haak recommended Olivo, the Pirates signed him. He was 40, they said, but his arm was 20. Olivo pitched in four games in 1960, played the entire 1961 season at Columbus, and made the Pirate roster the following year. He appeared in 62 games, had a 5–1 record, seven saves, and a fine 2.77 ERA.

The Pirates had a hot streak in July, winning 16 of 19, and on July 21 they had a 60–36 record and were in third place behind the Dodgers and Giants, just 3½ out of first. Their

.625 winning percentage was better than the .617 mark they'd posted during their championship season. The 1962 season was one of streaks, with hot spells alternating with deep slumps; by mid-July the Pirates already had four winning streaks of at least seven games.

During the second half of the season, the Pirates gradually fell out of the race, and if they weren't going to win the pennant, they, like the Pirates of the mid-1950s, were going to give their youngsters a shot. Many of the men who'd been future stars in the Rickey era were now fading veterans and a new generation of prospects was coming up. One of them was big, powerful Donn Clendenon.

In April and May, Clendenon platooned with Skinner in left field and often pinch ran for Stuart and played first base in the late innings. One day at the end of June, with Stuart continuing to slump, Murtaugh put Clendenon at first base and he hit a triple and a home run. When Murtaugh finally ran out of patience with Stuart, he sent Clendenon to Columbus to play first base every day for two weeks, with plans to bring him back to Pittsburgh and stick him in the lineup. When he returned to the Pirates, Clendenon pinch hit and pinch ran a few times, but on the 10th of August, with Stuart fighting a one for 21 slump, Clendenon replaced him at first and started almost every game for the rest of the season. By the end of the season, Stuart would start 100 games, Clendenon 41, and Marshall 20.

The youngster made the most of his opportunity. In his first three starts, he had eight hits in twelve at bats, including a grand slam homer, and stole three bases. It was the type of debut with which Stuart had driven Ted Kluszewski to the bench four years earlier. Like Stuart in 1958, Clendenon kept hitting for the rest of the year, raising his average from .239 to .302. Stuart got a reprieve for a brief period in late August and got seven hits in a three-game stretch, but when he hit just one home run (his 16th of the season and the last of his Pirate career), it was back to the bench.

By the end of the year, Stuart was Clendenon's biggest rooter, a uniformed version of Bill Spears. If the rookie did well, Stuart knew he'd be traded. If he floundered, the Pirates would probably keep Stuart around as insurance, and that meant sitting on the bench. No one was pulling harder for Clendenon during the final months of the 1962 season than Dick Stuart.[32]

During the month of September, Stuart started only three games, none after September 14. When Clendenon didn't start, Jim Marshall did. When Stu pinch hit at Forbes Field, he was booed. One day, the fans began booing as soon as he walked to the on-deck circle to hit for pitcher Jack Lamabe. Bill Mazeroski grounded into a double play to end the game, and Stuart had to absorb his abuse without even getting to bat.[33]

The handwriting on the wall was quite clear, and Stuart read it accurately. Clendenon was going to be the first baseman of the future and he was going elsewhere. His preference was to go either to the Red Sox or the Cubs, both of which had ballparks conducive to home runs.

Despite being anchored to the bench the last two months of the season, Stuart finished second on the Pirates in homers (Skinner led with 20). He had a .228 average, 94 strikeouts despite limited playing time, and tied for the lead among NL first basemen with 17 errors. That maintained his streak of leading the league's first basemen in errors every season since he'd come up in 1958,[34] despite averaging just 102 games a year in the field.

Stuart's fielding had always worn on the Pirate pitchers, and when he stopped helping them with his slugging, they became more impatient. After Stuart left Pittsburgh, Bob

Friend was asked at a fan club luncheon about his success during the first half of the 1963 season. He attributed some of it, only partly in jest, to the absence of Stuart. "I always tried to keep the ball away from Stuart as much as I could," he said.[35]

The first baseman who tied Stuart for the most errors in 1962 was Marv Throneberry of the New York Mets, who in the process usurped Stuart's long-standing reputation as baseball's most-publicized butcher. Stuart fielded as poorly as ever, but Throneberry made his errors in America's largest media market, while Stuart botched grounders in the relative obscurity of Pittsburgh. What was even more impressive (or unimpressive) about their league-leading error totals was that Stuart played only 101 games at first and Throneberry just 97.

Stuart and Throneberry had a lot in common, in addition to their propensity for fumbling ground balls. Both were prodigious minor league sluggers; Stuart had his 66-homer year at Lincoln, while Throneberry hit 118 home runs in three years at the AAA level in the Yankee system. Like Stuart, he also struck out a lot, and like Stuart, there were high hopes for him. After the 1956 season, George Sisler said Throneberry might be the Yankees' replacement for Lou Gehrig and would certainly compete for the Triple Crown. He didn't come close, and after putting in time with the Athletics and Orioles, wound up as a comic folk hero with the Mets.

Off the field, the man who stole Stuart's thunder was his diametric opposite. Stuart was voluble and shamelessly sought the limelight while Throneberry was a quiet country boy whose "Marvelous Marv" persona was created by teammate Richie Ashburn and the New York writers. The Mets were in the process of losing 120 games in 1962 and reporters were looking for entertaining stories. The Pirates had a relatively good season, finishing in fourth place with a very respectable 93–68 mark, and errors weren't funny.

Stuart received a full share of $585.62 for the Pirates' fourth place finish and spent the fall working in the investment business, going to Steeler games on the weekends, and wondering where he was going to play in 1963. The season was barely over before Pittsburgh and Boston writers began talking about the possibility of Stuart playing for the Red Sox. "Stuart could play Yankee Doodle Dandy on that short left field wall at Fenway Park," wrote Biederman. But he thought it was also possible that Stuart might not be going anywhere, since the Pirates had given Marshall his release to play in Japan and "this probably means Clendenon and Stuart will both be back at first base."[36]

The Red Sox were in a down cycle; in 1962 they finished eighth with a 76–84 record, their fourth straight sub-.500 season. Attendance was down 35 percent in two years. The team had been owned by Tom Yawkey, a wealthy sportsman in the mold of John Galbreath, since 1933. Unlike the self-made Galbreath, Yawkey inherited his money from his uncle and adoptive father William Yawkey, who once owned part of the Detroit Tigers.

Yawkey loved Fenway Park, which he also owned, and worked out on the field when the Red Sox were out of town. Sometimes when the Sox were on the road, he and his wife Jean would pack a meal, spread out a blanket on the outfield grass and listen to the game on the radio.

When Yawkey bought the Red Sox, they were at the bottom of the American League, and he tried using his wealth to buy a championship. He bought superstars like Jimmy Foxx, Joe Cronin, and Lefty Grove, and many owners resented his spendthrift ways, although they were willing to take his money in return for their players. They also resented the fact that Yawkey paid his players better than most owners, many of whom were cash-strapped entrepreneurs struggling through the Great Depression.

Dizzy Dean, asked about potential trades one year, said, "I'm trying to trade Branch Rickey for Tom Yawkey, and I'll give Rickey my next year's pay to boot."[37] Yawkey not only paid good salaries, he was known for slipping a player a few thousand dollars if he thought he deserved or needed it. Like Galbreath, Yawkey wanted a championship more than he wanted to make a profit, but thus far, he'd spent a lot of money without winning a World Series. Many thought Yawkey's generosity was a cause of the Red Sox's failure to win; they said his players weren't hungry.

"Because he liked ballplayers and was always in the clubhouse," said Carl Yastrzemski, "some people thought he spoiled us, that he wasn't demanding. Nothing could be further from the way it really was.... No one wanted to win more than he did."[38] When a reporter once asked Yawkey about his failure to win a title, he said, "How can you ever think failure when you've called men like Ted Williams and Carl Yastrzemski your friends?"[39]

The Red Sox already had a good first baseman, reigning AL batting champion Pete Runnels, but Runnels would turn 35 before the 1963 season began. He lived in Pasadena, Texas, about 120 miles from Houston, and had expressed a desire to be traded to the Colt 45s in order to finish his career near home.

Runnels was a left-handed spray hitter, and one of the major shortcomings of the Red Sox was a right-handed basher capable of tattooing the Fenway Park left field wall. They were supposed to be built to take advantage of the beckoning Green Monster, but in 1962 they hit 74 home runs on the road and just 72 at home. Third baseman Frank Malzone led the team with 21 homers; since Ted Williams retired following the 1960 season, Malzone had been the only member of the Red Sox to break the 20-homer barrier.

The Red Sox would have a new manager in 1963. Mike (Pinky) Higgins, a long time crony of Tom Yawkey,[40] moved to the front office, yielding the manager's job to former Boston player Johnny Pesky. Pesky was a Red Sox icon in later years, revered as a lovable old man, but in 1963 he was a fiery young man who described managing a big league team as a "fight for survival."[41] "A loafing ball player makes Johnny Pesky ill," wrote Bob Holbrook, which boded ill for Stuart if he ended up in Boston.[42] "I can't demand respect," Pesky said, "but I can command it.... I'll have guys in and out of there faster than you ever saw," he said, "if they are not producing."[43] Those were brave words, since Pesky didn't have a plethora of talent to choose from. It was also reminiscent of Bobby Bragan, who'd been Stuart's least favorite manager.

Stuart could not be traded to an American League team until the inter-league trading period commenced in mid–November. Once it did, it didn't take long for the Pirates to trade Stuart and pitcher Jack Lamabe to the Red Sox for pitcher Don Schwall and catcher Jim Pagliaroni.[44] Although the trade was announced on November 20, Brown and Higgins had been talking about it since the World Series.

Both players obtained by the Pirates were 25 year olds with promise. Schwall had been an all-star in his rookie year before fading in 1962 and Pagliaroni was a big receiver with power who'd gotten a sizable bonus. On the surface it looked like Brown had made a good trade. Schwall had more promise than Lamabe and with Clendenon at first, Stuart was expendable.

Stuart was pleased, for he would be playing half his games in the park he fell in love with at the 1961 All Star Game. "He's made for Fenway Park," Murtaugh said. "Had Stu played in Boston last summer he'd have hit 36 home runs instead of 16."[45] "Brown knew I wanted to go to the Red Sox," Stuart said, "and he did me a favor. I want to thank him publicly."⁴⁶ "I might be able," he said, "to realize my ambition of hitting 40 or 50 homers in Boston next summer."⁴⁷ "At least, on a foggy night, I'll be able to see [the fence]. Heck, at Forbes Field it was a five-dollar cab fare to get to the left field wall."⁴⁸ Fenway also had very little foul territory, and pop fouls that would be caught in other stadiums would land in the seats, giving the batter another swing.

The move to Boston would also allow Stuart to escape the hostile Pirate fans. "Wonder who the fans in Pittsburgh will boo now," he asked when the trade was announced.⁴⁹ Murtaugh added, "Stuart gave us the long ball, but the change will work wonders for him. He wanted to get away from the booing in Pittsburgh."⁵⁰ Of course, Stuart wasn't *that* upset about the Pirate fans, for he was like a professional wrestling villain who reveled in the abuse. One night, while he was being interviewed after a game, some fans were razzing him good-naturedly. "My hecklers," Stuart told the interviewer. "Other ballplayers have loyal fans. I have loyal hecklers."⁵¹

Many Pirate fans were sad to see Stuart go, and most of them were women. The first president of Pittsburgh's Dick Stuart Fan Club was a teenage girl named Meg Maslanik. When Meg matriculated to the University of Iowa, her sister Helen took over. Throughout the season, as Stuart struggled with his low batting average, women wrote to the newspapers urging fans to support the Pirate first baseman. When he was traded, his female fans sent letters to the press decrying the unfairness of it all. Eventually they gave up the ghost, and on February 25, 1963, the Dick Stuart Fan Club donated its remaining assets of $12.50 to Children's Hospital and disbanded.

Boston was happy to get Stuart, who was not only expected to fill the power void; he would liven up the city's sports scene. Bob Holbrook, the Boston correspondent to *The Sporting News*, wrote shortly after the trade was announced, "Lacking in the Red Sox picture is color. Stuart can provide that color and take up some of the slack left by the retirement of the incomparable Ted Williams."⁵² Stuart had always fantasized about being compared to Williams, and Holbrook's words were music to his ears. "I'm going to try to make Boston fans forget Ted Williams," he said.⁵³

The Stuart trade was part of a massive overhaul of the Pirate team. By the spring of 1963, only 11 members of the 1960 World Series champs remained. Stuart, Hoak, and Groat were traded within days of each other, leaving only Mazeroski from the infield that won the World Series. Hoak, who had an off-season and was about to turn 35, expected to be dealt, for the Pirates had 20-year-old Bob Bailey, who they'd given a $175,000 bonus, waiting in the wings.⁵⁴

Groat, who'd come to the Pirates directly from the Duke campus in 1952 and had been the team captain for several years, was devastated when he was traded to the Cardinals. "Dick never really got over it," said Bob Friend. "To this day he's never gotten over it."⁵⁵

"I'd taken a pay cut the year before," Groat said, "for the year I had in '61 and I thought that he [Joe Brown] would trade me in a minute. I told him, 'You'd better have a shortstop when you trade me. Contrary to what you and Howie Haak think, Schofield can't play every day. He's the best utility player in baseball today, but he can't play every day.' It worked out just the way I said it would. They said Schofield was faster, he was a switch hitter, and he should be playing shortstop, so they traded me. And when they traded me, that lit a fire under me and as good a year as I had with the Pirates in '60, I had a better year with the Cardinals in '63."⁵⁶

In 1963, with their revamped infield, the Pirates finished eighth, 14 games below .500. Schofield was traded to the Giants in 1965 and spent the rest of his career doing what he did best, serving as a top flight utility infielder and pinch hitter. Groat, after his excellent 1963 season, during which he batted .319, had 201 hits, and led the NL in doubles, played on a World Championship team the following year.[57]

The Sporting News devoted an editorial paragraph to Stuart in its December 8 edition. "Richard Lee Stuart," they said, "is a young man just turned 30 with as tremendous a potential as any player in the major leagues today. When he is on the beam, he can launch a baseball into orbit. A happy-go-lucky type who has refused to take some facets of the game seriously, he could be the most popular and the most colorful player in the game today. If he were living up to all of these potentials, he could also be one of the wealthiest men in baseball."

"Pittsburgh fans," they said, "generally are among the most tolerant in baseball, yet they made Richard Lee Stuart their particular target and virtually booed him out of town. Now he is moving to another city, Boston, where the fans chose up sides sharply on the matter of one of the greatest, Ted Williams. Stuart can enchant these fans, do the Red Sox an immense amount of good and help himself with a daily chips-down performance. He's the only one who can do it. Nobody can help him."[58]

Thus cautioned, Stuart went to Boston with as much confidence as ever, totally unbowed by his disappointing 1962 season. At first, he would find just about everything he was hoping for.

12

You Gotta Have the Park: 1963

On November 26, 1962, the Red Sox traded Pete Runnels to the Houston Colts for outfielder Roman Mejias, which left first base open for Stuart. The switch from Runnels to Stuart was likely to result in an increase in home runs, a decline in batting average and defense, and a significant upgrade in publicity. Runnels, who'd won two batting titles in the past three years, was a steady performer, a quiet, hard-nosed competitor who tended to keep his thoughts to himself. "In my book," said another player, "Pete's a pro all the way, but I'll bet if you asked the first six fans you met, five wouldn't know what club he played for."[1] Stuart would be a different type of animal and many thought it was a welcome change.

"The trade of Dick Stuart to Boston," wrote Sandy Grady in the *Philadelphia Bulletin*, "may be the noisiest event to hit Boston since Paul Revere.... Boston may not be ready for Stuart, but Stuart certainly is ready for Boston.... If he does nothing but show up at game time, Dick will wake up the museum called Fenway Park.... Last summer, it was the only graveyard in America with foul lines.... Stuart will remind Beantown loyalists of Ted Williams.... There are two piddling differences—Stuart likes sports writers and hits 100 points lower than The Splinter."[2] Another writer said Stuart would either be the most popular Bostonian since Revere or the most unpopular since Charles Ponzi.

Boston was a great sports town. It had ten newspapers and the Red Sox had a larger press contingent than just about any team not located in New York. All three major television networks had Boston affiliates. Red Sox play-by-play announcer Curt Gowdy was one of the most prominent sportscasters in the United States and while sports talk radio had not yet emerged, Boston's powerful stations reported on the Red Sox with an enthusiasm comparable to that given the Celtics, who were in the midst of winning eight straight NBA titles. Stuart had gained national notice in Lincoln, Nebraska, and with the Boston media stoking the fires, the possibilities were limitless.

"Stu was made for the headlines," said the *Pittsburgh Press*. "Everywhere he's gone during his baseball career, the newspaper ink followed."[3] Bud Collins of the *Boston Globe*, after talking about Stuart's power, said, "Stuart's forte is not the home run, however. It is his ability to get his name into the newspapers, principally in headlines telling how he is unhappy about something or other. This makes King Richard a 'personality' and 'colorful' and, according to him, leads people to buy tickets to see him occasionally hit and catch baseballs. Maybe he is right."[4]

One of Stuart's first appearances in Boston was the annual B'Nai B'rith banquet. "They gave me the VIP treatment," he said. "Put us up in a $75-a-day suite and made me feel I had already won the Most Valuable Player Award."[5] His only regret was that he was upstaged at the event by heavyweight boxer Cassius Clay, who had even more charisma than Stuart.

Stu had been a favorite of female fans in Pittsburgh and the women of Boston took to him quickly. One evening, he and Lois were having dinner in a fashionable Boston restaurant when a young woman came up and asked for his autograph. "You know, you look more like a movie actor than a baseball player," she told the handsome first baseman. "You come out to Fenway Park tomorrow or Sunday," he told her. "When you see me around first base you'll know I'm a movie actor."[6]

Stuart, always at ease in front of the camera, was hired by WBZ-TV to host "Stuart on Sports," which aired at 11:15 on Sunday nights during the season. The show was produced live when the Red Sox were home and taped when they were on the road. Stuart was paid $150 a week and teamed with WBZ announcer Gene Pell.[7] Pell asked Stuart about the day's game, they gave sports scores, and Stuart conducted interviews. Stuart's humor often shone through, but his inexperience in front of the camera initially created dead spots, such as the time he couldn't read a commercial on the teleprompter and stared in silence while the cameras rolled. A running gag on all of Stuart's shows was throwing him something, like a sponsor's product, and having him drop it. As he became more comfortable, the show got better; it wound up being Boston's highest rated sports show.

Stuart believed that his long term future lie in television. "I think I've got a good gift of gab," he said, "and, like anybody else who's been up for a while, I know a lot about the game…. Whenever I'd been interviewed on radio or TV, I'd always done a pretty good job. And I was also sort of controversial."[8]

Stuart had been with the Pirate organization since signing out of high school in 1951, but unlike Dick Groat, he wasn't upset to leave. Before heading for spring training, he stopped at the Pirates' offices to pick up his remaining belongings. Coincidentally, Danny Murtaugh and Don Schwall, the pitcher the Pirates had acquired in exchange for Stuart, happened to be there. "Remember me?" Stuart said to Murtaugh, "I used to work here."[9]

While Stuart had been a lesser light on the Pirates behind established players like Clemente, Friend, Groat, and Law, he was the big man on the Red Sox. Williams, the dominant player in Boston for two decades, had retired in 1960. Former MVP Jackie Jensen retired after the 1961 season, partly because of his terrible fear of flying. Carl Yastrzemski replaced Williams in left field, and in future years Yaz would be a Boston icon, but in 1963 he was just a 23 year old with potential. He tended to keep to himself and made little effort to assume a leadership role. Veteran Frank Malzone was well-respected but Malzone was not a superstar. And he didn't have the flash of Dick Stuart, who was, for the first time, what he'd always dreamed of being—The Man. There would be no competition for the starting position, no Kluszewskis or Nelsons waiting in the wings. Stu would, for the first time in his career, play every day for a full season, the wish he expressed to Harry Caray in 1961.

"We'll probably sink or swim with him," Johnny Pesky said in the early days of spring training. "People say Stuart might drive us nuts, but he'll help us. I'm sure he'll do his best. He likes money."[10] Pesky apparently knew his man, for no one was more motivated by money than Dick Stuart.

Sports Illustrated made Stuart the main topic of its pre-season report on the Red Sox. While pointing out his great power potential, they reminded Red Sox fans that they would need to get accustomed to Stuart's sloppy fielding and *sans souci* approach to the game. "Thus far," the report concluded, "Stuart's Boston teammates and his new manager have tolerated him. They are all waiting to see what happens in the early weeks. A good start for Stuart would likely mean a higher finish for the Red Sox—and vice versa."[11]

After the first week of camp, Tom Monahan wrote, "[Stuart] is the most talked about player Boston has owned since Ted Williams retired after the 1960 season. Red Sox camp followers wait for Stuart to hit his daily quota and then leave the park satisfied they have seen something like the U.S. beating Russia to the moon. Moreover, he is unlike the Stuart they had read about. He has not been popping off. He has been working hard as a fielder at first base. He has been running and sweating with the common ball players."[12]

Boston coach Billy Herman said, "I have been working with him for four days now and I'm positive he is not the worst fielding first baseman we ever had in Boston…. [H]e is definitely no lumber-foot out there around the bag."[13]

Pitcher Chet Nichols spoke in a similar vein. "As for his fielding, I don't think it can be as bad as everyone says."[14] That was faint praise, and Red Sox players should have been reminded that rumors of Stuart's fielding improvement in previous springs had proven false harbingers.

The Red Sox were one of only six major league clubs that trained in the western desert, and the light air at Boston's Scottsdale base made Stuart's hits take off like they had in Western League cities. He reported five days early and started pounding the ball over the fences more consistently than any Sox player since Williams.

Stuart hit so many balls over the fence off batting practice pitcher Harry Malmberg that reporters began keeping track of them. The first day he hit 15. The next day he hit seven in 10 minutes. In five days he hit 39 batting practice homers, and the following day the total increased to 45. Of course, Stuart wouldn't be hitting off Malmberg when the season started, but his exploits were reported breathlessly back to wintry Boston.

Stuart played almost every exhibition game but, like in past springs, he didn't hit that well. Pesky spoke highly of him, but indicated he wouldn't hesitate to put outfielder Gary Geiger at first if Stu didn't produce. He also said Geiger would probably replace Stuart for defensive purposes in the late innings.[15]

Ted Williams, who Stuart had idolized when he was in the minor leagues, was an instructor in the Red Sox camp. "Can you imagine the two of us on the same team," Stuart said. "There would never be a dull moment."[16] Reporters compared the two; they were about the same stature, both had controversial personalities, neither was known for their fielding, and both could hit, although Stuart was never the all-around hitter Williams was. A major difference was that while Williams always had a confrontational relationship with reporters, Stuart loved them.

During an exhibition game, with Williams watching, Stuart hit a home run that cleared a 12-foot fence about 430 feet from home plate. After he rounded the bases, Stuart shouted, "Hey, Williams, you ever hit one that far?"[17] He ducked into the dugout before Ted could reply. On another occasion, when Stuart was asked to pose for a picture with Williams, he said, "Heck, no. Can't you get a ballplayer for me to pose with?"[18] No one but Dick Stuart talked to Ted Williams that way, but Williams didn't seem to mind.

It wasn't long before the Boston media took to Stuart, for he gave them a lot to write about. He joked about his fielding, bragging that he now missed just one throw out of three, and gave them a tongue-in-cheek warning. "Get all those interviews out of the way now," he said. "I don't want any reporters bothering me with questions the last week of the season when I have 59 homers and all that pressure on me to break the record."[19]

That was the Stuart of 1956 talking, not the Stuart of 1962; his swagger was back.

When asked about the difference between the two leagues, he said "Pitchers are pitchers. Sooner or later they have to get the ball in the strike zone. It is then that I hit home runs. It's inevitable."[20] It was the kind of quote that made headlines, and at the end of training camp, the Boston writers voted Stuart the most personable newcomer.

While the media loved Stuart, it was also important that he get along with his manager. He'd had a relatively good relationship with Danny Murtaugh, but that was in large part because Murtaugh had gotten used to Stuart's foibles and was a patient man. Throughout his minor league career, Stu had found it difficult to get along with the man in charge.

Stuart had no previous experience with Pesky, who at first glance did not appear to be particularly patient. He was a fairly small man (5'9" and less than 170 pounds) who'd started as a clubhouse boy and as a player had gotten the most out of his talent, which was typical of men who become major league managers. Pesky was intense and when he did poorly it ate at him. He tried to master the little things and expected his players to be strong on fundamentals. That, however, was not the long suit of the 1963 Red Sox.

Pesky's team seemed to have great trouble with simple maneuvers, like cutting off throws from the outfield. That wasn't usually a problem when Yastrzemski was throwing, for Yaz never seemed to hit the cutoff man, preferring majestic, arcing, awe-inspiring throws that dazzled the fans while runners scooted around the bases.

In an exhibition game against the Giants, Stuart stood at first base instead of moving to the cutoff position and let a throw bounce through the infield. Yastrzemski misplayed a fly ball and turned it into a three-base error. The Sox made six errors in total, as well as several mental mistakes. Pesky was furious, blasted the players in the locker room, and said they were going to practice fundamentals until they got them right.

Pesky worked his team hard, but about a week later, in a game against the Houston Colts, disaster of a different nature befell them. One of the Colts hit a single to center field and Yastrzemski came up throwing to the plate to try to head off a runner coming in from second. Against the Giants, no one had been there to cut off the throw. Apparently, the team had taken Pesky's lessons to heart, for Yastrzemski threw the ball where he was supposed to and both Stuart and third baseman Frank Malzone sprinted toward the cutoff position. They collided, the ball squirted free, the runner scored, and the batter went to second while Pesky sat in the dugout fuming.

When the Red Sox appeared at Fenway Park for their April 16 home opener against the Orioles, Stuart had a pleasant reunion with the Green Monster, the 37-foot high barrier that stood just 315 feet from home plate at the foul line. There were other foul poles that were closer, but in those parks the fences curved out at a sharp angle. Fenway was built in the midst of Boston and its contours had to conform to the surrounding city streets. Landsdowne Street stood where a deep left center field would have been, so the fence cut almost straight across, creating an inviting target in the left center field power alley.

Fenway Park opened April 20, 1912, and six days later Boston's Hugh Bradley hit the first home run in the new grounds, launching a fly ball over the inviting left field barrier. For the next half century, batters and pitchers had been tempted, enticed and tortured by the unique edifice.

While most right-handed hitters loved Fenway (Jimmy Foxx was an exception, claiming that he lost many home runs when line drives banged off the wall), many baseball observers claimed the oddly-shaped park was the reason the Red Sox had not won a pennant since 1946 and had not been World Champions since 1918. Like the Pirates, the Red Sox were constructed to play well in their home park and they didn't usually do well on the road. In 1961, the Sox were 50–31 at home and a miserable 26–55 on the road. From the end of World War II through the mid-'60s, Boston played better than .600 ball at home and well under .500 on the road. In their last pennant-winning season in 1946, the Sox were an amazing 61–16 at Fenway.

Boston's hitters took aim at the left field wall and from 1946 to 1952 out-homered the opposition 509–351, but when they hit the same way in other parks, they weren't able to reach the more distant fences. The Red Sox didn't steal or use the hit and run play at home and therefore couldn't execute those plays on the road. They were partial to sluggers, and sluggers aren't always good base runners or slick fielders.

For pitchers, the Wall was another matter. "Think about The Wall?" said young Boston hurler Dave Morehead, "you don't think about anything else."[21] Pitching coaches tried to convince their charges to pitch the same regardless of the park, but that was a tough sell. Pitching had been a problem for the Sox in recent years.

Stuart celebrated his first game at Fenway with a home run off Robin Roberts, but despite the inviting left field wall, he hit just three home runs in April. At the end of the month, however, he was batting .302, and on April 20 against the Tigers, he did something he'd rarely done in all his years in Pittsburgh; he bunted. The score was tied 1–1 in the ninth when Yastrzemski led off with a single. Stuart, attempting to sacrifice, pushed a bunt past the pitcher and beat it out for a base hit. The Sox didn't score, but they eventually won the game, and the fact that Stuart passed up a chance for a game-winning homer indicated that, after all the false sightings, there might indeed be a new Dick Stuart this year.

There might also be a new Boston Red Sox. The club long had a reputation as a listless group of well-paid and coddled individualists, but Pesky had them fired up. "For the first time since I had been with the Red Sox," said Yastrzemski, "the boys were talking baseball, showing some life in the locker room, and acting like a single unit instead of a whole flock of small cliques with each group whispering in corners and looking suspiciously around at all the other cliques."[22]

Stuart was too self-centered to be a leader in the clubhouse, but he could lighten the mood. Yastrzemski once said that sometimes he wished he could be more like Stuart, letting criticism roll off his back rather than bristling when the press got on him. "Big Stu was so good-natured," he wrote, "that it was impossible to dislike him. And he didn't mind if you laughed at his fielding because he did himself."[23]

After several seasons of wallowing around in the second division, the Red Sox, who the writers had picked to finish eighth, got off to a flying start and on May 17 found themselves in first place with an 18–11 record, with the perennial champion Yankees fourth, a game and a half back. It was the first time since 1952 Boston had occupied first place after April.

The Red Sox had been 300–1 underdogs to win the pennant before the season started, but after the quick start, the Vegas odds were reduced to 15 to 1. The Fenway advantage was as strong as ever and the Sox won 13 of their first 16 games at home. Although the pitching was a bit shaky, Boston was scoring runs, led by Stuart and Yastrzemski, who would win his first batting title in 1963. The fans, who'd waited so long for a good team, were excited. "They gave me a standing ovation in Boston recently," Stuart said. "Being used to only boos, I turned around to see who they were cheering."[24]

The boos would come. "There's very little foul territory in Boston," Larry Claflin wrote, "so that puts the fans close to the playing field, where they can really razz [Stuart]. They'll drive him out of town if he doesn't hit."[25] When Stuart didn't tattoo the left field wall right off the bat, the fans started giving him the treatment Claflin had predicted. On April 28, he received his first boos in Boston. "It seemed like old times," he said.[26]

By the 16th of May Stuart had seven homers, but his average was plummeting and he was striking out a lot (44 times in 132 at bats). When his average dropped to .221, Pesky made good on his pre-season pledge and benched him in favor of future Red Sox manager Dick Williams. Geiger went to center field in place of Roman Mejias. Mejias had the best season of his career with Houston in 1962, and big things were expected of him in Boston. He'd been perhaps the most pleasant surprise in the Boston camp, but when the season started, Mejias was terrible. He was batting around .150 and would be a major disappointment, finishing with a .227 average and just 11 home runs in 111 games.

Stuart, disappointed by his slow start and thinking that his strikeouts might be caused by poor vision, tried wearing glasses for the first time. At Pesky's suggestion, he went to see Dr. Thomas Cavanaugh for an eye exam and, when he held his hand over his right eye, the numbers on the chart were blurry. "I didn't know this before," he said, "because I never batted holding my hand over my right eye."[27] The doctor told him he had astigmatism in his left eye.

Stuart refused to be photographed wearing his glasses, claiming to be self-conscious, but once the game started, the shyness vanished. Stuart loved to make a dramatic entrance and the glasses enhanced his act. In the first game after he got them, he walked up to the plate without them, stopped, turned and motioned to the batboy, who brought the case to him. Stuart took the spectacles out and made a big show of putting them on so everyone could see.

He drew a walk and beckoned the batboy again, handing him the glasses before going to first base. Later in the game Stuart homered off the Yankees' Ralph Terry, but he never felt comfortable with glasses, adjusting them after every pitch. He quickly discarded the spectacles and played the rest of his career without them.

Stuart's benching in favor of Dick Williams was brief. He helped the Sox win a game with a pinch-hit single and was back in the lineup two days later. His average didn't climb very quickly, but in mid–June he unleashed a barrage of home runs. On the 11th, he hit a 15th inning blast off the Tigers' Terry Fox in Detroit that capped a four-run inning. The Sox returned to Fenway Park the next day and Stuart hit three homers in three days off Washington and Baltimore pitching. Overall, he had seven home runs in ten days. In a doubleheader against the Angels, he hit a grand slam in the opener and a three-run blast in the nightcap to pace the Red Sox to a sweep. They won 10 of 11 games and were in third place with a 35–26 mark, two games behind the first-place Yankees.

For a while, it looked as though 1963 might be a repeat of the 1949 campaign, when the Sox battled the Yankees down to the last day of the season. New York was vulnerable, having suffered a myriad of injuries; Mickey Mantle broke his foot and injured his knee, limiting him to 65 games. Roger Maris suffered from a series of injuries and appeared in just 90 games. Shortstop Tony Kubek missed almost 30 games with an assortment of ailments. Starting pitcher Bill Stafford was injured in his first start and won just four games all year. If there was a season that the Yankees were ripe for the taking, it seemed like 1963 was the year.

But Boston's pitching wasn't up to the task, partly due to injuries. The most serious casualty was Gene Conley, a 15-game winner in 1962 who made only nine starts and finished with a horrible 6.64 ERA. Conley was a two-sport star who played pro basketball in the winter with the New York Knicks. Sports seasons were shorter in those days, and Conley played his final Knick game March 5, but that still put him into camp well behind the other pitchers, with the bumps and bruises accumulated over 70 NBA games. The Red Sox had never been happy about Conley's basketball career, and his injury-riddled 1963 season added to their distaste.[28]

The only reliable hurlers on Pesky's staff were starter Bill Monbouquette, ace reliever Dick Radatz, and Jack Lamabe, who'd come to Boston in the Stuart trade. Monbouquette was on his way to 20 wins, and the hulking, intimidating Radatz, who stood 6'6" and whose weight was estimated as high as 280, was in the midst of an incredible three-year streak during which he was baseball's dominant reliever and which permanently sapped the life out of his strong right arm. Radatz didn't really have a breaking pitch; all he did was wind up and fire his blazing fastball. Lamabe was a durable jack-of-all-trades who pitched whenever and however he was needed. Behind these three, however, there was little to choose from. Other than Monbouquette and Radatz, no pitcher won more than 11 games, and the team ERA of 3.97 was ninth in the league.

There were no "closers" in the early '60s; late inning relievers were known as short men, although by current standards, there was nothing short about their outings. As a rookie in 1962, Radatz pitched 124 innings in 62 games and amassed 144 strikeouts, a remarkable ratio. Today, nearly every reliever averages at least a strikeout an inning, but in 1962, only pitchers like Sandy Koufax were doing it.

Over the next two years, Pesky, who'd switched a disappointed Radatz to the bullpen at Seattle, used him even more than Mike Higgins had in 1962. He had a thoroughbred and was going to ride it until it broke down. In 1963, Radatz not only worked frequently, he worked long; on fourteen occasions, he pitched three innings or more (sometimes much more) and in only 21 of his 66 games did he pitch an inning or less, the standard workload for today's closers. On April 20, Radatz pitched the last seven innings of a 15-inning game. On June 9, he pitched six innings and two days later came back to pitch 8⅔ innings of another 15-inning affair.

In 1964, Pesky worked Radatz just as hard, and for the third consecutive year, the big right-hander was up to the task. He appeared in 29 of the Red Sox's first 51 games, and 17 of 26 at one point. He worked both games of doubleheaders and although he pitched for long stretches, Radatz seemed to have a "rubber arm."

At that time, very few star relievers had staying power. They had a great year or two and then flamed out. Pitch counts were ignored and any effective bullpen operative was imagined to have a rubber arm. "You can't overwork a workhorse," wrote Hy Hurwitz, under a column headlined, "Frequent Relief Missions Keep Fireballer Radatz Extra Sharp."[29] Pesky pledged not to let Radatz sit idle too long, a pledge he fulfilled faithfully.

While the rest of the pitching staff was shaky, the defense was no better than adequate and the team's 27 steals (12 less than individual leader Luis Aparicio) placed them last in the league. The strength of the 1963 Red Sox was power, and the epitome of their power was Dick Stuart.

After a couple of months of observing Stuart in action, Boston writers gave their assessments and one, veteran *Globe* columnist Harold Kaese, said that Stu wasn't getting along too well with his teammates. "Talk, talk, talk. Quote, quote, quote," Kaese wrote. That was why Stuart got so much attention and why he irritated some of his teammates.

Kaese then compared Stuart to Cassius Clay in a quote that would not stand the test of time. "Clay is a mediocre fighter, but a genius at being noticed. Stuart is a mediocre ballplayer, but a genius at making headlines."[30] Perhaps geniuses were as little appreciated in Boston as in Pittsburgh.

"The public image of Stuart as a big, awkward, good-natured, witty player is not quite how teammates see him.... If I had to guess, I'd say the Sox players somewhat resent (1) Stuart's ability to get publicity far out of proportion to his playing ability; (2) his salary of about $36,000, plus extras, such as his Sunday night TV show, and; (3) his general attitude." "Dick was very much into himself," said shortstop Ed Bressoud.[31]

On June 14, in a game at Fenway against the Orioles, Stuart hit a home run off right-hander Milt Pappas, his 14th of the season and fourth in four games, that was reminiscent of the one he hit off Glen Hobbie in 1959. The ball was still rising when it went over the 340 foot mark, over the screen, across the street and hit a building in the next block. Observers estimated it traveled 500 feet.

"I'll talk for an hour about that homer," Stuart told his old Pittsburgh friend Les Biederman. "They tell me that ball landed on a street beyond the ball park. And don't think I didn't give it the old home run trot going around the bases."[32] "Hope I can see you at the All Star game and hope you can see me," he added.

Pittsburgh reporters continued to follow Stuart's progress closely after he left the Pirates. While the Boston press found him entertaining, they rarely mentioned him after he left. The same was true of the other cities Stuart played in, but he was never forgotten in Pittsburgh.

One of the reasons Stuart was not as well-liked by the Red Sox players may have been the nature of the team. The Pirates were a close-knit group that won the World Series in 1960 and were generally a contending team. They had a strong leader in Groat and the players seemed to like each other.

The Red Sox of the early 1960s were a losing team without a leader. There was no one like Groat to tell them that Stuart could help them win and they should find a way to like him. It was not until Dick Williams arrived on the scene in 1967 that the team united, partly in hatred of Williams, and became a winning club. Williams was a teammate of Stuart in Boston, and got along with him, but he was a reserve, not a team leader.

On the 20th of June, Stuart's 17th home run gave him the American League lead. Mantle and Maris were both injured, but sluggers like Killebrew and Colavito were not, and Dick Stuart, in his first American League season, was ahead of them.

Predictably, it was Stuart's fielding that landed him in Pesky's doghouse, and it came at a most inopportune time. His fielding foibles were funny when his team was out of contention, but there was nothing amusing about blowing a game when the Red Sox were in a pennant race. On the 21st of June, the Yankees, who held a three game lead over the Sox, arrived at Fenway for a four-game series. If the Sox swept, they could move into first place.

The series started out well with a 7–4 win that moved Boston within two games of the lead. Radatz pitched a scoreless ninth to save Monbouquette's tenth win. The next day's doubleheader, however, was a disaster. Whitey Ford beat the Red Sox 6–5 in the opener when Radatz entered the game in the seventh but was unable to protect a one-run lead. The Yankees won the second game 3–2, beating 21-year-old Wilbur Wood. Wood eventually became a 20-game winner, but in 1963 he was an emergency starter looking for his first major league win. Instead, he got his third loss. In the ninth inning, trailing by a run, the Sox loaded the bases with no one out, but couldn't push across the tying run. They came excruciatingly close, as Geiger barely missed the right field foul pole with what would have been a game-winning grand slam.

The final game of the series featured the dubious fielding of Dick Stuart. While Stuart had gotten off to a slow start in the home run department, he'd also started slowly in accumulating errors, not making one until his 219th chance. Against the Yankees that Sunday, however, the old Stuart appeared and the results were disastrous.

The game was scoreless in the second inning and the Yankees had Elston Howard at second with two out when Johnny Blanchard lifted a pop fly to the infield. Second baseman Chuck Schilling called for the ball, but the wind started blowing it away from him and toward Stuart. As Schilling ran in frantic pursuit, pitcher Earl Wilson and shortstop Eddie Bressoud raced over, while Stuart stood motionless near first base. Wilson caught the ball just as Bressoud crashed into him and knocked it loose. The hit was ruled a single and Howard scored the first run of the game.

Wilson was shaken up and had the leave the game. The Yankees won 8–0 and afterwards Stuart was asked why he never made a move toward Blanchard's popup. "As soon as the ball went up," he said, "Schilling called for it so I stayed away. Then, when the wind started to take it, [catcher] Russ Nixon called again for Schilling to take it, so I stayed out of it."[33] Pesky said the ball should have been caught but stopped short of blaming Stuart.

The three losses put Boston five games behind, but they rebounded by winning four in a row against the Indians and crept back to within 2½ games of first on June 26. On the 27th, they commenced a five-game series with the Yankees, who were tied for first with the White Sox.

That series proved the undoing of the 1963 Red Sox. The highlight for Stuart came on Friday night when he became the first man at his position to record three assists in an inning. It was a questionable accomplishment, since it meant Stuart either wasn't able or willing to beat the runner to first base. Pesky was so unimpressed that he put Dick Williams at first in the late innings for defense.

Boston pitchers said they weren't worried about their arms wearing out; they were more concerned about their legs giving out from covering first base so often. "The joke was that you could lead the league in putouts if you pitched when he was playing first base," said Jack Lamabe, "because he wouldn't run to the base. He made Mazeroski lose 20 pounds because Maz had to cover the whole right side of the infield."[34] In 1963 Stuart led AL first basemen in assists with 134, with Baltimore's Jim Gentile a distant second with 110.

The Sox lost four of the five games to the Yankees. Stuart let in three runs when a soft ground ball went through his legs with two outs and the bases loaded in the second game of the June 30 doubleheader. The headline in the *New York Daily News* the next day read, "Thank you Rog, Pep, Whitey ... and Stu."[35]

Wilson, who was pitching when Stuart made his error, lost his temper and threw a tantrum on the mound, kicking dirt toward first base; it was the second time in a week he'd been victimized by Stuart, but at least this time he didn't get hurt. After the game, Wilson calmed down and apologized. If Schilling, Bressoud, or Malzone had made the error, he pointed out, everyone would have felt badly and then forgotten about it. "But Stuart makes the error and the whole thing becomes magnified."[36]

Although he had six hits in 15 times at bat during the series, that was Stuart's 14th error in 77 games. At that pace he would make about 30 errors for the season, a high total even for him. Wilson was mad, Pesky was losing his patience, and the rest of the Red Sox were getting aggravated by Stuart's sloppy play at first base. While the miscue against the Yankees was magnified because it came at a critical time, there were numerous other misplays.

"All the infielders," said Felix Mantilla, "Malzone, Bressoud and myself, we got really pissed off at the guy because it seemed he didn't give a damn about his fielding. He just wanted to hit. He was a good guy but it seemed like he just didn't give a damn."[37]

Stuart had been staying with his in-laws in Greenwich and was a little late getting to Yankee Stadium for the final game of the series. He arrived as the Red Sox were taking batting practice and noticed that Dick Williams was hitting with the regulars. Stuart went into the dugout to check the lineup card and saw that Williams was playing first base. He was furious and stormed into Pesky's office looking for an explanation. Stuart said Pesky had embarrassed him and Pesky reminded him that he had embarrassed the whole team on Sunday.

"He was almost in tears when he left my office," said Pesky,[38] who expressed his displeasure with Stuart over the same thing that had frustrated previous managers—his lack of attention in the field. Pesky felt that Stuart's talking to base runners, umpires, and players on the opposing bench caused him to lose concentration and when he lost his concentration, bad things happened.

"I hope [the benching] shakes him up a little," Pesky said. "I've got to get a little more hustle out of him.... I'm not going to have any player tell me how to run my ball club.... Stuart's a good boy and not difficult to handle, but this is one time we didn't see eye to eye."[39] Pesky also said he didn't plan to play Stu in the second games of doubleheaders, as he believed he got sloppy if he had to play two games in one day. After meeting with Pesky, Stuart went out to the Red Sox bullpen so that he was unavailable to the writers, and stayed there sulking until called on to pinch hit late in the game.

Pesky said that another reason for sitting Stuart down was that he didn't want to subject him to the booing he was likely to get from the fans. "I was afraid they might get on him good tonight."[40] Pesky was apparently unaware that Stuart had been booed his entire career and didn't seem to mind. "They booed me the first time I went to bat [in Boston]," Stuart said later, "and just to make it unanimous, I struck out. Later I hit a three-run homer and the crowd turned right around and cheered me. That's the story of my life."[41]

Yankee manager Ralph Houk was as unimpressed as Pesky with Stuart's defense, especially after watching him hand the Yankees two games in a week's time. As skipper of the previous year's pennant winner, Houk was the manager of the All Star team and, after the players selected the starters, he was responsible for selecting the pitchers and reserves. Although Stuart finished second to the Yankees' Joe Pepitone in the players' ballot (112 votes to 62), Houk left him off the team, selecting Kansas City's Norm Siebern instead.[42]

The All Star roster had to include at least one representative from each team, which Houk said was the reason he'd selected Siebern, although Kansas City infielders Wayne Causey and Ed Charles were having equally good seasons. "[Siebern] can play first base, the outfield, and pinch hit," Houk said. "I picked him over Dick Stuart for no other reason."[43] He didn't mention that Siebern could also catch a ground ball, but added, "I must admit [Stuart] frightens me with his bat, but his fielding is something else."[44]

Stuart didn't go quietly. Individual honors were important to Big Stu, and he had very much wanted to be an All Star, which would have made him part of a select group that had played for both leagues. "What does Houk know about how important it is for someone to be on the All-Star team," he fumed. "He was nothing but a third-string catcher all his life. The only way he got to an All Star game was when Casey Stengel got fired and they made him manager of the Yankees. This is a bush trick Houk played on me and I want him to know it."[45] He hinted that Houk picked Siebern because he was an old buddy from the Yankees and said that even Pepitone admitted Stuart should have been chosen. After all, he was among the league leaders with 17 homers and 50 RBI, while Siebern had just seven homers.

Stuart had something Houk did not have—a television show. One night, when a writer who was his guest gave him a picture of Houk as a joke, Stuart tore it up on camera. The controversy even reached Lincoln, Nebraska, where they still took slights to their old hero seriously. Hal Brown, sports editor of the *Lincoln Star*, wrote, "We had thought about running a black banner around the sports page in mourning for Stuart…. Houk's move regarding Stuart could be compared to forgetting your wife's birthday…. Leaving any of the other players off the squad may have brought a rebuttal, but none would have compared with that fired by Stuart."[46]

Les Biederman was in Cleveland covering the All-Star Game, and took the opportunity to have breakfast with Pesky and Boston business manager Dick O'Connell and ask them about Stuart. "YOU tell ME about Dick Stuart," Pesky countered, and Biederman laughed. "He's a likeable fellow," Pesky said, "and I get along with him fine although we did have a little flare-up the other day when I benched him…. I gave him the devil for challenging my authority to make up the lineup but I did admire his spunk. I know he wants to play and I know he had his heart set on being one of the few players to appear for both leagues in the All-Star game."[47]

The American League lost the All Star Game 5–3 and Siebern didn't play. Houk said that although there was a time or two he could have used him, he chose not to in order to spare Siebern the embarrassment of appearing in front of a national audience in his garish green and gold Athletic uniform.[48] That seemed a bit of a stretch, since Siebern wore the uniform in every game, and it wasn't *that* bad. Stuart always looked stylish in *his* uniform and if looking good was important to Houk, Stuart should have been his man.

Two members of the Minnesota Twins, Bob Allison and Harmon Killebrew, did see action, and Stuart opined that the two sluggers should hit a "million" homers because they played in such a friendly home park. Although the power alleys in Minnesota's Metropolitan Stadium weren't as deep as those in some other parks, it wasn't so much the distances that made it a homer haven; it was the wind, which blew toward the fences late in the summer. Even if the wind wasn't blowing out, there were never any tricky cross-currents like the ones that made hitting difficult in other parks. The hitting background at Metropolitan Stadium was also very good and Stuart thought the combination of those factors made things a lot easier for the Twins' sluggers.

Stuart proved his point by hitting two homers at Metropolitan Stadium during the first game after the All Star break, snapping a 20-day homerless drought and showing Houk that while he couldn't field, he was an All-Star hitter. His second homer was a three-run shot off Twins relief ace Bill Dailey that won the game in the tenth inning.

When the Twins came to Boston later in the month, Allison stood by the cage during batting practice and teased Stuart about what he'd said about him and Killebrew. Every time Stuart hit one into the left field screen, Allison said, "put out in Minnesota."[49] One didn't taunt Dick Stuart without living to regret it, and the first time he came to bat that night, he hit a three-run blast. By the end of July, Stuart had 23 homers, tied with Killebrew and one behind league leader Allison. He seemed certain to best his single season high and his 70 RBI led the American League.

August was a great month for Stuart but a terrible one for the Red Sox. After winning their first game, they lost the next nine, dropping them six games under .500 and ending their quixotic quest for the AL championship. The Yankees, despite their injuries, were running away with the pennant as substitutes like Blanchard, Hector Lopez, and Phil Linz filled the void left by Mantle and Maris. Whitey Ford was on his way to winning 24 games and second-year man Jim Bouton would win 21.

After the Sox's ninth straight loss, the Yankees had a nine-game lead over second place Chicago. Boston was sixth, 20 games back, and Pesky was baffled. "It's hard to figure out," he said. "This isn't a bad club, but we've sure been losing regularly."[50] "What happened to us then," wrote Yastrzemski, "is something I won't be able to explain to my dying day. We folded faster than I thought it was possible for any team to fold."[51] In the four weeks after July 15, Boston dropped from second to sixth, from 10 games over .500 to six under and from 5½ games out of first to 20. In one stretch the team lost 32 of 46 games. When the losing began, the atmosphere in the clubhouse reverted to that of previous years, with arguments and back-biting replacing the one-for-all spirit of the early season.

Pesky had used Radatz relentlessly and the big reliever was tired and ineffective. In late July he had a 12–1 record and a 1.13 ERA, along with 15 saves. He lost five of his last eight decisions and by the end of the year his ERA had risen to 1.97, still very good, but not as good as when the big fellow was fresh. "In the last three or four weeks of the season," he said, "it was an effort for me to walk from the bullpen to the mound."[52] It didn't help that Radatz was later diagnosed with tonsillitis.

No one could blame Stuart for the Boston collapse. He hit 12 home runs in August, giving him 35 for the season and matching his single season high. "I wish my slugging spree had come at a time we were winning," he said. "I can't talk much about it, since the club has been losing."[53] On the 10th, he regained the AL lead with his 27th homer, and on the 14th, he took out his revenge on Ralph Houk, rapping six hits (including a game-winning home run) and driving home six runs during a day-night doubleheader against the Yankees. When asked if he had extra motivation because of Houk's All Star snub, he modestly replied, "I've forgotten all about that. Of course, it's always nice to hit against those guys."[54]

Before the next day's game at Yankee Stadium, Stuart welcomed a couple of fans from Pittsburgh, Bob Mickey and his son Gene, who'd been a big Stuart supporter during Dick's Pirate days. Stu was the perfect host, giving the youngster an autograph and posing for his father's movie camera. Then he said he'd try to make young Gene's day a complete success by hitting a home run. It took until the ninth inning, but he did it. It was meaningless as far as the result, for the Yankees won easily, 10–2, but it was a day Gene Mickey would never forget.

For the season, Stuart wound up batting .385 against New York with five home runs. It was by far his highest average against any opponent and he only hit more homers against the Twins. Stuart pummeled Minnesota pitching, hitting four home runs in a four-game series at Metropolitan Stadium in mid–August and stroking ten homers against the Twins for the year, six in their home park.

On August 11, after his big series in Minnesota, Stuart led the league with 28 home runs, two ahead of Killebrew, and 78 RBI, one ahead of Al Kaline of the Tigers. When he hit home run #26, Stuart established a record, becoming the first player to hit more than 25 in both the National and American Leagues. It wasn't long before he became the first to hit 30 in each league and then 35.

On the 19th of August, Stuart hit the second inside-the-park home run of his career, off Pedro Ramos of the Indians. Yastrzemski called it the strangest thing he'd ever seen at Fenway Park. Like his inside-the-park job in Chicago, it wasn't an impressive drive, a high fly to left field that scraped the Fenway Park scoreboard. Catcher John Romano, playing left field for Cleveland, was unfamiliar with any left field, let alone the bizarre one in Fenway Park that was all angles and wall. Center fielder Vic Davalillo raced over to help and the ball rebounded off the wall, bounced off his cheek and headed back toward the corner. When Stuart was halfway between second and third, coach Billy Herman started waving him home. Romano lumbered after the ball as Stuart lumbered around the bases. "I didn't see Herman's sign at all," he said. "By the time I reached third base I couldn't see anything. I saw the ball go into the corner and decided to try for it."[55] He slid across the plate as the relay sailed over the catcher's head. As he had after hitting his first inside-the-parker at Wrigley Field, Stuart added a conventional home run later in the game, his 32nd of the year.

On September 3, Stuart's 36th homer, a two-run opposite field shot off the Orioles' Stu Miller, established a personal high and drove in his 100th run of the season, making him the first player to drive in 100 runs in each league. It would seem that, since 1901, someone would have already done that, but with much less inter-league player movement and no free agency, many ballplayers, particularly star players, spent their entire careers in one league. Wally Pipp, known primarily as the man Lou Gehrig replaced as the Yankee first baseman, drove in 100 for the Yanks and 99 for the Reds, but no one had ever reached 100 in each league—until Dick Stuart.

The honor Stuart really wanted was to lead the AL in home runs, for he was first and foremost a home run hitter. At the end of August, he led with 35, Killebrew had 33, and Allison was third with 30. By the 13th of September, Stuart and Killebrew were tied at 38, but on the 14th Stuart hit two in Kansas City to pull ahead. On the 21st, when the Twins arrived in Fenway for a three-game series and a head-to-head competition between Stuart and Killebrew, Stuart held a slim 41 to 40 lead.

Monbouquette, Boston's top starter, was on the mound for Saturday's first game. Killebrew clipped him for a home run into the left field screen in the first. He hit another off Pete Smith in the fifth and a third off Arnold Earley in the eighth to give him 43. Stuart hit one, leaving him one behind. In the second game, Killebrew homered again, and yet again the next day, giving him 45 to Stuart's 42, which is where they finished the season. Stuart failed to connect in his final 19 at bats, while Killebrew finished strong with 12 homers in the season's final month.

Stuart was particularly upset that Killebrew won the home run title with a barrage against Red Sox pitching. "Why should I feel bad about it," he said after the doubleheader. "I didn't throw four home runs to the guy.... [Killebrew] hit four fastballs and he's strictly a fastball hitter. You figure it out."[56] Killebrew was also a little surprised the Boston pitchers had challenged him. "I did get some pretty good pitches to hit at," he admitted.[57]

Stuart easily won the RBI title, as his 118 (one better than his previous personal high) were well ahead of Kaline's 101. He led the league with 319 total bases and finished 13th in the MVP voting with 22 points, receiving one third place vote. Stuart's final average was a respectable .261, but he broke Foxx's Boston single-season record for strikeouts with 144 (the third highest total in AL history[58]) and again led his league's first basemen in errors with a whopping 29. That was his all-time high and well ahead of Siebern, who was second with 12. No one mentioned whether it was the first time a first baseman had led each league in errors. When someone in Boston asked Danny Murtaugh about Stuart leading the league, he replied with a straight face, "I can't understand it. You mean Stuart didn't field well here?"[59]

Stuart barely missed tying Williams' single season home run high of 43 but fell well short of the all-time Boston record of 50 set by Jimmie Foxx in 1938. Led by Stuart, the Red Sox set a team record with 171 homers, breaking the old mark of 161 set in 1950.

For rebounding from his sorry 1962 season, Stuart was named AL Comeback Player of the Year, garnering 36 of the 64 votes.[60] Second place finisher Frank Lary was named on only six ballots. Stuart gave credit to Fenway, where he hit 24 of his 42 homers, for his improved showing. "You gotta have the park," he said. "There is no doubt in my mind that my hitting was helped by playing in Boston. I'm no better a hitter than I was with Pittsburgh. It's the park that helped me."[61]

Overall, it had been a banner season for Stuart and the excitement over his slugging, the amazement occasioned by his fielding, and the controversy created by his personality contributed to increased Boston attendance. The final total of 942,642 was up more than 200,000 from 1962 and was the highest it had been in three years. "You've got to say this for Dick," wrote Hurwitz, "He helped stimulate enthusiasm among the customers. He became a miniature edition of Ted Williams in the controversy department."[62]

Stuart enjoyed the Red Sox fans. "In Pittsburgh, they were 75–25 against me. In Boston they're only 60–40 against me."[63] "He's taken this town by—well, some kind of storm," said Red Sox publicity man Bill Crowley. "No one is indifferent to him." Crowley described an incident when a fan began slugging another fan who'd been heckling Stuart. "Stuart is out on the field," Crowley said, "going like this with his fist, as if to say, 'Attaboy, give it to him.' … They boo Stuart and they cheer him, but they come out to see him. He sells a lot of tickets for us."[64] "I have a controversial name," Stuart said. "Anything I say or do seems to attract attention. I don't mind. People know me, whether they like me or dislike me."[65]

The press hadn't decided whether they liked him. "The Boston press is about evenly divided on Stuart as a personality," wrote Larry Claflin. "Some find Stuart's straight-faced humor refreshing. Others feel his attitude is not serious enough."[66] When Stuart was informed that he had shattered Jimmy Foxx's team record for strikeouts in a season, he shouted triumphantly, "I knew I would break one of Foxxie's records."[67] Serious major league ball players did not get excited over setting records for strikeouts.

GM Mike Higgins had nothing but praise for his new first baseman. "He did a fine job for us," Higgins said. "He was better at first base than we were led to believe (one wonders what he had been led to believe) and he gave us power. Some of the fans booed him but they came out to see him and that's important."[68] "Had Stuart been a good fielder," he added later, "we never would have gotten him from the Pirates."[69]

Johnny Pesky, who Stuart had often driven to distraction during the season, said, "I'm naturally glad for him. I hope he hits 90 home runs next year. He was responsible for putting people in the ball park. He's quite a guy. He's controversial. I think he's a nice kid. But he has that kind of personality. People either like him or they don't."[70] For the time being, Pesky liked him, but 1964 would test his patience even further.

After their encouraging start, the Red Sox wound up seventh with a 76–85 record, the same number of wins they had in 1962. At home, Boston was 44–36 but they were a disappointing 32–49 away from Fenway. They were 44–37 during the first half of the season and 32–48 in the second half.

When Pesky was rehired for 1964, he admitted he made a number of mistakes in '63 and vowed to correct them. Yastrzemski was very critical of Pesky's managing and said he had done a terrible job the second half of the season. "[Pesky] couldn't have won the pennant for us," Yaz wrote later, "but I thought he certainly could have prevented the collapse of morale that followed our nosedive to oblivion.... Pesky, who had been the architect of our new-found spirit, practically lost control of the ball club."[71] The press latched onto Yaz's comments and controversy raged for a better part of the winter.

Harold Kaese fueled the fires by writing of the resentment several Red Sox players had for Pesky. After listing their complaints, Kaese wrote, "The new manager did not show enough authority, therefore did not command enough respect."

For years, the biggest problem with the Red Sox had been a listless atmosphere. When Yaz and Chuck Schilling joined the team as enthusiastic rookies in 1961, they were told to put a lid on their collegiate-like cheering and calm down. There was enthusiasm during the early 1963 run, but after it vanished the old listless behavior seemed better than the attitude with which the '63 Sox finished the season. They'd gone from listless to enthusiastic to rebellious.

Pesky lived to the age of 93 and became a grand old man of the Red Sox, beloved by baseball fans everywhere. He was a great storyteller, loved interacting with people and talking baseball, and it is hard to imagine anyone not liking sweet, funny, kindly old Johnny Pesky.

But Stuart and Yastrzemski were not dealing with the old Johnny Pesky. They were dealing with a man in his prime who had a temper. Ted Schreiber, who played for him in Seattle, told of Pesky's reaction to a tough loss one night and the show he put on in the clubhouse. "Pesky is an animated son of a bitch," Schreiber said. "There were boxes outside the clubhouse door. He kicked one of the boxes, got his foot caught in it, and all the boxes were falling on him. He was pissed now. He's really pissed. He finally gets into the clubhouse and there's a radio blasting music. He kicks the radio, stomps on it, and it won't shut off. Now he's more pissed than ever. He's kicking it and kicking it and it finally shuts off. Then he turns over a box filled with dirt where everybody put their cigarettes. Now the little bastard who's 5'5" or 5'6" (actually 5'9") stands on the box so he's 5'7". He's blasting everybody, challenging everybody. He wants to fight. We let him rant and rave for about five minutes. He said what he had to say and then goes in his office and sits down. He's a piece of work.... He reminded me of the Eddie Stankys of old.... If you missed a ball, he'd curse you out—make you feel like you were the lowest piece of crap on the face of the earth."[72]

Pesky and Stuart bickered frequently, and one night after a game at Yankee Stadium they had a long, unpleasant exchange on the team bus. Stuart, who'd homered that day, said, "How did you like that one, Pesky?" "Anybody can hit home runs off these guys," the manager retorted, and told Stuart about the great pitchers from his era.

"You don't know anything about it," Stuart taunted. "You couldn't hit anyhow." The dialogue continued at the same low level, with Pesky spouting his career statistics and Stuart replying, "Yah, what kind of hits? Dunkers and bleeders and dribblers and Texas leaguers. You never hit five home runs in a season. I hit 'em forty at a time."[73]

At other times, Stuart taunted Pesky by stating that he made more money than his manager. "Say, John" he once said. "I make $40,000. How much do you make, John—twenty? Maybe twenty-five? Is that what you make, John—Twenty-five?"[74] Even if it was said in fun, it was not the way a player talked to his manager. When Pesky didn't fine Stuart for insubordination, he lost the respect of the other players. He often said that the manager he most respected was Joe McCarthy, because McCarthy was able to get so much out of the immensely talented but eccentric Ted Williams. Thus far, Pesky hadn't done very well with his two biggest talents.

The Stuart trade had worked out well for the Red Sox. Not only did he have a terrific season; Jack Lamabe, who'd come to Boston in the same deal, was voted the unsung hero of 1963 by the Boston baseball writers. Lamabe pitched even more innings in relief than Radatz, working 151 in 65 games, and posted a respectable 7–4 record and 3.15 ERA, second only to Radatz on the Red Sox. Jim Pagliaroni, the catcher who'd gone from the Red Sox to the Pirates, hit just .230 in 90 games, and pitcher Don Schwall was 6–12. After a year, it appeared that the Red Sox had gotten much the better of the trade.

Stuart and his family spent the winter in the Boston suburb of Dedham. The fall was a warm one, allowing him the opportunity to play golf and attend sporting events as a spectator. Stuart's success on television led to a nightly radio show during the winter called, like its TV counterpart, "Stuart on Sports." Lois did some modeling and was an instructor in a charm school.

The Yankees lost the World Series to the Dodgers in four games and, ironically, the winning run in the final game was the result of All Star first baseman Pepitone missing a throw. Stuart's old friend Les Biederman assured his readers that Stuart would have caught it.

During the first weekend of February 1964, Stuart made a triumphant return to Pittsburgh for the Dapper Dan Dinner. "I'm like that French general," he told Al Abrams. "What's his name, DeGaulle, or something? Anyhow, he's the guy who said 'I shall return.' Or was it MacArthur? Those generals always confuse me."[75]

When Stuart saw Bob Friend he reminded him that he had been a 20-game winner just once and that Stu had given him his 20th win with a home run. He enjoyed kidding around with his old teammates, but the highlight of the evening was when Stuart presented an award to Ralph Houk. "This is for a man," he said, "who never rose higher than a third-string catcher with the Yankees and is now general manager."[76] Even Houk laughed. At another banquet, Stuart began by addressing "honored guests—and Mr. Houk"[77] and presented Houk with a steel-framed picture of himself, one that Houk couldn't tear up. Houk played along with the gag.

When he called his friends in Pittsburgh, Stuart announced himself as the president of the Donn Clendenon Fan Club. If it weren't for the presence of the big first baseman, he said, he would have been stuck in Pittsburgh. While Stuart hit 42 homers and led his league in RBI, Clendenon hit just 15 homers and drove in only 57 runs. "I like Clendenon," Stuart said, "but I'm afraid Forbes Field is too big for him, just as it was for me at times."[78] In 1966, Clendenon had his biggest home run season (28) and only three came at home.

The Pirates had complained about Stuart's strikeouts, but Clendenon led the National League with 136 and five years later he would fan 163 times, more than Stuart ever did during his career. And while Clendenon didn't make as many errors as Stuart, in

1963 he was second only to Orlando Cepeda among National League first basemen. He would lead NL first baseman in errors from 1965 to 1967.

It had been a satisfying year for Stuart, and he looked forward to a big raise and more success in 1964. He got the raise, but 1964 didn't exactly turn out as expected by either Stuart or Johnny Pesky.

13

It's About Time Stuart Grew Up: 1964

Stuart's banner 1963 season was worth an estimated $7,500 raise to $40,000 per year, well above the $27,500 paid to batting champion Carl Yastrzemski. The only Red Sox players who ever earned more were Ted Williams and Vern Stephens. That was very important to Stuart, who always equated success with monetary rewards. When someone questioned his value, he usually countered by telling them how much money he made. He was a $40,000 ball player.

On January 4, a few weeks before he signed, Stuart was stopped by a police officer near Boston because his car still carried its expired 1963 plates. Stuart's quick wit came to the rescue. "I had such a good year in 1963," he told the officer, "that I didn't want to jinx myself by changing the plates."[1] He was let off with a warning. The remark was widely publicized, and when Dick Radatz heard about it, he quipped, "I understand they're making a special plate for you this year. It's going to be E3."[2]

The most pressing needs of the 1964 Red Sox were pitching and catching. Pesky was hoping that Gene Conley, who ended his basketball season early so he could get to training camp on time, would rebound to his old form and that husky young Bob Tillman, who'd been a disappointment in 1963, would become a solid major league catcher. Tillman had batted just .225 and opponents stole 43 bases in 51 attempts against him.

Pesky was also displeased with the performances of outfielders Roman Mejias and Lu Clinton. If they didn't look better in the spring, he planned to take a good look at 19-year-old Tony Conigliaro, who had just one year of professional baseball but during that one season hit .363 with 24 home runs in just 83 games. Mike Higgins thought Conigliaro could use more seasoning but Pesky, after watching him hit some tape measure home runs in the spring, wanted to keep him.

Another promising youngster in camp was Tony Horton, also 19, who was reported to have received a $138,000 bonus package.[3] Ted Williams called Horton the best-looking hitting prospect in a Boston camp that included Conigliaro. He hit 21 homers at Waterloo in 1963 and was supposed to be Stuart's eventual successor at first base; the question was how soon the transition would take place. Both Conigliaro and Horton were "first year" players and only one could be sent to the minors without becoming subject to the draft. Therefore, it appeared that either Conigliaro or Horton would go north with the team.

Perhaps the biggest problem facing the Red Sox, more than any on-field issues, was what *Sports Illustrated* referred to the "powder keg relations" between Pesky and his best players.[4] By the end of the 1963 season, Pesky had problems with both Stuart and Yastrzemski. At the start of spring training, when asked about the situation, he said, "I'm just as friendly with Carl as I've ever been." He didn't say how friendly that was, but added, "I've seen him several times since the end of the season and he has not indicated to me he's sore about anything."[5] Pesky denied that there was a movement among the players to get rid of him.

"This is a poor ball club," wrote Bud Collins, "dismantled to a frightful state during Tom Yawkey's unimaginative and unaggressive ownership. The Sox are Inertia, Inc., and even Aladdin's genie would get a hernia trying to pull them into the first division."[6] "Several players did not like Pesky and probably still don't. He isn't crazy about all of them either. If that is dissension, the Red Sox have it...." Collins' next comment boded poorly for Pesky. "They know that a player with any ability will likely outlast any manager regardless of ability in the long run." It was much easier to change managers than to replace the 1963 batting and RBI champions.

Coming off the best season of his life, Stuart was in a good mood in Scottsdale. "I'm about 40 home runs behind my batting practice pace of this time last year," he joked. "Maybe this cold weather is harmful."[7] He said he was aiming for 50 homers and, if he got lucky, might beat Roger Maris's 61. "Of course it's far fetched," he admitted, "but you can dream. Maris told me he was awful lucky. I could get lucky."

The Giants trained in Phoenix, which gave Stuart the opportunity to banter with his old friend Willie Mays. "Willie," Stuart said, "I beat you in every department last year. More homers, more RBI, and even more errors." "Yes, I know all that," Mays replied. "You beat me in every department except salary."[8] That was hitting Stuart where it hurt.

It didn't take long for trouble to raise its head in the Red Sox camp, and Stuart was the cause. On March 18, Pesky decided to use his kids in the regular exhibition game and have some of the veterans play in a "B" squad game against the Giants. The "B" game was in the morning, and Pesky thought his vets might like to have the afternoon off.

Stuart felt otherwise. "I thought I was finished playing those kinds of games ten years ago," he told a reporter.[9] Stu showed his displeasure by not running out two ground balls and ignoring the third base coach and failing to score from second on a single. "What do you expect?" Stuart growled afterwards. "That's as good as I'm going to be in that kind of game."[10]

Pesky was angry. He denied calling Stuart "selfish," although many writers heard him use the word. He didn't take any disciplinary action, which set tongues wagging and typewriters clicking. Most reporters thought Stuart should have given a better effort and that when he didn't Pesky should have done something about it; they blasted both of them. "Would any club but the Red Sox," wrote Kaese, "have dismissed so lightly such a performance, particularly in view of Winter-long reports of team dissension."[11]

The Sporting News came down hard on Stuart in an editorial titled, "It's About Time Stuart Grew Up."[12]

"If Dick Stuart were a callow rookie," *TSN* said, "trying out in a major league camp for the first time this spring, there might be some excuse for his complete impertinence (and that's the kindest word we can think of).... But Dick Stuart is not a rookie. He is a veteran and consequently should be a mature individual. The fact that he obviously is not does not speak well of his attention to team effort.... [I]n case he's forgotten, we'd like to remind him that he is not a good first baseman and again that is the kindest way we can put it.... To be as blunt as possible, it's about time Dick Stuart grew up and started acting like a mature ball player...."[13]

Stuart and Pesky had a 45-minute closed-door discussion to clear the air. Stuart began by apologizing, which drained most of the anger from Pesky. "I am an employee of the Red Sox," Stu said afterward, "and I am paid by them. I will do anything I'm told to do. I didn't mean to cause any trouble. I'm sorry it happened."[14] The situation was defused, but it would not be the last time Pesky and Stuart clashed. Despite the apology and all the previous sightings of a "new" Dick Stuart, he was 31 years old, his attitude hadn't changed since he entered pro ball in 1951, and it wasn't about to change now.

Late in spring training, Stuart and Yastrzemski got under Pesky's skin by failing to run out ground balls. Stuart trotted to first three times and was doubled up each time. Yastrzemski tapped a ground ball back to the mound and made no attempt to run to first. It wasn't the first time Yaz made a half-hearted effort and Pesky said it was possible that he was bothered by an ingrown nail. He had no excuse for Stuart's failure to hustle, and the weariness of his response indicated he was tired of it.

A couple of days later, Arthur Siegel wrote a column in the *Globe* pointing out the lack of enthusiasm of the Red Sox as a team and Stuart in particular. He said Stuart thought he was only being paid to hit, and when he hit a grounder or popup, he didn't run hard. "We've had a few talks," Pesky said, "and lately he has shown a lot of hustle, *especially for him* (italics added)."[15] The danger, Siegel pointed out, was that Stuart's attitude might rub off on young players like Conigliaro. Two prima donnas were about all Pesky could stomach.

The relationship between Pesky and Stuart was uncomfortable but not vicious, for Stuart was more annoying than infuriating. One day in camp, he was in the dugout talking about how he expected to lead the league in home runs, RBI, and average. "What about strikeouts?" Pesky asked. He told Stuart that when Ted Williams got two strikes on him, he choked up on the bat. "Williams had it easier," Stuart replied. "He never had to face the tough pitchers that I do."

After a little more bantering back and forth, Pesky turned to a reporter and said, "Don't ask me why, but I like the guy. There isn't a mean bone in his body."[16] Shortly after the B game incident, an angry Stuart confronted Boston public relations man Bill Crowley and accused him of blowing the story out of proportion. "Then," Crowley said, "he lifted a cigar out of my pocket. 'And this makes us even,' he said. And he smiled and walked away."[17]

After leading the team with six exhibition home runs, Stuart got off to his traditional slow start. On the morning of April 28, as the Red Sox prepared to play the Orioles before a sparse crowd of about two thousand at Fenway, he was batting .229 and had only one home run.

In that game, Big Stu had his first big day of the season. In the ninth, he hit a long double off the center field fence to tie the score 2–2. After the Orioles scored twice in the top of the eleventh, the Sox loaded the bases and Baltimore brought Dick Hall in to face Stuart. He hit the ball into the left field net for a grand slam and a 6–4 Red Sox win.

The start of the regular season had not improved the Red Sox's morale. In early May, Harry Grayson of the *Globe* spoke with someone close to the Boston front office who told him that things were not good. "We have to get rid of Dick Stuart," he told Grayson.[18] The problem, he said, was that they couldn't get anyone to take Stuart due to his high salary and poor fielding.

How was Yastrzemski getting along with Pesky, Grayson asked? "Not at all. Yastrzemski doesn't like Pesky." The source said he thought Yaz was 15 pounds overweight and not trying, and that Higgins would protect him from Pesky. As if Pesky didn't have enough problems, he wasn't getting along with Higgins. He'd been forced to fire pitching coach Harry Dorish when the pitchers complained to Higgins about him.

The players got angry when reporters wrote about the dissension and voted to keep them out of the locker room for an hour before each game and 20 minutes afterwards. All in all, it was not a pretty picture, and it was becoming more likely that neither Pesky nor Stuart would be in Boston in 1965.

One controversy followed the next. During one game, Pesky gave Stuart the bunt sign, which Stuart regarded as a personal insult. "Bunting was against his principles,"[19] Pesky observed later. Stuart made a couple of half-hearted, unsuccessful efforts to lay down a bunt and then struck out. When he returned to the bench, he said, "I'm a slugger, not a bunter."[20] Pesky fined him $50. Shortly afterward, Stuart was fined $25 by the league for throwing his bat in disgust.

On May 21, there was an error committed in a game against the Angels. It wasn't charged to Stuart, but it got him in more hot water than many that were. The trouble started when he hit a line drive that bounced off the glove of Angel third baseman Felix Torres. Torres wasn't a much better fielder than Stuart and didn't make a great effort to get to the ball.

It was a close call, and most reporters thought it could have been either a hit or error. A year earlier, in a remarkably similar situation, Stuart hit a ball to Torres that was first ruled an error and later changed to a hit. This time Boston official scorer Larry Claflin (who had not been the scorer the previous year) ruled it an error and Stuart, who was in a slump, was livid. From first base, he directed several choice words toward Claflin. Stuart later scored, and as he crossed the plate he unleashed another barrage toward the press box. The second outburst got the attention of umpire Larry Napp, who reported it to the league office. Whether Stuart was right or wrong, abusing Claflin, who was a prominent local columnist and the Boston correspondent to *The Sporting News*, was probably not a good idea.[21]

Two days later, when the Athletics came to town, Stuart had another temper tantrum, throwing his bat high into the air after a strike out. When he thought Athletics' coach Mel McGaha was encouraging first base umpire Frank Umont to eject him, he got into a jawing match with McGaha.

The next day, during a doubleheader, Boston fans let Stuart know what they thought of his outbursts and his batting slump, especially after he grounded out his first three times up in the first game. It was 91 at bats since his last home run and his batting average, which was .219 when the game began, was inching toward .200.

In the eighth inning, with the score tied 2–2, Kansas City manager Eddie Lopat walked Yastrzemski intentionally to load the bases for Stuart. "That burned me up," Stuart said, and he retaliated by lining a grand slam home run into the center field bleachers to give Boston a 6–2 win.

Stuart was voted the most valuable Red Sox player of the first game and presented with a set of luggage by broadcaster Curt Gowdy between games. "I don't know where I am," he said to Gowdy, "the fans are cheering me."[22] The cheering increased when he won the second game with a two-run blast.

That was the start of one of Stuart's hot streaks; he hit six homers in seven games (two in one game against Washington on May 27), giving him nine for the season and 37 RBI, just three behind Cleveland's Leon Wagner for the AL lead. On May 29 and 30, Stuart hit home runs against the Twins at Metropolitan Stadium, giving him 12 homers against the Twins since the start of the 1963 season, eight of them in Minnesota.

On June 5, Eddie Lopat proved he hadn't learned his lesson, once more walking Yastrzemski to load the bases for Stuart. Stu delivered his third grand slam of the season, leaving him two short of the major league record held by Ernie Banks and Jim Gentile, with more than half a season to go.

Stuart attributed his hot streak to a new bat he'd been using. Unfortunately, the magic bat was declared illegal when the umpires inspected it during a game with the Twins and discovered that its powers had been enhanced by five nails. "It was so full of holes," said writer Jim Murray, "that it sounded like chimes every time he hit the ball."[23] Yastrzemski said that during day games, the sun reflected so brightly off the metal nails that anyone could see the bat was doctored.

Stuart, who readily admitted his guilt, suspected an inside job; someone from the Red Sox must have informed the Twins. They insisted not; Minnesota outfielder Lennie Green had spotted it and told manager Sam Mele. In any event, the bat was confiscated and Stuart was in trouble again.

Despite losing his favorite bat, Stuart's run of good hitting continued in July as he cleared the fences 12 times. On July 15, he hit two homers and drove in six runs against the White Sox and two days later he hit two more homers against the Senators. The entire Red Sox team came alive in July and hit 53 home runs, just two short of the all-time mark for a month.

No matter how well he hit, it was Stuart's fielding that always drew the most attention. After all, there were 18 Gold Glovers, but only one Dr. Strangeglove. Invariably, he would make a good play or two and people said he was getting better. But it wasn't long before there was another series of spectacular blunders that shattered the illusion.

Columnist Walt Riddle described Stuart's adventures against the Orioles. "You have to see Dick Stuart ... in the field to believe it," he wrote. Stuart botched four plays, three of which were errors and the fourth, in Riddle's judgment, should have been an error. "He had to move two steps to his right," Riddle said of the first incident, "and in the process over ran the ball. It hit his ankle and bounded off his head.... All the time he was running away from the ball with his glove over his face."

On the next play, Boston second baseman Dalton Jones made a great stop and threw a one-hopper to Stuart, who was so stunned he watched the ball go by with his glove at his side. "Finally he turned to chase it," Riddle continued, "and ran smack into the runner crossing the bag."[24] What made the sequence so unusual was that it wasn't unusual. Things like that happened to Stuart all the time.

Despite being among the league leaders in home runs and RBI, Stuart was again passed over for the All Star team. This time he placed third in the player voting behind Allison and Siebern. The latter had been traded to Baltimore and was in the midst of a very mediocre season that would end with a .245 average, 12 homers, and 56 RBI. Fielding aside, it was hard to imagine he was having a better season than Stuart. Even Earl Wilson, who'd been so upset over Stuart's fielding a year earlier, said Stu should have been chosen.[25] Yet when All Star manager Al Lopez of the White Sox[26] selected Siebern and Joe Pepitone of the Yankees, who'd finished fourth in the player voting, there was nary a protest from Stuart. He said he was hurt that the players hadn't voted for him, but he wasn't as upset as he'd been the previous year.

Others took up his case. Dick Young wrote, "Wonder which manager will fail to put Dick Stuart on the All-Star squad next time? When you consider that Stu is such a big RBI man, and such a colorful character, it does seem a bit foolish to leave him out of the game. Forget his glove; he could take a pinch swing. There's no knock on his bat—and the crowd would love it."[27]

Not if *Sporting News* reader Charles Grady of the USS Cascade was there. "King Richard Stuart annoys me with his constant complaints," he wrote in a letter to the sports weekly. "Last year Crying Dickie just could not believe that Ralph Houk did not pick him on the American League All Star team. This year Stuart finished third in the voting and again he pouted. I think Stuart ought to realize he lacks something in ability if he cannot improve his voting position among the players."[28]

Instead of being angry, Stuart decided that he needed to become a better all-around player. "I was hurt by the voting," he told Arthur Siegel of the *Globe* and said he didn't think Allison was any better defensively than he was, "But I was shaken up because for the first time I realized that power isn't enough. I've got my pride, although many people don't think so."[29]

Stuart said that fielding was a matter of concentration. "It's taken almost 15 years for me to thing (sic) about fielding. Now I know that I could be an outfielder because I'd concentrate on fielding. I was tried in the outfield in the minors and I was terrible. But that was because I didn't concentrate. Now I can handle pop flies around the infield. I could do the same in the outfield. And I can throw.... In the meantime however I just want to be known as a good all-around first baseman." There was, said Siegel, as so many had before him, a "New Stuart."

Unfortunately, three days after the announcement of a "New Stuart" Dick looked a lot like the old Stuart. "I was lucky to get out without being hurt," he said afterward. In the third inning, Cleveland's Leon Wagner hit a line drive that whizzed past Stuart's shoulder and was ruled a double, putting runners on second and third. Bob Chance then bounced a slow ground ball that somehow got between Stuart and second baseman Felix Mantilla for a two-run single. That gave Cleveland a 2–1 lead.

In the sixth, Wagner hit a grounder to Stuart but beat it out when Stuart and pitcher Bob Heffner couldn't connect. Two outs later, Wagner was at third when Tito Francona hit a grounder to Mantilla. Mantilla caught the ball and made a perfect throw to first. "But in some strange manner," reported the *Globe*, "Stuart, covering the bag, had succeeded in falling down. Laurel and Hardy, or Harold Lloyd, could not have done better. The stands rocked with laughter as Wagner scored."[30]

Before the night was over, another catchable grounder got past Stuart for a key hit and he cut off a throw from the outfield and threw it over the catcher's head. When Heffner, backing up the play, threw to Stuart, who'd returned to cover first, the ball got past him.

Stuart had more trouble on the basepaths. He was on first base with one out when the batter hit a fly ball to the outfield. Despite Stuart's recent vow to concentrate, he thought there were two outs and was trotting leisurely toward second before hearing his coach frantically tell him to get back to first. All in all, it was the type of game only Dick Stuart, old or new, could have. His reaction? "This just isn't my park."[31]

A couple of days after Stuart's escapades, there was an incident that foreshadowed a tragedy that would occur three years later. Boston, still in Cleveland, was playing the second game of a Sunday doubleheader. The sun was going down, visibility was poor, and the Cleveland pitcher was Pedro Ramos, who had a good fastball and a quick temper.

"I almost got hit in the head by a pitch," Stuart said afterward, "and that was enough for me. Ramos was throwing real hard and I couldn't follow the ball. None of us could.

The first time up, I couldn't see one pitch he threw me. ...I couldn't stand any further away from the plate because the umpire wouldn't let me.... I said to myself, Well, Ramos, you win today."[32]

Tony Conigliaro was a cocky 19-year-old rookie and wasn't about to concede to Ramos. In the third inning, he came up with two men on base and hit a long fly ball to center field that nearly left the park. When he came up in the fifth, Ramos decided to send him a message.

Conigliaro always crowded the plate and lunged in to attack the pitch. A couple of weeks earlier, coach Billy Herman had warned him to be more careful. "I told him if he kept charging the ball like that at the plate, he was going to get hit a lot."[33] Conigliaro didn't listen. "Tony just had too much courage for his own good," Stuart said.

Ramos threw an inside fastball, Conigliaro dove into it and it hit him squarely, breaking his arm and putting him out of action for several weeks. The lesson was lost on Conigliaro and he continued to hit in the same aggressive manner. Three years later, he would be hit in the face by a pitch that altered his career forever.

The Red Sox weren't having that bad a season. After hovering a few games under .500 for most of the year, they evened their mark at 52–52 on July 31, putting them in fifth place, 11½ games behind the league-leading Yankees.

The Boston offense, with Stuart, Yastrzemski, and young Conigliaro, was as productive as it had been in 1963. At the end of July, Stuart had 26 home runs and led the league with 85 RBI. Conigliaro, despite the time he'd missed, had 20 homers. By the end of the season, the Red Sox would break the team record they'd set in 1963 by blasting 186 home runs, second only to Minnesota's 221. Utility man Felix Mantilla, who'd never hit more than 11 homers in a season, connected for 30. Even pitcher Earl Wilson hit five.

In the spring, Pesky had been worried about pitching and catching. By the end of the year, the catching was much improved. Bob Tillman played 131 games and hit .278 with 17 homers and 61 RBI. He gunned down 23 of 84 base stealers, much better than the previous year.

Pitching was another story. Conley's arm never came around and he was released in April. Monbouquette, who'd won 20 games in 1963, won just 13 in '64. Jack Lamabe, who was rewarded with a position in the starting rotation after his splendid relief work in 1963, posted a horrible 5.89 ERA. Veteran Earl Wilson and young Dave Morehead were also disappointing as starters. About the only bright spot was Radatz who, in his third and last great season, appeared in 79 games, pitched 157 innings, won 16, saved 29, and had a 2.29 ERA.

It was too much to expect Boston's power to carry the team. As in 1963, they suffered a total collapse in August, losing 22 of 29 games, and Pesky was losing his cool. Rumors of his imminent dismissal began circulating again.

As the Red Sox fell hopelessly out of contention, they called up young Tony Horton and put him in left field. Horton hit .395 in his first ten games, but was not much of an outfielder; his future was at first base. And if Horton's future was at first, Stuart's future was in another city.

After his great July, Stuart had just four homers in August and batted only .198 for the month. One of his homers was against the Yankees with his old nemesis Ralph Houk, now the Yankee general manager, sitting in the stands. Stuart didn't realize Houk was there. "If I'd have seen him," he said, "I'd have stuck my tongue out at him."[34]

Pesky and Stuart had another dust-up in early September after Pesky benched

Stuart for the first two games of a series against Kansas City, ostensibly because two right-handers were pitching for the Athletics. But Stuart played against righties all season and hit .258 against them with 25 homers. Besides, neither of the two starters for the Athletics, Diego Segui or Orlando Pena, was a modern-day Walter Johnson. Stuart had four hits in nine at bats against Segui, including a home run. A third puzzler was that Pesky replaced Stuart with Horton, who was also a right-handed batter.

Stuart wasn't happy about sitting on the bench, mainly because he was one RBI behind Harmon Killebrew for the league lead. With the Red Sox going nowhere, individual honors were all they had to shoot for, and no one coveted individual honors more than Dick Stuart. When he learned he was not in the lineup, he threw his helmet down and stormed off.

There was apparently more to Pesky's decision than the fact that Segui and Pena were pitching, because when he reinstated Stuart to the lineup, he told him that he'd better hustle or he was coming out again. On September 5, in just his third game back, Stuart was hit on the right shin by a line drive but stayed in the game. In the fifth inning, he came up with two runners on and one out, popped up to the infield, and stopped running about halfway to first base. When he returned to the dugout, he and Pesky exchanged harsh words and Pesky sent Horton out to play first base in the sixth.

"People say I don't like Stuart," Pesky said, "but that isn't true. But I can't tolerate his loafing while other players are breaking their backs to win."[35] "That's the reward I get for playing while I'm injured," Stuart retorted. "The only reason I didn't run was because I didn't want to aggravate the injury."[36] He said he was angry because he felt Pesky was depriving him of a chance to lead the league in RBI.

The next day, Horton played first while Stuart stewed on the bench. When he learned he was not in the lineup, he stood at third base during batting practice and threw every ball that he caught into the stands. Baseballs were precious in those days and Stuart's actions were bound to infuriate Pesky. "Stuart and Pesky have been involved in frequent arguments in the past," wrote Larry Claflin, "but the situation seems to have reached the intolerable stage now."[37]

Stuart swallowed his pride and admitted he should have run harder to first base, and Pesky returned him to the lineup. The rest hadn't helped his fielding, as he dropped a pop foul and then reprised a play he'd used against Maury Wills several years earlier. Pitcher Pete Charton picked Lu Clinton off first and Clinton broke for second. Since Clinton was not as fast as Wills, Stuart apparently thought he could outrun him. He chased and chased, but never caught him and Clinton arrived safely at second.

It was not long before Stuart had company in Pesky's doghouse. A few days after his run-in with Stuart, Pesky benched Yastrzemski for failing to run out a ground ball. Yastrzemski, who was already unhappy because Pesky had moved him to centerfield, claimed he was ill. "If Pesky wants to call it loafing," said Yaz, "let him call it that. I wasn't feeling well. I had a cold and I almost had to come out of the game in the second inning."[38] "[S]ure he's had a virus," Pesky replied, "but don't tell me about it and try to use it for an alibi six innings later."[39] Regardless of who was right and who was wrong, being at odds with his two best hitters didn't bode well for Pesky's future.

It didn't help Pesky's cause when Boston finished the season in eighth place with a record of 72–90, 4½ games worse than the disappointing 1963 campaign. As always, the team struggled on the road, posting a 27–54 mark. The 1964 Sox were as powerful as the prior year's version, and just as slow. Eight players had 10 or more home runs, but the team's 18 stolen bases were the lowest ever for a team in the 162 game era. Moreover, attendance was down and on October 1, only 306 fans watched the Sox play the Indians at Fenway, the smallest crowd in the history of the old park.

Despite all the turmoil and occasional benchings, Stuart managed to appear in 156 games, batting .279 with 33 home runs and 114 RBI, second in the AL to the Orioles' Brooks Robinson. Stuart entered the final game of the season trailing Robinson 118 to 112. In the first inning he came up with runners on first and second, and was frustrated when the Senators walked him intentionally. In the sixth, he doubled in two runs to bring him within four RBI of Robinson. In the seventh he came to the plate with the bases loaded and Boston leading 14–7. A grand slam would tie him for the title.

Senator reliever Ron Kline thwarted Stuart by throwing a wild pitch. "Here comes Felix Mantilla," Stuart said, "dashing in from third—with one of my runs batted in. The ball is seven feet away from the catcher, but I have my hand up to stop Mantilla and I'm yelling 'No, no!' at him. But he scores and that leaves only two on base. If I hit a homer, I still only got 117 RBI and I lose by one. What good is that? I'm so teed off I just stand there and take three strikes down the middle, then sling the bat away.... Funny thing. When I came up I was almost tempted to tell [third base coach] Billy Herman not to send Mantilla in if it's a passed ball or a wild pitch. We don't need the runs—I do."[40]

Stuart set a record by leading his league's first basemen in errors for the seventh straight time, an impressive achievement for someone who'd only been in the major leagues for six full seasons. This was the year that the movie *Dr. Strangelove* appeared, and sometime shortly thereafter, Stuart acquired the nickname by which he was known ever after. No one was really sure who coined it. Some said it was Hank Aaron; others claim it was Bob Prince, but Stuart was long gone from Pittsburgh when the movie came out.

On a more positive note, Stuart got three votes for MVP and made up for his All Star snubs by being named the first baseman on *The Sporting News* American League All Star team, edging out Allison, Pepitone, and Bill Skowron of the White Sox in the closest race for any position.[41]

Stuart continued to torture the Yankees. He'd hit .382 against them in 1963, and had 17 hits in his first 31 at bats against New York in 1964. He even made some sparkling defensive plays, in contrast to his spectacular blunders against the Yanks the previous season. Stuart cooled off as the season went on, but still finished with a .342 average against the Yankees, although he hit just one home run.

While Ralph Houk may not have been a Stuart fan, apparently Yankee shortstop Tony Kubek was impressed. "Good for the game," he said. "The league needs more colorful guys like Stuart. I've always had a good time watching that guy play."[42] He'd had an especially good time in 1963 when his soft ground ball went through Stuart's legs and gave the Yankees a win.

By the end of the season, thanks in large part to Dick Stuart, Pesky had clearly lost control of his club. He said there were times during the year when he couldn't eat or sleep, and that his wife talked him out of quitting one time when he was disgusted with Stuart's lack of effort. While speaking to a Boston church group during the winter, Pesky wondered if the 1964 season might have been different had Stuart been traded the previous winter.

A couple of years later, Pesky, then coaching with the Pirates, said he'd forgiven Big Stu. Like many others, he found it difficult to stay mad at such an amiable irritant. "Dick almost drove me out of my mind with his fielding," Pesky said, "but he was no sneak. He didn't talk about you behind your back. He'd tell you to your face and not unpleasantly either. I really like the big joker."[43]

One day in the clubhouse, Pesky was reading the riot act to his team, which he felt was living it up a bit too much on the road. He said he was going to start enforcing the curfew—the first violation would cost the offender $500 and the second $1,000. At that point, Stuart piped up and asked, "John, is this tax-deductible?"[44]

"[E]veryone thought Stuart and I were at each other's throats," Pesky said. "That's far from the truth. He's a likeable guy. I just questioned his baseball ability. He questioned my managing ability.... If I could have managed him another year, I might have had better luck with him."[45]

Pesky hadn't been Higgins' first choice as manager, and if there was only room for one man in the lifeboat leaving the sinking Boston ship, Higgins was going to be the one at the oars. At the end of the season, he fired Pesky and replaced him with coach Billy Herman, who Yawkey thought would fall somewhere between Higgins' coddling of the players and Pesky's aggravating them.[46] Herman was popular with the players and perhaps they'd play harder for him than they had for Pesky.

Despite Pesky's problems, writer Jack Mann believed he might have been successful except for two things. First, he tried to change entrenched attitudes too quickly and second, he was too sensitive to the notoriously critical Boston press.[47] Stuart thought Pesky had trouble dealing with a losing team and would have done much better with a pennant contender. Pesky said that if he ever got another chance as a major league manager, he'd be more distant from his players.

It wasn't long before Stuart followed Pesky out the door. He had worn out his welcome with his selfish behavior, his inability to get along with his teammates, and his clashes with the manager. The Sox had Horton waiting in the wings and, as always, they desperately needed pitching.

Despite his fielding deficiencies and controversial personality, Stuart had trading value. The Pirates had unloaded him for two promising young players after a bad 1962 season, and after 75 homers and 232 RBI in two seasons, the Red Sox were certain they could swap him for a quality pitcher.

On November 29, Stuart was traded to the Philadelphia Phillies for 25-year-old left hander Dennis Bennett. On the surface, it didn't appear that Boston had gotten top value for one of the AL's biggest sluggers.

Stuart drove Red Sox manager Johnny Pesky crazy with his antics, but Pesky couldn't stay mad at him. After two years as the Boston manager, Pesky was fired because he didn't win and couldn't get along with his two best hitters, Stuart and Carl Yastrzemski. National Baseball Hall of Fame.

13. It's About Time Stuart Grew Up: 1964

Stuart had two great years in Boston, leading the American League with 118 RBI in 1964 and hitting 75 home runs and driving in 232 during his two years with the Red Sox. He had difficulty getting along with manager Johnny Pesky and his Boston teammates and was traded to the Phillies for pitcher Dennis Bennett after the 1964 season. National Baseball Hall of Fame.

Bennett was young and had promise, but he also had a history of injury, which was always problematic when pitchers and their fragile arms are concerned. Bennett had been in a serious auto accident while playing winter ball after the 1962 season, which resulted in a broken ankle and a badly damaged shoulder. The ankle healed, but the shoulder was never the same again.

Although Bennett was 12–14 in 1964, he went two months without a win and hardly pitched at all as the Phillies blew the pennant in the final days of the season. "By the time I got to the Red Sox in '65," he said, "I couldn't throw at all. I finessed my way through and then I had the operation in '66."[48]

Bennett and Stuart were alike in some ways. Both had outgoing personalities and reputations as being somewhat hard to handle and both were good-looking men with a large entourage of female fans. The women of Philadelphia were as distraught to see Bennett leave as Pittsburgh damsels had been when Stuart decamped to Boston.

Unlike Stuart's old fan club, which folded when he left, Bennett's club, consisting of 167 women between the ages of 23 and 32, planned to carry on.[49] "We feel terrible, shocked," said Irene Spitzer, the 24-year-old president. "We can't believe that we may not see Dennis again. We had fabulous plans for the Bennett Fan Club—dances to raise money for charity, and so on. But we won't disband, and we won't go for Stuart. He sounds conceited."[50]

Everyone in baseball knew about Bennett's health issues and many believed the Phillies had gotten a steal. Philadelphia manager Gene Mauch thought so and was enthusiastic about Stuart, who he'd played with in California winter leagues in 1957. It was that winter, Mauch said, that after seeing Stuart play the outfield, he told him to get a first baseman's glove. Mauch planned to play Stuart every day and predicted he would hit 40 home runs. "Nobody in this league can swing a quicker bat," he said.[51] "Everybody talks about his fielding and about how bad it is, but it didn't keep Pittsburgh from winning a pennant."[52]

When asked about Stuart's lackadaisical attitude, Mauch said, "I never saw Dick fail to hustle when he was in the National League."[53] That was hard to believe, since Mauch never missed anything. Stuart said he liked Mauch and would do whatever Gene told him to do. Of course, Mauch hadn't told him to do anything yet.

The odds were heavily stacked against a smooth relationship between Stuart and

Mauch, who had a reputation as a strategic genius with an explosive temper and no patience. "For Stuart," wrote Sandy Grady, "baseball is a carnival built around the home run. For Mauch, it's a Holy War."[54] When he went to his first major league camp with the Dodgers, Mauch said, "I figured right then that the only way I could make it big was to work ten times harder than anybody else. I would have to fight for every inch of ground."[55]

For the next two decades, Mauch fought and scrapped. Once, he jumped into the stands to challenge a fan to a fight. He engaged in fistfights with opponents and once with a teammate who missed a sign. He spared no one's feelings and was known for the deeply personal nature of the insults he flung at opposing players. They often backfired, motivating the opposition to do anything to beat his team.

Mauch prided himself on his ability to get under people's skin; he thought it unnerved his opponents and made his own players play harder.

Gene Mauch is smiling in this picture, but he was one of the most intense managers in the history of baseball. He thought he could "handle" Stuart, but their relationship quickly deteriorated and Stu lasted just one mediocre season in Philadelphia. National Baseball Hall of Fame.

"Like most managers," wrote Allen Lewis, "Mauch has never cared whether his players like him personally. All he wants is the respect and full effort of each."[56] Philadelphia catcher Clay Dalrymple said, "Most managers are disliked by 60 percent of the players. You figure it's almost inevitable that sometime over the course of a season a manager is going to do something that practically every player is going to resent. I found out that Gene Mauch's theory was to get all 100 percent of us mad at him and then go on from there."[57]

"What they don't like about me," Mauch said, "is that I violate their code. I don't go for the let's-play-nice-so-nobody-gets-hurt-and-everybody-gets-the-pension business. You don't get paid to play this game, you get paid to win."[58]

The managers who'd gotten along best with the laid-back Stuart had been even-tempered men like Larry Shepard and Danny Murtaugh. Former catcher Bob Oldis played for both Murtaugh and Mauch and served as a coach under Mauch for many years. "If a player did something wrong," said Oldis, "Danny would just sort of pick up a rock and say, 'son of a gun.' The guy knew he made a mistake and there was no use in getting on him. Gene was completely different. He wasn't afraid to get on a player if he did something wrong. He was intense all the time. Murtaugh didn't say a word during the game. Mauch would be up and down, yelling at the umpires or somebody all the time. He was a very intense gentleman."[59]

The low-key Murtaugh, who won two World Series and four divisional titles in

15 years, followed the baseball manager's Hippocratic Oath of "do no harm." He let his players win the games while Mauch tried to win by himself. Like Paul Richards before him and Joe Madden long after, Mauch liked making unorthodox moves. He constantly maneuvered his players, shuttling them in and out of the lineup and substituting constantly. "We used to have a little celebration in the locker room," said Phillies shortstop Ruben Amaro, "for anyone who lasted the whole nine innings."[60]

Although Mauch said winning was the only thing he cared about, he never won a pennant in 26 years as a big league manager. His 1961 Phillies lost 23 games in a row. Over his long managerial career, he lost over 100 more games than he won and when the chips were down in 1964, 1982, and 1986, his teams fell apart and blew commanding leads.

Although he was named the Associated Press Manager of the Year in 1964, many attributed the Phillies' embarrassing collapse to his over-managing and panic. "Mauch didn't like most of his players," said pitcher Gary Kroll. "He wanted 25 Johnny Callisons or 25 Richie Allens. You can't have a Jim Bunning for every pitcher."[61]

Most criticism was directed at Mauch's use of his starting pitchers. During the final two weeks, he had confidence in only two men—Bunning and Chris Short—and he used them repeatedly on short rest, rendering them ineffective. "I never saw a better job of managing," Lewis said, "than he did for 145 games this past season. But I never saw him manage as badly as he did in the last 16."[62]

Some men mellow with age, but Don Bosch, who later played for Mauch in Montreal, found pretty much the same man who'd managed the Phillies. "I don't want to bad-mouth anybody," he said, "but Gene wasn't like Gil [Hodges]. With Gil, everybody was equal, but Gene played favorites. From my perspective, it's the main reason he never went to the World Series, because he never had a team."[63]

One of the Phillies' biggest problems in 1964 had been a gaping hole at first base. They used eight different starters, with the undistinguished John Herrnstein's 61 starts leading the way. Late in the season, the Phillies acquired Stuart's former Pirate teammate Frank Thomas from the Mets and put him at first. Thomas hit well when he joined the club but broke his thumb in early September and missed the rest of the season. The Phils also had problems against left-handed pitchers, posting a 62–40 record against righties but a 30–30 mark versus lefties.

The addition of Stuart gave the club another right-handed bat and plugged the hole at first. With Stuart, Richie Allen, who was coming off an outstanding rookie year, and slugging young right fielder Johnny Callison, the Phillies had a powerful heart of the order. Many picked them to win the 1965 pennant.

Stuart had been happy to go to Boston and professed to be equally thrilled to leave. "I think it's wonderful," he said. "I hate like the dickens to leave Fenway Park, but I should do almost as well in Philadelphia, and it's good to be with a club that has a chance for the pennant."[64] The location was also good, for Stuart resided in Lois's tony home town of Greenwich, Connecticut, which was closer to Philadelphia than Boston.

Stuart couldn't resist a last dig at the Red Sox. "Do you think either one of them [Tony Horton and highly-touted rookie Bobby Guindon] will drive in 232 runs or hit 75 homers in the next two years?"[65] He also predicted that Bennett would be unable to win in Fenway Park because left-handers never did.

Harold Kaese, who'd never warmed to Stuart, wrote his final epitaph on the latter's Boston career. "In his two seasons with the Red Sox, Stuart was a powerful hitter, an amusing character and a terrible ball player."[66]

Stuart had been booed in Pittsburgh. He'd been booed in Boston and it wasn't likely to get any better in Philadelphia, whose fans weren't known for keeping their opinions to themselves. "Philadelphia is known as the angriest sports town in America," wrote Si Burick.[67] Their fans had just begun abusing Allen, a prodigious slugger with a controversial personality who made 41 errors at third in 1964. That sounded a lot like Dick Stuart, and perhaps Allen was hoping Phillie fans would start booing Stuart and leave him alone. Stuart professed not to be worried. "I played in Pittsburgh," he said, "and those fans boo as well as any, so I don't think the Philly fans will bother me."[68]

To replace Bennett in the rotation, Philadelphia acquired left-hander Bo Belinsky, whose playboy antics had rendered him *persona non grata* with the Los Angeles Angels. "When you get down to it," Belinsky said of his time with the Angels, "my escapades have been overplayed. So has my association with broads. If I turned away from girls who threw themselves at me, the club would think I'm a little lavender."[69]

The prospect of having Stuart and Belinsky on a team managed by Gene Mauch had Philadelphia sportswriters licking their lips all winter. The most optimistic view was that it would be much more difficult for Belinsky to find trouble in Philadelphia than it had been in Los Angeles and Hollywood.

Sports Illustrated sounded a cautionary note before the 1965 season began. "Stuart and Belinsky," they wrote, "are being counted on to give the Phils the edge in another tight NL pennant race. But neither player has been known for his team spirit in the past and Manager Mauch may have a tiger's tail in each hand."[70] Angel manager Bill Rigney, who'd had first-hand experience at that sort of thing, agreed. "I don't know why managers," he said, "myself included, think they can change a man's spots. When I traded Bo Belinsky to the Phillies everybody said Gene Mauch would make Bo behave. Maybe Gene can. I doubt it."[71]

For Boston, the trade turned out to be one of the worst Mike Higgins ever made as general manager. Bennett's arm was indeed shot; he won a total of eight games over the next three years and was out of the major leagues before he turned 30. Tony Horton, who was supposed to make Boston fans forget Big Stu, hit a total of seven home runs in 87 games over the next three seasons before being traded to Cleveland. Bobby Guindon, who received a reported $135,000 bonus, the largest ever given to a Red Sox signee, never played another major league game. Stuart, on the other hand, continued to be Dick Stuart, hitting home runs, missing ground balls, and making his manager's life difficult. He did it in Pittsburgh, he did it in Boston, and he would do it in Philadelphia.

14

They've Been Very Impartial Here—They Boo Everybody: 1965

Stuart just couldn't leave poor Johnny Pesky alone. "They made a trade for me," he said. "They just let him go outright. At least they got somebody in exchange for me."[1] "If a guy can't get along with a guy that in two years hits 75 home runs and drives in 232 runs," he added on another occasion, "then he can't get along with anybody."[2] Stuart repeated those two numbers (75 and 232) endlessly during the winter, in case anyone had forgotten them.

When Larry Claflin called Stuart at his Greenwich home, he answered, "Johnny Pesky's residence." Stuart never disappointed an interviewer and the conversation must have had a bittersweet tinge for Claflin, for there was no doubt the press, as well as the Red Sox, had gotten the short end of the Bennett for Stuart trade. "Farewell to Stu," he said, "from the Boston baseball writers. He made life a lot easier for us."[3]

In a wide-ranging interview, Stuart told Claflin he wished Billy Herman and the Red Sox well, he would miss Fenway Park, he still lamented the unfairness that kept him off the American League All Star team the past two years, and he had just purchased his latest Cadillac, a sierra gold model with a black top.

It was no ordinary Cadillac. The front driver and passenger doors were adorned with a coat of arms depicting crossed bats and the initials "RLS." The thing that most impressed Stuart about his new car, however, was the sound system. In an era when the normal automobile had an AM radio with erratic reception, Stuart's car was equipped with a sophisticated stereo system. "Ever hear one of these things," he asked a writer at the Phillies' Clearwater training site. The scribe had not, so Stuart proceeded to demonstrate.

The writer's ignorance of the finer things in life was evident from his description. "Stu inserted a long-playing capsule into an electronic gizmo in the dash board. The pear shapes of Frank Sinatra and Hello Dolly boomed out of speakers in each door."[4] He was suitably impressed, which was what Stuart wanted.

After a brief negotiation with general manager John Quinn, Stuart signed a contract that made him the highest paid Phillie (at an estimated $46,000 or $47,000). He then called Dennis Bennett to ask if he could help him get into Bennett's apartment building. "How do you like that?" Bennett said. "Stu steals my job and now he wants to take my apartment too."[5]

Stuart also made a silly remark that set the media to writing about an alleged feud between Bennett and Stuart. "When you trade a $50,000 player," Stu said immodestly and inaccurately, "you should get something equivalent in return, a player who can do much the same things I did. I only saw Dennis once and I hit a home run off him in Forbes Field. I don't understand it." Then came the comment that sparked the controversy. "I bet I pay more taxes than he gets in salary."[6]

"Any time you can get an established home run hitter in exchange for a .500 pitcher," he told another reporter, "you've made yourself a terrific deal."[7] "I know this much. Bennett isn't going to get the Red Sox out of eighth place.... Frankly, I don't see how the Red Sox benefitted from this deal."[8]

When asked about Stuart's comments, Bennett replied, "Stuart could have been traded for 10 players or three ball clubs and he would have said the Red Sox deserved more in return.... The Phillies are a team ball club and he's an individual and I just can't see him fitting in with that type of club."[9]

Someone pointed out to Stuart that Bennett's younger brother Dave, also a pitcher, was going to be his teammate in training camp. "Wow!" he replied and said he was only kidding about the comment on his taxes. The writer had suggested it and he had jokingly agreed. "That Bennett thing is all out of proportion," he said when he arrived in Clearwater for training camp. "Actually, he seems like a nice guy. I suppose he thinks I'm a pop-off. But it was a misunderstanding."[10] Bennett forgave him and the "feud" ended.

Stuart blasted Pesky in an interview with Milton Gross, who had a knack for getting Stuart to say controversial and unflattering things. Stuart told Gross that the coaching job Pesky had obtained with the Pirates was better suited to him than a manager's position. "He couldn't handle a losing team," Stu said. "I'm going to harass him when we play the Pirates. I'll have some fun."[11] "...Naturally, Pesky blamed me for everything and I blamed everything on him. Imagine the Red Sox trading someone like me who had two such big years for them."[12]

Stuart talked of how Pesky had hurt his chances for winning the RBI title by sitting him on the bench for a few games. "I had 50 more RBI's than anybody else on the team and he sticks a kid in my place.... I asked him what the hell he was trying to do. Players from the other clubs were talking about it. Our guys were talking about it. Obviously he was trying to show me up."[13]

"I've got nothing personal against Pesky," Stuart told Gross. "John and I get along fine until the game started and then we hated each other. I used to tell him, 'You like Dick Stuart, the person, but not the player.'"[14] He wondered how the Red Sox, with players like him, Yastrzemski, Radatz, and Conigliaro could have finished eighth. "The year before I'm first in RBI's and second in homers, Yastrzemski is the batting champion and Monbouquette wins 20 games and they finish seventh.... I liked Pesky, the person, but Pesky, the manager, ugh."[15]

Stuart continued to pile on Pesky throughout spring training, telling Philadelphia writer Larry Merchant how Pesky dropped him in the batting order because he said he wasn't driving in runs. "I told him that 499 other big leaguers must not be driving in any either, because I was leading the majors in RBIs. Another time he benched me. He said I was in a slump." I said, "I'm not in a slump; I'm leading the league. You're the one in a slump; we're in eighth place."[16]

Boston writer Hy Hurwitz came to Pesky's defense, stating that the deposed manager had been trying to win ball games while Stuart was only interested in personal accomplishments and cared nothing for team play. He quoted Dick Radatz, who had roomed with Stuart for a short time. "He made life so miserable for me," Radatz said, "that I almost lifted him off the bed and threw him out of a hotel room window."

When Radatz complained, the Red Sox gave Stuart a room to himself, which was what Radatz thought he wanted all along. "He didn't want any part of the ball club," Hurwitz wrote, "and vice-versa." He concluded that in trading Stuart for Bennett, "the Sox swapped a sore-head for a sore-arm."[17]

Stuart, who got shortstop Bobby Wine to give him his cherished #7, assumed he would be the Phillies' regular first baseman, not imagining they had traded for a man who, as he constantly reminded everyone, hit 75 home runs and drove in 232 runs in two years, to sit him on the bench. Frank Thomas thought otherwise, and vowed all spring to give Stu a battle for the starting position.

Thomas was as caustic as ever. When Stuart reported, he asked him when he was going to hold his first press conference. Then he proceeded to rib Stuart about his fielding. "Maz[eroski] said he didn't mind going to his left, but when he had to go to your left, too, that was too much."[18] When Stuart suffered a minor thumb injury, he said Stu would never get back in the lineup. "See this ring," Stuart replied, flashing his 1960 World Series ring, "I've got one and you've never even come close. That's the way it's going to be around first base, too."[19]

Stuart predicted he would hit 40 to 50 home runs and would be in the top five in the NL in homers and RBI, just like he'd been in the AL the past two years. "I've probably said a few things in my time that were out of the way," Stu admitted. "Now that I've accomplished something, though, they should give me more credit."[20]

One group he didn't think gave him enough credit was the Philadelphia press. "I came to Boston," he told Harold Kaese, "after a bad year in 1962 and they fell all over me—radio and TV shows, all kinds of interviews. Then I had two great years in Boston and Philadelphia pays little attention to me."[21]

One of the reasons Stuart wasn't the center of attention in Philadelphia was star players like Richie Allen, Johnny Callison, and Jim Bunning. Stuart had said he was pleased to join a contending team, but on a good team he wouldn't be the focus of media attention. It would be more like Pittsburgh than Boston, for he was no longer The Man.

No one could resist Dick Stuart's charm, and it wasn't long before he won the Philadelphia writers over. His new champion, taking on the role Les Biederman played in Pittsburgh, was Larry Merchant of the *Philadelphia Daily News*, who on April 1 wrote a long profile of the new Phillie slugger titled, "*Dick Stuart's Whacky World.*"[22]

"The world of Dick Stuart," Merchant began, "is mad, mad, mad, mad. It's a cockeyed, wonderful, wacky world, full of fun and games, homers and errors, self-indulgence and insanity. He is larger and giddier than life." That was more like it. Merchant went on to recite entertaining anecdotes like the time Stuart's five-year-old son Richie offered to belt a fan who booed Stuart's fielding and how Stuart planned to challenge top professional bowler Don Carter to a match.

"The big first baseman's three favorite subjects," Merchant wrote, "are his great hitting, his terrible fielding, and his lousy managers. He laughs at them all." He quoted one of Stuart's favorite lines: "I have refined the art of fielding to the point where I can catch two out of every three." Now that he was in a new city, Stuart could recycle the old jokes they were tired of hearing in Pittsburgh and Boston.

A year earlier, the Phillies had acquired catcher Gus Triandos, another character and the perfect foil for Stuart. Once, Triandos said he had played five innings at first base the previous day before fans realized he wasn't Stuart and stopped booing him. He asked Stuart how many career hits he had and Stuart gave him the exact number. "And you know every one of them, don't you?" Triandos said. "Come around to the lobby tonight," Stuart replied, "and I'll tell you some fabulous stories about my hits." And so it went, with Merchant dutifully reporting every word. Apparently, Philadelphia wasn't going to ignore big Stu after all.

One detriment of the move to Philadelphia was leaving cozy Fenway Park, to which Stuart made a sentimental farewell visit during the winter. "Good-by (sic) wall," he said. "It was nice knowing you."[23] Connie Mack Stadium, where the Phillies played their home games, was much more spacious. The left field fence was a distant 360 feet and center field was an unreachable 466 feet, even farther than Forbes Field. Stuart tended to hit to the power alleys rather than down the lines and Connie Mack would be a challenge for him.

The biggest challenge facing the talented young Phillie team was trying to forget the horrific finish of 1964, when they blew a seemingly insurmountable lead in the last two weeks. "Too bad I wasn't here last year," Stuart said in the spring, "they could have blamed the whole thing on me."[24] Mauch tried to dismiss the impact. "I don't see how anything in baseball can have a lasting effect on anybody," he said. "What you did last year or didn't do no longer counts. You've got to start all over again."[25]

That was brave talk, but the scars remained, scars that could only be exorcised through success, which perhaps would be sparked by the "new Dick Stuart" of 1965. This year's new Stuart, like the past incarnations, was a team player, no longer an individualist concerned only with his own statistics. He said he would even be willing to play in B squad games in spring training if asked and added, "[I] would like to hit as many home runs as I possibly can ... but those things are secondary to us winning the pennant this year.... People always quote me as saying I am a great hitter. I am not. Take Hank Aaron. Now there is a great hitter.... What I am is a great home run hitter."[26] That showed at least a touch of modesty and perhaps, at the age of 32, Stuart was mellowing a bit.

While it would be a stretch to say there was also a new Bo Belinsky, Bo said he was delighted to be in Philadelphia and play for a team with a chance at the pennant. In the happy glow of springtime, Mauch said Belinsky and Stuart were two reasons he thought his team would be in the World Series. What about their rebellious personalities? "Every ball club has a personality itself," Mauch replied, "and the personality of the Phillies is so strong that individualism is not tolerated on the field.... Everybody plays for the team, not himself."[27] The question was whether the team personality was stronger than the personalities of Bo Belinsky and Dick Stuart and, it turned out, it was not.

Stuart's fear of being ignored in his new city proved groundless. He got a television show on Channel 6, titled "Stuart on Sports" and the Philadelphia writers found him just as entertaining as those in Boston had found him.

At the end of spring training, Al Cartwright wrote a lengthy article about Stuart and his love of home runs. He tried to hit a homer every time up, he told Cartwright, and wasn't interested in nuances like hitting to the right side to move a runner up, or bunting, although he told Cartwright he was an excellent bunter. Stuart said he didn't like getting the take sign and often ignored it. He expressed surprise that the Philadelphia single season record for home runs was only 43 (by Chuck Klein), and the most any Phil had hit since the team moved to Connie Mack Stadium was 32. He predicted he would break both records. Cartwright concluded by speculating about Stuart's relationship with

Mauch. "The prediction here," he wrote, "is that they will get along swimmingly—as long as Stuart connects."[28]

The honeymoon didn't last long, for in the second game of the season, Stuart's fielding problems and lack of concentration contributed to a Philadelphia loss to the Giants. In the seventh inning, there were two men on base when Jesus Alou hit a slow bouncer to Stuart's right. "I have seen the seasons change faster than Stuart moved toward the ball," wrote one reporter.[29] The soft grounder found its way into right field and a run scored. It was judged a hit, but a better first baseman would have stopped it.

During the next inning, another Alou gave Stuart trouble. Matty was on first base with one out when Willie Mays hit a line drive to right field on which Johnny Callison made a fine running catch. Alou never thought Callison would get to the ball and was well past second. Callison's throw to first base beat him by a mile, but unfortunately Stuart was nowhere in the vicinity; he was headed for the dugout. Fortunately, Alou was so far from the base that shortstop Ruben Amaro managed to corral the throw and touch first to complete the double play.

"I saw the runner at third," Stuart said after the game, "so I thought Callison's catch was the third out.... Even if the ball had rolled in the dugout, we would have gotten the runner. He had to back track to return to first."[30] Stuart came to bat in the ninth to a lusty round of boos and struck out. "I was beginning to wonder where they were all night," he said. "Then they finally showed up. They don't bother me, though. I'm kind of used to getting booed."[31] After just two days, it appeared there had been another false sighting of a "new Dick Stuart."

Mauch remained uncharacteristically calm. "I'm not worried about Stuart," he said. "He'll hit a couple on that roof, and everybody will come down from the stands and start hugging him."[32] "He's had a couple of tough days around the bag, but he's trying harder than he ever did in his life."[33]

When the Phillies started slowly, however, Mauch's ferocious temper flared. After a third straight loss in Los Angeles, he closed the clubhouse door and blasted his players. "I've seen more mistakes in the first nine games this year," he screamed, "than I did in the first 130 last year."[34]

It wasn't long before Stuart landed in Mauch's doghouse. Not only was Stu fielding poorly, he was batting in the low .200s, had just two home runs and many of his hits were going to right field. "[T]here's nothing wrong with getting an occasional hit to right field," he said. "Not unless you're Dick Stuart. When someone else gets one, it's fine. When I try it, they say, 'Stuart's over the hill. He can't get around on the ball any more.'"[35]

Mauch's pre-season optimism about Stuart's fielding proved false and it wasn't long before he looked like the same old Stu. He made four errors in a four-game stretch and one of them let in four unearned runs against the Dodgers. Mauch couldn't understand why Stuart could make difficult plays and then botch the easy ones. "I just know he can improve," he said. "I've seen him make enough good plays to know he can field. But he's got to work at it."[36] Stuart insisted he was trying. "My basic movements are nonchalant," he said. "All tall guys have a tendency to look nonchalant."[37]

After Stuart made three errors in two games against the Braves, Mauch gave him a chance to look nonchalant on the bench for a few days. He inserted Thomas at first and told Stuart to come out early for extra fielding practice. "He makes a lot of money," Mauch said, "and if he isn't going to earn it by playing for a while, he'll earn it practicing."[38] Perhaps more practice was the answer and perhaps it wasn't. "The chances of turning him into a respectable fielder," said the *Philadelphia Daily News,* "are slim, none and ho-ho-ho, but there's no harm in trying."[39]

Stuart thought he was being made a scapegoat for the team's slow start and couldn't believe that he was on the bench with the season less than a month old. "I'm used to manager problems," Stuart told Merchant.[40] "I've had everything bad happen to me that could possibly happen to a ballplayer. I've been booed, benched, ridiculed for my fielding and been traded. I've been sat on every way you can think of. My mother always told me, 'try to think everything happens for the best.'"[41] Perhaps fewer bad things would have happened to Stuart if Mom had taught him how to field a ground ball or keep track of the number of outs.

Stuart said a lot of things when Mauch sat him on the bench, but one thing he insisted he did *not* say was that Mauch was a "rat fink," as one writer claimed. When he heard about the quote, he immediately went to Mauch's office and told him he never said it, went on television to deny it, and said he didn't want to have the type of problems with Mauch that he'd had with Pesky.

Stuart was not the only Phillie having trouble catching the ball; defense was not the team's long suit. They made 31 errors in their first 22 games and had a number of questionable defensive operators in the lineup. One of their leading sluggers was outfielder Wes Covington, who, while he didn't have Stuart's reputation, made an adventure of every ball hit to left field. During his career, Richie Allen was moved from one position to another in the hope he could master one, and Thomas, Stuart's replacement at first, was no Hal Chase. In spring training, one reporter noted that several defensive caddies would be needed for the late innings. "[A] team with Dick Stuart, Richie Allen, Wes Covington, Alex Johnson, Tony Gonzalez and Frank Thomas needs glove men the way generals need chauffeurs."[42]

The benching of Dick Stuart (the man who hit 75 home runs and drove in 232 runs in two years) was always news, and Phillies beat writer Allen Lewis asked Stu for his reaction. Characteristically, Stuart appeared unconcerned and thought he was being treated unfairly. Lewis pointed out that many people thought he didn't take his fielding seriously. "[W]hat's the use of getting upset when you can't do anything about it once the play is over?" Stu replied. "It's the same about striking out and I've been criticized for not arguing with the umpires."[43]

When Dick Stuart was in the news, it was inevitable that the provocative Milton Gross would show up and equally inevitable that the intent of his story would be to create some sort of controversy. With Stuart, he had a good chance of success. "If I'm not playing," Stuart once said, "statements just flow out of my mouth."[44]

Gross gave a play-by-play description of a Stuart-Mauch confrontation that supposedly took place earlier. At 6:55 he got Stuart's denial. Then he reported that Stuart was going to meet with Mauch, presumably to resolve the issue. Stuart emerged from the meeting and told Gross he didn't have time to talk to him because he had to take batting practice, which apparently meant that he was back in the starting lineup. At 7:15 Mauch emerged from his office and Gross asked him why he reinstated Stuart and what he thought Stuart had said about him. Mauch was non-committal and Gross brought his tale to a fortunately inconclusive end.

There would be other opportunities for controversy, however. In 1966, when Mauch was blasted by Johnny Callison and some of his other players, reporters went to Stuart, by then in Los Angeles after the Phillies had practically given him away, hoping for some inflammatory comments. They were surprised when Stuart said nice things about

Mauch. "No manager ever helped me more than Gene did last year," he said. "He would pitch to me for 20 minutes then hit me grounders for 20 minutes and by that time both of us would be ready to drop. Gene was happy to do that. I can't criticize the man for getting rid of me."[45]

Stuart returned to the lineup, got a few hits and managed to hit his third home run, off the Cardinals' Ray Sadecki on May 9. Apparently, his time on the bench hadn't affected Stu's sense of humor, as he said after his homer that if he hadn't been so tired after all the fielding practice, he might have pulled the ball foul. A few days later, he hit two homers against the Braves, and by the end of May his average had climbed to .268.

The Phils had expected to challenge for the pennant, but for the first two months of the season they certainly didn't look like contenders, ending May with a 20–24 record. On May 24, they reached their nadir, losing a doubleheader to the downtrodden Mets. Mauch was never one to take defeat gracefully, and as the losses mounted, he had a number of meltdowns. One day, after starter Chris Short gave up six runs in the first inning, Mauch came to the mound to remove him, took the ball and *fired* it angrily at the incoming relief pitcher.

During the game in which Stuart's error let in four unearned runs, Mauch became incensed when a balk was called on Belinsky. Later in the game, while standing on the mound awaiting a relief pitcher, Mauch got so angry he took the ball and hurled it against the screen. The next day he got a message from Dodger manager Walt Alston, not known for his sense of humor. "When you threw the ball against the screen," Alston wrote, "you definitely balked."[46] After the game, Mauch locked the clubhouse door and blasted his team; it was beginning to look as though it might be a long season in Philadelphia.[47]

Much of the blame for the Phillies' sorry performance came to Stuart's doorstep. Mauch questioned his intensity and there were rumors he couldn't get along with his teammates. "I guess I'll always go through life being blamed for all the bad things that happen to others," he told his old friend Les Biederman.[48] The always sympathetic Biederman wrote, "Stu is personable, he can hit a baseball out of any park ever built, and is no dummy. But he was labeled when he first came up and a player seldom changes anybody's mind no matter how much he improves."[49]

A long article in the *Philadelphia Daily News*[50] discussed the Phillies underachieving performance ("They haven't been hitting and they haven't been fielding and they haven't been pitching") and Stuart's culpability for it. "They've got to put the rap on someone," the *News* explained, "so they've picked Stuart…. They blame him for errors … and they blame him for men left on base (all he talks about is how many home runs he hit in Boston) and they blame him for the ferocity of Gene Mauch's post-game tirades."

"It isn't only the way Stuart has played, of course," the *News* explained. "He has a knack for saying the wrong thing at the wrong time, and the only time he discusses baseball is when he is reciting an heroic anecdote about himself." The best thing about the situation, the writer summarized, was that Bennett's sore arm and inability to pitch effectively made the trade look good despite Stuart's lackluster performance.[51]

"I've been this way ever since I first put on a uniform," Stuart explained. He admitted he wasn't having a great season, but said, "I don't think the way I've played has affected the way the other guys have played. I'm surprised to hear that everybody thinks that." He also thought that too much was expected of him, although he had no one to blame for that but himself. "If I could field and run bases and do all the other things besides hit home runs," he said, "I'd be in Cooperstown."[52]

The egotistical Stuart's relationship with his teammates was always a matter of curiosity. "A guy comes to a new club," he said, "and he isn't gonna make 25 friends right away. But I think all the guys have been real good to me." At a luncheon in Pittsburgh, Phillie catcher Clay Dalrymple was asked about Stuart's popularity in Philadelphia. Dalrymple's reply was diplomatic and cryptic. "His popularity is about the same there as in any town he goes."[53] Stuart was never close to his teammates off the field and the question was whether Phillie players would like and tolerate him as the Pirates eventually had or if he would face the resentment he found in Boston.

Stuart's continuing popularity in Pittsburgh was evidenced by the number of questions Pirate fans asked about him at the gathering. One inquired of coach Bob Oldis, a former Pirate, whether Stuart still signed his autograph with a star dotting the "i" in his name. "I don't know," Oldis replied, "I have never gotten Dick Stuart's autograph."[54]

After his team won 17 of 23 games during the second half of June, Mauch felt a little better about things, including his first baseman, who'd hit his 200th career home run on June 10. "I think about what Dick Stuart can do," he said, "and try not to get too excited about what he doesn't do. And the things he reputedly cannot do, he's doing a lot better.... He looks like Hal Chase."[55]

It was June 22 before the Phils finally climbed over the .500 mark, at 33–32. On July 2, they won their sixth game in a row, giving them a record of 40–34, which put them in fourth place but just 3½ games out of first. No team was running away from the field and the Phillies were in a good position. Stuart hit his 13th home run that day, an eighth inning game winner off lefty Gerry Arrigo of the Reds, and was batting .248, with 43 RBI. He was known as a second half hitter, and if he got hot in 1965, it might be enough to put his team in the World Series.

If Stuart could have played all his games against the Dodgers, he would have had a great year. In mid–June, when he had a total of nine home runs and 32 RBI, five of the home runs and 14 of the RBI were against the Dodgers, who boasted the best pitching staff in baseball.

When the Phillies played the Dodgers on June 18, Stuart hit a first inning home run, which he said was for his brother Daryl, who was at the game. Daryl had graduated from the University of Washington School of Journalism, but became fascinated with photography and spent most of his career as a photo-journalist for the Edmonds School District. He'd been living in the Seattle area since 1957.

It was only the second time the brothers had seen each other in seven years. Dick told reporters all about Daryl, who was then a part-time sportswriter. "Can you imagine," he said, "all the trouble I've had with sportswriters and I've got a brother who's a sportswriter."[56]

From Los Angeles, the Phillies flew to Houston for a doubleheader. This was the first year the Houston team played in the Astrodome, and the stadium was not just a baseball field, it was an entertainment venue that foreshadowed future sports palaces. It was the first park to cater to people who weren't that interested in watching baseball. The food was top notch, there were luxury suites, there was a huge, magnificent scoreboard, and there was plenty to entertain the fans.

Stuart was always up for promotions, and between games of the doubleheader, he and pitcher Chris Short participated in a cow milking contest against Astro third baseman Bob Aspromonte and coach Clint Courtney. Stuart and Short lost badly, getting just a few drops from their animal, but Stuart made up for it by hitting a home run in the second game, which was a 7–1 Philadelphia win.

From Houston, the team flew back to the West Coast to play the Giants, and it was in San Francisco that Stuart hit a rough patch. San Francisco was home territory for him; he left several tickets for family and friends and desperately wanted to do well for them. "I was around .260 or .270 [actually it was .252].... I hit a two-run homer off Juan Marichal [it was actually off Bob Bolin] in a late inning of the opening game. It broke a 1–1 tie and we won 3–1 [the score was 2–1 when Stuart hit his homer].... That homer was the only hit I got. I went 1-for-19 [actually 1-for-15] in the series. It hurt my pride and depressed me terribly to make such a bad show before my own people. It bothered me for weeks."[57] Stuart's average didn't plunge; it just declined a point at a time until it dipped into the .230s.

Stuart also believed his performance was affected when Mauch dropped him from fourth to sixth in the batting order. He was a cleanup hitter, he told Mauch, and simply couldn't hit in the sixth position. On one occasion, when a reporter asked Mauch why Stuart had been benched, he replied, "I told Stu to sit here and help me manage."[58]

Larry Merchant came to Stuart's defense. "He should play," Merchant wrote, "because the Phillies don't have anyone better to replace him, because his background shows that when he plays regularly he has a good chance of bursting out in a long ball streak, and because he's a spectator sport all by himself."[59]

Merchant then shared some banter from the team bus that demonstrated why the writers found Stuart such an enjoyable subject. The two leagues were about the same, Stuart told everyone, because American League pitchers struck him out just as much as National League pitchers. He then took issue with an official scorer who failed to give him an error on a questionable play. "It was an error," he insisted. "But I've been building a reputation as such a good glove man lately that they think it has to be a hit if I don't get it."[60] Airport banter was just as entertaining. When the team boarded a flight from Ramp E-3 in Chicago, Stuart announced, "I guess this flight is in honor of me."[61]

Stuart soon had first base to himself, thanks to Frank Thomas. Thomas's difficult personality had gotten him traded in Pittsburgh and this time it cost him his job.[62] The groundwork for the incident was laid one day when the Phillies were checking out of a hotel. Thomas, trying to be funny, said to Richie Allen, "Hey, boy, can you carry my bags."[63] Even in 1965, that was way over the line, but Allen, who had been subjected to vicious racial abuse when he played in Little Rock, did nothing.

A couple of weeks later, Thomas failed to execute a sacrifice bunt in a key situation. When he laid down a good bunt in batting practice the next day, someone said, "Twenty-four hours too late, Lurch." Thomas thought Allen said it and that he was ridiculing him. Others thought it might have been John Callison. But Thomas focused on Allen, who he said had laughed at him a couple of days earlier when he was bruised by a ground ball during batting practice. Thomas began jawing with Allen, comparing him to either Cassius Clay or Malcolm X, depending on the source.

The scene degenerated into classic playground taunts. "You got a problem? Come down here and do something about it." "You know where to find me." "Come here and call me that," and similar clever remarks. Allen walked toward the plate and Thomas struck him on the shoulder with his bat, claiming afterward that Allen had sucker-punched him first. Teammate Ruben Amaro separated the two men, taking a stray punch to the jaw and being hit on the elbow with a bat in the process.[64] Eventually, several teammates arrived on the scene and restrained the enraged Allen.

When reporters came around, Allen refused to talk about the incident. "What fight?" he asked.[65] That gave Thomas the opportunity to control the narrative, and he gave his side of the story in great detail, dismissing it all as his usual harmless horseplay. "I'm one of the biggest agitators around," he said, "always have been, but I never try to hurt anybody. I do it to try to keep the club loose."⁶⁶ He accused Allen of being able to dish it out but not take it and said he had apologized twice but Allen refused to accept the apology.

Both Thomas and Allen played in that night's game and both did well. Allen got three hits and drove in four runs while Thomas connected for a pinch-hit home run into the upper left field stands that tied the game in the eighth inning. When he returned to the dugout, Allen joined the line of Phillies who shook his hand.

After the game, Mauch told Thomas the Phillies were asking waivers on him for the purpose of giving him his unconditional release. Mauch and Quinn said they weren't releasing Thomas just because of the fight; they'd been trying to trade him for some time. Mauch also said Thomas, as the veteran, should have showed more maturity and that he had broken the code. One could use their fists to settle differences—Mauch had done so many times—but using a bat on another player was clearly out of bounds.⁶⁷

It was a "zero tolerance" policy before the term was commonly used. One can only wonder, however, what the Phils might have done if Thomas had been a 23-year-old All Star slugger and Allen a 35-year-old reserve. Many fans blamed Allen for the incident and their razzing of him increased.

Frank Thomas, Stuart's teammate in Pittsburgh and Philadelphia, was one of the top power hitters in the National League in the 1950s and early 1960s. He was also a great agitator who often got under his teammates' skins. Thomas's Phillies career ended when he had an on-field fight with Richie Allen. National Baseball Hall of Fame.

With Thomas gone, Stuart played nearly every day. When the Phillies went to Pittsburgh in June, Pirate fans showed that perhaps absence really does make the heart grow fonder, for while Phillie fans were booing Stuart, those in Pittsburgh had warmed to him during the three years he'd been gone. His friends Miles Span and Dr. Phil Antonucci organized a day for Stuart at Forbes Field. His old fan club sold 600 tickets and contributed money and a 300-pound cake to the Children's Hospital in Dick's name. Unfortunately, the game was rained out. "Well," Stuart said, "I set another record. First man ever to have his Day rained out."⁶⁸

While the players were sitting around, hoping the rain would stop, Stuart chatted with Pirate coach Johnny Pesky. "You got a raise," Pesky told Stuart, "and I get fired and a (salary) cut." "I got your cut," Stu replied. "That evened it out."⁶⁹ It would have been appropriate, Larry Merchant suggested, if Pesky could have jumped out of the cake.

While Pesky was jocular with Stuart in public, he spoke more bluntly with reporters.

"All four of us (Bragan, Murtaugh, Pesky, and Mauch) can't be wrong, you know," he said.[70] "He says I'm a great guy and a terrible manager, and I say he's a great guy and a terrible ballplayer. He really is a great kid, but he kills you out there on the field. He takes good care of himself, but he thinks only about himself. Sure, he's got a great wit. But it's not funny when you're paid to win and you're losing. I honestly don't believe you can have a pennant contender with him."[71]

The Stuart fan club was not daunted by the postponement, and when Philadelphia returned in late July, they showed up in full force and presented their hero with a number of gifts. After receiving kisses from three female members of the club, he said, "This is one of the best nights I ever had at Forbes Field."[72]

In the meantime, Stuart had created a little excitement when the Pirates visited Connie Mack Stadium on July 5. After hitting a home run earlier in the game, he was batting in the seventh inning when Pirate pitcher Don Schwall (who'd been traded for Stuart in 1962) threw him a slider. During his follow-through, Schwall held up one finger. Although *The Sporting News* didn't indicate which finger, one can assume it was the one typically used to convey a crude message. After Stuart struck out on the next pitch, he headed for the mound to confront Schwall. Players streamed onto the field from both benches but nothing happened other than a lot of milling around. Schwall said later that he always raised his middle finger after delivering a slider, although he didn't explain why. Stuart said he misinterpreted the gesture and all was forgiven and forgotten.

There were also light moments, including a couple with Stuart's old antagonist Bobby Bragan, then managing the lame-duck Milwaukee Braves. When he was told that someone had suggested eliminating infield practice, Stuart said he was all for it. Then they told him it was Bragan's idea. "But if it's Bragan's idea," he said, "I don't like it."[73]

On another occasion, as the Braves and Phillies waited out a rain delay, the phone rang in the Braves dugout. Bragan answered it, and someone started asking him his opinion of some of the Philadelphia players. When he asked about Stuart, Bragan was suspicious and gave a non-committal answer. Then he looked over at the Philadelphia dugout and saw Stuart talking on the phone and laughing.[74]

On July 24, Stuart hit his 17th homer of the year off Mets' pitcher Tom Parsons at Shea Stadium, which had opened the previous year. Shea was the 23rd different stadium in which Stu had homered, an all-time record. It also made him the only active player to have hit a home run in all 19 current major league parks (the Dodgers and Angels shared a stadium in 1965).

As seemingly happened every season, Stuart had a period of flashy fielding. "I'm having a ball down there at first base," he said. "I'm getting a kick out of making plays, and I've made some that even astonish me." "I feel like this is the way he should have been playing it all his life," Mauch said.[75]

On August 13, just when things seemed to be going smoothly, the big first baseman had an evening during which things happened that only seemed to happen to Dick Stuart. The Phillies were in San Francisco to play the Giants, whose starting pitcher was venerable Warren Spahn, finishing his final major league season at age 44. While batting in the third inning, Stuart asked the umpire to take a look at the ball. That apparently perturbed Spahn. On the next pitch he decided to give Stu a really close look at it and buzzed a pitch past his head.

Stuart hollered to Spahn that he didn't throw hard enough to hurt him even if he hit him. "If I hit you I may shake some brains into you," Spahn replied and suggested that if Stuart didn't think he threw very hard, he should take his helmet off. Stuart promptly took off his helmet and skimmed it toward third base. Umpire Ken Burkhart put an end to the foolishness by telling him to put the helmet back on and get in the batters' box. Stuart grounded out to the third baseman.

In the bottom half of the inning, Spahn singled, and when he got to first base asked Stuart why he'd gotten so upset. "I don't like anybody needling me when I'm hitting .230,"[76] Stu replied. Two innings later, with the Phillies trailing 2–0, Stuart came up with the bases loaded and struck out on a pitch well out of the strike zone.

Spahn pitched probably his best game of the year, striking out nine and shutting out the Phils for six innings, but he was running out of steam. In the seventh, Philadelphia scored a run and loaded the bases with none out and Giants manager Herman Franks brought in reliever Frank Linzy. After the tying run scored on a double play, Stuart came to the plate with Cookie Rojas on third base. With a 2–2 count, he turned and looked toward the dugout just as Linzy delivered. Stuart could not have swung if the ball was a strike, but fortunately it was not. On the next pitch, he lined a single to center field to score Rojas with the winning run.

In early September, Stu's big bat came alive, and he hit five homers in eight days. His average for that stretch was .350 and he drove in 16 runs, including six in one game. Perhaps there would be another finish like 1961, when Stu hit 13 home runs in the final month.

Unfortunately, there was not, and Dick hit just two more home runs, finishing with 28 homers, 95 RBI and a disappointing .234 average in 149 games. His batting average was 45 points lower than the previous year and the worst of his major league career except for 1962, when he hit .228.

Stuart summarized his season for reporter Stan Hochman. He gave himself a plus for helping the team, since it finished nine games over .500. He also gave himself good marks for his home runs and RBI, as well as his improved fielding, calling it his best year ever in the field. "I get a minus on batting average," he said, but added, "Don't forget I got a lot of big hits. I was on the 'star of the game' show eight or nine times."[77]

Stu managed one more moment of glory in a return to Forbes Field late in the season, and surprisingly it was with his glove rather than his bat. Stuart ranged about 15 feet in the hole to grab a ground ball hit by Bill Virdon, leaped in the air, and threw to pitcher Ray Culp for the out. The Pittsburgh fans gave him a standing ovation and Johnny Pesky, who had a front row seat in the first base coach's box, said, "You never did that for me with the Red Sox."[78]

Toward the end of the season, Stuart had a run-in with Los Angeles reporter Jim Murray. Sarcasm was Murray's forte, and he'd stung Stuart with his bitter pen in the past. When Stu came into the Phillie locker room one day and saw Murray interviewing Johnny Callison, he told Callison not to talk to him. "If he can think of something bad about you," Stuart said, "he'll say it. And he'll hunt until he finds it."[79]

That remark was like waving the red cape in front of a bull—a bull with a regular newspaper column. The next day, Murray wrote that he was determined to find something positive to write about the Phillie first baseman. "With Stuart," he began, "this isn't easy." Finally, in the ninth inning, when Stuart struck out on a wild pitch, Murray found his "positive" moment.

"Now, this is by no means a career first for Stuart," he wrote, "but this had to be the farthest distance a swinging bat came from a thrown ball in the history of the game. At that, it wasn't a great deal worse than the first two pitches Stu swung at but this pitch was so far away from everybody with a glove or bat the first impression in the press box was that Stuart had swung at a pickoff attempt. But it did get him down to first base where he hasn't been much lately and which is something his 800 other major league strikeouts didn't get him. And I am happy to report this minor triumph of Dick Stuart."[80]

On September 26, against the Mets, Stuart got the thousandth hit of his major league career. He'd gotten number 999 in the first inning, and came up in the bottom of the tenth with the Phillies trailing 4–3 and a runner at second base. The reason the Phils were trailing was that Stuart had botched a bunt in the top half of the inning. With a chance to redeem himself, he looped a pop fly into short center field, driving in the tying run. A minute later, he scored the winning run on a double by Tony Gonzalez. "I put it into second gear," he recounted, "if I have a second gear."[81]

Stuart was a hero in the locker room. The media wanted to hear all about his 1,000 hits and Stu, as always, was happy to oblige. He never thought he'd get there, he said, pointing out all the tribulations (mostly self-inflicted) he'd had during his professional career. The reporters heard about Bobby Bragan, the 66 home runs in Lincoln, and the rest of the journey.

Overall, the season was a disappointment. The Phillies, who had such high hopes before the season, finished sixth and Stuart, despite decent home run and RBI totals, didn't live up to Mauch's expectations or his own predictions. "He hit 40 points less," Mauch said, "and struck out 50 times more than I thought he would. Outside of that, he played the way I thought he would."[82] Mauch also talked about team morale. "The club personality was never the strong personality it was last year."[83] Part of the reason was the acquisition of Stuart and Belinsky, which Mauch later called two of the worst moves he ever made.

"Stuart did not have a year to be proud of," wrote Allen Lewis.[84] "His fielding faults were expected, but the simple truth is that Stuart has not produced with the bat ... it is no exaggeration to say that the most pleasant phase of Stuart's play with the Phillies has been his fielding."[85]

Lewis, noting that Stuart had committed just one error in a 30-game stretch, credited the improvement to Mauch. "I thought Dick improved a great deal on defense last year," Mauch said, "and probably fielded better than he ever did in his life."[86] For the first time in his major league career, Stuart didn't lead his league in errors. He had a mere 17, well behind the 28 miscues committed by Donn Clendenon, the man who replaced him in Pittsburgh to strengthen the defense.[87]

Mauch wasn't *that* thrilled with Stuart's fielding, for he often replaced him in the late innings for defensive purposes, usually with Amaro. That upset Stuart, who felt Mauch was embarrassing him, particularly on one occasion when Stuart had already taken his position and had to unceremoniously leave the field, and another when Amaro later came up with the bases loaded, taking Stuart's RBI opportunity away from him.

While Stuart may not have met expectations, the Philadelphia fans behaved exactly as expected. They were on Stuart all year, although he was not their only target. "[T]hey've been very impartial here," he said late in the season. "They boo everybody."[88]

The Red Sox thought they would be better in 1965 without Stuart, but when the season was over, they were ten games worse than they'd been in 1964. For the first time since 1932, the Red Sox lost 100 games, hitting the mark squarely with a 62–100 record. They dropped from eighth to ninth in the standings and finished 40 games behind the pennant-winning Twins. Dennis Bennett was 5–7 with a 4.38 ERA as both a starter and reliever.

When the Red Sox hit five home runs in their opening game, it looked like they wouldn't miss Stuart. But they did. Young Tony Horton couldn't hold the first base job, which went to veteran Lee Thomas. Thomas had a good year, batting .271 with 22 homers and 75 RBI, but led AL first basemen with 18 errors. Perhaps Stu had damaged Fenway Park's first base so badly no one could play it.

Certainly Tony Horton couldn't. A couple of years later, Boston writer Ray Fitzgerald said, "Dick Stuart at his worst never committed the atrocities at first base that Horton has this young season."[89] That evening Horton had gone after a foul pop and ended up on top of the tarpaulin with his feet sticking straight up in the air. Stuart couldn't play first base, said Fitzgerald, because he didn't try. Horton was trying and was even worse.

The Red Sox took a lot of heat for the Stuart trade. All season long, there was talk that the transaction might be voided because of Bennett's bad arm, or that the Phillies would send another player to Boston, but nothing was ever done. Most of the blame was directed at general manger Mike Higgins, but the *Globe* claimed that Higgins had traded Stuart only at the insistence of Tom Yawkey and his wife, who were tired of his errors.

The entire Boston organization was in disarray. Apparently Johnny Pesky hadn't been the problem; there was just as much dissension under Billy Herman as there had been under Pesky. A new direction was needed and the Red Sox reached out to Danny Murtaugh, who had resigned as Pirate manager after the 1964 season, to take the job of Director of Player Personnel and straighten out the mess. Murtaugh wisely declined.

Meanwhile, back in Philadelphia, Stuart was on the trading block again. As writer Milton Richman put it, "For the third time in four years, big Stu will be forced to get behind the wheel of his snazzy Caddy convertible and drive it somewhere else."[90] The Phils didn't have any promising first basemen on the roster or in their minor league system, but there was talk of moving outfielder Johnny Briggs to first base if Stuart went elsewhere.

Stu said he had been happy in Philadelphia and that Mauch was the first manager he'd never had any trouble with. The benchings were forgotten, the removals for defense were forgotten, but Stuart said he wanted to be traded if the Phillies planned to cut his salary.

It had been a disappointing summer in Philadelphia and there was growing sentiment to back up the truck and load up a batch of veteran players. Wes Covington and Tony Gonzalez had irreconcilable differences with Mauch and Stuart, infielder Tony Taylor, and pitcher Art Mahaffey were also rumored to be heading out of town.

Stuart's departure became a certainty when the Phillies obtained veteran first baseman Bill White from St. Louis. The Cardinals, who'd won the World Series in 1964, did what the Pirates had done three years earlier. They traded three-fourths of their championship infield—White, third baseman Ken Boyer, and Dick Groat, who came to Philadelphia along with White.

White was 31 years old, about two years younger than Stuart, and had been an All-Star four times. Although his performance declined slightly in 1965, he still hit .289 with 24 homers. White was also a slick fielder and had speed (he stole 16 bases for the Phillies in 1966); there was no question he was going to be Philadelphia's starting first baseman.

After the Phillies obtained White, Mauch made it clear that Stuart was "available" and all the nice things Stuart said about the Phillie manager went out the window. "Maybe Mauch should be available," Stuart replied and said Mauch cost him 100 at bats by taking him out of games. "Baseball has always been a lot of fun for me," he claimed, "but Mauch sort of ruined it." Mauch said he thought Stuart had been a bad influence on Allen and Callison.

"I know I'm going somewhere," Stuart said when he heard about the White trade. "I won't be in spring training with the Phillies. There is no way in the world they can play two $50,000 players at the same position."[91] Especially if one was an all-around star and the other a one-dimensional slugger.

It was a difficult winter for Philadelphia general manager John Quinn, who had to peddle a lot of damaged merchandise. Moving Covington was even more difficult than getting rid of Stuart, for Wes would be 34 before the next season began and had balky knees and a defensive reputation almost as bad as Stuart's. When coach Peanuts Lowery chided Covington about his defense, Wes replied, "Hub, they pay me for what I do with the wood. If I got the wood smoking, nobody notices a little mistake with the glove."[92] Every general manager in baseball knew Stuart and Covington had to be traded, and although there were a lot of rumors, no team was willing to offer very much for players the Phillies had to get rid of.

Stuart mocked the idea that the Phillies were going from a power team to a speed team. "I sure get a big laugh out of that one." He said that while the Dodgers won the 1965 World Series with speed, it was the speed of Sandy Koufax and Don Drysdale, not that of Maury Wills and Willie Davis that propelled them to the top. "Take those guys away from the Dodgers and they would be in the second division (which they were the year after Koufax retired)."[93]

Stuart said he would like to return to Boston and Fenway Park, but didn't think that would happen. In August, Stuart had told a Los Angeles reporter that he had an offer from Japan, but now he dismissed the possibility. "Forget that," he said with a laugh. A player needed to be released to play in Japan, and when he asked the Phillies to release him in January, they refused.

The Phillies sent Stuart a contract calling for a $5,000 cut and he returned it unsigned. Just after the dawn of the new year, New York columnist Dick Young suggested that since the Phils weren't likely to get any good players for Stuart, they should sell him, and that the Mets, who had lots of cash, should buy him. "Stu would be perfect for New York," Young wrote. "He's colorful copy and would help fill the publicity void left by Casey Stengel [who'd retired the previous September], or at least part of it. He also can hit a ball over a few fences."[94]

Stuart was still a Phillie when he returned to Boston for the annual baseball writers' dinner in early February. He came out wearing a mask that was dramatically removed by broadcaster Curt Gowdy and was as clever and loquacious as ever. Stu turned to Billy Herman and said, "I sure hope you have a good winter, Billy, because you sure had a lousy summer." That was a favorite line of Stuart's, adaptable to many situations. He described Dick Radatz, who'd had the worst season of his career, as a "former fastball pitcher," and saved his best remark for Pesky. "I made you what you are today—a coach."[95]

When spring training began, Stuart was still in limbo. Although he feigned indifference (as always) he had to be getting a little concerned. He'd just turned 33, which was approaching old age for a major league player in the '60s.[96] Stuart had no education and no preparation for any career outside of baseball other than broadcasting. No one was going to make him a coach. He needed to find a place to play.

15

I'm Not in a Position to Give Anyone an Ultimatum: 1966

Despite spending the entire winter on the trading block, Stuart was still a Phillie when the team gathered for spring training. Bill White graciously said he was going to have to compete with Stuart to win the first base job but Gene Mauch quickly confirmed what everyone knew. "Well, I'll guarantee this. Only one will be in Clearwater when spring training starts—me or Stuart. And I'm gonna show up."[1]

White, an educated, erudite, personable man who was later a long-time Yankee announcer and then president of the National League, was a more than adequate replacement for Stuart on the banquet circuit. Speaking at one Philadelphia event during the winter, he said, "I received a telegram telling me to be sure and make it to Philly. The telegram said it might be the only time I get any applause here. It was signed Dick Stuart."[2]

Stuart had more than angry fans to deal with over the winter; apparently he had an angry wife. Stuart, as always, made a joke of the situation. He and Lois had a fight just before the start of spring training, he told Larry Merchant. "She threw a bowling ball at me and it went right through a $500 picture window. What got me mad, though, was that she should have known I would have dropped it anyway."[3] Reducing marital discord to money and a quip about his fielding was the essence of Dick Stuart and the incident was a harbinger of his eventual divorce.

It didn't make a lot of sense to pay Stuart nearly $50,000 a year to sit on the bench and finally, on February 22, he was traded to the New York Mets for three minor leaguers—infielders Bobby Klaus and Wayne Graham and catcher Jim Schaffer. It was a giveaway. Klaus, Graham, and Schaffer were all assigned to San Diego of the Pacific Coast League and none ever played in the major leagues again.[4]

"It shall go down in American history," wrote Dick Young in the *New York Daily News*, "that on this day George Washington was born and Dick Stuart became a Met."[5] From Boston to Philadelphia to New York, Stuart's welcomes were becoming less effusive. In New York there were no predictions of 50 home runs or leading his team to the pennant. "We needed a bat," said Met manager Wes Westrum, "and this is the best we could get."[6]

Philadelphia General Manager John Quinn was equally unenthused and admitted he hadn't gotten much for a man who'd hit 103 home runs the past three seasons. "It was the best deal we could make," he said. "We tried to talk to many major league clubs but none was interested."[7] He said the Phils could have gotten cash but Eddie Leishman, who ran the San Diego club, was a friend of Quinn's and he wanted to help him out by sending him some good Triple-A players. Besides, Quinn said, by trading Stuart to the Mets, he avoided having to send him to the minor leagues. He didn't mention his

In February 1966, the Phillies practically gave Stuart away to the New York Mets, who'd never finished out of the basement in their first four National League seasons. He was injured, never found his groove, and was released in June. National Baseball Hall of Fame.

primary objective, jettisoning Stuart's hefty salary. By going to the Mets, Stuart avoided the pay cut Quinn had planned, for the Mets agreed to pay him the same salary he received in 1965.

While Stuart was happy to get off the Philadelphia bench, he was angered by Quinn's comments. "You don't treat a guy like me, making $50,000, like this,"[8] Stu told legendary

Ed Kranepool was the Mets' incumbent first baseman when Stuart was traded to New York in 1966. Kranepool, the first big Met bonus baby, was unhappy playing left field, which led to Stuart's departure. National Baseball Hall of Fame.

New York columnist Jimmy Cannon. "A player as established as I am, I don't worry about staying in the major leagues. You don't drive in 95 runs and hit 28 homers and worry about the minor leagues. I thought it was a bush statement. I guess he was trying to make himself a big man with the home town fans. I'll show Quinn what kind of a ball player I am when I come to Philadelphia with the Mets. Minor leagues…. I'd hate like hell for him to hold his breath until I reported to a minor league.... Mentioning my name in connection with the minor leagues makes me want to throw up."[9]

"Look, if I were 36 or 37 I'd worry. But I'm 33. Don't make it sound like they gave me away for nothing. Those three guys aren't total losses. The price of a minor leaguer is $12,000. That's $36,000 plus my salary that the Mets have invested in me. Ballplayers who hit 28 homers and drive in 95 runs just don't grow on trees."[10]

The Mets were just a notch above the minor leagues. They had finished last in all four of their National League seasons, losing more than 100 games each year. Their greatest success had been carving out a niche as America's most loved losers, drawing more than 1.7 million fans in each of the two seasons they'd played in Shea Stadium. It would seem that the talent-challenged Mets had plenty of room for someone of Dick Stuart's baseball pedigree.

The problem was that, in 1962, the Mets had given an $80,000 bonus to a New York high school phenom named Eddie Kranepool, who was expected to be the new team's first home grown star. Kranepool seemed to have all the ingredients for success. He was a local boy. He was a good-sized young man at 6'3" and more than 200 pounds. He was a left-handed hitter with a smooth swing who'd broken Hank Greenberg's home run records in high school.

Kranepool was just 17 when he made his first appearance with the Mets in the final days of the 1962 season. He played in three games, got his first major league hit, and would be forever known as an "original" Met.[11] The next season, despite the fact that nearly everyone else thought Kranepool needed minor league seasoning, manager Casey Stengel made him the opening day right fielder. Stengel hopefully compared the raw rookie to Hall of Famer Mel Ott, who'd joined the New York Giants at 17.

Players like Mel Ott come along perhaps once in a generation, and Ed Kranepool was not the one for his generation. Although he got off to a quick start, he soon became overmatched by big league pitching. Once National League hurlers found out he could be jammed effectively, he saw nothing but inside pitches and his average dropped to around .200. Kranepool was sent back to the minor leagues a couple of times, and didn't return for good until 1965, when he settled in as the Mets starting first baseman.

Kranepool got off to a sizzling start that year, made the All-Star team, but then went into a deep slump. When the season was over, he'd batted .253 in 153 games, while hitting 10 home runs. The modest home run total was somewhat disappointing, given the youngster's size and potential.

When Stuart arrived on the scene, Kranepool was just 21, although he was starting his fifth major league season. If he was going to be the star the Mets hoped he would be, Kranepool needed a change in attitude. He wasn't as voluble as Stuart had been as a young player, but he was almost as cocky. He'd cashed a big bonus check and played in the major leagues as a teenager and didn't seem to have the relentless drive that creates truly great players. He brushed off Hall of Famer Duke Snider when the latter tried to give him some batting advice. He was aloof and, despite his youth, had a certain *ennui* about him. "Kranepool," observed the recently retired Stengel, "if he really gets mad and serious, ought to be one of the best players in the league."[12]

Before acquiring Stuart, Met president George Weiss received Kranepool's assurance that he wouldn't mind playing the outfield, where he had just six games of major league experience, on days when Stuart played first.[13] What about playing Stuart in the outfield, where he'd begun his minor league career? "I wouldn't want to be the guy that was pitching that night," Stuart said with a twinkle.[14] "I've already decided to vote for [Kranepool] at All-Star time. He's my All-Star left fielder."[15]

Even if Kranepool was a part-time outfielder, that still left Stuart playing only against left-handed pitchers, who were in the distinct minority. It would be the first time since his early days in Pittsburgh that he wouldn't be a regular and he wasn't happy.

Westrum, a former Giants catcher, assured reporters he would be able to deal with the ticklish situation of Stuart and Kranepool. "Westrum seems to think he will be able to handle Stuart," wrote Young. "They all do."[16] He recounted how Gene Mauch, Johnny Pesky, and Bobby Bragan all thought they could get along with Stuart and summarized the sorry results.

"I'm going to convince Dick," said Westrum, "how important it is to have a good man on the bench." Stuart, on the other hand, wanted to convince his manager that he should be playing every day. "I wouldn't be worth a thing," Stuart said, "if I were to be strictly platooned. I don't want to sound like I'm issuing any orders. Nothing could be further from the truth. I'll do anything the Mets want. But I think Wes Westrum should know what I've produced everywhere I played regularly."[17]

Another ticklish situation was Stuart's uniform number. Next to 66, his favorite number was 7, the one he'd worn on his back ever since joining the Pirates in 1958. Since he had taken his position, Stuart didn't think he could take number 7 away from Kranepool, who'd given his original number (21) to Warren Spahn when the latter joined the Mets a year earlier. Stuart kiddingly said he'd ask for 007, then 37, which was Casey Stengel's old number. Finally, he decided that 17 was as close to 7 as he was going to get.

The 1966 team was the first Mets club to escape the cellar, and while there were some promising young players on the roster, there were a lot of veterans who were nearing the end of the line. "Clearly," wrote Phil Pepe, "the trades for [Ken] Boyer and Stuart were a last-ditch attempt by [Met president] George Weiss to escape the cellar before retiring."[18] Philadelphia had acquired Stuart with the hope he would help them win a pennant. If the Mets ever became pennant contenders, Stu would be long gone. Still, he could be very useful to the Mets if he could do what he'd done for the Phillies in 1965. Rookie Ron Swoboda led the '65 Mets with 19 home runs, and no Met had hit more than 20 since 1962. Kranepool, at .253, had the highest average of any 1965 regular.

The people most eager to welcome Stuart to New York were the writers. There was no dearth of material when Casey Stengel managed the Mets, but Westrum's specialty was the platitude, particularly those involving teamwork and positive thinking. That didn't make for scintillating copy and the press was hoping that Stuart would liven up the scene.

A trade that neither team seemed terribly excited about received a tremendous amount of coverage in both New York and Philadelphia. "Dick Stuart and the Mets," wrote one reporter, "a match made in heaven."[19] If Met fans liked Marv Throneberry, he said, they'd love Stuart. "Forget Marvelous Marv. Now the Mets have Stupendous Stu."[20] Larry Merchant, who would miss having Stu to write about, assured New Yorkers they'd love him. And Stu, he said, would love New York. "It has to be the best thing that ever happened to him," Merchant wrote, "because his goofs will not only be tolerated but celebrated, giving him a chance to indulge in his greatest passions: hitting homers and making money."[21]

Stuart thought he'd fit in well with the raucous Met fans, who were known as The New Breed. "I'm as wild as they are," he said with a laugh.[22] He was asked whether, with the retirement of Stengel and the closing of the nearby World's Fair, the Mets needed a new image. "They've got a new image and a new World's Fair," he replied. "They got me."[23] "With Ken Boyer, Ed Kranepool, Ron Swoboda and me in the lineup, I guarantee you the Mets won't finish last."[24]

While the writers welcomed Stuart for his outrageous quotes, columnist Phil Pepe questioned his value as a ballplayer. "In baseball," he wrote, "to get nothing you must give up nothing,"[25] and pointed out that the Phillies had been desperate to get rid of him. "He has the reputation of being something of a kook and it has been said he wears a glove merely for protection and to comply with the rules." "The trouble with Dick Stuart," he wrote on another occasion, "is nobody understands or appreciates him as much as Dick Stuart.... Stuart discusses home runs with the same passion as Picasso discussing art, Oleg Cassini discussing fashions and Jack Benny discussing money...."

Stuart, true to form, arrived at the Met camp in St. Petersburg with both lips blazing. His first extensive interview occurred, however, when he traveled to Fort Lauderdale to visit his old teammate Bob Friend, who'd been traded to the Yankees over the winter. Friend was still working out when Stuart arrived, so Stu sat down in front of Mickey Mantle's locker and asked if he could see the bandages Mantle wrapped around his damaged legs. They weren't there, but reporter Milton Richman was and took the opportunity to chat with the Mets' new first baseman.

"I'm an established player," Stuart said. "I get half the salary Mantle does.... Admit my batting average was terrible last year. How about the 28 homers I hit, though, and my 95 RBI?"[26] He pointed out that there was only one first baseman (the Giants' Willie McCovey) who hit more home runs and only one (the Cubs' Ernie Banks) who had more RBI. "Look it up if you don't believe me."[27]

Stuart told Richman that he and his wife were happy to be in New York because it was so close to their new home in the Indian Harbor section of Greenwich, Connecticut. "Cost me 50 grand," he said.[28] "It's the cheapest house in the neighborhood. You know how ritzy Greenwich is. They got one house in my neighborhood for $500,000 and a few others for $300,000. I'm in a very exclusive area. You have to go through gates to get to my house. There's a big cop at the gate and he stops you. He asks you whom do you want to visit. If you say Dick Stuart, he calls me on the phone and I tell him if it's OK or not." Stuart finished the interview by telling Richman that while he'd done a lot of talking in the past, "I'm not gonna talk much in New York."

Not talking proved impossible for Stuart, and Richman caught him in an expansive mood a few weeks later. The subject was Stu's reputation as a horrible fielder. After stating that Bill White was the best fielding first sacker in the NL, Stuart compared himself to some of the others. "Take Lee Thomas (of Atlanta)," Stuart said. "He's a very good friend of mine and I don't mean to single him out, but since we're on this subject, I don't think he's better than me defensively. Neither of us is ever gonna win the Gold Glove Award." He then proceeded to denigrate the fielding of Baltimore's Boog Powell, who he also described as a good friend.

Being a conscientious reporter, Richman contacted Thomas to see what he thought of being compared to Stuart as a fielder. Thomas told Richman he had just one comment. "He thereupon," wrote Richman, "made his two-word comment but they don't permit it in this newspaper."[29]

Stu made an immediate hit with Met fans during one of the first intrasquad games. He hit a double and two singles, driving in two runs, but what wowed the crowd was his great catch of a line drive off the bat of Lou Klimchock. The fans cheered and Stuart acknowledged them with a deep bow from the waist and a doffing of his Mets cap.

"We were playing pepper one day in spring training," recalled Klimchock. "I was beside him and Dick says, 'Look at that photographer over there just waiting for me to boot one so he can take a picture.' Yeah, I said, he'll probably stay there all day if he has to. Dick said, 'It's not going to take that long.' He could field. He just didn't want to. He thought playing the infield was something you did while you were waiting to hit."[30]

In his first at bat as a Met in the opening exhibition game, Stuart homered off Bob Gibson. But then he cooled off and went 50 at bats without a homer. Westrum professed not to be worried. "Lou Gehrig didn't hit in the spring," he said hopefully. "Neither did Babe Ruth."[31] And neither did a lot of players who wound up on Triple A rosters. Dick Young, who'd always been a Stuart fan, said, "He is brooding. He has a star complex and when he is anything less than a star, he gets angry with himself."[32]

When the regular season began, it looked as though Stuart had won the battle with Westrum. In their opening game, the Mets faced left-hander Denver Lemaster of the Braves and Stuart was at first base. That gave the Mets an All-Star at every infield position, quite an accomplishment for a last place team. The problem was that only second baseman Ron Hunt was in his prime. Stuart made the All-Star squad in 1961; shortstop Roy McMillan was 36 and had last been an All-Star in 1957. Third baseman Ken Boyer had been the National League MVP just two years earlier, but he was about to turn 35 and had a bad back.

Stuart started the first four games, while Kranepool played left or replaced him for defensive purposes in the late innings. Then disaster struck. Throughout his career, Stuart had been remarkably free of injury, but he'd never been 33 years old before. On Monday, April 18, while taking batting practice, Stuart tore a muscle near the left side of his rib cage. He had his ribs taped and tried to play the next night, but in the first inning he had to be taken out before he could complete his turn at bat.[33] Stu was placed on the disabled list and didn't play another game until May 8.

Clif Keane of the *Boston Globe* caught up with Stuart shortly after he came off the disabled list and painted a sorry picture, that of a fallen star dealing with injury, old age, and declining production. "Stuart used to pride himself on his strength," Keane wrote, "but his locker was so filled with bandages that he couldn't find room for a couple of his combs."[34]

Stuart made a couple of lame jokes, but they didn't have the sting of the old Stuart humor. He told Keane that he and Ed Bressoud were staging a fierce battle for home run supremacy (each had one) but no one was noticing. Then he asked how much money rookie Red Sox first baseman George Scott was making.

Kranepool played first in Stuart's absence, but didn't set the world on fire. He had a batting average of just .189 when Stu made a dramatic return from the disabled list, hitting a home run off the Cubs' Dick Ellsworth in his first at bat. It was his first circuit blow of the season.

The next few weeks were disappointing. Stuart started nearly every day, and although he raised his batting average over .200, he didn't hit consistently and wasn't delivering the long ball. On May 31, he finally managed to hit his second home run. It came against the Phillies, and Stuart blew kisses at the Philadelphia dugout as he rounded the bases.

The next night, he homered against the Pirates, but the game had a bad ending. In the bottom of the ninth he came up with the bases loaded, two out, and the Mets trailing

3–1. It was the dramatic setting Stuart always coveted, but former teammate Al McBean struck him out on three sliders to end the game.

In describing that night, Dick Young provided a fitting eulogy to Stuart's Met career. "Lovable Dick Stuart," he wrote, "television actor, made them cheer, and laugh, and weep on the big stage at Shea last night.... Stuart, if he weren't such a righthanded imitation of Marv Throneberry, would be sensational. He tries so hard. He blows into the cornet so hard and it comes out so sour. He excites the people with his tall presence, and they root for him so hard, just as the 11,795 New Breeds did last night, and they are so let down, just as the 11,795 were last night."[35]

Stuart started his last game for the Mets on June 9. Six days later, after four more pinch hitting appearances, he was released.[36] "Stuart, with his power," said Westrum, "might have been valuable to us as a pinch hitter. But he had it in his head that he couldn't hit unless he played regularly. So there was no use keeping him on our roster."[37]

Stuart wasn't doing that badly, and the Mets were playing at, for them, a record pace, but there was another reason Stuart had to go. "Everything was just great," he said, "and then Ed Kranepool decides that he wants to play first base. The run to the outfield was too tiring for a 20-year-old [sic]."[38]

"Many players have to play every day to keep their eye sharp," Kranepool said. "[T]hat's not the whole story with me. There's another thing that's very important to me. I have to feel that the ball club has confidence in me."[39] Kranepool was the first baseman of the future and the Mets wanted him to be happy; he wasn't going to be happy as long as Stuart was on the team.

Stuart later said the release had been at his request. When he'd hit his last two home runs, he'd gone to Westrum and asked to play regularly. When Westrum told him that wasn't going to happen, he suggested, he claimed, that the Mets give him his release. "I don't know for sure it was because I asked," he said, "but three or four days later they gave it to me."[40] He also said he would never forgive Westrum for costing him the $10,000 he was making from his television show.[41]

The show was called "Stump Stuart." Fans asked Stuart questions about baseball, and if he didn't know the answers, they won prizes. While Stuart was very aware of his own accomplishments, he didn't know a lot about baseball history and proved to be easily stumped. "It got so bad they had to rig the show," Stuart admitted.[42]

One day Stuart had old sparring partner Johnny Pesky as a guest, and on another he had a New York City policeman who asked him a question about home runs by a Red Sox shortstop. Stuart was stumped by the correct answer of Rico Petrocelli, who happened to be the officer's brother.[43] After people started doing research and coming up with difficult queries, the producers asked for easier questions.

At the same time Stuart was released, first baseman Jim Gentile was traded by the Astros to the Indians after he smashed his bat and threw it at umpire Ed Vargo when Vargo called him out on strikes. By the next season Gentile would be in the minor leagues. In the early 1960s, Stuart and Gentile had been two of the premier power hitters in the major leagues. In 1961, while Stuart was hitting 35 homers, Gentile had 46, while driving in 141 runs. Five years later, although Gentile was just 32 and Stuart a year older, both were staring at the end of their careers.

The Sporting News published a righteous editorial that took the form of a homily on attitude. "Talent can take a player a long way up the success ladder," *TSN* said, "but talent alone does not insure against a painful tumble. Jim Gentile and Dick Stuart displayed enough skill to scale baseball's salary heights, but they lacked what it takes to stay there…. Both might well anticipate several more years of high earnings—if only they could conquer some glaring shortcomings of temperament…. While Gentile's boiling point was unbelievably low, no one has determined whether Stuart even has one. The Iron Glove could be—and frequently was—peerless at the plate, but he steadfastly refused to acknowledge that baseball consisted of anything but swinging a bat. Nonchalant was the most charitable description ever offered of his fielding. Though temperamental opposites, these two were found wanting in the same category. Neither could subordinate his own feelings to strive for a common goal. They failed because baseball is a team game and they were not team players."[44]

For the first time in his baseball career, Dick Stuart was unemployed in the middle of the summer.[45] "Big Stu Now a Warmed-Up Leftover," read the headline in the *Philadelphia Inquirer*.[46] There were no player agents in those days, so Stuart contacted a few teams directly to see if they might have any interest in a veteran right-handed power hitter. In the meantime, he tended his garden in Greenwich, where Boston reporter Bud Collins caught up with him.

Collins described Stuart as a $4,000 a month gardener, a position that was good for a month, since the Mets were only obligated to give him 30 days pay when they released him. "If no team wants me," Stu told Collins, "I'm available as a gardener. Like everything else I try I'm very good at it."[47] That showed a touch of the old bravado but other comments were more telling. "It sure hurts your ego," he told another writer, "when you can't play for the Mets."[48]

Stuart called his old friend Miles Span and told him he'd be interested in going back to Pittsburgh. Joe Brown offered a place on the Pirates' AAA farm club at Columbus, but Stuart thought he had a chance at a major league job and declined. Old adversary Bobby Bragan, manager of the Braves, told GM John McHale that Stuart could help his team, but McHale wasn't interested. Neither were the Cleveland Indians.

A friend said he'd seen an interview with Sandy Koufax in which Koufax said Stuart hit him pretty well.[49] Therefore Stuart called Dodger GM Buzzie Bavasi. The Dodgers had switch-hitting Wes Parker at first base, and while Parker wasn't a great hitter, he was an excellent fielder and quick on the bases. On the other hand, the Dodgers had a woeful bench, so thin that in one game in the 1965 World Series they used pitcher Don Drysdale as his first pinch hitter. Bavasi told Stuart he wanted to talk to manager Walt Alston and asked him to call back the next day. When Stuart called, Bavasi offered him a contract and Stuart agreed immediately. Alston planned to use him as a pinch hitter and occasional fill-in at first base against left-handed pitching.

In the spring, Stuart had told Wes Westrum he wouldn't be satisfied or effective as a part-time player, but now he was willing to accept whatever role Alston had in store for him. One reason for the change in attitude was the shock of his release, and the second was that the Dodgers were in the middle of a pennant race while the Mets had been in ninth place. When Stuart signed, the Dodgers were third, five games behind the first place Giants, with the Pirates sandwiched between them. "It's hard to accept being a scrubeenie," he said, "but it's easier to accept with the Dodgers than with the Mets. I just have to face the facts. I'm not in any position to give anyone an ultimatum. I don't know if the Dodgers need me, but I sure need them."[50] It was no disgrace, he said, to sit on the bench of a world champion.

Had Dick Stuart finally discovered humility? Had he learned the meaning of hustle?

One of the famous advertising tag lines of the mid–1960s was that of Avis car rental, second in size to Hertz. The Avis slogan was "We Try Harder." When Stuart arrived in the Dodger locker room, he found the Avis slogan taped to his locker as a hint.[51] "He may find the atmosphere with the Dodgers a little strange," said Los Angeles columnist Sid Ziff. "They don't mind characters as long as they give out 100 percent."[52]

Stuart had to try a little harder to get to the locker room. The air conditioning on his flight from New York to Los Angeles malfunctioned and it was a long and extremely uncomfortable journey. Fellow passenger Milton Berle, returning to California from a film festival in Berlin, walked up and down the aisles passing out washcloths soaked in ice water.

Stuart's first hit as a Dodger was a pinch single in the 11th inning against the Mets at Shea Stadium. Batting with the bases loaded against New York's best reliever, right-hander Jack Hamilton, Stuart looped a single into short center field to score Ron Fairly from third with the winning run.

It wasn't long before Stuart began playing much more frequently than anyone expected. Between July 24 and August 14 he played in 19 games, 17 of them at first base. After starting three games in a row, he asked, "What does Alston think I am? A machine?"[53]

In the 19 games, Stuart made 16 hits in 58 at bats, with three home runs. After one of his home runs, Stuart was the recipient of something he'd rarely experienced in the major leagues: a standing ovation. "I've had standing boos a lot of times," he observed.[54] Perhaps most remarkable of all, wrote Dodger beat writer Bob Hunter, "Dick Stuart's fielding has been outstanding."[55] Stu said he'd been overweight when he reported to the Mets, but had shed 15–20 pounds, which made him more agile in the field.

Stu was also a popular figure in the Dodger clubhouse. He'd never hesitated to tease his teammates, and in Los Angeles he even tweaked the great Sandy Koufax. In two Koufax starts, the Dodgers scored just two runs. In his next start they exploded for 12 and after Alston removed Koufax after six innings to rest him, Stuart quipped, "We get you 14 runs in three games and you can't even finish one."[56]

On another occasion, after Stuart was hit on the helmet by the Phillies' Larry Jackson, trainer Bill Buhler came out and asked if he was dizzy. "No more than usual," Stuart replied, before kissing his helmet and heading for first base. Former Pirate teammate Dick Schofield, acquired by the Dodgers from the Yankees in early September, was reunited with Stuart for the first time since 1962. Had he changed? "He was the same guy," Schofield said.[57]

The Dodgers went on a six-game winning streak in late July, bringing them to within a half-game of first place on July 27. In one of the victories, Stuart contributed a home run off Phillie left-hander Chris Short that gave the Dodgers the lead and then drove in an insurance run with an eighth-inning single. He also made a fine defensive play.

But perhaps the most notable change was in his attitude. "I looked at the scoreboard," Stuart said after the game, "and saw that San Francisco had beaten Pittsburgh and I knew that this would be a big one for us to win." When Wes Covington, another former teammate who'd joined the Dodgers, reminded him in the locker room that he had beaten the man who'd traded him, Stuart was all graciousness, saying that Gene Mauch had been good to him and he was sorry to see he was having trouble with a couple of his players.

After all the false starts over the years, this really *was* a new Dick Stuart—willing to come off the bench, fielding like a wizard, and talking about his team winning rather than his home runs. "This is like when I was with the '60 Pirates and we won the pennant," Stuart said. "Every hit means something in this race."[58] He even executed a perfect hit and run play, hitting the ball expertly behind the runner. "I might be another Willie Keeler," he said.[59] He went from first to third on a single to left field and even tried stealing a base, although he wasn't successful.

The 1966 Dodgers prided themselves on their spirit and desire. Like the 1960 Pirates, they made a practice of pulling games out of the fire in the late innings. They had great pitching, mediocre defense, and a pop-gun offense—only the Mets hit fewer home runs. "They have a few good players," said the Pirates' Donn Clendenon, "and Alston is a real good manager ... but they have to be the ungodliest luckiest team alive."[60]

By 1966, Clendenon had become Stuart's replacement in more ways than one. In his fourth year as the Pirates' regular first baseman, he was having an excellent season, but was regularly incurring the wrath of Pirate fans. When Stuart came to Pittsburgh with the Dodgers, he was cheered while Clendenon was booed.

Walter Alston, who had managed the Dodgers since 1954, was a lot like Danny Murtaugh. Alston was Stuart's type of manager, a quiet undemonstrative sort who didn't lose his cool on the bench. He let his players play, and they came through for him. Alston did not fancy himself a strategic genius and generally made orthodox moves. Although he was quiet, Alston was so physically strong that many of his players feared him. When he managed at St. Paul, he beat up two of his players (at the same time) for lying about curfew violations. Once, after Jackie Robinson disparaged his managing ability, he challenged Robinson to meet him anytime and anywhere. Robinson declined but retained an undying enmity for the Dodger skipper.

The players responded to Alston and the veterans made certain that the youngsters played and acted like Dodgers, as the Yankee veterans of the great 1950s teams had done. When they joined the Dodgers, long-time individualists like Stuart and Covington caught the vibe and began cheering for their teammates. "C'mon, Stuart," Covington shouted on one occasion, "Yell it up a little."[61]

On the final day of July, the Dodgers beat the Cardinals 6–4 to move into first place by a single percentage point. Stuart, who'd had two hits the previous day, singled in the Dodgers' first run in the second inning and tied the game 2–2 in the third with a home run off Steve Carlton. With the Dodgers trailing 4–3 with two outs in the top of the ninth, Stuart doubled in Maury Wills to tie the game. John Roseboro singled in Stuart to put the Dodgers in front. Reliever Phil Regan retired the Cardinals in the bottom of the ninth to gain his ninth win against one loss.

The 29-year-old Regan was a major reason the Dodgers were in first place. He had some success as a starting pitcher with the Tigers in the early '60s but had regressed so badly by 1965 that he was sent to the minor leagues. Regan saw the demotion as a blessing in disguise, for he was able to get steady work, hone his control, and regain his earlier form.

In December, Regan was traded to the Dodgers for utility infielder Dick Tracewski. He would finish the 1966 season with a 14–1 record, a league leading 21 saves, and a 1.62 ERA. Sandy Koufax gave him the nickname "The Vulture" for his knack for coming out of the bullpen to pick up late-inning victories. Many thought the reason for Regan's resurrection had something to do with the Vaseline he was rumored to use to doctor the ball, and for the rest of his career he was accused and inspected but never convicted.

15. I'm Not in a Position ... 1966

The presence of Stuart in New York hadn't motivated the lethargic Kranepool, but when Alston put him in the Dodger lineup it lit a fire under urbane, cerebral Wes Parker. Kranepool had received a large bonus from the Mets while Parker had gotten nothing from the Dodgers. In fact, no one wanted him when he graduated from USC with a degree in history. But Parker had money to fall back on; he came from the kind of family one would expect a young man named Wesley Maurice Parker to come from. He was a member of the prestigious Los Angeles Country Club and a tournament bridge player. Many thought he was too sophisticated and financially secure to take baseball seriously.

When Stuart began taking his place, Parker went to GM Buzzie Bavasi and said, "If the Dodgers want to win the pennant again, I've got to play." That was what Bavasi wanted to hear, and for the rest of the season, Parker saw the majority of playing time at first. After his initial burst, Stuart rarely left the bench. When he started a game on September 16, it was his first start in 35 days.

For the third year in a row, the National League pennant race went down to the wire. On the first of September, the Giants and Pirates were tied for first with identical records and the Dodgers were three games behind. The Dodgers began the month with five straight wins, bringing them to within a game and a half of the Pirates, while the Giants dropped to third. After two losses, the Dodgers won eight more times, giving them 13 wins in 15 games and propelling them into first place by 3½ games.

The Pirates didn't go down easily. After sweeping a doubleheader from the Phillies on Wednesday, September 28, they were just 1½ games behind with three games left. The Dodgers, who were shut out that day by Cardinal rookie Larry Jaster, had four games remaining.[62]

The next day, Sandy Koufax beat the Cards while the Pirates were idle. Each team now had three games left and the Dodgers led by two games. On the season's final weekend, the Dodgers were scheduled to play in Philadelphia while the Pirates hosted the Giants. The Giants weren't officially eliminated, but one loss or one Dodger win would seal their fate.

The last road trip of the year featured an old Stuart tradition. Reporter Bud Tucker received a call from the Dodger first baseman, who said, "You are invited to the suite which I have rented in this hotel. The joint is loaded with booze and sandwiches and anything you don't see, just order. I always do this on the last road trip of the season. I only invite guys I like."[63] Stuart liked a lot of guys, and for three days people trooped in and out of the suite, enjoying Stuart's hospitality for the final time.

On Friday, the Phillies beat the Dodgers 5–3 while the Pirates and Giants were rained out. On Saturday, the Giants swept a doubleheader from the Pirates, eliminating them from the race, while the Dodgers and Phils were rained out. The Giants, who had been on the verge of elimination, were still on the verge and could force a playoff if they won their remaining two games and the Dodgers lost theirs.

On Sunday, the Dodgers played a doubleheader while the Giants played a single game. If the Dodgers lost both games and the Giants won, the latter would make up a previously rained out game against the Cincinnati Reds on Monday. Sure enough, the Dodgers lost the first game, as the Phillies came from behind with two runs in the bottom of the eighth inning. At Pittsburgh, the Giants rallied for four runs in the 11th to keep their slim hopes alive.

In the second game of the doubleheader, Alston asked Koufax to pitch on two days rest for the first time all season. By that time, Koufax's elbow was hurting so badly that he was surviving on massive amounts of medication. It was his 41st start of the season and the last regular season appearance of his major league career.

Koufax entered the ninth inning with a 6–0 lead, a throbbing elbow, and a displaced vertebra that had been popped back into place by the trainer. Nothing came easily for the Dodgers in the 1960s, and the Phillies, on an error, two singles, and a double, closed to within 6–3 with no outs. Koufax was Alston's ace, the best Dodger relievers had pitched in the first game, and Alston was going to win or lose with his ace. The next batter was catcher Bob Uecker, who is a baseball legend, but not for his hitting. Koufax got him out and retired the next two batters to clinch the Dodgers' second consecutive pennant.

For the second time in his major league career Stuart would be in a World Series. For the Dodgers, he'd batted .264 in 38 games and 91 at bats, with three home runs and nine RBI. He hadn't played much down the stretch, but everyone acknowledged that in such a tight race, the Dodgers might not have won without him. He'd played a key role in a couple of wins, and in the end one win made the difference.

The Dodgers' opponent in the 1966 Series was the young Baltimore Orioles, led by MVP Frank Robinson, third baseman Brooks Robinson, and first baseman Boog Powell. The Orioles had a young, talented pitching staff, but nearly all of them had suffered from arm miseries. In an era of complete games and 20-game winners, none of the Oriole hurlers had thrown more than 213 innings nor won more than 15 games. Lefthander Dave McNally was probably the Orioles' best pitcher, which meant that Stuart might see some action at first base.[64]

The Dodgers started out as if they were going to rout the young Oriole staff, knocking out McNally in the third inning of the first game. The Oriole hitters had done even more damage to Dodger ace Don Drysdale, however, and Stuart was called on to hit for him in the bottom of the second. The Dodgers were trailing 4–1 and there were runners on first and second with one out. Stuart gave a good ride to a McNally pitch, but it was caught by Frank Robinson in deep right center field, just in front of the 390 foot sign on the fence.

The two runs the Dodgers got off McNally were the only ones they would score in the entire Series. They were shut out in the final three games as Baltimore swept the Series and set a plethora of pitching records, holding the Dodgers to a .142 team batting average. "The watery performance of Los Angeles in the World Series," wrote Melvin Durslag, "was totally repulsive and must take its place among the all-time pratfalls of sports."[65]

Oriole scouts had noticed that the Dodgers had trouble hitting good fastballs, and that was about all they saw. "Fast ball after fast ball," said Dodger infielder Jim Gilliam. "Right here. Above the belt, in the wheelhouse. One after the other. And we don't hit it."[66] By starting McNally twice, the Orioles moved the speedy Dodger switch hitters a step farther from first base and neutralized lefty Ron Fairly, one of the Dodgers' few power hitters. When the speedsters tried to bunt, they had to cope with Brooks Robinson. The Dodgers had an uncanny ability to get runners in from third base, so the Oriole pitchers didn't let anyone get to third base.

In Game Two, which was the final appearance of Koufax's illustrious career, the Dodgers suffered the dual indignity of being shut out and seeing their defense completely collapse. Even without Stuart on the field, they made six errors, three in one inning by center fielder Willie Davis. "If they had started Dick Stuart," wrote Clif Keane, "they could have recorded ten errors and immortality."[67]

Although some thought Stuart should have started the final game against left-hander McNally, he didn't. He appeared as a pinch hitter leading off the ninth inning and when the count reached two balls and two strikes, rookie catcher Andy Etchebarren thought Stuart would be looking for a fast ball. He called for a curve. "[T]he pitch hung," Etchebarren said after the game, "it got up there just begging to be hit out of the park. But Stu couldn't pull the trigger."[68]

Although 1966 was Stuart's worst season in the big leagues, it had been a relatively good year financially, even with the loss of his New York television show. The Phillies had wanted to cut his salary, but when the Mets acquired him, they agreed to pay him the same amount he'd earned the previous year. The Dodgers paid him a reported $16,000 to finish the season. In addition, he picked up a two-thirds World Series share of $5,459.57. Stuart estimated he earned $60,000 for his fragmented year, probably the most lucrative season of his career.

But the future was not as promising. Stuart would turn 34 in November and had no guarantee of a major league job for 1967. Although he was obsessed with money and measured his worth by his salary, he'd never been especially careful with it. The Cadillacs, the alimony, the child support, and the hospitality suites had prevented him from accumulating a nest egg. He had not gone to college and his best job skill was swinging a bat. When Stuart accompanied the Dodgers on their post-season tour of Japan, he hoped to play well enough to persuade either the Dodgers or another major league team to offer him a 1967 contract. Or perhaps the old Japanese offer would be revived. If a team in Japan wanted him now, it was doubtful that anyone would stand in his way.

16

I Don't Think I Could Play Here One More Minute: 1967–1968

A few days after the end of the World Series, the Dodgers left for a goodwill exhibition tour of Japan. Attendance was optional and some of team's biggest stars, including pitchers Sandy Koufax and Don Drysdale, elected to stay home.[1] First baseman Wes Parker also declined to make the trip, and 20-year-old minor leaguer Tom Hutton took his place. Stuart would back up Hutton.

When American teams first started going to Japan, they were expected to win every game. The Japanese gradually became more competitive, but in 1956, the last time the Dodgers had been there, they were 14–4–1. By 1966, things had changed. Minus their two best pitchers, the Dodgers were 9–8–1 in 19 games.[2] After winning the first game, they were shut out in the second by the Yomiuri Giants' Akio Masuda, just as they had been shut out by the young Oriole pitchers.

The eight losses were by far the most ever by a visiting American team. In one game, the Dodgers surrendered 13 runs, the most ever scored by a Japanese team against American major leaguers and in two consecutive games, they struck out a total of 26 times. Stuart played in 11 games, several as a pinch hitter, and batted just 19 times with six hits, including three home runs.[3] If he was auditioning for a job, Stuart made a good impression.

Commissioner William Eckert and Dodger owner Walter O'Malley accompanied the players and the visit was a public relations success, even without the missing stars. The Emperor and Empress attended one of the games and the players and other members of the traveling party were given medals and awards at every stop. The previous year, the major leagues had been involved in a bitter dispute with Japan over the services of pitcher Masanori Murakami, and the Dodger tour helped to mend the rift.[4]

When the Dodgers returned to the United States, Stuart was cut adrift on two fronts. The first was the home front. As columnist Dick Young put it, "Dick Stuart has been given his release by Mrs. Stuart."[5] Lois had finally tired of Stuart's behavior and he told reporters there was no chance of reconciliation. The marriage, which had endured nearly nine years, was over. Stuart was also given his release by the Dodgers, the third team to discard him within a year. Although he had performed creditably during the second half of the season, the club needed to free up a roster spot to protect a young player.

Bill White tore his Achilles tendon playing handball during the winter, and there were rumors that the Phillies would sign Stuart to take his place while he recovered. Instead, the Phillies signed Jim Gentile, who'd often been compared to Stuart. Before Phillie minor league manager Frank Lucchesi suggested signing Gentile, he told him, "I'm not going to recommend you, Jim, if you're going to have the attitude of another Dick Stuart." "I'm not an egotist," Gentile assured him. "I'm just a hard-headed paisano."[6]

Since the power-starved Dodgers desperately needed a long ball hitter, they invited Stuart to spring training. Stu said he and Buzzie Bavasi had agreed on the salary ($35,000) he would be paid if he made the opening day roster. It was less than Stuart had been paid in 1966, but he was in no position to bargain.[7]

In February, Stuart reported to Vero Beach to attempt to win a spot on the Dodger roster. He appeared often as a pinch-hitter that spring and played first on a few occasions. Overall, he managed six hits in 24 at bats; on his biggest day he had three hits, including his only homer, drove in three runs, and didn't make an error at first base.[8]

While Stuart labored in Vero Beach, a little further down the east coast of Florida, at the Yankee camp in Fort Lauderdale, Mickey Mantle was attempting to get an extra year or two out of his badly-damaged legs by making the transition from the outfield to first base. A reporter asked him if there was any particular first baseman he was trying to emulate. "No," Mantle said, "I'm not patterning myself after anyone in particular but I sure look like Dick Stuart."[9] It was a turnabout, for after the all the years of Stuart comparing himself to Mantle, Mickey was now comparing himself to Stuart, though not in a flattering way.

For a couple of years, there had been rumors that Stuart would go to Japan, but at that time he was under contract and could not obtain his release. In the spring of 1967, he had no contract and could sign with a Japanese team at any time. But first he needed an offer and after his 1966 decline, Stuart was a less valuable commodity than he'd been a year earlier. When rumors surfaced in March of a Japanese overture that included a $10,000 bonus and a $40,000 salary, Stuart said, "It's news to me."[10]

As spring training came to an end, it did not appear there was a place on the Dodger roster for Stuart. Parker was going to be the starting first baseman and Los Angeles still had veteran Ron Fairly, who played both the outfield and first base. In addition, the Dodgers had acquired Bob Bailey, the old Pirate bonus boy who'd dislodged Don Hoak from third base in 1963. Bailey hadn't lived up to his immense hype, but he was a solid right-handed batter who, unlike Stuart, could play several positions.

The Dodgers faced a most unusual situation in the spring of 1967—a defending league champion embarking on a rebuilding program. The main reason the Dodgers were rebuilding was that Sandy Koufax had yielded to the pain in his aching left elbow and retired at the age of 30, taking his 27 wins with him. Further, Walter O'Malley, furious when Maury Wills left the team in Japan, traded Wills to the Pirates in the deal that brought Bailey to the Dodgers. Without the best pitcher in baseball and one of the top shortstops, the Dodgers were facing a difficult season in 1967. It would take a series of miracles to make them pennant contenders, and on a rebuilding team, there was no room for an aging pinch hitter who couldn't field.

Thus, when the Japanese came calling again, Stuart was ready to listen. He accepted what was reported as $30,000 to $35,000 per year to play for the Taiyo Whales of Japan's Central League for the next two seasons.[11] "It was a sudden decision," he said, "but I didn't have a contract this spring and I felt I would be foolish not to take the offer.... I can't stand being a nobody and going over there I might be a somebody again."[12] Stuart said he had asked Walter O'Malley for his opinion and the Dodger owner told him that if he was offered a two-year guaranteed contract, he should take it. "When the Japanese kept after me with this two-year contract," he said, "I just had to take it, as much as I regretted being forced to make the move. Believe me, I gave the matter plenty of thought."[13]

Stuart's farewell remarks were delivered in his typical flip fashion, and included one of his old standby stories, which he told on several occasions while changing the name of the batter. "[I] could tell I was slowing up the other day," he said when explaining why he was going to Japan, "when Eddie Mathews hit a smash which I caught. A couple of years ago, I could have got out of the way of it."[14]

Stuart departed with kind words for most of the people he'd been associated with in professional baseball, singling out Pirate GM Joe Brown and his old minor league manager Larry Shepard for special praise. When the interview was interrupted by his phone ringing, he quipped, "It's probably President Johnson." It wasn't, but perhaps it should have been, for the prospect of Dick Stuart in Japan might have foreign policy implications.

Baseball had been introduced to Japan by American teachers in the 1870s and by the early 20th century had become very popular in Japanese universities. Interest in the game was further abetted by a series of tours of American major leaguers, beginning in 1908. Former player and long-time manager Lefty O'Doul arranged several visits and was a major factor in bridging the gap between Americans and Japanese.[15]

Following a gala 1934 tour that included Babe Ruth, Lou Gehrig, and Connie Mack, a group of Japanese baseball men formed the Nippon Professional Baseball League, the country's first venture into professional baseball. The league was dormant during the latter stages of World War II, but revived after the war, encouraged by American occupation forces. At the time Stuart joined the Taiyo Whales, there were two six-team professional leagues, the Central League (which included the Whales) and the Pacific League.

Shortly after World War II, Wally Yonamine, a Hawaiian native, became the first American to play in Japan, and in 1953, pitcher Phil Paine, while serving in the U.S. military, pitched a few games and became the first former major leaguer to play in a Japanese professional league.

In 1962, former major league stars Don Newcombe and Larry Doby were signed by the Chunichi Dragons but both were well past their prime and lasted just a year. The first American star in Japan was a former minor league pitcher named Joe Stanka, whose major league career consisted of two appearances with the White Sox in 1959.

Stanka, huge by Japanese standards at six foot six and more than 200 pounds, joined the Nankai Hawks in 1960 at the age of 28. Over the next seven years, he won exactly 100 games, including 26 in 1964, when he became the first American to win the MVP award. Stanka was one of the highest paid players in Japan.[16]

The Japanese took their baseball seriously, a little more seriously than Dick Stuart was accustomed to taking *his* baseball. Also, as in most aspects of Japanese life, there was an emphasis on selflessness and team play. Tetsuharu Kawakami, manager of the Yomiuri Giants, said in the early '60s, "Lone wolves are the cancer of a team."[17] That didn't bode well for Stuart.

"The most cherished ability in a Japanese high school ball player," wrote Robert Fitts, "was not ability but spirit or heart."[18] It wasn't long after baseball became popular in Japan that young players were encouraged to adapt the samurai warrior spirit to the game. Practices were brutal endurance contests, with pitchers throwing hundreds of pitches per day and players working until they literally dropped.

The Yomiuri Giants were the best team in Japan, dominating the Japanese leagues like the Yankees ruled the American League for so many years. In their initial seasons, the Giants didn't do that well, and in 1936 the team was playing so poorly that their manager put them through nine grueling days of intense workouts, so demanding that many players came in after practice and vomited; the sessions became known as the "Vomit Practices." Perhaps scared into success, the Giants followed the Vomit Practices with a series of victories, which convinced the Japanese that the road to success was paved with vomit.[19]

Former Pirate pitcher Vernon Law was a pitching coach for the Seibu Lions in 1979 and 1980, and his son Vance played there in 1990. Vern was amazed by how hard Japanese players practiced, even before a game. "They'd work your tail off," Law said. "If [American players] did as much as they did before a ballgame, we'd have to sit down and rest, but they're not like that. They keep pushing and pushing. I'd get two carts of balls and they'd have two guys hitting—one to right field and one to left. They'd put one guy out there and keep him running back and forth until the guy is bent over and throwing up. Then they'd holler out, 'Do you want more?' and the guy will say, 'Yeah, I want more.' They're not going to give up."

Law was also appalled at how hard the club worked his pitchers. He played in an era where pitch counts were more a matter of curiosity than strategy and prided himself on pitching complete games, but he never saw anything in America like what he witnessed in Japan. "I saw a guy throw batting practice for 35 or 40 minutes," he recalled, "then see the same guy get up to throw two or three times in the bullpen, and finally in the seventh inning, he gets in the game and pitches three innings. The next night he's the starter.... You don't see many 32- or 34-year-old pitchers over there. You're done when you're 30. You've got nothing left."[20]

The career of Tadashi Suguira is a case in point. Sugiura was 38–4 for the Nankai Hawks in 1958, appearing in 69 games, including 35 starts, and threw 371 innings. The next year he was 31–11 in 59 games. Suguira had his last big season at the age of 28 and won only 23 games during the next six years. His arm was dead.

More ominously for lone wolf Dick Stuart, Law noted the Japanese insistence on conformity. "They expect you to fit in," Law said. "If you're a nail sticking up, they'll pound you down." Stuart never conformed in America, wasn't likely to start doing so in a foreign country and it remained to be seen whether the Japanese could pound him down like the protruding nail.

The phrase about the nail is taken from a Japanese saying. Robert Whiting, author of "You've Gotta Have Wa," wrote, "The U.S. is a land where the stubborn individualist is honored and where 'doing your own thing' is a motto of contemporary society. In Japan, kojinshigi, the term for individualism, is almost a dirty word. In place of 'doing your own thing,' the Japanese have a proverb. 'The nail that sticks up shall be hammered down.' It is practically a national slogan."[21]

Kent Hadley, a first baseman who was briefly with the Yankees and Athletics, played in Japan from 1962 to 1967 and was the first American voted to the All-Star team by the fans. Hadley had a degree in anthropology, was very interested in Japanese culture, and adapted well to life in a foreign country. He never spoke the language fluently but learned enough to function. "After the first year of acclimation," he said, "I loved it. I wasn't a Dick Stuart type—or a Joe Pepitone. I kept my mouth shut and did my job. My teammates liked me, unlike some other guys who were in Japan at the time. At that time, each team could have three Americans, and two of the three were usually jerks who mouthed off, saying things like, 'Who are these Chinks?' and 'All I want is the money, just pay me.'"[22]

Although Stuart's ego would be out of place, his placid temperament would fit in well. In the 1960s, Japanese players and fans considered on-field outbursts of temper shocking and offensive. Prior to Stuart's arrival, Americans like Stanka, Ken Aspromonte, and Norm Larker argued with umpires, smashed batting helmets, and acted as immaturely as most players did in the U.S., which the Japanese considered appalling.

Stanka, the first American to star in Japan, spoke no Japanese and came from a rural Midwestern background. He had never been to a foreign country before and when he first arrived, he was frequently criticized for his displays of temper. The Japanese nicknamed him "Big Thunder" and his 1961 contract contained a provision requiring him to practice better behavior on the playing field.

Stanka eventually adapted to Japanese norms, but many Americans did not and antagonized the Japanese with their tantrums. At least Stuart, who was generally criticized for not showing enough emotion, wasn't likely to smash any helmets or attack any water coolers.

Another obstacle facing Americans playing in Japan was loneliness. None spoke the language when they arrived and almost none had ever been to the country. They left their entire social network behind except for perhaps their immediate family. Stuart, with his recent divorce, went to Japan alone. The only other American on the Taiyo roster, Francis Agcaoili, was a Hawaiian who never played professional baseball in the U.S. He was a veteran of the Japanese leagues, having played there since 1962.

Stuart, although he liked kidding around with his teammates in the clubhouse, was never one to socialize with them off the field. He preferred to go his own way, and although that would be more difficult for him in a foreign country, he wouldn't miss the camaraderie as much as other Americans.

Fortunately for Stuart, he hadn't signed until April, and therefore missed Taiyo's grueling training sessions, which in Japan usually began in January and, unlike the leisurely pace of the American training camps, consisted of daily eight-hour sessions. By the time he arrived, the season had already begun.

Stuart wasn't in Japan long before he learned about the protruding nail. In one game shortly after he arrived, Stuart made three outs with men on base in his first three at bats and was summarily yanked from the game. No player was more important than the team, and no one's ego, even one as large as Stuart's, was inviolate. He said the manager took him out every time he hit two home runs in a game so he wouldn't hit three. "I used to call him a few choice names in English," Stuart related, "and the guy would just grin and bow. I'd bow back and go to the clubhouse."[23]

There were ways of teaching Americans their place. Umpires often made questionable calls against them. Some players were thrown at, particularly if they were threatening to break a record held by a Japanese player or competing with a native player for a batting or home run title. Even if they weren't made human targets, they found themselves discriminated against in other ways.

"They had a different strike zone for foreigners and the Japanese players," said former major leaguer John Miller.[24] "It was comical," said George Altman, an American who starred in Japan for several years. "They would not allow foreigners to win any batting titles or anything like that. It was sort of us against them, no matter what team you were on. The guy I was battling for the batting title [Michivo Arito] was on our club and he was batting right in front of me. We were one or two games out of first place and it was a tight pennant race. Arito hit a lot of balls to right field, so they moved the second baseman over to the shortstop side and pitched him low and away. He hit four ground balls to second base and went four for four. He was a big lumbering guy who couldn't run, but every time he got to first he took off for second and they threw him out. That's the kind of game they were playing in the middle of a pennant race. It was more important to them to keep the foreigners from winning any titles."[25] When Darryl Spencer was fighting for the home run title one year, he was walked 12 times in a row while his Japanese competitor overtook him.

Changing continents didn't seem to take any of the wind out of Stuart's sails. As always, he made pre-season predictions, and when Stu looked into his crystal ball, he saw a batting average between .270 and .300 and a league-leading 40 home runs. Leading the Central League in homers would be difficult, first because Stuart had already missed a few games and, second, because the 1966 league leader had been the legendary Sadaharu Oh with 48. Two years earlier, Oh hit a record 55 home runs. Stu might hit his 40 and still not lead the league.

Stuart made a dramatic debut, hitting a home run in his first at bat to lead the Whales to a 5–0 win. His second and third homers followed in rapid succession and it appeared that perhaps he could make good on his predictions.

Stuart had nine homers by early June, but then went into a slump and didn't hit another for 18 days. He was getting nothing from Japanese pitchers but outside breaking pitches, which he wasn't able to drive or get into the air. Stuart finally broke his drought with two homers on June 29, but he was not doing as much for the Whales as they had hoped. They anticipating that signing Stuart would help them unseat the powerful Giants, but in late June they were lodged in fifth place in the six-team league with a 21–33–3 record.

Publicity had always been important to Stuart, and it was more difficult to get noticed in America when he was half a world away. Therefore, he wrote to former teammates like Jim Campanis and sent letters to baseball writers who'd covered him in the States to make certain they wouldn't forget about him. "Since I hit a 500-footer," he wrote, "they call me Moby Dick,[26] the great white whale. Each pitcher has at least four different pitches over here, all for strikes. Nobody has the overpowering fast ball, but they have the best 3-2 sliders I've seen anywhere."[27]

Stuart's former Pirate teammate Jim Marshall played for the Chunichi Dragons from 1963 to 1965. "The [Japanese] pitchers were more breaking ball pitchers," he said. "They had good location but they weren't overpowering. Japanese are different in their approach to pitching. They like to pitch from behind in the count."[28] Stuart had always been a good breaking ball hitter, and he saw a lot of them in Japan.

When he was laid up with a leg injury, Stuart dispatched a letter to Les Biederman, informing the Pirate beat writer that Japan was a beautiful country and he was enjoying his time there. He was staying at the pleasant Hotel New Otani and while Tokyo was expensive, Stuart said it was a wonderful city and he loved exploring it. Moreover, Japanese fans didn't boo. Stu also liked the fact that almost all games were at night, leaving his days free, and he spent a lot of his free time shopping for clothes. "They sell clothing here," he wrote, "for about half what they charge in the United States and I'm stocking up. I've bought so many suits I don't know how I'll get them home."[29]

After Stuart had been in Japan about three and a half months, sportswriter Kent

Nixon of the *Pacific Stars and Stripes* sat down with the big slugger to get his impressions of life in Japan. The article was titled, "If You're Dick Stuart, Things Happen for You."[30] Stuart began by telling Nixon that he had a hard time getting motivated against Japanese pitchers. In America, he said, he got pumped up when he knew he would be facing Bob Gibson or Sandy Koufax, but in Japan, he didn't know one pitcher from another.

At the time he spoke with Nixon, Stuart was batting .272 with 13 home runs, which was somewhat below expectations, and while he admitted he might not reach his goal of 40 homers, he predicted a strong finish. "You know why I'm confident?" he told Nixon. "I know myself. I've always been a better hitter over the second half of the season." He pointed out that he'd missed some time with his leg injury and was just getting to know the pitchers.

Stuart also told Nixon he was no longer the braggart he'd been early in his career. "I'm 34 now," he said. "I've mellowed." Over the years, Stuart had told many reporters he'd become less brash and more modest. And often, as he did with Nixon, he followed the comment with a boast. "I just don't know if the Japanese appreciate what it is to hit a tape measure home run. There's a place in the Kawasaki park (where the Whales played their home games) where no one has ever hit the ball out of the park. Superman couldn't do it. But you know, I almost had one out of there. I didn't miss by much."

Nixon described the drama of a Stuart at bat, which he hadn't misplaced while crossing the ocean. "He strides to the plate like Gary Cooper going down the street alone in 'High Noon,'" Nixon wrote. "Passing in back of the batters' box, he pivots and casually flips the leaden warmup bat away. He smoothes the rear area of the box with his right foot, with which he digs in first, and leans to the side to spit languidly. Then he digs in the left foot, with his left hand adjusts his batting helmet, then pumps his bat once, twice, once more and he's ready."[31]

Stuart's old buddy Milton Richman didn't forget him, and called to see how he liked Japan. Stu told Richman he knew he'd never play in the major leagues again, but proudly informed him that he'd made only one error in his last 50 games. "When I first came over here, I made seven or eight errors in the first couple games because I wasn't used to these infields," he said. "They use soft dirt on them.[32] Anyway, the manager and me had a little meeting. His name is Miahara. That's his last name. I can't even pronounce his first one."

Stuart told another story that had the scent of a Stuart tall tale. He said that during a game at Hiroshima, a rival player had a crowd gathered around him and was drawing something on a piece of paper. Stuart asked what he was doing and was told that the player was drawing a sketch of the parts of the city that had been destroyed by the atomic bomb. Stuart said he began drawing circles in the dirt with his bat. When an English-speaking player asked what he was drawing, he said, "Pearl Harbor."[33]

During his first year in Japan, Stuart put his broadcasting experience to good use. When ABC decided to cover one of the Japanese All Star games at Tokyo's Maiji Jingu Stadium, Stuart provided the color commentary for legendary broadcaster Red Barber's play-by-play. That was not Barber's first Japanese rodeo. He'd broadcast two games during the Dodgers' 1966 tour for *ABC's Wide World of Sports*.

As he had predicted, Stuart picked up his pace during the second half of the season. On August 13 he hit two homers, his 18th and 19th, but then went a couple of weeks before hitting #20. Number 21 came the very next day, and for the rest of the season Stuart hit homers like he did in September 1961. During a game in early October he touched up the Sankei Atoms for his 28th, 29th, and 30th and drove in seven runs. For the season, he fell short of 40 home runs, but not by much, finishing the season with 33 in just 110 games. His final batting average (.280) was just about what he forecast.

At the end of the season, Stuart returned to the United States and late that winter made a surprise appearance at the annual dinner of the Boston chapter of the Baseball Writers' Association. The Red Sox had won the pennant the previous season, and while the audience hailed the architects of the Impossible Dream, one of the biggest cheers of the evening was for Dick Stuart, who hadn't played in Boston since 1964. "I finally found a manager I can get along with," he told the crowd. "My manager in Japan can't speak English and I can't speak Japanese. We get along fine."[34] That brought down the house.

Stuart returned to the Whales for the 1968 season, which saw several more Americans playing in Japan. Each Japanese team was allowed two foreign players, and nearly all the foreigners were Americans.

Two new arrivals, outfielders George Altman and Willie Kirkland, had been, like Stuart, prominent major league power hitters in their prime.

An increasing number of Americans playing in Japan were African-Americans. Black teams had undertaken a number of Japanese tours, including visits by the Philadelphia Royal Giants in the late '20s and early '30s. Japanese baseball historian Kazuo Sayama believes that the Royal Giants helped bring professional baseball to Japan. Many of the white American players who went on tour held the typical American condescending opinion of the Japanese and were not always respectful. It would be difficult for any African-American player to acquire a feeling of racial superiority while playing in the segregated United States, and they were more respectful to their hosts.[35] The Japanese liked the black players and enjoyed their visits, for if their teams were going to lose almost every game, it was more palatable to be thrashed by a group of nice guys.

One Japanese player said, "At heart, perhaps we have prejudice too, but there is something irritating to us about white pride. But there is also something almost cute about the Negro players. They try to learn a little Japanese; they are more informal; perhaps they can't communicate so well with whites, so they try in Japan."[36]

In the 1940s, the Washington Senators signed a number of Latin players, not in a quest for diversity but because they could be obtained cheaply. The same attitude prevailed in Japan, where the owners thought that black players could be signed for less money than whites, and that older blacks were in better shape than older whites. Perhaps they had heard about Satchel Paige.

Whatever the reasons they were signed, the blacks that came to Japan in 1968 provided a good return on investment. Altman, although he was 35 when he got there, stayed eight years and hit 205 home runs, with a season high of 39. Kirkland, 34, hit 37 homers his first year and stayed for six seasons. Another African-American, Dave Roberts, hit 40 homers his first season (the most ever by an American) and hit 183 in seven seasons. Further, the newcomers made an effort to fit in with the Japanese system and were respected by their teammates.

While many Americans complained about the grueling workouts, Altman found they helped him. A heavily-muscled man, he had been plagued by injuries in the States, but the stretching and flexibility exercises the Japanese teams did before the games kept him loose, and he rarely missed a game.

Stuart had a strong spring in 1968 batting, per his account, over .400 with six home runs in 15 exhibition games. He said he'd done more running in Japan than he'd ever done in the States and was in good shape. On opening day, he rapped three singles, earning a headline in *Pacific Stars and Stripes* that read, "Is Dick Learning to Hit? At 35?" "I haven't played in a week," he said. "I just wanted to meet the ball."[37]

Stuart's 1968 season was not as good as the previous year. In 83 games, he had a sorry .217 average with just 16 home runs. There was also a lot of dissatisfaction with his frequent defensive lapses. Much later, when a group of Japanese players came to the United States, Danny Murtaugh asked them if they remembered Stuart. One of them stooped down in a fielding position and then looked back toward right field, as if the ball had gone through his legs. "Oh, yes," he said with a laugh.[38]

Stu found himself on the bench more often than he liked and rarely played during his final month. He blamed his benching on the team's new manager, who he said was a World War II pilot that hated Americans.

Late in the summer, Stuart played host to 14 Boy Scouts from the U.S. Naval Air Station in Atsugi. The boys were the children of Americans from the base and their assistant scoutmaster was Yeoman Second Class Jude Pohl, who was a Pittsburgh boy. Pohl got in touch with Stuart, who got the youngsters into Kawasaki Stadium, which was not far from the base, to watch his Whales play the Chunichi Dragons. After the game, he gave each boy an autographed baseball. They were excited and Big Stu was probably just as excited to play hero to some Americans.

At the end of September, Kent Nixon caught up with Stuart at his hotel as he was packing to return to the United States. The season wasn't over but Stuart had had enough of Japan. "Bewildered Dick Stuart," Nixon began, "clad only in a towel, looked like a beachboy who'd forgotten where a luau was."[39] Stu said he thought he could probably play baseball for another two or three years—in the U.S. "In Japan?" he said. "I don't think I could play here one more minute." The honeymoon was over and so was Stuart's career as a Taiyo Whale. Although he was leaving early, Stuart was allowed to save face by saying he had "illness in the family." Since he was divorced, it was a transparent ruse, but no matter.

Given Stuart's free-wheeling personality and his lack of intellectual curiosity, it was difficult to imagine him fitting into the regimented Japanese system, and he had not. After he returned to the States, Stuart told a reporter, "The people were extremely nice and courteous. But to live alone in a foreign country for nine months a year requires an adjustment that I just couldn't make … the conditions in the league are like one of our minor leagues."[40]

Stuart told Nixon he wasn't sure what the future held for him. He was unemployed and divorced, saddled with alimony and child support payments and nothing to fall back on outside of baseball. For years, the prospect of playing in Japan had been his ace in the hole, and now that was gone. He'd contacted the Detroit Tigers, who were en route to the American League pennant, to see if they needed a pinch hitter for the stretch run. They didn't. Stu said he didn't want to play in the minors and thought he might be interested in television if the money was right.

Then a bellboy appeared to gather Stuart's bags, and it was time to leave. Nixon asked him where he was going. "To get a final fitting on a suit," Stu replied. "It's always nice," Nixon concluded, "to look your best when job hunting."[41]

17

The Old Dick Stuart Is Just That, a Thing of the Past: 1969

Stuart returned to the United States to look for a job at the same time the California Angels were looking for a first baseman. In the nine years the Angels had been in the American League, they had never had an established starter at first. They began their first season with two old competitors of Stuart, Ted Kluszewski and Steve Bilko, but both were at the end of their careers. Lee Thomas, Joe Adcock, Vic Power, and Don Mincher were all good major league players, but none lasted very long as an Angel. Mincher was the only one to play as many as 110 games in a season.

Bill Rigney was the Angels first and only manager, hired for the difficult task of building the team from scratch in 1961. The early expansion drafts were designed to ensure that the existing clubs wouldn't lose much talent, and the new teams were expected to struggle for their first several years. But in their second season, the Angels were the surprise of baseball, leaping from eighth place to third with 86 wins and astonishing everyone by leading the league in early July.

After the excitement of 1962, the third Angel season was a major disappointment. They dropped to ninth place with the same record they'd posted in 1961. There were good times and bad times during the next few seasons, and in 1968 the Angels finished a disappointing eighth, losing 95 games. Mincher played the most games at first (113) but he had been lost to the Seattle Pilots in the expansion draft. That left veteran utility men Chuck Hinton and Bob Chance, along with promising 21-year-old left-handed hitting Jim Spencer. Spencer hit 28 home runs at AA El Paso in 1968 and was a slick fielder, but he was an unproven commodity with just 19 games of big league experience.

Dick Walsh, who'd known Stuart when both were with the Dodgers, had just been named general manager of the Angels. After Stuart left Japan, he contacted Walsh and was invited to spring training with no guarantees. Rigney wasn't sure what to do about first base and wanted options. "I just have doubts," he said as spring training began, "that we can ask Stuart or Hinton or Chance to play 162 games. Maybe we can find the right combination. We've had some luck that way before."[1]

Stuart reported to the Angels' training camp in Palm Springs in late February, hoping to squeeze one more season out of his once powerful bat. "I'm happy to be back where the players speak English," he said.[2] One might think that fighting for a job and trying to hang on in the big leagues would have caused Stuart to take things a bit more seriously than he had in the past, but at least on the surface he was the same old Stu, making jokes about going four games in a row in Japan without an error and laughing when shortstop Jim Fregosi teased him about his hands of steel. He said that while some players aimed for 3,000 hits, he was shooting for 3,000 errors.

Two years in Japan had also not diminished his knack for the colorful quote; in fact, two years out of the American limelight probably made him more eager than ever to court the press. Stu told Los Angeles writer Ross Newhan that when he played first it was "Tinker to Evers to take a Chance."[3] Then he told him how he won the Triple Crown in Japan by leading the league in strikeouts, errors, and quotes.[4]

When the end is near, people tend to reminisce about better days, and it wasn't long before Stuart returned to his favorite topic, his 66 home runs in Lincoln. "Looking back," he told Newhan, "it has been only the last few years that I've realized the significance of those 66 home runs [as if they had ever been out of his mind, even for a minute]. I was the youngest player to hit more than 60 and I'm one of the few to go on and have a good career. It was the start of all the publicity and it was the big year for me."[5]

The Stuart of 1969, however, was not the confident young slugger fresh off a big season in Lincoln. This Dick Stuart was more like the one who'd joined the Dodgers for the 1966 stretch run. He was willing to start, platoon, pinch hit, or do just about anything Rigney wanted him to do. A UPI dispatch was headlined, "Dick Stuart Bombast Gone; He Just Wants to Belong." "Time was," the article stated, "when if he couldn't have his way on a team, he didn't play. Those were the salad days when his big bat matched his personality, but those days are gone. Now it's twilight time and the urge for just one more chance is overwhelming." "I have no illusions," Stuart said, "and the old Dick Stuart is just that, a thing of the past."[6]

One of Stuart's best hits of the spring was a batting practice line drive that felled teammate Bill Voss, who took a solid shot to the head and dropped like a rock. Trainer Freddie Frederico raced to the outfield to render assistance and the youngster was soon back on his feet, having escaped serious injury. "Lucky thing it was you who hit him," needled Fregosi, hinting that Stuart couldn't hit a ball hard enough to hurt anyone.[7]

The staid world of baseball had been shaken by the lack of offense in 1968 and during the off-season decided to do what baseball rarely did, experiment with the rules. They lowered the mound, maybe juiced up the ball, and in the spring they allowed teams to use what was called the "designated pinch hitter," or the "wild card pinch hitter," which became known as the designated hitter when it was adopted by the American League for the 1973 season.

By the time the DH was adopted for regular season play, it was too late to save Dick Stuart's career, but in the spring of '69, it helped him earn a spot on the Angels' roster. On March 10, he served as the designated pinch hitter and had a great day. "I like the new rule," he said. "I hope it's adopted."[8] He kept reminding everyone, however, how much his fielding had improved during his time in Japan and how much he was concentrating on defense. Once the season started, there would be no designated pinch hitters, only pinch hitters, and Stu preferred not to be one of them.

Stuart had a reputation as a bad spring hitter, but in 1969, when he needed it, he came through. It was the first time since his rookie year he'd had to make a club in spring training and he said he was approaching every at bat as if it was the World Series. This was not like prior springs when he could assure everyone he would hit once summer rolled around. If he didn't hit in the spring, he'd be spending the summer at home.

Stuart hit the first pitch he saw in the first intrasquad game for a home run. In his first exhibition game, against the new San Diego Padres, Stu had a single, a double, and two walks in four trips to the plate. On the 22nd of March, Stuart homered, doubled, and singled against the Giants, driving in three runs. On April 1 he had a pinch hit, grand slam home run off Jack Aker of the Pilots and excitedly pumped his fist in the air while rounding the bases. The next day he started at first and hit another homer. For the spring, Stu had 14 hits in 43 times at bat, for a .323 average, and led the Angels with four homers and 14 RBI.

Despite his strong performance, the Angels hadn't signed him. "If they don't make a decision soon," Stuart moaned, "I may need a heart transplant."[9] Finally, the day before the season began, he was signed to a $35,000 contract and given an opening night start against the Pilots, who were playing their first major league game. The fact that Stuart started against Pilot right hander Marty Pattin was a bit of a surprise, and perhaps Rigney considered him more than just a platoon player. When he took the field, he became the first former big leaguer to play in Japan and then return and appear in a major league game.

Opening night was not a good one for Dick Stuart. During the loss to the Pilots, he struck out three times and made a bad error at first base.[10] Outfielder Roger Repoz played first the next night and Stuart didn't start another game for six days, although he did make a couple of unsuccessful pinch-hitting appearances.

On the 14th of April, against lefty Tommy John of the White Sox, Stuart got his second start and drove a ball over the right center field fence at Anaheim Stadium, his first major league home run in three years. Even more remarkably, Stuart sparkled in the field, making three good defensive plays. "They may call me Dr. Strangeglove," he said after the game, "but you can't play first base any better than I did."[11] Then he struck a hopeful note. "Back in '63," he said, "I was 0 for 7 at the beginning of the season [he had been 0 for 7 before hitting his first 1969 homer] and then I got my first hit, also a homer. I hit 42 homers that year. I'm a part-time player now and I'll settle for half that many."[12]

But it was not 1963. Stuart was six years older and had trouble getting around on a good major league fastball. Near the end of April, when he was batting .087, he managed a joke. "For the first time in my career," he said, "my fielding average is higher than my batting average."[13] But when his average remained below .200, he stopped joking about his fielding and began to talk about how he had improved and now considered himself competent.

One night in late May, Stuart was on the bench watching the Angels play the Red Sox. With the score tied 2–2, Rigney asked him how he'd fared against Boston pitcher Lee Stange. "Pretty good," Stu replied. "I've had some home runs off him." He had indeed, four in just 25 at bats. Rigney therefore sent him up to pinch hit for pitcher Andy Messersmith. Stuart reached for an outside slider and tapped a soft one-hopper back to the mound. "I forgot to tell you, Rig," he said when he returned to the bench, "that was quite a while ago."[14] That quote summarized Stuart's situation, for he was not the hitter he'd been quite a while ago.

On May 23, Stuart started for the last time, striking out four times in four at bats against Tiger lefty Mickey Lolich. Stuart wasn't the only one Lolich struck out that night; he had 16 in all, a single game record for a Tiger pitcher. He fanned Stuart in the ninth to set the record. Stu had always been prone to the strikeout, and with the Angels he had 21 in 51 at bats.

Stuart was still cracking jokes, and they were more self-deprecating than ever, for there was a lot to deprecate. When the Angels returned after a poor road trip and went through the mail that had accumulated during their absence, Stuart said, "I'm afraid to start looking at mine." Then he asked Jim Fregosi, "What time do the regulars hit tonight? I'd like to watch. It might build up my confidence."[15]

On the 27th, Stuart made the final appearance of his major league career, striking out as a pinch hitter against fire-balling Sam McDowell. That made it six strikeouts in a row and marked the end of the line. The Angels released him on June 3. He'd played in 22 games, 13 at first base and 9 as a pinch hitter, with only eight hits in 51 at bats, and just the one home run against the White Sox. On the plus side, he didn't come close to leading the league in errors, making just one in 107 chances. His .991 percentage was his best ever; just as Stuart was learning to catch the ball, his career ended.

If the Angels had been playing better, they might have stayed with Stuart a bit longer. But the 1969 team got off to a horrible start; they had a 16–30 record and were deep in the basement of the American League's Western Division when Stuart was cut adrift. The poor start got Rigney fired and he was replaced by former Dodger pitching coach Lefty Phillips. Phillips was on the Dodger staff the year Stuart played in Los Angeles, but apparently he was not a big fan, for it was only about a week after he assumed command that Stuart was released.

Stuart said he understood why the Angels let him go, but added, "I still believe I can hit. I had a fine spring and then I lost it during the last week when they let Jim Spencer play his way to Hawaii."[16] He said he'd talked to another major league team and thought they might be interested. He may have been speaking of the Pirates, managed by his old friend Larry Shepard. Stuart was still popular in Pittsburgh, but the Pirates had a phalanx of young sluggers and didn't need an old one.

No major league team offered Stuart a contract, so he signed with Phoenix of the Pacific Coast League, the AAA affiliate of the San Francisco Giants. The last time Stuart played in the PCL was 1958, when he was a cocky youngster expecting to become a major league star. Now he was on the way down, hoping that a major league club would pick him up for the September stretch run and give him a chance at part of a World Series share.

Stuart wasn't the only veteran on the Phoenix roster. Thirty-three-year-old Jesse Gonder, who spent eight years in the major leagues, was the Dick Stuart of catching, a man who frightened his managers when he put on the chest protector and shin guards. In 1964 he played in a career high of just 94 games behind the plate but managed to lead the league in passed balls. One of the Phoenix outfielders was 35-year-old Leon Wagner, one of baseball's great characters, known for his awesome power, quick wit, and unenthusiastic fielding. He and Stuart had been up-and-coming young power hitters in the PCL of 1957; now they were aging veterans hoping for one last chance. There was no designated hitter in the PCL that year, and putting Gonder, Stuart, and Wagner on the field at the same time required a great deal of courage on the part of manager Charley Fox.

Wagner was a lot like Stuart. He'd hit 211 homers over 12 major league seasons and, like Stuart, made no secret of his disdain for defense. "Left field is merely a place," one writer commented, "he may be reached between times at bat. He was supposed to have played so deep that he could only be reached by mail."[17] When a pitcher complained about his failure to handle a long fly ball, Wagner replied, "The ball's got no business out there 400 feet away, anyway."[18] Like Stuart, Wagner drove a big white Cadillac and didn't subscribe to the notion that baseball was a life or death proposition. "It's a game, not a religion," he said, "and if you can't have fun at it, what good is it?"[19]

One other thing Wagner and Stuart had in common was that they were both in the minor leagues, and Big Stu wasn't excited about it. "The minor leagues are really bad," he said. "I can't get 'up' for many games here before 2,000 people. I'm the type that plays better before 30,000."[20] Stuart didn't even have his old number 7; he was wearing a non-descript 31 on his back.

Stuart had been in Phoenix only a couple of weeks when he made three errors in a game against Tucson. Since he was the famous Dr. Strangeglove, *The Sporting News* spread the word across the country. There were a few highlights, such as a home run in his first game, the 450-foot grand slam homer he hit on June 30, and the two home runs he hit on July 16 against Eugene. The previous night, however, he'd struck out twice, made an error, and been pulled out of the game.

The grand slam was particularly satisfying, since Eugene had walked Wagner intentionally in order to pitch to Stuart, just like they had walked Yastrzemski in Boston. "I guess they figured I'm over the hill and I can't do any damage," he said afterward. "I considered it an insult."[21]

In 74 games with the Giants, Stuart batted .244, hit 12 home runs and drove in 44 runs. His home run total led a team that hit only 48 all season. On the negative side, Stuart made 22 errors in 72 games at first for a miserable .966 fielding mark.

Nineteen-sixty-nine was the first year of divisional play, which meant four pennant races. Stuart had nine years in the pension plan, wanted to be a ten-year man, and hoped that perhaps a contender would pick him up to pinch hit in the final month. Unfortunately, only the National League West race was close. The Giants were in the thick of the fight, but the veteran they called up for the stretch run was Leon Wagner, not Dick Stuart. There would be no dramatic swan song for Dr. Strangeglove, no World Series heroics to make up for his near-miss in 1960.

With the close of the 1969 season came the end of Dick Stuart's baseball career. He finished with a .264 batting average, 228 home runs and 743 RBI. His 169 errors gave him a career fielding percentage of .982, not very good for a first baseman. After 19 years as a baseball player, Stu would have to move on to his next career, and no one, including Stuart, knew what that might be. Fielding coach was out of the question, and his best hope was for a job in television or radio. That was a very competitive business and openings were rare. Big Stu hoped to land one of them.

18

A Nobody: 1970–2002

Dick Stuart spent his entire life trying to be *somebody*, a famous man who would be recognized and admired wherever he went. Whatever fame he acquired was based on his ability to hit a baseball and when he could no longer hit long home runs off major league pitchers, he became what he most feared becoming—a *nobody*.

Phoenix released Stuart in December 1969 and he became a free agent. He appeared to have no chance at a spot on a major league roster, but that didn't necessarily mean his baseball career was over. The Hawaii Islanders of the Pacific Coast League had a loose major league affiliation but the majority of their players were over-the-hill veterans whose familiar names would draw fans.

There were a lot of connections for Stuart in Hawaii. The team had been moved to the islands by Nick Morgan, the Salt Lake City owner at whose home Stuart had been married. The 1970 roster included a number of players with whom he'd previously been associated, including Dennis Bennett, 42-year-old Roy Face, and Leon Wagner. Plus, the climate in Hawaii was pretty appealing.

But Stuart wasn't interested in playing in the minor leagues. When he was on his way up in places like Lincoln and Hollywood, he'd been a famous minor leaguer, but after being a famous major leaguer, the life of a veteran Triple-A player had little appeal. By the end of the year, he was selling life insurance for John Hancock, joking that he hadn't dropped a policy yet.

Stuart had always been popular in Pittsburgh and went there in early 1970, hoping to use some of his contacts to help him find a job. His old friend Miles Span was running for the Pennsylvania State Senate and Stuart lent his presence to the campaign. Apparently, Span was unable to help Stuart find a job, for there is no indication that Stu found the public relations position he was looking for.

For most of his post-baseball career, Stuart worked for NFC Services, Ltd. a commercial collection agency in the New York/Connecticut market, trading on his diminishing fame to gain entrance to businesses and attempt to sell them his company's services. Gehr Brown, a financial executive for Cadbury-Schweppes, USA Corporation in Danbury, Connecticut, recalled Stuart calling on Cadbury.

"He pulled up in a big white convertible," Brown recalled, "either a Cadillac or a Lincoln (given Stuart's history of Cadillac ownership, it was probably the former). He took us out to lunch and the thing I remember most was that the name of our company was Cadbury-Schweppes and Dick just couldn't get a handle on that. He'd say, 'I'd really like to do business with Cad-a-berry.' We'd say, 'No, it's Cadbury,' and he'd say, 'I know, Cad-a-berry.'"

At lunch, Stuart mostly talked about baseball. "I don't think he knew a lot about the business," Brown said. "He was very proud of his baseball career and talked about his 66 home runs. He was very proud of the fact that he knew Mickey Mantle and intimated that they were good buddies. He gave me a couple of 8×10 photos of him and Mantle and signed his name and Mantle's name, as if we wouldn't know who Mantle was. Then I think he went out and played golf. I imagine he worked a few hours in the morning and then went to play golf."[1] The 8×10 photos were a staple. Stuart always carried them to distribute to customers rather than business cards.

In 1971, the *Boston Globe* noted that Stuart had suffered from some financial reverses, but did not go into detail; perhaps they had none. In 1972, someone said he was living in Fort Myers, Florida, but if so it was only for a brief period.

Occasionally Stuart would show up at a major league ballpark, always meticulously attired, with stylishly long hair and sunglasses. The closest big league city was New York and he often went to Shea Stadium when the Pirates were in town. They hadn't forgotten Stu in Pittsburgh. During the 1974 National League Championship Series, in which the Pirates lost to the Dodgers, a man in denim overalls paraded through the stands carrying a sign that read: "Bring Back Dick Stuart."[2]

Prior to the 1975 season, Stuart was a candidate for the broadcasting job he'd wanted since his playing days. Boston's Channel 38, which televised Red Sox games, was looking for a color commentator and Stuart, along with former Sox players Mike Andrews and Ken Harrelson, was a candidate. The station chose Harrelson, launching him on a long, controversial television career.

It was ironic that Harrelson rather than Stuart was able to carve out a prominent post-baseball career because Stuart was the original prototype for characters like Harrelson. Both were enamored of the home run, both led the American League in runs batted in while playing for the Red Sox and both were very popular and highly publicized in Boston. Both wore flashy clothing and were popular with women.

It was almost as if Harrelson had studied Stuart's career as a model for his own. When he was interviewed by Joe Garagiola on the *Today* show, Garagiola mentioned the great success of actor Dustin Hoffman in *The Graduate*. "He had a pretty good year last year," Garagiola noted. In a reply almost identical to Stuart's rejoinder to Jayne Mansfield in Hollywood in 1957, Harrelson said, "Yes, but he didn't hit 35 home runs and drive in 109 runs, did he?"[3]

Harrelson's line of braggadocio followed Stuart's example; his autobiography was one that Stuart would have written about himself.[4] Like Stuart, Harrelson was good at bowling and golf, eventually attempting to make a living at the latter sport. He succeeded Stuart as baseball's champion arm wrestler.

Harrelson was able to capitalize on his outrageous personality after he retired. With so many parallels, it would seem as though Stuart should have been able to achieve something similar, but he did not, spending his post-playing career in a mundane sales job trying to play on his fading name recognition.

Stuart had great aspirations, but his work ethic was always questionable. He didn't work on the baseball skills he wasn't good at. When he was employed by brokerage firms during the off-season, he spent most of his time taking clients out to play golf and never bothered to learn anything about the business.

Shortly after retiring, Stuart met a reporter in Florida who mentioned the name of Archie Litman. "I know Archie very well," Stuart said. "He owns a brewery in Pittsburgh. Get word to him that I need a job. Tell Archie I'll work for $500 a week." The reporter asked what he wanted to do. "Oh, I won't do anything," Stuart replied. "I just need the money."⁵ In every non-baseball job he held, Stuart merely wanted to capitalize on his celebrity without contributing anything else. Not caring was part of his image.

Harrelson acted as if he didn't care, but he apparently cared enough to do what it took to be successful. In 1968, when he had a season that was very reminiscent of Stuart's 1963 campaign, it was noted that despite their similarities, Harrelson was much more of a team player than Stuart had been. You wouldn't find Hawk Harrelson criticizing his own pitchers for giving up home runs. He also started a number of business ventures designed to capitalize on his fame, while Stuart merely appeared in ads for the Magic Cradle.

When he began his major league career, Stuart fancied that he could be one of the greatest sluggers of all time, a Hall of Famer. But when he first became eligible for the Hall in 1974, it wasn't even a possibility. As always, he turned the situation into a joke. "I won't get many votes," he said, "because I haven't announced my retirement."⁶

In 1981, when Stuart took part in a home run hitting contest in San Diego, Philadelphia columnist Bill Conlin reported that he was working as a securities analyst but that is unlikely, and more probable that Stuart told him that to make what he was actually doing sound more glamorous and important. It was just two years after Dick Young reported him as working for NFC, and that was what he appeared to be doing in 1981.

The only recorded instance of Stuart having any association with baseball after his retirement was when, at the request of his friend Moe Resner, he served as batting instructor for the 1981 Mount Vernon Generals of the Atlantic Collegiate Baseball League. Resner recalled that Stuart loved telling old stories and joking about himself, particularly his fielding. The old stories were all he had, for not much had happened in his life since 1969.

Most retired ballplayers drift away from their former teammates after they retire. They were brought together by baseball from a variety of backgrounds and baseball is usually the one common thread that held them together. Once they retire, the thread is gone and very few remain close. Stuart had always been an outsider in baseball locker rooms, for he was too concerned with promoting Dick Stuart to worry much about anyone else. He wasn't close to his teammates when they played and he didn't keep in touch as they got older.

Stuart did go to Old Timers' Games, playing the part of Dr. Strangeglove to perfection. He took part in a Mets ceremony in 1974, but he was remembered most fondly in Pittsburgh and it was to that city he returned most frequently. He went to a Pirates' Old Timers celebration in August 1980 and played in the brief game. In the first inning there was a pop-up between first and second. "Get it, Maz," Stuart yelled loud enough for everyone to hear, and they all laughed when Mazeroski ran over and caught the ball.

Ten years later he returned to Three Rivers Stadium for another Old Timers affair and entertained the crowd by booting the first ball hit to him (probably intentionally) and then driving in the winning run with a long drive off the left field wall. That was the Stuart Pirate fans remembered and they loved it.

Between his two appearances in Pittsburgh there was an unsavory event. In 1985, when the Pirates marked the 25th anniversary of the 1960 World Series champions, Stuart did not appear. He announced that he would not be coming because the Pirates had refused his request for a first-class ticket from San Francisco to Pittsburgh. Stuart told reporters that, because of his size, he needed the room afforded by a first-class accommodation. Kathy Saba, the Pirates' director of promotions, told a different story. She said no other players were flying first class and that Stuart told her he wanted to get a first-class ticket, cash it in, buy a coach ticket and pocket the difference. When she wouldn't agree, he refused to come.

Stuart always focused on the amount of money he made, and had he played a generation later and been able to take advantage of free agency, he would have made a lot more. "Right now," he said in 1976, "I would have been one of those $4.5 million, five-year, no-cut ballplayers, too. But I'm not interested in that. Baseball was good to me."[7] in 1985, player agent Tom Reich was more conservative. When asked to estimate the salaries of the 1960 Pirates under current conditions, he put Stuart's at $750,000.[8]

The surge of the memorabilia market gave the autographs of former players more value than they'd ever had during their playing days. Many players from Stuart's era were able to earn more appearing at autograph shows than they had during their playing careers. For several years, Stuart refused to work the card circuit, but around 1990 he changed his mind. He appeared at the 30th reunion of the 1960 World Series champions and signed autographs for four dollars each at a huge card show and appeared at several other shows over the next few years. But Stuart had a short attention span and sitting at a table for several hours was not for him. A newspaper reporter recalled seeing him at a show and noticed that he appeared bored. After a while, he excused himself to go out for a smoke and never returned.

He pulled a similar disappearing act at the Boston Baseball Writers Dinner in 1981. When master of ceremonies Ken Harrelson introduced Stuart, no one stood up, and when Harrelson looked over, he saw that Stuart's seat was empty. "His Red Sox pitchers used to wonder where Dick was, too," Harrelson ad-libbed, and it was reported later that Dick had back trouble and had to return to his room for treatment. Perhaps the treatment, as before, was a cigarette.

Stuart's life after baseball is difficult to trace because he made it so. The man who'd wanted everyone to know *who* he was now wanted no one to know *where* he was. He cultivated a mysterious image and was very secretive about his whereabouts, claiming that his ex-wives were chasing him for money. He and Lois had separated sometime around the end of 1966 and divorced in 1967, but that was not the end of their relationship.

"He told me," said former teammate Bob Oldis, "that he was walking down the beach in Florida one day and he saw a pretty woman lying there getting some sun. He walked over and tapped her on the shoulder and when she turned around he saw it was his ex-wife. He wound up marrying her again."[9] The story may have been true or it might just have been another Dick Stuart fabrication. In any event, they married again, but that union didn't fare any better than the first one. He and Lois were divorced for the second time on June 30, 1971, with "cruelty" cited as the cause.

When retired players lose touch with their old teammates, they have their family to fall back on, but Stuart did not have that comfort. He never remarried, and it does not appear that he was close to any of his children. When they were young, he was focused on his career, and when his career was over, he was divorced and no longer part of the family. When his brother came to see him play in 1965, it was just the second time they'd seen each other in seven years. His brother never met either of Stuart's sons. "He knew and loved his niece Debbie," said Daryl's wife Laurel, "but never met or had any contact with Rick or Robbie. I don't believe Dick had a close relationship with his sons."[10] Lois had not appeared interested in getting to know Dick's family, and they spent their time almost exclusively with her family.

Stuart's oldest son, Dick, Jr., was a baseball star at Greenwich High School and had a brief professional career, playing for Johnson City, the Appalachian League affiliate of the St. Louis Cardinals, in 1981. He was an outfielder, the same position in which his father had begun his professional career, and like his father he didn't seem to be much of a fielder, posting a fielding average of .935 in his only professional season. In other ways, however, the son was different than the father. He threw left-handed, and more importantly, he did not have his father's size or power. The *Pittsburgh Post-Gazette,* describing young Dick's exploits at Greenwich High, said he was a strapping 6'2", but *Baseball Reference* listed him at just 5'10" and weighing only 180 pounds. At Johnson City, he played in 29 games and batted .209 with one home run and nine runs batted in.

In 1982, the *Pittsburgh Press* contacted Stuart for a "where are they now" story. He said he was in the finance business, which was a generous way of describing his position, for a company, which he would not identify, in Long Island. He said he lived near Hartford, Connecticut. "That's enough," he cautioned. The Pirates reached him in 1985 by leaving a message with a relative (probably his brother) in Seattle. When Stuart called the *Pittsburgh Press* shortly afterward, he wouldn't tell them what state he was calling from. "Somewhere in the United States," he said.[11] When the *Pittsburgh Post-Gazette* got in touch with him in 1998, he narrowed the possibilities by saying he lived in "California."[12] He was in Redwood City, where he'd gone to high school, living in an apartment on Woodside Road.

That year, John I. Bird published a biography of Bill Mazeroski that contained a number of lengthy interviews with Mazeroski's former Pirate teammates. Bird approached 23 people with requests for interviews and 22 agreed to speak with him. The only one who refused was Dick Stuart, perhaps still stinging from having Maz steal his glory in 1960.

"In 1998, as Mark McGwire and Sammy Sosa pursued Roger Maris's single season home run record, reporters looked up the man who had once hit 66 home runs in a season."[13] It was the first time in years that the press sought his opinion, so unlike the days in Lincoln when he was the biggest attraction in the minor leagues, and he was happy to receive the attention. "[*Life*] called me an irrepressible egotist," he told reporter Rick Shum. "That hasn't changed any."[14]

Stuart said that although he didn't follow baseball much anymore, he was well aware of the home run chase. "What I did in 1956," he said with unfamiliar modesty, "was small potatoes compared to McGwire and Sosa. Lincoln is a long way from St. Louis and Chicago. They've been outstanding.... I hit 75 homers in two years (with the Red Sox) which is what McGwire is going to get this year. And they traded me."[15] He also noted that McGwire and Sosa were much bigger and stronger than him and other players from his era (assisted, as we later learned, by chemicals). "I was Big Stu, but being 6–3, 6–4 is nothing these days."

The McGwire/Sosa interview was the last time the sporting public showed an interest in the former Pirate slugger. He was just another senior citizen going about his day-to-day routine. A receptionist in the office of a doctor Stuart visited in Redwood City recalled him as a very nice, pleasant man who would bring his old baseball cards to the ladies in the office and sign them.[16] Apparently Stuart had evolved from the brash egotist of 1957 to the likeable one of 2000.

Stuart's name was not totally absent from the newspapers. He was mentioned

Dick and his brother Daryl clowning around long after the end of Dick's playing career (left). The last photograph Stuart's family has of him, taken a year or two before his death in 2002. He's wearing the cap of the St. Louis Cardinals, although he never played for the Cardinals during his nine-year big league career (right). Courtesy Daryl and Laurel Stuart.

whenever someone wanted to compare a notoriously bad fielder to one who was just as bad or even worse. When Boston first baseman Danny Cater got hit in the eye with a popup, it was noted that not even Stuart had done that. Yankee Ron Blomberg, who fittingly became baseball's first designated hitter, also reminded writers of Stuart with his bumbling at first base.

The comparisons weren't limited to baseball. Football receivers who dropped passes were compared to Stuart. When basketball player John Brisker of the Pittsburgh Condors let a pass go through his legs, it was compared to Stuart's play at first base. Hockey goalies who whiffed on save attempts dredged up memories of his worst misplays.

Stuart's recalled ineptitude was so noteworthy that it even transcended the world of sports. In panning Neil Simon's movie "Last of the Red Hot Lovers," the *Pittsburgh Press* called Simon "the most famous strikeout artist since Dick Stuart."[17] An investment advisor opined, "A perfect market timer doesn't really have to do much else right; he or she could pick stocks like Dick Stuart played first base and still be a winner."[18]

Occasionally, Stuart was remembered for something good, such as the time when an important goal by Pittsburgh Penguin star Mario Lemieux was compared to Stuart's long home run off Glen Hobbie. In 1995, when Jose Canseco homered in five consecutive Boston games, it was pointed out that he tied the team record held by four others, including Stuart.

Some of the records Stuart established stood long after he retired. It wasn't until 2019

Dick and brother Daryl with their mother Phyllis. As Daryl's wife Laurel said, the two brothers were very different, in stature and every other way. Courtesy Daryl and Laurel Stuart.

that Josh Bell broke Stuart's record for home runs by a Pirate first baseman. In 1982, Willie Stargell, finishing up his legendary Pirate career, tied Stuart's record of three pinch hit home runs in a season. The lasting legacy of Dick Stuart, however, was not the mammoth home runs he hit, but his outsized personality, his atrocious fielding, and the way the fans treated him. When Pirate star Dave Parker was booed in Pittsburgh, it was compared to the abuse Stuart had taken from the same fans.

Like he did as a minor leaguer, Stuart sometimes made headlines for doing nothing. When Stargell was named the first baseman on an all-time Pirates team selected in 1987, the headline read, "No Room for Dick Stuart on This Team."[19] There was room, however, on Les Biederman's team. When the Pirates left Forbes Field in 1970, Biederman was asked to select his all-time favorite Pirate players by position. Biederman, who always had a fond place in his heart for the eccentric first baseman, named Stuart and Dale Long as the first basemen.

In 1975, the *Pittsburgh Post-Gazette* polled its readers and asked them to identify the Most Memorable Personality in Pittsburgh Pirate History. To no one's surprise, Roberto Clemente was the readers' top choice. Shockingly, Willie Stargell was no better than #7, behind Mazeroski (#2) and Harvey Haddix. Stuart was ninth, between Smoky Burgess and Roy Face.

After leaving NFC, Stuart moved back to northern California, where he'd grown up and was reported to be working there as a salesman in 1990, although he refused to say exactly where he lived. Roy Stuart passed away in June 1978 and Phyllis in July 1985. Both were cremated and their ashes were scattered in the Pacific Ocean. His daughter Debbie, from his first marriage, is also deceased, as is her mother Diane, who had remarried.

One of the ironies of Stuart's life is that he grew up in a highly-functional, loving family, which produced a brother who has been married to his high school sweetheart for 61 years, yet Dick was unable to maintain healthy relationships with either of his two wives or his children. His brother Daryl and his wife were closer to

Stuart manning the barbeque, reminiscent of the time, as part of a promotion, he assisted Big Boy Professor Frank Marvin during his days as a Pirate hero. Now he was just another senior citizen at a backyard picnic. Courtesy Daryl and Laurel Stuart.

Stuart relaxes with his ever-present cigar and a newspaper. In the late 1950s he liked reading articles about himself, but it's unlikely that the newspaper in Stuart's hand had any articles about him. Courtesy Daryl and Laurel Stuart.

18. A Nobody: 1970–2002

Stuart's daughter Debbie than he was. "He was very different from Daryl," said Daryl's wife Laurel, "physically and in every other way."[20]

Big Stu eventually ended up where he started, Redwood City, California. "He lived a quiet life," said Laurel Stuart, "and continued relationships with some old friends."[21] One local writer tried repeatedly to contact Stu in order to write about him, but Stuart ignored him. He lived in virtual anonymity until he passed away December 15, 2002, from cancer.

APPENDIX

Dick Stuart Home Run Log

Appendix. Dick Stuart Home Run Log

Home Run #	Date	Opponent	Location	Day/Night/DH	Pitcher	Inning	On Base	Comments
1	7/10/58	Chicago	Chicago	Day	Elston	9	1	
2	7/11/58	Chicago	Chicago	Day	Drabowsky	5	3	grand slam
3	7/15/58	Los Angeles	Los Angeles	Night	Drysdale	6	0	
4	7/20/58	San Francisco	San Francisco	Night	Giel	6	0	
5	7/24/58	Los Angeles	Pittsburgh	Day	Williams	4	1	
6	7/31/58	Chicago	Pittsburgh	Night	Solis	5	0	
7	8/16/58	Cincinnati	Cincinnati	Day	Lawrence	7	1	
8	8/17/58	Cincinnati	Cincinnati	Day/Game 2	Nuxhall	6	1	
9	8/17/58	Cincinnati	Cincinnati	Day/Game 2	Nuxhall	8	0	2nd of game
10	8/19/58	Chicago	Chicago	Day	Phillips	6	1	
11	8/20/58	Chicago	Chicago	Day	Hillman	4	1	
12	8/24/58	St. Louis	St. Louis	Day/Game 2	Brosnan	5	0	
13	8/27/58	St. Louis	St. Louis	Night	Chittum	1	0	
14	8/29/58	Milwaukee	Milwaukee	Day	Spahn	1	0	
15	9/10/58	San Francisco	Pittsburgh	Night	Grissom	10	1	two-out HR won game 6–4
16	9/20/58	Philadelphia	Philadelphia	Day	Roberts	6	0	
1	4/24/59	Philadelphia	Philadelphia	Night	Owens	1	1	
2	4/26/59	Philadelphia	Philadelphia	Day/Game 2	Short	3	1	
3	5/1/59	St. Louis	Pittsburgh	Night	Brosnan	9	1	
4	5/11/59	San Francisco	San Francisco	Night	Sanford	9	0	Pinch-hit Homer
5	5/13/59	Los Angeles	Los Angeles	Night	Drysdale	8	1	put Pirates ahead 5–4/won 6–4
6	5/14/59	Los Angeles	Los Angeles	Night	Labine	9	0	game winner
7	6/5/59	Chicago	Pittsburgh	Night	Hobbie	1	1	
8	6/8/59	San Francisco	Pittsburgh	Night	Worthington	8	1	

Appendix. Dick Stuart Home Run Log

9	6/9/59	San Francisco	Pittsburgh	Night		Antonelli	9	0	
10	6/11/59	San Francisco	Pittsburgh	Day		Worthington	2	0	
11	6/14/59	Los Angeles	Pittsburgh	Day/Game 2		Erskine	1	1	
12	6/14/59	Los Angeles	Pittsburgh	Day/Game 2		Fowler	5	0	2nd of game
13	6/18/59	Chicago	Chicago	Day		Drabowsky	7	1	
14	6/23/59	San Francisco	San Francisco	Night		Muffett	9	0	
15	6/24/59	San Francisco	San Francisco	Day		Antonelli	2	0	
16	6/26/59	Los Angeles	Los Angeles	Night		Podres	8	1	
17	7/10/59	Chicago	Pittsburgh	Night		Elston	11	2	Game winner/Pirates trailed 6–3 in 11th
18	7/18/59	San Francisco	Pittsburgh	Day		Fisher	1	2	
19	8/16/59	Milwaukee	Pittsburgh	Day		Pizarro	1	1	
20	8/25/59	San Francisco	Pittsburgh	Night		Antonelli	4	1	
21	8/30/59	Philadelphia	Pittsburgh	Day/Game 2		Farrell	9	0	
22	9/2/59	Cincinnati	Cincinnati	Night/Game 1		O'Toole	1	1	
23	9/5/59	Philadelphia	Philadelphia	Day		Cardwell	6	0	
24	9/11/59	Los Angeles	Los Angeles	Night/Game 1		Koufax	6	0	
25	9/13/59	Los Angeles	Los Angeles	Day		Podres	3	0	
26	9/26/59	Cincinnati	Cincinnati	Day		O'Toole	2	0	
27	9/27/59	Cincinnati	Cincinnati	Day		Hook	3	2	
1	5/13/60	Milwaukee	Milwaukee	Night		Willey	7	1	
2	5/15/60	Milwaukee	Milwaukee	Day/Game 1		Spahn	1	1	
3	6/5/60	Philadelphia	Philadelphia	Day/Game2		Owens	8	0	
4	6/8/60	Chicago	Chicago	Day		Anderson	5	1	
5	6/11/60	St. Louis	St. Louis	Day		Bridges	7	1	

Appendix. Dick Stuart Home Run Log

Home Run #	Date	Opponent	Location	Day/Night/DH	Pitcher	Inning	On Base	Comments
6	6/12/60	St. Louis	St. Louis	Day/Game 1	Kline	1	1	
7	6/12/60	St. Louis	St. Louis	Day/Game 1	Simmons	7	0	2nd HR of game
8	6/19/60	Los Angeles	Los Angeles	Day	Koufax	5	3	grand slam
9	6/30/60	San Francisco	Pittsburgh	Night/Game 2	McCormick	1	2	
10	6/30/60	San Francisco	Pittsburgh	Night/Game 2	Loes	3	0	2nd HR of game
11	6/30/60	San Francisco	Pittsburgh	Night/Game 2	Miller	5	0	3rd HR of game
12	7/4/60	Milwaukee	Milwaukee	Day/Game 1	McMahon	7	1	
13	7/16/60	Cincinnati	Pittsburgh	Day	Brosnan	9	0	game-winning walk off
14	8/18/60	Cincinnati	Cincinnati	Night	McLish	8	2	Pinch hit HR—winning runs
15	8/21/60	Cincinnati	Cincinnati	Day	Hook	6	0	
16	8/21/60	Cincinnati	Cincinnati	Day	Hook	8	0	2nd HR of game
17	8/24/60	Chicago	Chicago	Day	Elston	9	1	
18	9/5/60	Milwaukee	Pittsburgh	Day	Jay	4	2	
19	9/10/60	Chicago	Pittsburgh	Day	Anderson	2	0	
20	9/12/60	San Francisco	Pittsburgh	Night	Sanford	4	1	
21	9/18/60	Cincinnati	Cincinnati	Day	McLish	4	0	
22	9/24/60	Milwaukee	Milwaukee	Day	Burdette	9	0	
23	9/27/60	Cincinnati	Pittsburgh	Night	Purkey	1	2	
1	5/7/61	Los Angeles	Pittsburgh	Day	Koufax	7	0	
2	5/12/61	Cincinnati	Pittsburgh	Night	Bridges	5	2	
3	5/16/61	St. Louis	Pittsburgh	Night	Simmons	6	0	Game winning RBI
4	5/24/61	Chicago	Chicago	Day	Wright	8	0	
5	5/28/61	St. Louis	St. Louis	Day	Sadecki	3	1	
6	6/14/61	Cincinnati	Pittsburgh	Night	O'Toole	1	0	

Appendix. Dick Stuart Home Run Log

#	Date				Pitcher			Notes
7	6/17/61	St. Louis	Pittsburgh	Day	Broglio	2	2	
8	6/20/61	Philadelphia	Philadelphia	Night	Mahaffey	1	1	
9	6/25/61	Philadelphia	Pittsburgh	Day/Game 1	Ferrarese	1	1	
10	7/3/61	Cincinnati	Cincinnati	Night	Maloney	9	0	
11	7/15/61	San Francisco	San Francisco	Day	McCormick	4	0	
12	7/16/61	Los Angeles	Los Angeles	Day	Craig	5	0	
13	7/17/61	Los Angeles	Los Angeles	Night	Williams	1	1	
14	7/23/61	Milwaukee	Pittsburgh	Day/Game2	Willey	4	0	
15	7/28/61	Los Angeles	Pittsburgh	Night	Podres	7	1	
16	8/3/61	St. Louis	St. Louis	Night	Miller	5	3	grand slam
17	8/4/61	Cincinnati	Cincinnati	Night	Purkey	8	1	
18	8/14/61	Milwaukee	Milwaukee	Night	Buhl	2	0	
19	8/17/61	Chicago	Chicago	Day	Drott	1	1	
20	8/23/61	Milwaukee	Pittsburgh	Night	Burdette	6	0	
21	8/26/61	Chicago	Pittsburgh	Day	Ellsworth	6	1	
22	8/28/61	Chicago	Pittsburgh	Day	Drott	2	0	
23	9/2/61	St. Louis	St. Louis	Day	Broglio	1	2	
24	9/2/61	St. Louis	St. Louis	Day	Broglio	4	0	2 home runs
25	9/5/61	Chicago	Chicago	Day	Hobbie	1	1	
26	9/9/61	Milwaukee	Milwaukee	Day	Willey	6	0	
27	9/11/61	San Francisco	San Francisco	Day	Sanford	6	0	
28	9/12/61	San Francisco	San Francisco	Night	McCormick	1	1	
29	9/12/61	San Francisco	San Francisco	Night	McCormick	4	0	2 home runs
30	9/13/61	Los Angeles	Los Angeles	Night	Golden	8	1	
31	9/18/61	St. Louis	Pittsburgh	Night	McDaniel	7	1	

Appendix. Dick Stuart Home Run Log

Home Run #	Date	Opponent	Location	Day/Night/DH	Pitcher	Inning	On Base	Comments
32	9/26/61	Los Angeles	Pittsburgh	Night/Game 1	Williams	8	1	
33	9/28/61	San Francisco	Pittsburgh	Night	Duffalo	2	0	
34	9/30/61	Cincinnati	Pittsburgh	Day	Jay	3	1	
35	9/30/61	Cincinnati	Pittsburgh	Day	Hunt	5	1	
1	4/21/62	New York	Pittsburgh	Day	R.L. Miller	6	1	
2	4/29/62	Los Angeles	Los Angeles	Day/Game 2	Moeller	7	0	
3	5/16/62	Milwaukee	Pittsburgh	Night	Cloninger	5	0	
4	5/24/62	St. Louis	St. Louis	Night	Broglio	6	0	
5	5/30/62	St. Louis	Pittsburgh	Day	Washburn	1	1	
6	6/2/62	Houston	Pittsburgh	Day	Anderson	6	1	
7	6/7/62	Los Angeles	Pittsburgh	Night	Sherry	9	2	walk off win
8	6/11/62	Chicago	Chicago	Day	Cardwell	1	1	
9	6/11/62	Chicago	Chicago	Day	Cardwell	6	2	2 home runs/5 RBI
10	6/23/62	Chicago	Pittsburgh	Night	Cardwell	6	0	
11	7/2/62	Houston	Houston	Night	McMahon	9	0	
12	7/8/62	Philadelphia	Pittsburgh	Day/Game 1	Bennett	1	1	
13	7/12/62	Houston	Pittsburgh	Day	Golden	1	1	
14	7/19/62	New York	New York	Night	Jackson	3	1	
15	7/22/62	San Francisco	Pittsburgh	Day	Marichal	6	1	
16	8/25/62	St. Louis	St. Louis	Night	Simmons	8	0	
1	4/13/63	Washington	Washington	Day	Rudolph	2	0	
2	4/16/63	Baltimore	Boston	Day	Roberts	6	2	
3	4/28/63	Chicago	Boston	Day/Game 2	Fisher	1	1	
4	5/10/63	Washington	Boston	Night	Cheney	5	1	

Appendix. Dick Stuart Home Run Log

5	5/13/63	Washington	Boston	Night	Bronstad	4	0	
6	5/15/63	Los Angeles	Boston	Night/Game 1	Fowler	3	3	grand slam
7	5/15/63	Los Angeles	Boston	Night/Game 2	McBride	3	2	
8	5/21/63	Minnesota	Boston	Night	Perry	4	0	
9	5/30/63	New York	Boston	Day	Terry	2	1	
10	6/2/63	Chicago	Chicago	Day/Game 1	Herbert	2	1	
11	6/11/63	Detroit	Detroit	Day	Fox	15	0	
12	6/12/63	Washington	Boston	Night	Stenhouse	4	0	
13	6/13/63	Washington	Boston	Day	Duckworth	2	0	
14	6/14/63	Baltimore	Boston	Night	Pappas	2	0	
15	6/16/63	Baltimore	Boston	Day/Game 1	Hall	6	0	
16	6/18/63	Detroit	Boston	Night	Fox	8	0	
17	6/20/63	Detroit	Boston	Day	Bunning	4	0	
18	7/10/63	Minnesota	Minnesota	Night	Kaat	4	1	
19	7/10/63	Minnesota	Minnesota	Night	Dailey	10	2	Game-winner/2nd of game
20	7/24/63	Kansas City	Boston	Night	Wickersham	6	1	
21	7/26/63	Los Angeles	Boston	Night	Newman	6	1	
22	7/29/63	Minnesota	Boston	Night	Perry	1	2	
23	7/31/63	Minnesota	Boston	Day	Stange	4	1	
24	8/7/63	Detroit	Detroit	Day	Bunning	5	1	
25	8/9/63	Minnesota	Minnesota	Night	Perry	4	1	
26	8/10/63	Minnesota	Minnesota	Day	Stange	4	0	
27	8/10/63	Minnesota	Minnesota	Day	Stange	6	0	
28	8/11/63	Minnesota	Minnesota	Day	Pascual	6	1	
29	8/14/63	New York	Boston	Night	Bridges	8	1	

Appendix. Dick Stuart Home Run Log

Home Run #	Date	Opponent	Location	Day/Night/DH	Pitcher	Inning	On Base	Comments
30	8/15/63	New York	Boston	Day	Williams	9	0	
31	8/19/63	Cleveland	Boston	Night	Ramos	2	0	
32	8/19/63	Cleveland	Boston	Night	Ramos	9	0	2 home runs
33	8/22/63	Chicago	Boston	Day	Fisher	3	1	
34	8/28/63	New York	New York	Day	Ford	2	0	
35	8/29/63	New York	New York	Day	Williams	4	1	
36	9/3/63	Baltimore	Boston	Day	S. Miller	8	1	
37	9/6/63	Baltimore	Baltimore	Night	Pappas	3	2	4 RBI game
38	9/10/63	Los Angeles	Los Angeles	Night	Belinsky	2	0	
39	9/14/63	Kansas City	Kansas City	Night	Santiago	3	0	
40	9/14/63	Kansas City	Kansas City	Night	Fischer	5	0	2 home runs
41	9/18/63	Chicago	Chicago	Night	Herbert	3	1	
42	9/21/63	Minnesota	Boston	Day/Game 1	Stange	6	0	
1	4/24/64	Chicago	Chicago	Night	Pizarro	4	0	
2	4/28/64	Baltimore	Boston	Day	Hall	11	3	walk-off grand slam/Sox were trailing 4–2
3	5/24/64	Kansas City	Boston	Day/Game 1	Drabowsky	8	3	game-wining grand slam
4	5/24/64	Kansas City	Boston	Day/Game 2	Segui	4	1	2 home runs in doubleheader
5	5/27/64	Washington	Boston	Day	Koch	3	1	
6	5/27/64	Washington	Boston	Day	Ridzik	7	0	2 home runs
7	5/29/64	Minnesota	Minnesota	Night	Roland	2	1	
8	5/30/64	Minnesota	Minnesota	Day	Pascual	9	0	
9	6/1/64	Los Angeles	Los Angeles	Night	Latman	8	1	
10	6/5/64	Kansas City	Kansas City	Night	Monteagudo	2	3	grand slam

Appendix. Dick Stuart Home Run Log

11	6/6/64	Kansas City	Kansas City	Day	O'Donoghue	1	0	
12	6/19/64	Baltimore	Baltimore	Night	Estrada	4	0	
13	6/21/64	Baltimore	Baltimore	Day	Hall	6	2	
14	6/28/64	Cleveland	Boston	Day/Game 1	Ramos	2	0	
15	7/5/64	Los Angeles	Boston	Day	B. Lee	7	0	
16	7/10/64	Detroit	Detroit	Night/Game 1	Regan	1	1	
17	7/13/64	Washington	Washington	Night	Duckworth	4	2	
18	7/14/64	Chicago	Boston	Night	Pizarro	8	0	
19	7/15/64	Chicago	Boston	Night	Talbot	1	2	
20	7/15/64	Chicago	Boston	Night	Fisher	7	2	2 home runs/6 RBI
21	7/17/64	Washington	Boston	Night	Koch	1	1	
22	7/17/64	Washington	Boston	Night	Koch	6	1	2 home runs
23	7/19/64	Washington	Boston	Day/Game 1	Hannan	6	0	
24	7/21/64	Detroit	Boston	Night	Lolich	7	2	broke 4–4 tie
25	7/25/64	Cleveland	Cleveland	Day	Kralick	2	0	
26	7/25/64	Cleveland	Cleveland	Day	Siebert	6	0	2 home runs
27	8/9/64	Chicago	Chicago	Day/Game 1	Mossi	7	1	
28	8/21/64	New York	Boston	Night	Terry	4	0	
29	8/25/64	Detroit	Boston	Night	McLain	4	0	
30	8/28/64	New York	New York	Night	Downing	8	0	
31	9/10/64	Cleveland	Cleveland	Night	Siebert	1	1	
32	9/13/64	Los Angeles	Boston	Day	Gatewood	4	0	
33	9/16/64	Kansas City	Boston	Day	Odom	5	0	
1	4/18/65	Los Angeles	Philadelphia	Day	Koufax	6	1	
2	4/25/65	Los Angeles	Los Angeles	Day	Drysdale	4	1	

Appendix. Dick Stuart Home Run Log

Home Run #	Date	Opponent	Location	Day/Night/DH	Pitcher	Inning	On Base	Comments
3	5/9/65	St. Louis	Philadelphia	Day	Sadecki	1	1	
4	5/14/65	Milwaukee	Philadelphia	Night	O'Dell	5	0	
5	5/15/65	Milwaukee	Philadelphia	Day	Fischer	3	3	grand slam
6	6/6/65	Chicago	Chicago	Day	McDaniel	5	0	Callison had 3 homers/Phils 5
7	6/7/65	Los Angeles	Philadelphia	Night	Koufax	1	1	
8	6/10/65	Los Angeles	Philadelphia	Night	Podres	6	0	
9	6/18/65	Los Angeles	Los Angeles	Night	Podres	2	0	
10	6/20/65	Houston	Houston	Day/Game2	Coombs	7	0	
11	6/24/65	San Francisco	San Francisco	Day	Bolin	9	0	
12	6/29/65	St. Louis	Philadelphia	Night	Sadecki	8	2	
13	7/2/65	Cincinnati	Philadelphia	Night	Arrigo	8	1	
14	7/3/65	Cincinnati	Philadelphia	Night	Ellis	2	0	
15	7/5/65	Pittsburgh	Philadelphia	Night/Game 2	Wood	5	0	
16	7/15/65	Cincinnati	Cincinnati	Night	Nuxhall	4	0	
17	7/24/65	New York	New York	Day	Parsons	6	1	
18	7/31/65	New York	Philadelphia	Day	Fisher	2	0	
19	8/4/65	Chicago	Philadelphia	Night	Buhl	2	1	
20	8/8/65	Pittsburgh	Philadelphia	Day	Sisk	6	0	
21	8/22/65	Cincinnati	Philadelphia	Day	Craig	8	0	
22	9/3/65	Cincinnati	Cincinnati	Night	O'Toole	3	0	
23	9/5/65	Cincinnati	Cincinnati	Day	Ellis	1	3	grand slam
24	9/5/65	Cincinnati	Cincinnati	Day	Davidson	7	1	2 home runs/6 RBI
25	9/8/65	Milwaukee	Milwaukee	Night	Johnson	4	1	
26	9/10/65	St. Louis	Philadelphia	Night	Gibson	6	1	

Appendix. Dick Stuart Home Run Log 223

27	9/16/65	Milwaukee	Philadelphia	Night	Sadowski	4	0	
28	9/25/65	New York	Philadelphia	Day/Game 1	Bearnarth	4	0	
1	5/8/66	Chicago	New York	Day	Ellsworth	2	0	
2	5/31/66	Philadelphia	New York	Night	Short	1	1	
3	6/1/66	Pittsburgh	New York	Night	Cardwell	5	0	
4	6/7/66	Atlanta	New York	Day	Lemaster	3	1	
5	7/25/66	Philadelphia	Los Angeles	Night	Short	6	0	
6	7/26/66	Philadelphia	Los Angeles	Night	L. Jackson	4	0	
7	7/31/66	St. Louis	St. Louis	Day	Carlton	3	0	
1	4/14/69	Chicago	Anaheim	Night	John	7	0	

Chapter Notes

Introduction

1. John Kuenster, "What They Thought When the Pressure Was Greatest," *Baseball Digest*, June 1961, p. 5.
2. *Ibid.*
3. Interview with Bob Oldis, August 27, 2018.
4. Interview with Dick Schofield, January 8, 2019.
5. *Lincoln Journal Star*, June 17, 2006.
6. *Sports Illustrated*, September 2, 1963.
7. Modern statistical analysis is based on the understanding that fielding percentage is not necessarily the most important statistic in determining ability. The new statistics confirm, however, that Stuart was truly miserable with the glove.
8. "Like Williams," *Baseball Digest*, July 1962, p. 12.
9. *True*, September 1959, p. 74.
10. *Lincoln Star*, July 5, 1956.
11. *Salt Lake City Tribune*, April 8, 1958.
12. Interview with Dick Groat, July 13, 2018.
13. *The Sporting News*, April 18, 1964.
14. Email from Jan Finkel, June 27, 2018.
15. William Faulkner, *The Sound and the Fury* quoted in Finkel email of June 27, 2018.
16. *Boston Globe*, June 26, 1963.
17. *Pittsburgh Post-Gazette*, September 18, 1960.
18. Bill Bryson, "They Remember Dick Stuart," *Baseball Digest*, July 1960, p. 33.

Chapter 1

1. Letter from Laurel Stuart, received April 27, 2020.
2. *Lincoln Journal Star*, June 17, 2006.
3. Information on Sequoia High School can be found at https://en.wikipedia.org/wiki/Sequoia_High_School_(Redwood_City,_California).
4. *San Mateo Times*, May 16, 1950.
5. *Life* magazine, September 2, 1957.
6. *San Mateo Times*, June 23, 1951.
7. The current Modesto minor league team is called the Nuts, in recognition of one of the city's primary agricultural products. That would suit Stuart better.
8. During his lengthy career, Freitas was involved in some landmark moments. He played in the first PCL night game at Sacramento in 1930 and was a member of the Cincinnati Reds when they played the first major league game under the lights in 1935.
9. Curtis suffered no serious injuries, and four days later, in his next start, struck out 19, including the first nine batters, to set a California League record.
10. *Modesto Bee*, August 31, 1951.
11. Wilson went to training camp with the Pirates and began the 1952 season in Hollywood, but finished it back in Modesto, where he also played in 1953. He continued toiling in the minor leagues until 1960, when he was 37, usually in a B or C league. Warner played three more seasons and finished his career in D ball in 1954.

Chapter 2

1. *Saturday Evening Post*, April 28, 1962, page 68.
2. Although the *Billings Gazette* stated in its April 24, 1952 issue that all Pioneer League clubs had major league affiliations, *Baseball Reference* indicates that neither Idaho Falls nor Magic Valley was affiliated.
3. Gerry Hern, "There Are Still Too Many Minors," *Baseball Digest*, April 1954, p. 45.
4. Les Biederman, "Life at $135 a Month," *Baseball Digest*, July 1954, p. 67.
5. *Billings Gazette*, April 18, 1952.
6. *Billings Gazette*, April 20, 1952.
7. *Billings Gazette*, April 22, 1952. Stuart and Dapper proved a potent 1–2 punch but Van Burkleo was plagued by injuries and batted just .206 with three home runs. Despite his big bonus and high expectations, he never came close to the major leagues. His son, Ty Van Burkleo, played a total of 14 games with the Angels and Rockies in 1993 and 1994.
8. The *Gazette* frequently spelled Stuart's name "Stewart" in box scores and game coverage.
9. *Billings Gazette*, June 5, 1952.
10. Tasby played in the major leagues from 1959 to 1963 with the Orioles, Red Sox, Senators, and Indians.
11. Ken Kimball of Idaho Falls, who led the league with 15 wins, started for the All-Stars. Earlier that day, Kimball's five-year-old daughter fell off a swing and broke both arms, but his wife didn't tell him until after the game.

12. *Billings Gazette,* December 28, 1952.
13. Elliott returned to manage Billings in 1955 and 1956 and played in a few games each season.
14. *Billings Gazette,* September 4, 1952.
15. *Billings Gazette,* September 8, 1952.
16. *Billings Gazette,* June 18, 1952.
17. Like Stuart, Pinckard played a couple of seasons in Japan and dabbled in Hollywood, with bit parts and stunt roles, and after he retired as an active player, he designed and marketed baseball gloves.
18. The Shaughnessey System was implemented in 1933 by Frank Shaughnessy, a longtime minor league executive. Under his system, the first and fourth place teams typically played one semi-final series and the second- and third-place teams played each other in a second series. The two winners then played for the championship. The format was sometimes implemented differently, and in the 1952 Pioneer League playoffs, the third-place Mustangs faced the first place Pocatello club while second-place Idaho Falls played fourth place Great Falls.
19. Idaho Falls beat Pocatello in three straight games to win the Pioneer League championship.
20. *San Mateo Times,* November 3, 1952.
21. *Humboldt Standard,* June 25, 1953.
22. *The Daily Chronicle,* July 10, 1954.
23. *The Akron Beacon Journal,* April 8, 1967.
24. Ibid.

Chapter 3

1. *The Sporting News,* March 9, 1955. As a minor leaguer, Stuart was often described as having good speed, although he rarely stole a base. By the time he reached the major leagues, he was invariably characterized as a ponderous base runner.
2. *The Sporting News,* March 9, 1955.
3. *Times-Picayune,* March 4, 1955.
4. Ibid.
5. *Times-Picayune,* April 5, 1955.
6. *Times-Picayune,* February 26, 1955.
7. Interview with Paul Pettit, January 30, 2020.
8. Ibid.
9. *Time Magazine,* September 2, 1957.
10. Information on the Mustangs' season is taken primarily from the *Billings Gazette.*
11. *Billings Gazette,* September 3, 1955.

Chapter 4

1. https://www2.census.gov/library/publications/decennial/1950/pc-02/pc-2-21.pdf.
2. Interview with Bob Wirz, January 8, 2020.
3. Interview with Bob Wirz, January 8, 2020. The competition between the Chiefs and Cornhuskers included the social scene. Stuart and Nebraska quarterback Don Erway dated the same woman, which may explain Stuart's 1957 divorce. Wirz believed, but was not certain, that the young woman was Miss Nebraska.
4. Shepard became very popular during his two seasons as manager of the Chiefs. Although he was promoted to Salt Lake City of the Pacific Coast League in 1958, he built a new house in Lincoln. The home was being constructed during the summer, while Shepard was in Salt Lake, and just before he returned to see the finished product, the sports editors of the two Lincoln newspapers, Don Bryant and Dick Becker, organized a "Schlitz a weed" party and brought their staffs to Shepard's new home to drink a few beers and finish the landscaping.
5. https://en.wikipedia.org/wiki/Dick_Wagner_(baseball).
6. *Lincoln Star,* April 11, 1956.
7. For some reason, Rowe was called "Bomark Misslehead," a moniker given him by teammate George Witt (Interview with Larry Foss, January 18, 2002).
8. *Lincoln Star,* April 18, 1956.
9. Les Biederman, "Life at $135 a Month," *Baseball Digest,* July 1954, p. 67.
10. Interview with Larry Gerlach, February 18, 2020.
11. *Pittsburgh Press,* October 10, 1965.
12. *Lincoln Star,* May 16, 1956.
13. Information on Stone was obtained from the *Los Angeles Daily News,* May 15, 2011. At the time the article appeared, Stone was working for the Los Angeles Dodgers ticket office at the age of 90.
14. "Between Innings," *Baseball Digest,* April 1959, p. 4.
15. *Lincoln Star,* July 13, 1956. Stone did a service to the umpiring profession when he gave an autograph to young Larry Gerlach and got him interested in the profession of umpiring. It was the first baseball autograph Gerlach obtained, and the fact that it was from a minor league umpire was a clue that Gerlach had unusual interests. He joined the Society for American Baseball Research in 1978 and became its foremost expert on the history and profession of umpiring.
16. *Lincoln Star,* June 9, 1956.
17. *Lincoln Star,* June 12, 1956.
18. Ibid.
19. Hobbs' problems weren't over. A few days later, Albuquerque, one of three new Western League teams, said they had a tax problem and threatened to withdraw if the league didn't give them a $10,000 loan. The concept of a loan from the Western League was not new. Lincoln had previously obtained one and Wichita had an outstanding debt when it left to join the American Association. This time the league declined Albuquerque's request and the latter, its bluff called, decided to stay. Although the league had agreed to Sioux City's request, the split season didn't help them. They lost 13 of their first 17 games in the second half and quickly found that local interests were not going to raise $15,000. Despite that, the club managed to finish the season and returned the following year.
20. *Lincoln Star,* June 16, 1956.
21. Pueblo was a Dodger farm club whose roster included future Hall of Famer Maury Wills and pitcher Larry Sherry, who would star in the World Series three years later.

22. *Pittsburgh Press*, March 6, 1959.
23. *Pittsburgh Post-Gazette*, December 8, 1964.
24. *The Sporting News*, July 4, 1956.
25. *Lincoln Star*, June 29, 1956.
26. Ibid.
27. Ibid.
28. *Lincoln Star*, July 6, 1956.
29. *Pittsburgh Press*, February 28, 1958.
30. *Lincoln Star*, July 25, 1956.
31. *Lincoln Star*, July 27, 1956.
32. *Lincoln Sunday Star and Journal*, September 2, 1956.
33. *The Sporting News*, July 18, 1956.
34. This was not the first time Hopper ran off at the mouth and lived to regret it. He was the manager of the Montreal Royals in 1946 when Jackie Robinson was assigned there. When Hopper, a native of Mississippi, learned he was to manage an African American player, he told Branch Rickey he couldn't do it. If he did, he said, he'd have to move his family out of Mississippi. Rickey told him Robinson was staying, and one day when the latter made a superlative defensive play, said to Hopper, "Have you ever seen a human being make a play like this?" Hopper replied, "Mr. Rickey, do you really think a nigra is a human being?" By the end of the season Robinson won Hopper over, and the manager not only praised his character but recommended that he be promoted to Brooklyn (https://nationalpost.com/42/how-clay-hoppers-attitude-was-transformed-by-jackie-robinson).
35. *Lincoln Journal Star*, June 17, 2006.
36. *Lincoln Star*, July 18, 1956.
37. Interview with Bob Wirz, January 8, 2020.
38. *Lincoln Star*, July 21, 1956.
39. *Lincoln Star*, July 26, 1956.
40. *Lincoln Star*, August 10, 1956. Of the first 500 Western League homers, 176 were hit in Amarillo (*The Sporting News*, August 1, 1956).
41. On August 12, Daniels pitched a no-hitter and lost, 1–0. Daniels walked a batter, who stole second, but infielder John McDevitt, covering the base, thought the runner had been called out. He started to throw the ball around the horn but threw it wildly, enabling the runner to reach third. He scored the only run of the game when Daniels threw a wild pitch.
42. *Saturday Evening Post*, April 28, 1962.
43. Interview with Don Rowe, June 1, 2001.
44. *Lincoln Star*, August 28, 1956.
45. *True, the Men's Magazine*, September 1959, p. 74.
46. The dialogue cited here is taken from an article by Jimmy Breslin in *True* magazine, September 1959. Breslin had a reputation for inventing and embellishing, so it is not certain that these exact words were spoken, but the essence of the story is plausible.
47. *Lincoln Star*, August 29, 1956.
48. *True, the Men's Magazine*, September 1959, p. 73.
49. Brown never reached the major leagues. He was forever damned by a scouting report in which Branch Rickey said he was stupid and never had a thought in his life. Rickey greatly valued intelligence in a ballplayer, and his ridicule of Brown's intellect pretty much guaranteed he would never make the majors.
50. Toothman was promoted to AAA in 1957 and played at that level through 1962 but never made it to the major leagues. Like Sam Miley, Toothman was considered a much better offensive than defensive player. Of the others rated as top prospects, Maury Wills and Larry Sherry of Pueblo, Sammy Taylor and Marshall Bridges of Topeka, and Don Rowe of Lincoln eventually played in the majors.
51. Although he is not counted as a 60-home run man, Bill Serena deserves at least an asterisk. In 1947, Serena hit 57 regular season homers for Lubbock of the West Texas-New Mexico League and added 13 more in seven playoff games for a total of 70.
52. *Baseball Research Journal*, Number 24 (1995), published by the Society for American Baseball Research, *Minor League Big Guns*, Ernest J. Green. A curious fact presented by Green was that none of the teams featuring a record setting slugger (other than Lincoln) finished first in its league.
53. George K. Leonard, "37 Stars Hit 50 Homers in a Year," *Baseball Digest*, October 1954, p. 43.
54. SABR Bioproject article on Lennon by Warren Corbett, https://sabr.org/bioproj/person/3f2ba3b4.
55. *Sports Illustrated*, September 17, 1956.

Chapter 5

1. *Salt Lake City Tribune*, April 8, 1958.
2. *Baseball Digest*, March 1957 p. 45. In fairness, the scouting reports published in *Baseball Digest* were not always on the mark. A March 1962 report on Richie Allen (p. 68) said, "Tools are pretty good but bat is a question mark. It's slow." Tony Oliva (March 1964, p. 104)—"Can make somebody a real good utility outfielder. Fair hitter." Tony Perez (March 1965, p. 109)—"Weak hitter. Fair fielder. Must hit higher to have chance." Rod Carew (March 1965 p. 102)—"Overall just an average player." Gaylord Perry (March 1963 p. 110)—"A borderline case." Ron Hunt, one of the scrappiest players of the 1960s (March 1963 p. 101)—"…doesn't try hard enough. Could be a better player with more desire."
3. *The Sporting News*, March 20, 1957.
4. *Press-Telegram*, April 12, 1957.
5. *The Sporting News*, March 20, 1957.
6. *Chicago Tribune*, March 21, 1957.
7. There were no cheap home runs in Fort Myers, where the field dimensions were nearly identical to those at spacious Forbes Field.
8. Interview with Dick Groat, July 13, 2018.
9. https://sabr.org/bioproj/person/83f33669-- SABR Bioproject article on Bragan by David Fleitz and Maurice Bouchard.
10. *The Sporting News*, March 27, 1957.
11. *The Sporting News*, June 26, 1957.

12. *The Sporting News*, March 27, 1957.
13. *Pittsburgh Press,* March 18, 1957.
14. *Salt Lake City Tribune*, June 7, 1964.
15. *Pittsburgh Press,* March 18, 1957.
16. *The Sporting News*, April 3, 1957.
17. *New York Daily News*, February 25, 1966.
18. *Pittsburgh Press*, March 9, 1963.
19. *Salt Lake City Tribune*, June 7, 1964.
20. *The Sporting News*, May 8, 1957.
21. *Pittsburgh Post-Gazette*, January 22, 1963.
22. *The Sporting News*, April 10, 1957.
23. Interview with Paul Pettit, January 30, 2020.
24. The relationship between King and Stuart appeared amicable on the surface, but years later, when he was named manager of the Giants, King was asked if he thought he'd have trouble with any of the Giant players. "I've managed some of the toughest players around," he replied, "including Leon Wagner and Dick Stuart, and never had any problems" (*Pacific Stars and Stripes*, October 13, 1968).
25. Interview with Ed Bressoud, June 1, 2002.
26. Interview with Dick Beverage, January 11, 2020.
27. Interview with Paul Pettit, January 30, 2020.
28. Interview with Dick Beverage, January 11, 2020.
29. Bill Conlin, "Crisis in the Coast League," *Baseball Digest*, March 1954, p. 72.
30. *The Sporting News*, March 26, 1958.
31. *Pittsburgh Press*, July 24, 1963.
32. *Press-Telegram*, April 16, 1957.
33. *Press-Telegram*, April 17, 1957.
34. *Ibid.*
35. *Press-Telegram*, April 19, 1957.
36. Interview with Paul Pettit, January 30, 2020.
37. *Press-Telegram*, April 9, 1957.
38. *Ibid.*
39. Quoted in *Press-Telegram*, April 9, 1957.
40. Interview with Paul Pettit, January 30, 2020.
41. *Press-Telegram*, April 15, 1957.
42. *Press-Telegram*, April 16, 1957.
43. *Press-Telegram*, April 22, 1957.
44. Interview with Paul Pettit, January 30, 2020.
45. SABR Bioproject article on Paul Pettit by Dan Taylor (https://sabr.org/bioproj/person/1a542859).
46. Jack Hernon, "The End Nears for $100,000," *Baseball Digest*, April 1954, p. 43.
47. Interview with Paul Pettit, January 30, 2020.
48. *Press-Ledger*, April 26, 1957.
49. As a further blow to Stuart's sizable ego, he entered a home run hitting contest on April 13 at San Diego and was defeated, two home runs to one, by San Diego pitcher and future major league star Jim (Mudcat) Grant.
50. *Lincoln Sunday Journal and Star*, May 12, 1957.
51. At Atlanta, Stuart joined outfielder Ken Guettler, who'd hit 62 home runs for Shreveport in 1956, giving the Crackers two 60+ home run hitters in their outfield. For the 1957 Crackers, Stuart hit just eight homers while Guettler managed only two.
52. *Albuquerque Journal*, June 10, 1957.
53. *Lima News*, June 11, 1957.
54. *The Atlanta Constitution*, May 18, 1957.
55. *Ibid.*
56. Interview with Ken MacKenzie, April 28, 2020.
57. *The Sporting News*, June 5, 1957.
58. Stuart managed to play ten games in the outfield without making an error.
59. Interview with Ken MacKenzie, April 28, 2020.
60. *The Sporting News*, June 19, 1956.
61. *Lima News*, June 11, 1957.
62. *The Atlanta Constitution*, June 11, 1957.
63. *Ibid.*
64. *Ibid.*
65. *Ibid.*
66. *Ibid.*
67. Interview with Ken MacKenzie, April 28, 2020. Stuart was probably referring to the home run he hit in Pueblo that was generously estimated at 650 feet.
68. *Kenosha Evening News*, June 14, 1957.
69. *The Atlanta Constitution*, June 17, 1957.
70. *The Atlanta Constitution*, June 27, 1957.
71. *Big Spring Herald*, May 21, 1957.
72. *Lima News*, June 11, 1957.
73. *Press-Telegram*, June 16, 1957.
74. *The Sporting News*, June 26, 1957.
75. *True, the Men's Magazine*, September 1959, p. 75.
76. *Amarillo Globe Times*, June 21, 1957.
77. *Amarillo Globe Times*, June 23, 1957.
78. Information on Bell is taken from the biography written by Warren Corbett for the SABR bioproject: https://sabr.org/bioproj/person/e5dfd9fc.
79. SABR Bioproject article by Warren Corbett (https://sabr.org/bioproj/person/e5dfd9fc).
80. Interview with Harry Dunlop, January 11, 2020.
81. When Bell continued to struggle, the Pirates released him in 1959. He died from injuries suffered in a car crash in 1962 at the age of 28.
82. He was not about to win the safe driver title, pleading guilty to four parking violations and an illegal U-turn during the season. Apparently, the Lincoln police showed no favoritism toward the city's most famous resident.
83. Interview with Harry Dunlop, January 11, 2020.
84. *The Sporting News*, July 24, 1957.
85. *The Sporting News*, March 19, 1966.
86. *Albuquerque Journal*, July 24, 1957.
87. *Albuquerque Journal*, August 14, 1957.
88. *Albuquerque Journal*, August 16, 1957.
89. *Ibid.*
90. *Williamsport Sun Gazette*, July 27, 1957.
91. Interview with Harry Dunlop, January 11, 2020.
92. *True, the Men's Magazine*, September 1959, p. 74.
93. The contents of the September 2, 1957 issue of *Life* can be found at https://www.oldlifemagazines.com/september-02-1957-life-magazine.html.
94. *Amarillo Daily News*, August 29, 1957.

95. *Amarillo Daily News*, August 31, 1957.
96. Interview with Harry Dunlop, January 11, 2020.
97. *The Sporting News*, November 6, 1957.
98. The next year, when Stuart played in Salt Lake City, veteran pitcher Max Surkont noticed that Stuart was laying off high pitches, something he'd begun to do in winter ball.
99. *The Sporting News*, March 5, 1958.
100. *The Sporting News*, November 6, 1957.
101. The official league record was for the three years in which it was affiliated with Organized Baseball. Pedro Formental hit 13 home runs in 1951.
102. *Kittanning Simpson Leader Times*, November 21, 1957.
103. *Pittsburgh Post-Gazette*, February 18, 1958.

Chapter 6

1. *The Sporting News*, March 26, 1958.
2. *Salt Lake City Tribune*, April 10, 1958.
3. *The Sporting News*, March 26, 1958.
4. Sy Burick, "All Muscle and Brawn," *Baseball Digest*, January 1969, p. 68.
5. Herbert Burskey, "And You Can Quote Me," *Baseball Digest*, March 1955, p. 66.
6. *The Sporting News*, September 23, 1959.
7. "Klu's Outfield Career Wound up with a Bang," *Baseball Digest*, June 1956, p. 39.
8. *Sports Illustrated*, March 24, 1958.
9. R.C. stood for R.C. Stevens had no first or middle name.
10. *Pittsburgh Press*, June 17, 1966.
11. *Burlington Daily Times News*, March 11, 1959.
12. *Salt Lake City Tribune*, April 25, 1958.
13. *Salt Lake City Tribune*, April 14, 1958.
14. *Ibid.*
15. *Salt Lake City Tribune*, January 19, 1958.
16. The stadium was named after longtime sports editor John C. Derks of the *Salt Lake City Herald Tribune*.
17. *The Physics of Baseball*, Alan M. Nathan, University of Illinois: http://baseball.physics.illinois.edu/Denver.html.
18. *Salt Lake City Tribune*, April 2, 1958.
19. *Salt Lake City Tribune*, April 25, 1958.
20. *Salt Lake City Tribune*, April 30, 1958.
21. After Stuart was recalled to Pittsburgh, Rossitto and Anton sent him a money order for a steak dinner when he hit his first major league home run.
22. *Burlington Daily News Times*, March 11, 1959.
23. Interview with Paul Pettit, January 30, 2020.
24. Stuart, who liked to compare himself to Babe Ruth and Ted Williams, must have been horrified when the *Tribune* called him the most exciting minor league player since Lou ("the Mad Russian") Novikoff.
25. *Salt Lake City Tribune*, May 28, 1958.
26. Information on Bernier is taken from the SABR bioproject article written by Charles F. Faber: https://sabr.org/bioproj/person/a54d927b.
27. Baseball-reference/bullpen/Carlos_Bernier.
28. *Sports Illustrated*, June 2, 1958.
29. *Ibid.*
30. *Ibid.*
31. *Ibid.*
32. *Salt Lake City Tribune*, September 9, 1958.
33. *Salt Lake City Tribune*, July 5, 1958.
34. *Ibid.*
35. *Salt Lake City Tribune*, June 13, 1964.

Chapter 7

1. *Pittsburgh Sun-Telegraph*, July 10, 1958.
2. *Pittsburgh Press*, July 7, 1958. See later section on former Pirate Dino Restelli.
3. *Pittsburgh Post-Gazette*, July 11, 1958.
4. *Pittsburgh Press*, July 11, 1958.
5. Unidentified article in Dick Stuart player file at the Giamatti Research Center, National Baseball Hall of Fame.
6. Some suggested that the trade of Kiner was prompted by Rickey's ownership interest in the Pirates and his desire to rid the club of Kiner's large salary.
7. Al Abrams, "Rickey Flopping! He's Lost His Touch," *Baseball Digest*, May 1953, p. 5.
8. Maraniss p. 59.
9. *Sports Illustrated*, July 1, 1957. The 1957 article provided detailed information on each team, while a June 7, 1958, SI article about Galbreath placed the aggregate loss at $1.5 million, citing figures provided to the House Judiciary Subcommittee that was investigating baseball.
10. Gordon Cobbledick, "Galbreath's Party," *Baseball Digest*, February 1956, p. 32.
11. Interview with Bob Friend, September 27, 2018.
12. *Sports Illustrated*, April 21, 1960.
13. Interview with Vernon Law, February 4, 2019.
14. Interview with Bob Friend, September 27, 2018.
15. In his lone season, Groat averaged a very respectable 11.9 points in 26 games, the second highest average on the team.
16. Interview with Bill Virdon, February 5, 2019. Although Groat was considered a good fielder in his day, his style is not one that is appreciated by today's analysts. Even under current standards, however, Groat was one of the better defensive shortstops of his era. His career range factor was a hair above average and he led NL shortstops in putouts and assists several times. Fan Graphs Total Zone credited him with 46 fielding runs for his career and 16 in 1960.
17. *Baseball Digest*, December 1963–January 1964 p. 59.
18. Interview with Dick Groat, July 13, 2018. To Bragan's credit, he later admitted he had been wrong about Groat.
19. One theory was that the Dodgers, who were well-stocked with talent at the time, didn't mind

losing Clemente to the lowly Pirates. Their only concern was that he not end up with the rival Giants.
20. *Baseball Digest*, April 1957, p. 33.
21. *Sports Illustrated*, February 17, 1958.
22. *Ibid.*
23. *Sports Illustrated*, August 12, 1957. Bragan made a number of enemies with his brash behavior, and they delighted in pointing out the times he was very wrong. Former Brave Lou Klimchock recalled, "Bobby Bragan told [Phil Niekro] to stick that knuckleball you know where, because he'd never win in the major leagues with it" (interview with Lou Klimchock, May 30, 2002). Hall of Famer Niekro won 318 games with the knuckler.
24. *Sports Illustrated*, March 16, 1959.
25. *Pittsburgh Press*, February 19, 1959.
26. *Sports Illustrated*, April 14, 1958.
27. *Sports Illustrated*, July 14, 1958.
28. Unidentified clipping from the Dick Stuart player file at the Giamatti Research Center, National Baseball Hall of Fame.
29. *Ibid.*
30. *Pittsburgh Sun-Telegraph*, July 13, 1958.
31. *Pittsburgh Post-Gazette*, July 14, 1958.
32. *The Pittsburgh Press*, July 20, 1958.
33. Pirate slugger Frank Thomas, a dead pull hitter, found the California stadiums greatly to his liking. He hit seven homers in the Coliseum and six at Seals Stadium, for a total of 13 home runs in 22 games.
34. Interview with Vern Law, February 4, 2019.
35. *Los Angeles Herald & Express*, July 12, 1958.
36. *Pittsburgh Sun-Telegraph*, July 21, 1958.
37. *Pittsburgh Sun-Telegraph*, September 16, 1958.
38. *Pittsburgh Post-Gazette*, August 2, 1958.
39. *The Sporting News*, June 22, 1960.
40. After Stuart was traded from the Pirates, he never hit a home run as a visiting player at Forbes Field.
41. Some of the information on Forbes Field was taken from https://en.wikipedia.org/wiki/Forbes_Field
42. *The Sporting News*, June 28, 1961. The infield was the Pirates' friend in the seventh game of the 1960 World Series, when a ground ball off the bat of the Bucs' Bill Virdon took a bad hop and hit Yankee shortstop Tony Kubek in the throat, keying an eighth inning rally.
43. Jack Hernon, "Then He Got Bounced," *Baseball Digest*, July 1961, p. 16.
44. Interview with Dick Groat, July 13, 2018.
45. Interview with Vern Law, February 4, 2019.
46. Interview with Bill Virdon, February 5, 2019.
47. Interview with Dick Groat, July 13, 2018.
48. Interview with Bob Friend, May 28, 2002.
49. *The Pittsburgh Press*, July 30, 1958.
50. *The Sporting News*, February 25, 1959.
51. *Pittsburgh Post-Gazette*, September 23, 1958.
52. *The Pittsburgh Press*, September 4, 1958.
53. *The Sporting News*, September 24, 1958.
54. *Pittsburgh Press*, June 15, 1989.
55. *The Sporting News*, October 1, 1958.
56. *Sports Illustrated*, September 22, 1958.
57. Stuart was one of only four men to homer in every National League park. The others were future Hall of Famers Ernie Banks, Eddie Mathews, and Hank Aaron.
58. *The Sporting News*, October 1, 1958.
59. *The Pittsburgh Press*, November 13, 1958.
60. Stuart later joked that although he got the same amount as the bat boy "that was alright because he was a very good bat boy" (*Pittsburgh Press*, March 9, 1963).
61. *Pittsburgh Post-Gazette*, December 25, 1958.
62. *The Pittsburgh Press*, November 13, 1958.
63. Interview with Bob Friend, September 27, 2018.
64. Stuart did not repeat the achievements of his record-setting 1957–58 season. After hitting seven homers in 34 games, he was forced to return to the States in December due to a hand injury. At first it was feared the hand might be broken, but it turned out not to be the case.

Chapter 8

1. *Sports Illustrated*, June 22, 1959.
2. *The Sporting News*, October 14, 1959.
3. Nelson related this remark during a broadcast of May 13, 1969.
4. Interview with Vern Law, February 4, 2019.
5. One of Thomas' idiosyncrasies was his habit of assisting flight attendants in serving meals during team flights. Another was his standing challenge to catch anyone bare-handed, which he did for money. Thomas rarely lost.
6. *Sports Illustrated*, July 28, 1958.
7. Interview with Frank Thomas, August 28, 2001.
8. *Sports Illustrated*, July 28, 1958.
9. *The Sporting News*, March 18, 1959.
10. *Sports Illustrated*, March 16, 1959.
11. *The Sporting News*, March 11, 1959.
12. *Ibid.*
13. *Sports Illustrated*, April 13, 1959.
14. "Words That Showed a Prophet or a Loss," *Baseball Digest*, February 1960, p. 57.
15. *Salt Lake City Tribune*, December 17, 1958.
16. *Los Angeles Times*, July 25, 1963.
17. *Baseball Digest*, September 1960, *Status Quote* p. 4.
18. Nelson was married at home plate at the Lynchburg, Virginia ballpark in 1947.
19. *Sports Illustrated*, August 18, 1958.
20. *Ibid.*
21. *Sports Illustrated*, August 25, 1958.
22. *Sports Illustrated*, August 18, 1958.
23. *Ibid.*
24. *Sports Illustrated*, August 25, 1958.
25. *Sports Illustrated*, August 18, 1958.
26. R.C. Stevens had been drafted into the Army and was temporarily out of the picture.
27. *Florence Morning News*, March 5, 1959.
28. *Sports Illustrated*, April 17, 1960.

29. *The Sporting News*, March 25, 1959.
30. *Florence Morning News*, March 5, 1959.
31. *Ibid.*
32. *Pittsburgh Press*, February 19, 1959.
33. *Pittsburgh Post-Gazette*, March 3, 1959. Stuart's recollection of his performance against Milwaukee was accurate. He was four for eight against Burdette, three for 12 with a home run against Spahn, and 0 for 14 against the other Braves pitchers.
34. Stevens was expected to be released from the Army and join the Pirates by May.
35. *Pittsburgh Press*, June 3, 1959.
36. *The Sporting News*, April 8, 1959.
37. One of the highlights of Kluszewski's season was that owner John Galbreath named one of his horses Big Klu.
38. Interview with Bob Friend, September 27, 2018.
39. A 1957 scouting report referred to Witt as a "peculiar type" (*Baseball Digest,* March 1957 p. 45). In a 1987 interview with Ron Cook of the *Pittsburgh Press,* Witt said he never liked baseball and found playing it to be an unpleasant chore. Basketball and track had been his two favorite sports, but baseball was the only one in which he had a professional future. And in baseball he preferred playing the outfield but wound up as a pitcher. Witt's chronic arm injuries made pitching a painful experience that he preferred to forget. "I hardly ever talk about baseball now," he told Cook (*Pittsburgh Press*, May 11, 1987). His wife apparently shared Witt's dislike of baseball and never went to see him pitch.
40. In 25 career at bats against Brosnan, Stuart had nine hits, including two triples and three homers.
41. *True, The Men's Magazine*, September 1959, p. 43.
42. *Pittsburgh Post-Gazette*, June 26, 1959.
43. *Pittsburgh Post-Gazette*, July 3, 1959.
44. *Pittsburgh Post-Gazette*, September 27, 1960.
45. *Pittsburgh Post-Gazette*, July 9, 1961.
46. Edgar Williams, "Right Face," *Baseball Digest*, September 1959, p. 11.
47. *The Sporting News*, July 22, 1959.
48. *Pittsburgh Sun-Telegraph*, July 13, 1959.
49. Pirate traveling secretary Bob Rice was apoplectic when Stuart told him how many passes he wanted. Rice came up with them, but said, "Don't try this again" (*The Sporting News*, May 27, 1959). In 1966, when the Pirates played in Atlanta, first baseman Donn Clendenon's home town, he asked for 26 passes. "Attention, Dick Stuart," Les Biederman wrote, "your record is safe.... You still hold the Pirate mark of 27 in Los Angeles" (*The Sporting News*, April 30, 1966).
50. A group of legislators from Allegheny County introduced a resolution recognizing Haddix's feat in the Pennsylvania legislature. House Speaker Hiram Andrews quashed it, saying, "Sometime or other the leadership must place some bounds on the range of resolutions that are presented" (*The Sporting News*, June 17, 1959). Ironically, the Pirates won 15 of their first 16 extra inning games, Haddix's defeat being the only loss. For the season, they were 19–2 in overtime.
51. *The Sporting News*, May 27, 1959.
52. *Pittsburgh Sun-Telegraph*, July 21, 1959.
53. *Pittsburgh Press*, March 31, 1983.
54. *San Mateo Times*, June 24, 1959.
55. *Pittsburgh Press*, June 7, 1959.
56. *Ibid.*
57. *Ibid.*
58. *The Sporting News*, August 5, 1959.
59. *Kittanning Simpsons Daily Leader Times*, August 4, 1959.
60. *Ibid.*
61. *The Sporting News*, July 22, 1959.
62. Interview with Bob Oldis, August 27, 2018.
63. *The Sporting News*, October 14, 1959.
64. *The Sporting News*, September 23, 1959. Actually, the discrepancy in power wasn't that pronounced. Of the Pirates 112 home runs, 47 were hit at home and 65 on the road. The bigger difference was in batting average, which was .277 at home and .251 away from home.
65. In those days, there was a Sophomore of the Year award, and Stuart placed a distant third behind Orlando Cepeda and Vada Pinson.
66. Interview with Felix Mantilla, February 8, 2002.
67. *True*, September 1959, p. 68.
68. *True*, September 1959, p. 72.
69. An excellent article on the Home Run Derby series was written by Don Zminda for the 2011 issue of *The National Pastime*, published by the Society for American Baseball Research. It can be found online at https://sabr.org/research/home-run-derby-tale-baseball-and-hollywood.
70. Video of the Stuart-Post contest can be found on you tube at https://www.youtube.com/watch?v=HKLuPCsK83Y.
71. Video of the Stuart-Triandos contest can be found on you tube at https://www.youtube.com/watch?v=UN9dsm5dhZo.
72. Video of the Stuart-Robinson contest can be found on you tube at https://www.youtube.com/watch?v=1ZESIXtRz9Y. Although the show was fairly popular, it lasted just one season. Scott, the major force behind it, died of a heart attack in July 1960, about halfway through the showing of the taped episodes. With Scott gone, the show was dropped.
73. Interview with Ken MacKenzie, April 28, 2020.

Chapter 9

1. *Sports Illustrated*, April 17, 1960.
2. Burgess continued to play through 1967, appearing almost exclusively as a pinch hitter in his later years, and set a record for career pinch hits.
3. Interview with Dick Groat, July 13, 2018.
4. *Cumberland Evening Times*, January 8, 1960.
5. *DuBois Courier Express*, February 6, 1960.
6. *Delaware County Daily Times*, April 2, 1960.

7. *Ibid.*
8. *The Sporting News*, October 21, 1959.
9. *Saturday Evening Post*, April 28, 1962.
10. Interview with Dick Groat, July 18, 2018.
11. *Saturday Evening Post*, April 28, 1962.
12. Interview with Bob Oldis, August 27, 2018.
13. Interview with Dick Schofield, January 8, 2019.
14. Interview with Bob Friend, September 27, 2018.
15. *Ibid.*
16. Interview with Vernon Law, February 4, 2019.
17. Interview with Dick Groat, July 18, 2018.
18. *Pittsburgh Press*, March 21, 1959.
19. *Pittsburgh Press*, August 15, 1960.
20. *Pittsburgh Post-Gazette*, January 31, 1961.
21. *Pittsburgh Post-Gazette*, March 7, 1961.
22. *Boston Globe*, June 12, 1964.
23. *Pittsburgh Post-Gazette*, March 29, 1961.
24. *Pittsburgh Press*, May 10, 1961.
25. *Pittsburgh Press*, July 3, 1961.
26. *Boston Globe*, November 30, 1964.
27. *Saturday Evening Post*, April 28, 1962.
28. *Pittsburgh Press*, February 15, 1960.
29. *Pittsburgh Press*, March 3, 1960.
30. *The Sporting News*, April 13, 1960.
31. *Sports Illustrated*, April 17, 1960.
32. *The Sporting News*, May 4, 1960.
33. *The Sporting News*, May 11, 1960.
34. *Pittsburgh Press*, April 29, 1960.
35. *Pittsburgh Post-Gazette*, May 3, 1960.
36. *Corpus Christi Times*, April 29, 1960.
37. *The Sporting News*, May 11, 1960.
38. SABR Bioproject article by Mike Jaffe, https://sabr.org/bioproj/person/e4fb7b3a.
39. Interview with Ken MacKenzie, April 28, 2020.
40. *The Sporting News*, July 6, 1960.
41. *Sports Illustrated*, May 30, 1960.
42. *Pittsburgh Press*, August 3, 1980.
43. *Baseball Digest*, May 1962, *Status Quote* p. 89.
44. Leonard Shecter, "Same But Different Pirates," *Baseball Digest*, August 1961, p. 52.
45. *Los Angeles Times*, July 19, 1960.
46. *Stars and Stripes*, July 17, 1960.
47. *The Sporting News*, July 27, 1960.
48. *Saturday Evening Post*, April 28, 1962.
49. *The Sporting News*, July 13, 1960.
50. "It's not the weight or length of the bat that counts," Clemente told Stuart, "It's the name on it that means something" (*The Sporting News*, July 13, 1960). Bob Stevens, San Francisco correspondent to *The Sporting News*, indicated that Stuart had been spared a trip to the minor leagues by hitting the three homers. "He was, it was believed, within a few steps of the plane leaving for Salt Lake City," Stevens wrote (*The Sporting News*, July 13, 1960). Murtaugh later admitted he was thinking of sending Stuart down and bringing up R.C. Stevens, who had been released from the service and was playing well. Then he considered that Stevens and Stuart each had about 50 RBI and decided that 50 RBI in the majors was better than 50 in the minors (*The Sporting News*, August 10, 1960).
51. Interview with Dick Groat, July 13, 2018.
52. Interview with Dick Schofield, January 8, 2019.
53. *The Sporting News*, October 26, 1960.
54. Brosnan, *Pennant Race*, p. 47.
55. In late August, Benack and his band were temporarily banned from Forbes Field because the Pirates thought they were a jinx. When the Pirates proceeded to lose five of seven games, they were invited back. Joe Christopher suggested that Benack's band play "Donkey Serenade" every time Stuart came to bat, anticipating the "walk-up" music prevalent in today's game.
56. Keene, p. 94.
57. *Pittsburgh Press*, August 21, 1960.
58. *Pittsburgh Press*, August 17, 1960.
59. *Pittsburgh Post-Gazette*, September 18, 1960.
60. *Ibid.*
61. *Pittsburgh Post-Gazette*, July 17, 1960.
62. Interview with Dick Schofield, January 8, 2019.
63. While he was recuperating, Groat received a get-well message from Richard Nixon, whose brother Ed had been Groat's roommate at Duke. Nixon was sidelined from the presidential campaign trail by a knee injury and expressed the wish that both he and Groat would soon be back in action.
64. *Sports Illustrated*, August 8, 1960.
65. Interview with Dick Schofield, January 8, 2019.
66. Interview with Dick Schofield, May, 2002.
67. Interview with Clem Labine, August 10, 2000.
68. *Sports Illustrated*, September 26, 1960.
69. Interview with Dick Groat, July 13, 2018.
70. *Pittsburgh Post-Gazette*, January 21, 1971. Prince was known to exaggerate, and it is unlikely that a third-floor window was 90 feet above the ground. Still, leaping from the third floor into a pool was nothing to sneeze at.
71. It was often written that Hoak was an ex-Marine, but Jack Morris, who wrote the SABR Bioproject article on him, said he was unable to corroborate the facts that Hoak was a Marine or the assertion that he participated in any professional boxing matches.
72. Interview with Vern Law, February 4, 2019. MVP voters agreed with Law's assessment and placed Hoak second in the voting behind Groat. Willie Mays and Ernie Banks, whose offensive statistics were far more impressive than Hoak's, finished third and fourth, respectively. Modern statistics would question the writers' choice, as Mays had a WAR of 9.5, Banks 7.9, and Hoak 5.4.
73. *Sports Illustrated*, July 18, 1960.
74. "A. Hoak K," *Baseball Digest*, July 1963, p. 32.
75. *Sports Illustrated*, July 3, 1961.
76. *Ibid.*
77. *Ibid.*
78. Interview with Dick Schofield, January 8, 2019.

79. Interview with Gil McDougald, January 7, 2002.
80. Interview with Dick Schofield, January 8, 2019.
81. *The Sporting News*, October 19, 1960.
82. *Pittsburgh Press*, October 4, 1960.
83. Interview with Vern Law, February 4, 2019.
84. *Cumberland Evening Times*, October 7, 1960.
85. *Pittsburgh Press*, April 1, 1961.
86. One remarkable aspect of that game was that neither team registered a strikeout.
87. For a detailed account of the game, see Ryczek, *The Yankees of the Early '60s*, pp. 38–43.
88. *Pittsburgh Press*, May 11, 1987.
89. Interview with Dick Groat, July 13, 2018.
90. Interview with Bob Friend, September 27, 2018.
91. Interview with Dick Schofield, May, 2002.
92. *Sports Illustrated*, October 2, 1960.
93. Interview with Bob Oldis, August 27, 2018.
94. *Pittsburgh Post Gazette*, December 20, 2002.
95. *Pittsburgh Press*, October 14, 1960.
96. *The Sporting News*, October 26, 1960.
97. Murtaugh wasn't swept up in the glory of being the manager of a World Championship team. When the Series ended, he went back home and resumed his long-time job of clerking in a men's store.

Chapter 10

1. *The Sporting News*, November 2, 1960.
2. *Pittsburgh Press*, April 1, 1961.
3. *Ibid*.
4. *Pittsburgh Press*, April 6, 1961.
5. *Pittsburgh Press*, August 24, 1961.
6. Frankie Frisch, "My 1961 Gashouse Team," *Baseball Digest*, July 1961, p. 35.
7. Interview with Vern Law, February 4, 2019.
8. *Ibid*.
9. Brosnan, *Pennant Race*, p. 48.
10. *Ibid*.
11. *The Sporting News*, May 31, 1961. It was not exactly true that Stuart couldn't hit coming off the bench. In his first three seasons with the Pirates, Stuart, in 32 pinch-hit at bats, had nine hits, including five homers and 14 RBI.
12. Leonard Shecter, "Same But Different Pirates," *Baseball Digest*, August 1961, p. 52.
13. *Pittsburgh Press Telegram*, June 8, 1961.
14. Brosnan, *Pennant Race*, p. 98.
15. *Indiana Evening Gazette*, July 7, 1961.
16. *Pittsburgh Press*, May 31, 1961.
17. *Pittsburgh Press*, July 6, 1961.
18. *The Sporting News*, August 9, 1961.
19. Pittsburgh's Children's Hospital was a beneficiary of Stuart's power surge. Since Bill Spears donated five dollars to the hospital each time Stuart hit a homer, the hospital received $175 from Spears in 1961.
20. *Saturday Evening Post*, April 28, 1962.
21. *The Sporting News*, February 23, 1963.
22. *The Sporting News*, November 1, 1961.
23. Interview with Paul Pettit, January 30, 2020.
24. *The Sporting News*, July 9, 1966.

Chapter 11

1. *The Sporting News*, December 13, 1961.
2. *The Sporting News* loved alliterative headlines, and that over a drawing of Stuart read, "Boomed to Bloom as Buc Boundary Belter Next Year" (*The Sporting News*, December 27, 1961).
3. *The Sporting News*, December 27, 1961.
4. *The Sporting News*, February 28, 1962.
5. *Pittsburgh Post-Gazette*, February 1, 1962.
6. *The Pittsburgh Press*, April 30, 1962.
7. *Saturday Evening Post*, April 28, 1962.
8. *Ibid*.
9. *Ibid*.
10. *Ibid*.
11. *Ibid*.
12. *Pittsburgh Post Gazette*, April 24, 1962.
13. *Pittsburgh Press*, June 7, 1962.
14. *Sports Illustrated*, April 30, 1962.
15. *Sports Illustrated*, April 9, 1962.
16. On April 29, Stuart fouled a ball that broke the mask of Dodger catcher John Roseboro. Roseboro sued the manufacturer of the mask and in 1967 was awarded a $20,000 judgment.
17. *Pittsburgh Post-Gazette*, May 10, 1962.
18. *Pittsburgh Press*, May 17, 1962.
19. *Sports Illustrated*, June 18, 1962.
20. *Pittsburgh Press*, June 20, 1962.
21. *The Sporting News*, May 23, 1962.
22. *Pittsburgh Post-Gazette*, June 28, 1962.
23. Ryczek, *The Amazin' Mets* p. 132.
24. *Pittsburgh Press*, August 19, 1962.
25. *Pittsburgh Press*, June 8, 1962.
26. *Pittsburgh Press*, June 12, 1962. On July 1, 1958, Tony Taylor of the Cubs hit a ball similar to Stuart's that rolled around the Cubs bullpen. Giant left fielder Leon Wagner arrived in his usual tepid fashion and, as he searched for the ball in vain, Cub relievers stared and pointed where the ball wasn't in order to confuse him. By the time he found it Taylor, like Stuart, had rounded the bases for a home run (Ritter Collet, "Why the Eye-Dea," *Baseball Digest*, August 1962, p. 28).
27. *Pittsburgh Press*, July 21, 1962.
28. *The Sporting News*, September 8, 1962.
29. *Ibid*.
30. Olivo's biographical sketch on SABR's Bioproject page was written by Rory Costello. https://sabr.org/bioproj/person/9154766a. Olivo's brother Chi-Chi played briefly in the majors, as did his son Gilbert Rondon, born out of wedlock in 1953.
31. *Sports Illustrated*, July 16, 1962, quoted in Costello.
32. In early September, Stuart suffered yet another affront to his ego when Felix DeLeon broke his Pioneer League record by hitting 37 home runs. Worse yet, DeLeon played for Billings, which meant Stuart's team record was shattered as well.

33. Les Biederman laced into the fans for the way they treated him. "Fans?" he wrote, "who calls 'em fans?" (*The Sporting News*, September 1, 1962).
34. In 1958, despite not being called up to the Pirates in mid–July, Stuart tied Orlando Cepeda for the lead with 16 errors.
35. *Pittsburgh Press*, July 12, 1988.
36. *The Sporting News*, October 27, 1962.
37. Nowlin p. 67.
38. Nowlin p. 303.
39. Nowlin p. 331.
40. Yawkey employed so many of his buddies that the Red Sox offices were referred to as Crony Island.
41. *The Sporting News*, November 24, 1962.
42. Ibid.
43. *The Sporting News*, February 2, 1963.
44. There was a slight resemblance between Stuart and Pagliaroni, and when the latter was issued Stuart's old number 7, someone said, "Pagliaroni has two strikes on him now; he looks like Stuart and he has his old uniform number" (*The Sporting News*, March 9, 1963).
45. "Status Quote," *Baseball Digest*, February 1963, p. 4.
46. *The Sporting News*, December 1, 1962.
47. Ibid.
48. *The Sporting News*, December 8, 1962.
49. *The Sporting News*, December 1, 1962.
50. *The Sporting News*, December 8, 1962.
51. *Sports Illustrated*, September 2, 1963.
52. *The Sporting News*, December 1, 1962.
53. *Pittsburgh Post-Gazette*, December 7, 1962.
54. Hoak lost a bet to Stuart and Groat. He'd bet them he would be the first of the three to be traded, but it turned out that he was the last, being sent to the Phillies on November 28. Groat was traded on the 19th and Stuart on the 20th.
55. Interview with Bob Friend, September 27, 2018. Joe Brown told Les Biederman about an angry fan who called to cancel his season tickets after he learned that Groat had been traded. "No amount of reasoning could persuade this fan to sit tight," said Brown. When Stuart was traded a day later, Brown said, the fan called and asked if he could have his seats back (*The Sporting News*, December 8, 1962).
56. Interview with Dick Groat, July 13, 2018.
57. Brown was correct in his belief that Hoak was finished as a major league player. He completed one sub-par season with the Phillies and was released early the next year. He later managed in the minor leagues and served as a Pirate broadcaster. When the Pirates fired Larry Shepard as manager near the end of the 1969 season, Hoak openly campaigned for the job. Joe Brown had other ideas, however, and brought back Danny Murtaugh for a second tour of duty. The day Murtaugh's appointment was announced, Hoak was at home when he saw someone attempting to steal his brother-in-law's car. He jumped in his own car, took off in pursuit and suffered a fatal heart attack.
58. *The Sporting News*, December 8, 1962.

Chapter 12

1. Sam Greene, "The Champion Nobody Knows," *Baseball Digest*, February 1963, p. 31.
2. Quoted in *The Sporting News*, December 22, 1962.
3. *Pittsburgh Press*, December 12, 1962.
4. *Boston Globe*, March 22, 1964.
5. *Pittsburgh Press*, December 12, 1962.
6. *The Boston Globe*, April 24, 1963.
7. Stuart claimed it was $200 a week and a new car.
8. *Greenfield Recorder Gazette*, March 10, 1964.
9. *Pittsburgh Press*, January 22, 1963.
10. *Sports Illustrated*, April 8, 1963.
11. Ibid.
12. *The Sporting News*, March 9, 1963.
13. *The Sporting News*, March 16, 1963.
14. Ibid.
15. Geiger had graciously given up his #7 to Stuart.
16. *Boston Globe*, April 1, 1964.
17. *The Sporting News*, April 6, 1963.
18. *Scottsdale Progress*, March 5, 1963.
19. *The Sporting News*, April 20, 1963.
20. *Hagerstown Daily Mail*, March 16, 1963.
21. *Sports Illustrated*, June 28, 1965.
22. Yastrzemski and Hirshberg, p. 130.
23. Yastrzemski and Hirshberg, p. 134.
24. *The Sporting News*, January 5, 1963.
25. *Sports Illustrated*, April 8, 1963.
26. *Boston Globe*, April 29, 1963.
27. *The Sporting News*, June 15, 1963.
28. Conley returned to the Knicks for the 1963–64 season and, his arm still not recovered, was released by the Red Sox in the spring of 1964. He never played in the NBA again, although he played and coached minor league basketball for several years.
29. *The Sporting News*, September 14, 1963.
30. *Boston Globe*, June 2, 1963.
31. Interview with Ed Bressoud, June 1, 2002.
32. *Pittsburgh Press*, June 21, 1963.
33. *Boston Globe*, June 24, 1963.
34. Interview with Jack Lamabe, June 3, 2002.
35. quoted in *The Sporting News*, July 13, 1963.
36. *Boston Globe*, July 1, 1963.
37. Interview with Felix Mantilla, February 8, 2002.
38. *The Sporting News*, July 13, 1963.
39. *North Adams Transcript*, July 2, 1963, and *Boston Globe* July 2, 1963.
40. *Boston Globe*, July 2, 1963.
41. *Pittsburgh Press*, February 3, 1964. That wasn't exactly true. The Boston fans didn't boo Stuart in the opener. It took them a couple of weeks to get around to razzing him.
42. Joe Brown was one man who was glad Stuart was left off the All-Star team. Groat had been named to the NL squad and Don Leppert, who Brown had traded to the Senators, was on the AL team. It would have been worse, he said, if he had traded three all stars.

43. *Boston Globe*, July 2, 1963.
44. *The Sporting News*, November 2, 1963.
45. *The Sporting News*, July 13, 1963.
46. *Lincoln Star*, July 5, 1963.
47. *Pittsburgh Press*, July 9, 1963.
48. "Unsuited," *Baseball Digest*, April 1964, p. 45.
49. *The Sporting News*, August 10, 1963.
50. *The Sporting News*, August 24, 1963.
51. Yastrzemski and Hirshberg, p. 132.
52. *Sports Illustrated*, April 13, 1964.
53. *The Sporting News*, August 24, 1963.
54. *Ibid*.
55. *Newport Daily News*, August 20, 1963.
56. *The Sporting News*, October 5, 1963.
57. *Boston Globe*, September 22, 1963.
58. A year earlier, Stuart's strikeouts would have been an American League record, but in 1963 Dave Nicholson of the White Sox fanned 175 times and Don Lock of the Senators also bested the old mark with 151. Although Stuart always laughed about strikeout records, he was pleased when Nicholson outdid him. One time when the White Sox visited Boston and Nicholson was suffering from a bruised hand, Stuart fixed him up with a sponge pad. When a teammate teased him about helping the opposition, he replied, "Maybe so, but I've got to keep him in the lineup" (Earl Lawson, "Self-Defense," *Baseball Digest*, June 1965, p. 9).
59. *Boston Globe*, January 29, 1965.
60. Larry Merchant, who would become a big booster of Stuart when he was traded to Philadelphia, wrote a satirical column on various hypothetical all-star teams. Although Ralph Houk left Stuart off the American League team, Merchant put him on the "All-Angry" squad (Don Hoak was the third baseman) and the All-Star Worst Fielding Team (Larry Merchant, "Everybody's Some Sort of All Star," *Baseball Digest*, September 1963, p. 80).
61. *The Sporting News*, November 2, 1963.
62. *The Sporting News*, October 12, 1963.
63. *The Sporting News*, November 2, 1963.
64. *Sports Illustrated*, September 2, 1963.
65. *Ibid*.
66. *The Sporting News*, November 2, 1963.
67. *Ibid*.
68. *Pittsburgh Press*, October 9, 1963.
69. *Pittsburgh Post-Gazette*, October 21, 1963.
70. *Lake Charles American Press*, October 11, 1963.
71. Yastrzemski and Hirshberg, p. 132.
72. Interview with Ted Schreiber, January 9, 2002.
73. Yastrzemski and Hirshberg, p. 134.
74. Yastrzemski and Hirshberg, p. 135.
75. *Pittsburgh Post-Gazette*, January 9, 1964.
76. *Pittsburgh Press*, February 3, 1964.
77. *Boston Globe*, January 31, 1964.
78. *Pittsburgh Press*, February 3, 1964.

Chapter 13

1. *The Sporting News*, January 18, 1964.
2. *The Sporting News*, January 25, 1964.
3. SABR Bioproject article by Mark Armour and Mark Kanter (https://sabr.org/bioproj/person/e1dbb148).
4. *Sports Illustrated*, April 13, 1964.
5. *The Sporting News*, February 29, 1964.
6. *Boston Globe*, March 4, 1964.
7. *Boston Globe*, March 3, 1964.
8. *Pittsburgh Press*, March 18, 1964.
9. *The Sporting News*, April 4, 1964.
10. *High Point Enterprise*, March 19, 1964.
11. *Boston Globe*, March 20, 1964.
12. *The Sporting News*, April 4, 1964.
13. *Ibid*.
14. *High Point Enterprise*, March 19, 1964.
15. *Boston Globe*, April 8, 1964.
16. *The Sporting News*, April 18, 1964.
17. *Ibid*.
18. Quoted in *Pittsburgh Press*, May 3, 1964.
19. *Pittsburgh Press*, June 10, 1965.
20. *Boston Globe*, May 22, 1964.
21. One Boston writer pointed out that earlier in the game a grounder had gone through Stuart's legs and was ruled a hit. He didn't protest that decision.
22. *The Sporting News*, June 6, 1964.
23. *Salt Lake City Tribune*, June 7, 1964.
24. *Burlington Daily News Times*, June 26, 1964.
25. *The Sporting News*, July 4, 1964.
26. The manager of the previous season's pennant winner managed the All-Star team, but Ralph Houk, who'd skippered the Yankees to the flag in 1963, had resigned to take the general manager's job. Lopez, who brought the White Sox home second in 1963, was selected to manage the team.
27. *The Sporting News*, August 8, 1964.
28. *The Sporting News*, July 18, 1964.
29. *Boston Globe*, July 22, 1964.
30. *Boston Globe*, July 25, 1964.
31. *Ibid*.
32. *Boston Globe*, July 27, 1964.
33. *Boston Globe*, July 27, 1964.
34. *The Sporting News*, September 5, 1964. One night, Stuart was sent home from the park with a throat infection and swollen glands. While listening to the game on the radio, he heard the announcer say he had been benched for poor hitting and called the station to tell them the true story.
35. *The Sporting News*, September 19, 1964.
36. *Ibid*.
37. *Ibid*.
38. *The Sporting News*, September 26, 1964.
39. *North Adams Transcript*, September 12, 1964.
40. *The Sporting News*, April 3, 1965.
41. Reader Selby Martin of Toronto wrote a letter to *The Sporting News* that was highly critical of Pepitone. "Joe Pepitone is ninth in fielding among first sackers," Martin wrote, "only because Dick Stuart is in the American League, too" (*The Sporting News*, September 19, 1964).
42. *Boston Globe*, June 10, 1964.
43. *The Sporting News*, April 16, 1966. In 1968, Pesky filed a lawsuit for defamation of character against a Boston journalist who'd written a series of articles Pesky claimed contained false information

about conversations he allegedly had with Stuart and Yastrzemski.
44. *Boston Globe*, June 29, 1997.
45. *Pittsburgh Press*, June 10, 1965.
46. Stuart got five hits in Herman's first game as a manager.
47. *Sports Illustrated*, June 28, 1965.
48. Interview with Dennis Bennett, April 9, 2004.
49. It seemed as though the president of every ballplayer's fan club was a female.
50. *Boston Globe*, December 1, 1964.
51. *Star News*, June 11, 1965.
52. *The Sporting News*, December 12, 1964.
53. *Sarasota Daily Times*, November 30, 1964.
54. Sandy Grady, "They Kicked Stuart in His Ego," *Baseball Digest*, May 1966, p. 73.
55. "Will Gene Mauch Outmanage Himself?" *Baseball Digest*, September 1963, p. 19.
56. Allen Lewis, "How Phils Blew Big Lead, Flag," *Baseball Digest*, December-January 1965, p. 91.
57. *The Sporting News*, April 5, 1969.
58. *Sports Illustrated*, July 26, 1965.
59. Interview with Bob Oldis, August 27, 2018.
60. "Will Gene Mauch Outmanage Himself?" *Baseball Digest*, September 1963, p. 19.
61. Interview with Gary Kroll, February 27, 2002.
62. Allen Lewis, "How Phils Blew Big Lead," *Baseball Digest*, December-January 1965, p. 91.
63. Interview with Don Bosch, January 14, 2003.
64. *The Sporting News*, December 12, 1964.
65. *Ibid*. The five games Guindon played in 1964 were the only ones he would play in the major leagues. Although he was a talented youngster who, as an 18-year-old in 1962, hit 37 homers and drove in 121 runs in the New York-Penn League, he lacked the confidence of a Dick Stuart. In 1963, Guindon told the Red Sox he would rather report to the minor league spring camp than train with the parent club. He'd gone to the Red Sox camp the previous year and, not knowing anyone, had been lonely. He thought he'd be more comfortable with minor leaguers. That was fortunate, for the minor leagues were where Guindon spent almost his entire baseball career.
66. *Boston Globe*, November 30, 1964.
67. Si Burick, "Philadelphia Boo-Boo," *Baseball Digest*, December 1968-January 1969, p. 63.
68. *The Sporting News*, February 20, 1965.
69. "Status Quote," *Baseball Digest*, January 1963, 4. Lavender was a term suggesting homosexuality.
70. *Sports Illustrated*, April 19, 1965.
71. "Status Quote," *Baseball Digest*, August 1965, p. 4.

Chapter 14

1. *The Sporting News*, January 2, 1965.
2. *Ibid*.
3. *The Sporting News*, February 27, 1965.
4. *Pittsburgh Post-Gazette*, March 9, 1965.
5. *The Sporting News*, February 13, 1965.
6. *Lowell Sun*, February 10, 1965.
7. *Salt Lake City Tribune*, March 1, 1965.
8. *The Sporting News*, February 27, 1965.
9. *Bradford Era*, March 3, 1965.
10. *Lawton Constitution*, March 9, 1965.
11. Stuart did have fun when he encountered Pesky. After he waved at a ground ball hit by a Pittsburgh batter, he turned to Pesky in the first base coach's box and said, "That would have bothered you in Boston, John, but now you can laugh about it" (*Boston Globe*, March 26, 1965).
12. *Boston Globe*, March 17, 1965.
13. *Ibid*.
14. *Ibid*.
15. *Ibid*.
16. *Philadelphia Daily News*, April 1, 1965. Pesky took most of Stuart's remarks in good humor. At an event in Pittsburgh, he revealed that members of the Dick Stuart Fan Club of Pittsburgh made a trip to Cleveland in 1964 and signed Pesky up as a member (*Pittsburgh Press-Gazette*, April 16, 1965).
17. *Boston Globe*, March 18, 1965.
18. *Philadelphia Daily News*, March 3, 1965.
19. *Pittsburgh Post-Gazette*, March 22, 1965.
20. *Zanesville Town Recorder*, January 14, 1965.
21. *Boston Globe*, March 26, 1965.
22. *Philadelphia Daily News*, April 1, 1965.
23. *Lowell Sun*, February 10, 1965.
24. *The Sporting News*, March 20, 1965.
25. *Appleton Post Crescent*, March 30, 1965.
26. *Sarasota Herald Tribune*, April 6, 1965.
27. *The Sporting News*, April 3, 1965. Having Stuart and Belinsky on the same team would put a strain on the clubhouse mirrors, for *The Sporting News* reported that the two shared the record (35 minutes) for the longest time spent in front of a mirror getting ready for a game.
28. *Ibid*.
29. *Chester County Daily Times*, April 15, 1965.
30. *Bristol Daily Courier*, April 15, 1965.
31. *Chester County Daily Times*, April 19, 1965.
32. *Ibid*.
33. *Boston Globe*, May 2, 1965.
34. *The Philadelphia Inquirer*, April 26, 1965.
35. *The Sporting News*, May 8, 1965.
36. *Lebanon Daily News*, May 6, 1965.
37. *Ibid*.
38. *The Sporting News*, May 15, 1965.
39. *Philadelphia Daily News*, May 6, 1965.
40. *Ibid*.
41. *Boston Globe*, May 6, 1965.
42. *Philadelphia Daily News*, March 4, 1965.
43. *The Sporting News*, May 15, 1965.
44. *Pittsburgh Press*, June 10, 1965.
45. *Lubbock Avalanche Journal*, July 26, 1966.
46. *The Sporting News*, May 8, 1965.
47. It was also turning out to be a long season for Bo Belinsky. In July, he declared himself disgusted with the Philadelphia social scene. It was "for the birds," he said, and indicated that it would take him about two minutes to get out of town after the season ended (*Sports Illustrated*, July 19, 1965). After the season he added, "I am going to spend my winter forgetting about my summer" (Larry Merchant, "Oh,

Woe is Bo!" *Baseball Digest*, December 1965-January 1966, p. 55).

48. *Pittsburgh Press*, May 27, 1965.
49. *Ibid.*
50. *Philadelphia Daily News*, May 25, 1965.
51. Early in the season, when Mauch was booed by Philadelphia fans, a reporter wrote, "The fans booed so loudly it sounded as if they thought Gene was Dick Stuart in disguise" (*Philadelphia Inquirer*, April 21, 1965).
52. *Pittsburgh Press*, May 27, 1965.
53. *Pittsburgh Press*, June 2, 1965.
54. *Ibid.*
55. *Lebanon Daily News, July 3, 1965.*
56. *Philadelphia Daily News*, June 19, 1965.
57. *The Sporting News*, March 19, 1966.
58. Ryczek, *The Amazin' Mets*, p. 134.
59. *Philadelphia Daily News*, June 25, 1965.
60. *Ibid.*
61. *Philadelphia Daily News*, July 23, 1965.
62. I have interviewed a few hundred former baseball and football players over the years and Thomas is the only one who ever complained about what I wrote about him. After *The Amazin' Mets* came out, I sent Thomas a copy as thanks for doing an interview. Shortly afterward, I received a lengthy, handwritten letter. Frank thought that he deserved a picture, since he hit 34 home runs during the Mets' first season, and he was upset that I had quoted another player who said Frank was not a very good fielder.
63. A good retrospective account of the fight is in *The Philadelphia Enquirer*, posted by Frank Fitzpatrick, July 2, 2015, https://www.philly.com/philly/sports/phillies/311524701.html
64. Another version of the story had Thomas making racist comments to teammate Johnny Briggs and Allen interceding.
65. *Philadelphia Inquirer*, July 5, 1965. According to Allen's autobiography, Mauch threatened to fine him $2500 if he ever spoke about the incident (Dick Allen and Tim Whitaker, *Crash, The Life and Times of Dick Allen*, Ticknor and Fields, 1989, pp. 8–9).
66. *Philadelphia Inquirer*, July 5, 1965.
67. The bat was used as a weapon more often in 1965 than perhaps in any other big-league season. In the most notorious incident, Giant pitcher Juan Marichal skulled Dodger catcher John Roseboro and in a less-publicized fracas, Cleveland infielder Pedro Gonzalez clubbed Tiger pitcher Larry Sherry.
68. *Philadelphia Daily News*, June 3, 1965.
69. *Ibid.*
70. *Ibid.*
71. *Philadelphia Daily News*, June 3, 1965.
72. *The Sporting News*, August 14, 1965.
73. Stan Hochman, "Eliminate Infield Practice," *Baseball Digest*, June 1965, p. 31.
74. John P. Carmichael, "Hidden Call Trick," *Baseball Digest*, February 1966, p. 72.
75. *Philadelphia Daily News*, August 5, 1965.
76. *El Paso Herald Post*, August 14, 1965.
77. *Philadelphia Daily News*, January 27, 1966.
78. *The Sporting News*, October 2, 1965.
79. *Phoenix Republican*, September 1, 1965.
80. *Ibid.*
81. *Philadelphia Daily News*, September 27, 1965.
82. *Philadelphia Daily News*, October 4, 1965.
83. *Ibid.*
84. *The Sporting News*, October 30, 1965.
85. *The Sporting News*, September 4, 1965.
86. *The Sporting News*, March 5, 1966.
87. *Sporting News* reader Art Richardson wrote a letter claiming that Clendenon was a better fielder than Stuart, even though he made more errors. He went over putout and assist figures and summarized, "[M]any of Clendenon's errors came on off-balance throws. He reached ground balls that Stuart wouldn't get close to. Just watch Clendenon play a game. Watch his smooth, agile motion and his unmatched stretch on close plays and you will know why he is never booed for his fielding (*The Sporting News*, April 30, 1966).
88. *The Sporting News*, September 4, 1965.
89. *Boston Globe*, June 1, 1967.
90. *Xenia Daily Gazette*, November 27, 1965.
91. *The Sporting News*, November 13, 1965.
92. Sandy Grady, "Ol' Kingfish a Swinger," *Baseball Digest*, June 1963, p. 37.
93. *Salisbury Daily Times*, November 2, 1965.
94. *The Sporting News*, January 8, 1966.
95. *The Sporting News*, February 12, 1966.
96. Of the 19 non-pitchers who played for Philadelphia in 1965, only Covington, Thomas, and catcher Gus Triandos were older than Stuart. All three were out of the major leagues by the end of the 1966 season.

Chapter 15

1. Sandy Grady, "They Kicked Stuart in His Ego," *Baseball Digest*, May 1966, p. 73.
2. *Philadelphia Daily News*, February 1, 1966.
3. *Philadelphia Daily News*, April 25, 1966.
4. After Graham retired from playing baseball, he became a very successful coach at San Jacinto Junior College and Rice University. At San Jacinto, he won five national junior college titles in six years and coached future major league stars Roger Clemens and Andy Pettitte. Graham then led Rice to the College World Series title in 2003.
5. *New York Daily News*, February 23, 1966.
6. *Ibid.*
7. *Philadelphia Inquirer*, February 23, 1966.
8. *Oneonta Star*, March 12, 1966.
9. *Philadelphia Daily News*, February 23, 1966.
10. *Ibid.*
11. Kranepool stayed with the Mets through 1979, the last active link to the club's initial season.
12. *The Sporting News*, April 16, 1966. By 1966, young players were subject to military service and part of Kranepool's value was the fact that, as the sole support of his widowed mother, he was ineligible for the draft.
13. "It may be," wrote one reporter, "the first time in the history of the Ford Motor Company that a

pair of Lincoln Continental owners have been platooned at first base by the worst team in the history of baseball." It is not certain if Stuart had traded in his Caddy or if the writer just disregarded the facts in the interest of creating a *bon mot* (unidentified article in Stuart's player file at the Giamatti Research Center, dated February 23, 1966).
14. *The Sporting News*, March 19, 1966.
15. Unidentified clipping in Stuart's player file at the Giamatti Research Center. In early 1966, Pepe was writing for *The World Telegram and Sun*.
16. *New York Daily News*, February 23, 1966.
17. *The Sporting News*, March 19, 1966.
18. Unidentified clipping in Stuart's player file at the Giamatti Research Center.
19. *Oxnard Press Courier*, February 23, 1966.
20. *Daily Review,* Hayward, California, March 10, 1966.
21. *Philadelphia Daily News*, February 23, 1966.
22. *The Sporting News*, March 19, 1966.
23. *The Sporting News*, April 16, 1966.
24. *Philadelphia Daily News*, February 23, 1996.
25. Unidentified clipping in Stuart's player file at the Giamatti Research Center.
26. *Bennington Banner*, February 25, 1966.
27. He was correct, although Banks had the same number of home runs.
28. The average home in the United States at that time sold for just over $20,000.
29. *Redlands Daily Facts*, April 19, 1966.
30. Interview with Lou Klimchock, May 30, 2002.
31. *Pittsburgh Press*, April 8, 1966.
32. *New York Daily News*, April 3, 1966.
33. Kranepool completed the at bat and took a third strike, but the strikeout was charged to Stuart, one of the 957 of his career for which he couldn't be given all the blame.
34. *Boston Globe*, May 14, 1966.
35. *New York Daily News*, June 2, 1966.
36. Stuart taped about 20 episodes for future viewing but most would never be shown.
37. *The Sporting News*, July 2, 1966.
38. *The Sporting News*, March 22, 1969.
39. *The Sporting News*, May 7, 1966.
40. *Los Angeles Times*, July 6, 1966.
41. Ironically, Stuart was released to make room for his old teammate, Bob Friend, who was acquired from the Yankees.
42. *Mount Vernon Register News*, July 31, 1966.
43. Post by Mike Simpson on October 25, 2001 on Ultimate Mets Database (ultimatemets.com).
44. *The Sporting News*, July 2, 1966.
45. While he was unemployed, Stuart received one bit of good news. He had made a major fuss over being left off the American League All Star team in 1963, but after he was released by the Mets, he received one vote for the 1966 NL team. The vote was cast by Pirate pitcher Al McBean, who also voted for light-hitting infielders Hal Lanier and Tito Fuentes of the Giants. McBean said he voted for them because they couldn't hit him.
46. *Philadelphia Inquirer*, June 18, 1966.

47. *Boston Globe*, June 26, 1966. "When a guy has ten thumbs," Collins quipped, "at least one of them has to be green."
48. *Pittsburgh Press*, July 6, 1966.
49. In 63 career at bats, Stuart hit .286 off Koufax, with five home runs. That was better than most major league hitters fared against the overpowering Dodger lefty.
50. *The Sporting News*, August 6, 1966.
51. *Sports Illustrated*, July 18, 1966.
52. *Los Angeles Times*, July 7, 1966.
53. *The Sporting News*, January 7, 1967.
54. *Sports Illustrated*, August 7, 1966.
55. *The Sporting News*, August 13, 1966.
56. *Ibid.*
57. Interview with Dick Schofield, January 8, 2019.
58. *Boston Globe*, August 3, 1966.
59. *Ibid.*
60. *Sports Illustrated*, September 26, 1966.
61. *Sports Illustrated*, September 19, 1966.
62. Jaster had been a particular nemesis to the Dodgers. He posted an 11–5 record in his rookie season of 1966, with five shutouts, all against the Dodgers. He didn't have a long major league career but nine of his 35 wins came against Los Angeles.
63. *Oxnard Press Courier*, August 13, 1968.
64. *Boston Globe*, October 8, 1966.
65. Melvin Durslag, "Pity Too Good for Dodgers," *Baseball Digest*, December 1966-January 1967, p. 29.
66. Bob Stevens, "Orioles Won on One Pitch," *Baseball Digest*, December 1966-January 1967, p. 25.
67. *Boston Globe*, October 7, 1960.
68. *The Sporting News*, October 22, 1966.

Chapter 16

1. Captain Maury Wills had suffered from nagging injuries all season and accompanied the team to Japan on the condition that he would partake in the social aspects of the tour but not play. When Alston put him in the lineup, he became upset and left for the States after just four games, saying he needed medical treatment for his knee. O'Malley was so angry he told GM Buzzie Bavasi to trade Wills, who was soon sent to the Pittsburgh Pirates.
2. A good summary of the tour can be found at www.walteromalley.com/en/dodger-history/international-relations/1966-Japan-Tour_Page-1.
3. Stuart also won a home run hitting contest with six other players.
4. Even so, no Japanese player went to the major leagues until Hideo Nomo signed with the Dodgers in 1995.
5. *The Sporting News*, January 7, 1967.
6. Sandy Grady, "Mauch Can't Kick the Habit—Now He has Gentile!" *Baseball Digest*, March 1967, p. 61.
7. In *The Sporting News* of February 11, 1967, it was stated that Stuart had signed a contract, but of

course the Dodgers could release him at any time. He was not on the Dodger roster.

8. The Dodgers had to fill the shoes of Maury Wills that spring, and after watching a number of prospects fail at shortstop, partly because none of them could hit, Alston joked to his coaches that perhaps they should try Stuart at the position.
9. *Ottumwa Courier*, July 27, 1967.
10. *Pacific Stars and Stripes*, March 6, 1967.
11. Most Japanese contracts also provided some fringe benefits, especially for Americans. Some included a provision that the team would pay the income taxes incurred in Japan and/or the United States. Joe Stanka's contact called for the team to pay his rent, travel expenses, utilities, and medical expenses. In addition, if he or any member of his family died in Japan the team would pay to ship the body back to the United States.
12. *Kittanning Simpson Leader Times*, April 6, 1967.
13. *The Sporting News*, April 22, 1967.
14. *Los Angeles Herald Examiner*, April 5, 1967.
15. Robert Fitts has written extensively about Japanese baseball, and I have relied heavily on two of his books, *Mashi*, a biography of Masanori Murakami, and *Banzai Babe Ruth*, an account of the 1934 tour, for background on Japanese baseball.
16. In its June 25, 1962 issue, *Sports Illustrated* ran a feature story on Stanka's experience in Japan.
17. Fitts, *Mashi*, p. 20.
18. Fitts, *Mashi*, p. 9.
19. In 1977, a former Giants player wrote an expose about the team and its training methods. Perhaps the most shocking revelation was that the players' wives were unhappy about the team's rule that in order to conserve energy, players were to refrain from sexual relations during the season. Although it's unclear how this rule could be enforced, Yomiuri management apparently thought the team was more important than the players' marriages (Whiting, p. 5).
20. Interview with Vernon Law, February 4, 2019.
21. Robert Whiting, "You've Gotta Have Wa," www.japanesebaseball.com/writers/display.gsp?id=18777. While he was in Japan, Stuart talked with former Phillies teammate Bo Belinsky about playing there. Had he done so, Bo would undoubtedly have added more fuel to the anti-American argument.
22. Interview with Kent Hadley, February 16, 2001.
23. Al Abrams, "Off the Record Conversation," *Baseball Digest*, June 1968, p. 89.
24. Interview with John Miller, May 24, 2002.
25. Interview with George Altman, July 3, 2001.
26. Stuart was known to exaggerate, and it is questionable how many Japanese had read the American classic.
27. *Star News*, Pasadena, California, May 25, 1967.
28. Interview with Jim Marshall, April 1, 2019.
29. *Pittsburgh Press*, June 14, 1967.

30. *Pacific Stars and Stripes*, July 30, 1967.
31. *Ibid.*
32. There were only two grass infields in the Central League; the rest were dirt.
33. Rick Talley, "Dick Stuart Scores Again," *Baseball Digest*, June 1969, p. 18.
34. *The Sporting News*, February 10, 1968.
35. Excellent sources for the early visits of African American teams to Japan are *Biz Mackey in Japan* by Bill Staples, Jr., in *The Newark Eagles Take Flight: The Story of the 1946 Negro League Champions* (SABR, 2019) and Kazuo Sayama, "Their Throws Were Like Arrows—How a Black Team Spurred Pro Ball in Japan," *Baseball Research Journal* 16 (1987) pp. 85–88.
36. *Pacific Stars and Stripes*, October 28, 1968.
37. *Pacific Stars and Stripes*, April 8, 1968.
38. *Pittsburgh Post-Gazette*, April 3, 1975.
39. *Pacific Stars and Stripes*, September 29, 1968.
40. *The Sporting News*, March 22, 1969.
41. *Pacific Stars and Stripes*, September 29, 1968.

Chapter 17

1. *The Sporting News*, March 8, 1969.
2. *The Sporting News*, April 26, 1969.
3. *The Sporting News*, March 22, 1969.
4. There was no television show for Stuart in Los Angeles. The best he could do was a guest appearance on *Hollywood Squares*.
5. *The Sporting News*, March 22, 1969.
6. *Bedford Daily Gazette*, March 21, 1969.
7. *Los Angeles Times*, March 24, 1969.
8. *Mount Vernon* (IL) *News*, March 11, 1969.
9. *Los Angeles Times*, April 2, 1969.
10. About the only positive mention Stuart received was when he hit a foul pop into the stands that was caught by the wife of Angel broadcaster Dick Enberg, who was making his debut as a major league baseball announcer.
11. *El Paso Herald Post*, April 15, 1969.
12. *The Sporting News*, April 26, 1969. Stuart's memory was not quite accurate, for in 1963 he was 0 for 5 before getting his first hit.
13. *Kansas City Star*, May 9, 1969.
14. *Boston Globe*, May 21, 1969.
15. John Hall, "Why Losers Find It a Long Season," *Baseball Digest*, July 1969, p. 85.
16. *Los Angeles Times*, May 29, 1969.
17. Bob August, "The One-Handed Fielding of Leon Wagner," *Baseball Digest*, May 1965, p. 31.
18. "Status Quote," *Baseball Digest*, February 1969, p. 58.
19. Bill Libby, "Daddy Wags—And Gags," *Baseball Digest*, November 1964, p. 67.
20. *The Sporting News*, August 9, 1969.
21. *Fairbanks Daily News Miner*, July 1, 1969.

Chapter 18

1. Interview with Gehr Brown, February 1, 2020.
2. *Pittsburgh Press*, October 6, 1974.

3. "Harrelson with Garagiola on Today Show," *Baseball Digest*, July 1969, p. 18.
4. Harrelson's autobiography is *Hawk,* by Ken Harrelson and Al Hirshberg, Viking Press, 1969.
5. *Pittsburgh Post-Gazette*, June 13, 1985.
6. *Boston Globe*, August 11, 1974.
7. *Pittsburgh Post-Gazette*, April 21, 1976.
8. *Pittsburgh Press*, July 7, 1985.
9. Interview with Bob Oldis, August 27, 2018.
10. Letter from Laurel Stuart, received April 27, 2020.
11. *Pittsburgh Press*, June 12, 1985.
12. *Pittsburgh Post-Gazette*, September 20, 1998.
13. *Ibid.*
14. *Ibid.*
15. *Ibid.*
16. Post by LR, January 23, 2013 on Ultimate Mets Database (ultimatemets.com).
17. *Pittsburgh Press*, June 15, 1976.
18. *Boston Globe*, November 8, 1992.
19. *Boston Globe*, June 28, 1987.
20. Letter from Laurel Stuart.
21. *Ibid.*

Bibliography

Newspapers

Akron Beacon-Journal
Albuquerque Journal
Amarillo Daily News
Amarillo Globe Times
Appleton Post Crescent
Atlanta Constitution
Bedford Daily Gazette
Bennington Banner
Big Spring Herald
Billings Gazette
Boston Globe
Bradford Era
Bristol Daily Courier
Burlington Daily Times News
Chester County Daily Times
Chicago Tribune
Corpus Christi Times
Cumberland Evening Times
The Daily Chronicle
Daily Review (Hayward, CA)
Delaware County Daily Times
DuBois Courier Express
El Paso Herald Post
Fairbanks Daily News Miner
Fitchburg Sentinel
Florence Morning News
Greenfield Recorder-Gazette
Hagerstown Daily Mail
High Point Enterprise
Humboldt Standard
Indiana Evening Gazette
Kansas City Star
Kenosha Evening News
Kittanning Simpson Leader Times
Lake Charles American Press
Lawton Constitution
Lebanon Daily News
Lima News
Lincoln Journal
Lincoln Journal-Star
Lincoln Star
Lincoln Sunday Star and News
Los Angeles Daily News
Los Angeles Herald & Express
Los Angeles Herald-Examiner
Los Angeles Times
Lowell Sun
Lubbock Avalanche Journal
Modesto Bee
Mount Vernon News
Mount Vernon Register-News
New York Daily News
Newport Daily News
North Adams Transcript
Oneonta Star
Ottumwa Courier
Oxnard Press-Courier
Pacific Stars and Stripes
Philadelphia Daily News
Philadelphia Inquirer
Phoenix Republican
Pittsburgh Post-Gazette
Pittsburgh Press
Pittsburgh Sun-Telegraph
Press-Ledger
Press-Telegram
Redlands Daily Facts
Salisbury Daily Times
Salt Lake City Tribune
San Mateo Times
Sarasota Daily Times
Sarasota Herald Tribune
Scottsdale Progress
Star News (Pasadena, CA)
Stars and Stripes
Times-Picayune
Williamsport Sun-Gazette
Xenia Daily Gazette
Zanesville Town Recorder

Magazines

Baseball Digest
Baseball Research Journal (Society for American Baseball Research)
Life
The National Pastime (Society for American Baseball Research)
Saturday Evening Post
The Sporting News
Sports Illustrated
Time
True, the Men's Magazine

Interviews

George Altman
Dick Beverage
Don Bosch
Ed Bressoud
Gehr Brown
Harry Dunlop
Larry Foss
Bob Friend
Larry Gerlach
Dick Groat
Kent Hadley
Lou Klimchock
Gary Kroll
Clem Labine
Jack Lamabe
Vernon Law
Ken MacKenzie
Felix Mantilla
Jim Marshall
Gil McDougald
John Miller
Bob Oldis
Paul Pettit
Don Rowe
Dick Schofield
Ted Schreiber
Frank Thomas
Bill Virdon
Bob Wirz

Books

Bratkovich, Stephen M. *Bob Oldis: A Life in Baseball*. Minneapolis: Levins, 2015.
Brosnan, Jim. *Pennant Race: The Classic Game-by-Game Account of a Championship Season, 1961*. New York: Harper & Row, 1962.
Faulkner, William. *The Sound and The Fury*. New York: Vintage, 1990.
Fitts, Robert K. *Banzai Babe Ruth: Baseball, Espionage, and Assassination During the 1934 Tour of Japan*. Lincoln: University of Nebraska Press, 2012.
_____. *Mashi: The Unfulfilled Baseball Dreams of Masanori Murkami, the First Japanese Major Leaguer*. Lincoln: University of Nebraska Press, 2014.
Harrelson, Ken, with Al Hishberg. *Hawk: I Did It My Way*. New York: Viking Press, 1969.
Keene, Kerry. *1960: The Last Pure Season*. Champaign: Sports Publishing, 2000.
Lowenfish, Lee. *Branch Rickey: Baseball's Ferocious Gentleman*. Lincoln: University of Nebraska Press, 2007.
Mariness, David. *Clemente: The Passion and Grace of Baseball's Last Hero*. New York: Simon & Schuster, 2006.
Nowlin, Bill. *Tom Yawkey: Patriarch of the Boston Red Sox*. Lincoln: University of Nebraska Press, 2018.
Ryczek, William J. *The Amazin' Mets 1962–1969*. Jefferson, NC: McFarland, 2008.
_____. *Yankees of the Early '60s*. Jefferson, NC: McFarland, 2008.
Staples, Bill, Jr. "Biz Mackey in Japan." In *The Newark Eagles Take Flight: The Story of the 1946 Negro League Champions*, edited by Frederick C. Bush and Bill Nowlin, 106–108. Phoenix: Society for American Baseball Research, 2019.
Whalen, Thomas J. *Spirit of '67: The Cardiac Kids, El Birdos, and the World Series That Captured America*. Lanham, MD: Rowman and Littlefield, 2017.
White, Gaylon, *The Bilko Athletic Club, The Story of the 1956 Los Angeles Angels*. Lanham, MD: Rowman and Littlefield, 2014.
Yastrzemski, Carl, with Al Hirshberg. *Yaz*. New York: Grosset and Dunlap, 1970.

Other

Baseball Reference
nationalpost.com
The Physics of Baseball, website, Alan M. Nathan, University of Illinois: http://baseball.physics.illinois.edu/Denver.html
Retrosheet.org
SABR Bioproject
sabr.org
U.S. Census
Wikipedia
youtube.com

Index

Aaron, Hank 86, 91, 104, 118, 153, 162, 230
Abrams, Al 39, 66, 83, 90, 97, 119, 143
Adcock, Joe 86, 114, 197
Agcaoili, Francis 192
Aguilas Cibenas 51–52
Aker, Jack 199
Albuquerque Dukes 29–31, 33, 226
Allen, Richie 157–158, 161, 164, 167–168, 173, 227, 237
Allison, Bob 138–140, 149, 153
Alou, Felipe 56, 75
Alou, Jesus 163
Alou, Matty 163
Alston, Walter 86, 165, 182–184, 238–239
Altman, George 192–193, 195
Amarillo Gold Sox 27, 32, 34–35, 48, 50
Amaro, Ruben 163, 167, 171
Anderson, Vic 31, 33
Andrews, Hiram 231
Andrews, Mike 203
Anton, Phillip 56, 229
Antonucci, Phillip E. 116, 168
Aparicio, Luis 134
Arito, Michivo 192–193
Arrigo, Gerry 166
Ashburn Richie 124
Aspromonte, Bob 166
Aspromonte, Ken 192
Atkinson, Paul 46
Atlanta Crackers 13, 45–47

Bailey, Bob 126, 189
Baker, Bill 64
Balobeck, Joseph J. 101
Balter, Sam 68
Baltimore (IL) 36
Baltimore Orioles 135, 147, 149, 186
Banks, Ernie 75, 149, 179, 230, 232
Barber, Walter (Red) 13, 194
Barone, Dick 14
Barr, Joseph 107
Bates, Buddy 45–47, 49
Bauman, Joe 32, 35–36
Bauta, Ed 98
Bavasi, Emil (Buzzy) 182, 185, 189, 238

Becker, Dick 226
Beene, Charley 22, 24
Beiderman, Les 38, 40, 54, 61, 75, 80, 93, 96–97, 100, 108, 110, 113, 116, 120, 135, 138, 143, 161, 165, 193, 209, 234
Belinsky, Bo 158, 162, 165, 171, 236, 239
Bell, Bill 48
Bell, Josh 209
Benack, Benny 100–101, 232
Bennett, Dave 160
Bennett, Dennis 154, 155, 157–161, 165, 172, 202
Benny, Jack 16, 42, 179
Berle, Milton 183
Bernhardt, Jim 46
Bernier, Carlos 57–58,
Berra, Yogi 62, 69, 89, 107
Beverage, Dick 41–42
Biebel, Don 70
Bilko, Steve 41, 43–44, 57, 79, 197
Billings Mustangs 11–17, 19–20, 22–24
Bird, John I. 206
Blackwell, Ewell 63
Blanchard, John 2, 136, 139
Blanton, Hugh 34
Blomberg, Ron 206
Boise Yankees 13
Bolin, Bob 167
Bonds, Barry 8
Bonds, Bobby 8
Boone, Aaron 12
Bosch, Don 157
Boston Celtics 128
Boston Red Sox 4–5, 124–125, 128, 130, 132–136, 139, 142–143, 145–148, 151–153, 157–158, 161, 171–172, 199, 234
Bouton, Jim 139
Boyer, Ken 172, 178–180
Bradley, Hugh 131
Bragan, Bobby 39–41, 49, 64–65, 69, 71, 100, 112, 169, 171, 178, 182, 229, 230
Brennan, Dave 50
Breslin, Jimmy 34, 90, 227
Breslow, Lou 90
Bressoud, Ed 41, 135–137, 180
Brett, George 12
Bridges, Marshall 227

Briggs, John (Cubs) 72
Briggs, Johnny (Phillies) 172, 237
Bright, Harry 109
Brisker, John 207
Brooklyn Dodgers 13, 39, 40, 42, 103
Brosnan, Jim 82, 100, 102, 112–113, 231
Brown, Gehr 202–203
Brown, Hal 138
Brown, Joe E. 64
Brown, Joe L. 33, 47–49, 59, 62, 64–65, 72, 74, 76–78, 89, 93, 96, 98, 102–103, 108–109, 112, 114, 119, 125–126, 182, 234
Brown, John Mungo (Jackie) 34, 227
Brown, Paul 101
Brown Derby Restaurant 12
Bryant, Clay 43
Bryant, Don 28–32, 34–35, 47, 80, 226
Bryson, Bill 5
Buell, Bob 11
Buhler, Bill 183
Bunning, Jim 157, 161
Burdette, Lew 80–81, 85, 102, 231
Burgess, Forrest (Smoky) 64, 76–77, 89, 98, 113, 122, 209
Burick, Si 158
Burkhart, Ken 170
Burwell, Bill 63
Byerly, Bud 100

Cadbury-Schweppes 202
Cagney, Jimmy 50
California Angels 197, 199–200; see also Los Angeles Angels
California League 9–11
Callison, Johnny 157, 161, 163–164, 167, 170, 173
Camp Roberts 19
Campanella, Roy 13, 76
Campanis, Jim 193
Candlestick Park 99, 114
Cannon, Jimmy 176
Canseco, Jose 207
Caray, Harry 82, 112, 129
Carew, Rod 227
Carlton, Steve 184
Carter, Don 161
Cartwright, Al 162

243

Index

Cassini, Oleg 179
Cater, Danny 206
Causey, Wayne 137
Cavanaugh, Dr. Thomas 133
Cepeda, Orlando 75, 88, 115, 118, 144, 231
Cernkovic, Rudy 69
Chance, Bob 150, 197
Charles, Ed 137
Charleston Senators 65
Charton, Pete 152
Chase Hotel 104
Cheney, Tom 92
Chicago Cubs 66, 72, 86–88
Chicago White Sox 18
Christopher, Joe 48, 88, 99, 121, 232
Cimoli, Gino 1, 92, 95, 99, 105
Cincinnati Reds 10, 26, 53–54, 58, 72, 77, 99–102, 112, 113, 115, 185
Ciutti, Art 27, 34
Clabaugh, John (Moose) 36
Claflin, Larry 133, 141, 148, 152, 159
Clark, Jim 11
Clarke, Fred 101
Clay, Cassius 128, 135, 167
Clemens, Roger 237,
Clemente, Roberto 51, 64, 71–74, 80, 88–89, 98, 100, 102, 105, 111, 113, 116, 129, 209, 230, 232
Clements, Bob 55, 119
Clendenon, Donn 117, 123–125, 143, 171, 184, 231, 237
Cleveland Indians 150
Clinton, Lu 145, 152
Cobb, Bob 12, 23
Cobb, Ty 86
Cobb Field 12–17, 23
Cobbledick, Gordon 62
Cobos, Marcos 32
Cohen, Andy 21
Colavito, Rocky 135
Collins, Bud 128, 146, 182, 238
Colorado Rockies 55
Colorado Springs Sky Sox 28, 32, 33, 49
Condon, David 38–39
Conigliaro, Tony 145, 147, 151, 160
Conley, Gene 134, 145, 151, 234
Conlin, Bill 42, 78, 204
Connie Mack Stadium 162
Cook, Ron 231
Cope, Myron 5, 75, 93, 101, 119–120, 122
Corey, Jill 119
Courtney, Clint 166
Covington, Wes 73, 164, 172–173, 183–184, 237
Craig, Roger 73
Creamer, Robert 3
Cronin, Joe 124
Crosby, Bing 2, 62–63
Crosetti, Frank 8
Crowley, Bill 141, 147
Crues, Bob 36
Culp, Ray 170
Curtis, Al 11, 225

Dailey, Bill 138
Daley, Arthur 43
Dalrymple, Clay 101, 156, 166
Daniels, Bennie 23–24, 26, 28, 30–32, 34–35, 82–83, 109, 227
Dapper, Cliff 13–17, 22, 225
Darby Dan Farm 62
Dark, Alvin 64
Darnell, Bob 43
Dascoli, Frank 64–65, 88
Davalillo, Vic 140
Davis, Tommy 113
Davis, Willie 122, 173, 186
Dean, Dizzy 63, 98, 125
DeLeon, Felix 233
DeLimur, Charlie 2
Dent, Bucky 107
Derks, John C. 229
Derks Field 55–56, 70
Des Moines Bruins 29, 33
Desmond, Connie 13
Detore, George 87
Detroit Tigers 196
Devaney, Bob 25
Dick Stuart Fan Club 126, 236
DiMaggio, Joe 8, 41, 43
Ditmar, Art 106
Doby, Larry 190
Dolby, Ray 8
Dominican Winter League 51–52, 75, 91, 104, 122
Donatelli, Augie 23
Donohue, Mike 18
Dorish, Harry 148
Dotterer, Henry (Dutch) 79
Drabowsky, Myron (Moe) 66
Dressen, Charlie 39
Dreyfuss, Barney 69
Drysdale, Don 84, 173, 182, 186, 188
Duffalo, Jim 48
Duhem, Joe 45
Duke University 63
Dunlop, Harry 48–51
Dunn, William (Red) 22, 24
Duquesne University 100
Durante, Jimmy 42
Durocher, Leo 39, 82
Durslag, Melvin 186
Dyer, Braven 99

Earley, Arnold 140
East Texas League 36
Easter, Luke 42
Eastern League 25
Eckert, William 188
Elliot, Bob 73
Elliot, Buck 16
Ellsworth, Dick 113
Elston, Don 66
Enberg, Dick 239
Enright, Maury 14, 15, 22
Erskine, Carl 86
Erway, Don 226
Esposito, Sammy 18
Etchebarren, Andy 187

Face, Elroy 72, 78, 83–87, 94, 102, 106, 108–109, 111, 113, 122, 202, 209

Fairly, Ron 183, 186, 189
Faulkner, William 4
Fenway Park 114, 124–126, 128, 131–132, 140–142, 157, 173
Finegold, Dr. Joseph 82
Finkel, Jan vi, 4
Fitts, Robert 190, 239
Fitzgerald, Ray 172
Foiles, Hank 73, 76, 80, 92
Fondy, Dee 54
Fontaine, Bob 9, 20
Forbes, John 69
Forbes Field 1, 2, 39–40, 69–72, 74, 77, 80, 82–83, 86, 89, 100–102, 104–106, 113, 115–116, 118, 121, 126, 143, 162, 169, 170, 230
Ford, Whitey 18, 106, 114, 139
Formental, Pedro 229
Fort Lewis Explorers 18–19
Fort Ord Braves 17
Fort Ord Warriors 18–19
Fort Wayne Pistons 63
Foster, Stephen 121
Fox, Charley 200
Fox, Kenny 27
Fox, Nelson 31
Fox, Terry 133
Foxx, Jimmie 124, 131, 141
Francis, Earl 102, 122
Frank Street and Company 116, 119
Franks, Herman 170
Frederico, Freddie 198
Freeman, Moran 23
Fregosi, Jim 198, 200
Freitas, Tony 10, 225
Frick, Ford 57, 115
Friend, Bob 54, 63, 70–75, 77–78, 82, 87, 92, 94, 96–98, 102, 107, 111, 122, 124, 126, 129, 143, 179, 238
Friend, Pat 74
Frisch, Frank 110
Fuentes, Tito 238

Galbreath, John 62–63, 124, 229, 231
Garagiola, Joe 62, 82, 114, 203
Garber, Marty 33
Gehrig, Lou 4, 124, 140, 180, 190
Geiger, Gary 130, 136
Gentile, Jim 136, 149, 181–182, 188–189
Gerlach, Larry 27, 226
Gibbon, Joe 48
Gibson, Bob 180, 194
Gilbert, Buddy 24
Gilbert, Larry 20
Gillan, Max 87
Gilliam, Jim 186
Gilmore Field 44
Giltroy, Lillian 15
Goldman, Doron (Duke) vi
Gomez, Ruben 73
Gomez, Vernon (Lefty) 36
Gonder, Jesse 200
Gonzalez, Pedro 237
Gonzalez, Tony 164, 171–172

Index

Goss, Howie 30, 34–35
Gowdy, Curt 128, 148, 173
Grady, Charles 150
Grady, Sandy 128, 156
Graham, Billy 50
Graham, Jack 42
Graham, Wayne 174, 237
Grant, Jim (Mudcat) 228
Gray, Dick 98
Grayson, Harry 147
Great Falls, Montana 12
Great Falls Electrics 13, 15–16, 23
Grebe, Jim 56
Green, Ernest J. 35, 227
Green, Fred 97
Green, Lennie 149
Greenberg, Hank 70, 86, 116
Greenwich High School 205–206
Grenald, Reg 26, 28, 32, 48
Grimes, Burleigh 74
Grissom, Marv 74
Groat, Dick 4, 39, 63–64, 70–72, 80, 86–89, 92–95, 98, 100, 102–105, 107, 109, 111, 126–127, 129, 135, 172, 229, 232
Grob, Connie 18
Gross, Don 72
Gross, Milton 80, 109, 110, 160, 164
Grove, Robert (Lefty) 124
Guettler, Ken 36–37
Guindon, Bobby 157–158, 236

Haak, Howie 122, 126
Haddix, Harvey 1, 76–77, 84–86, 107, 120, 209, 231
Hadley, Kent 191–192
Hall, Dick 147
Hamilton, Jack 183
Hamlin, Ken 48
Haney, Fred 40
Harrelson, Ken 117, 203–205
Harris, Mark 50
Harwell, Ernie 13
Hathaway, Ray 37
Hauser, Joe 36
Hawaii Islanders 202
Heffner, Bob 150
Hemus, Solly 82–83
Henry, Bill 112
Herman, Babe 43
Herman, Billy 130, 140, 151, 153–154, 159, 172
Hern, Gerry 13
Hernon, Jack 20, 61–62
Herrnstein, John 157
Higgins, Mike (Pinky) 125, 134, 141, 145, 148, 154, 158, 172
Hill, Sam 21
Hinchberger, Don 11
Hinton, Chuck 197
Hoak, Don 76–77, 80, 86, 89, 94, 97–98, 103–105, 109, 119–120, 126, 189, 232, 234–235
Hobbie, Glen 86, 106, 114, 135, 207
Hobbs, O'Neal 29, 32
Hochman, Stan 170
Hodges, Gil 94, 157

Hoffa, Jimmy 50
Hoffman, Dustin 203
Hoffman, Trevor 12
Hogan, Ben 57
Holbrook, Bob 125–126
Hollingsworth, Hank 42–43
Hollywood Stars 5, 12, 24, 26, 31, 38, 40–44, 52, 55
Home Run Derby 90–91, 96, 110
Hopper, Clay 31, 227
Horne, John vi
Horton, Tony 145, 151–152, 154, 157–158, 172
Hotel Cornhusker 2, 26, 29
Hotel New Otani 193
Houk, Ralph 137–139, 143, 150–151, 153, 235
Houston Astrodome 166
Houston Astros 166
Houston Colt 45s 118, 128, 131
Howard, Elston 136
Howard, Frank 91
Huggins, Miller 53
Humboldt Crabs 18
Hunt, Ron 180, 227
Hunter, Bob 183
Hurwitz, Hy 134, 141, 160–161
Hutchinson, Fred 70, 100
Hutton, Tom 188

Idaho Falls, Montana 12
Idaho Falls Russets 13, 23, 226
Iron City Six 100
Ivor-Campbell, Fred vi

Jackson, Al 48
Jackson, Bill 26, 30, 32, 34
Jackson, Larry 98, 183
Japanese Baseball 173, 187–196, 239
Jaster, Larry 185, 238
Javier, Julian 98
Jay, Joey 115
Jefferson High School 9
Jensen, Jackie 129
John, Tommy 199
John Hancock Life Insurance Company 202
Johnson, Alex 164
Johnson, Lyndon 105–106, 190
Johnson, Roy 46
Johnson City Cardinals 206
Jones, Dalton 149
Jones, Vernal (Nippy) 79
Jorgenson, Merlin 23
Juan Carlos, Prince 50
Junior Celebrity Bowling 119

Kaese, Harold 134–135, 142, 146, 157, 161
Kaline, Al 139–140
Kansas City Athletics 102, 148, 152
Kawakami, Tetsuharu 190
Keane, Clif 180, 186
Keck, Harry 109, 118
Keefe, Bill 20–21
Keeler, Willie 184
Kent, Dick 23

Killebrew, Harmon 135, 138–140, 152
Kimball, Ken 225
Kiner, Ralph 53, 59, 62, 66, 70, 86, 97, 115–116, 229
King, Clyde 41, 43–45, 49, 228
Kirkland, Wille 52, 56, 195
Klaus, Bobby 174
Klein, Chuck 162
Klein, Lou 37
Klimchock, Lou 180, 230
Kline, Ron 71, 73, 78, 92, 95, 153
Kluszewski, Ted 14, 53–54, 59, 66–68, 74, 78–79, 81–82, 88–89, 123, 129, 197, 231
Konstanty, Jim 102
Koufax, Sandy 99, 134, 173, 182–187, 189, 194, 238
Kranepool, Ed 176–181, 185, 237–238
Kranz, Dick 50
Kravitz, Danny 40
Kress, Ralph (Red) 79
Kroll, Gary 157
Kubek, Tony 133, 153, 230
Kurowski, George (Whitey) 79

Labine, Clem 84, 103, 105, 113
Lamabe, Jack 48, 123, 125, 134, 136, 143
Landenberger, Ken 32
Landes, Stan 64–65
Lanier, Hal 238
Lardner, Ring 80, 110, 119
Larker, Norm 192
Larsen, Don 18
Lary, Frank 141
Law, Vance 191
Law, Vernon 63, 68, 71–72, 77–78, 84, 87, 94–95, 97–98, 101–102, 104, 106, 108, 110–111, 122, 129, 191, 232
Lawrence, David 74, 105
Lazzeri, Tony 8, 35–36, 55, 57, 59
Leishman, Eddie 174
LeJohn, Don 24
Lemaster, Denver 180
Lemieux, Mario 207
Lennon, Bob 36, 45
Leppert, Don 120, 234
Levy, Len 83
Lewis, Allen 156–157, 164, 171
Lewis, Buddy 98
Limmer, Lou 28
Lincoln, Abraham 4
Lincoln Chiefs 1, 3, 5, 23, 25–32, 34–35, 38, 47–52, 58
Linz, Phil 139
Linzy, Frank 170
Litman, Archie 203
Lock, Don 235
Loes, Billy 100
Logan, Johnny 73
Lolich, Mickey 199
Long, Carl 23
Long, Dale 209
Longhorn League 35–36
Lopat, Eddie 148–149

Lopez, Al 79, 149, 235
Lopez, Hector 139
Los Angeles Angels (PCL) 44
Los Angeles Angels (AL) 148; *see also* California Angels
Los Angeles Coliseum 68
Los Angeles Dodgers 55, 68, 71, 84, 94, 96, 99, 113, 143, 166, 173, 183–187, 189, 239
Lucchesi, Frank 188
Luscutoff, Jim 19

Mack, Connie 190
MacKenzie, Ken 45–47, 91, 98
Maddon, Joe 157
Magic Valley Cowboys 13
Mahaffey, Art 172
Malcolm X 167
Malmberg, Harry 130
Malzone, Frank 125, 129, 131, 136–137
Manier, Larry 16
Mann, Jack 154
Mansfield, Jayne 5, 42, 203
Mantilla, Felix 86, 89, 137, 150–151, 153
Mantle, Mickey 40, 43, 69, 71, 90, 105–107, 114–115, 118, 133, 135, 139, 179, 189, 203
Maraniss, David 62
Marichal, Juan 75, 167, 237
Maris, Roger 1, 35, 57, 95, 102, 105–106, 114–115, 118, 133, 135, 139, 146, 206
Marshall, Jim 121, 123–124, 193
Martin, Selby 235
Marvin, Frank 81, 209
Marx Brothers 42
Maslanik, Helen 126
Maslanik, Meg 126
Masuda, Akio 188
Mathews, Eddie 118, 190, 230
Mauch, Gene 155–158, 162–165, 167–169, 171–174, 178, 183, 237
Mays, Willie 18, 88, 95, 98, 115, 118, 122, 146, 163, 232
Mazeroski, Bill 1, 2, 64, 66, 69, 74, 80, 87–89, 92, 96, 99, 103, 107–108, 120, 123, 126, 136, 161, 204, 206, 209
McBean, Al 122, 181, 238
McCarthy, Joe 143
McCormick, Mike 54, 100, 114
McCovey, Willie 56, 75, 179
McCullough, Clyde 65
McDaniel, Jim 57
McDaniel, Lindy 115
McDevitt, John 227
McDougald, Gil 105, 107
McGaha, Mel 148
McGwire, Mark 206
McHale, John 182
McKechnie, Bill 54
McLish, Cal 101
McMillan, Roy 180
McNally, Dave 186–187
McNamara, John 18, 50
Mejias, Roman 133, 145

Melendez, Willie 51
Merchant, Larry 160–61, 164, 167–68, 174, 178, 235
Messersmith, Andy 199
Metropolitan Stadium 138–39, 148
Mexico City Azuls 21–22
Mickey, Bob 139
Mickey, Gene 139
Miley, Sam 26, 28, 30, 32, 35, 48, 227
Miller, John 192
Miller, Stu 100, 140
Milwaukee Braves 73, 84, 89, 98, 169, 182
Mincher, Don 197
Minneapolis Millers 36
Minnesota Twins 138–39, 149
Minoso, Orestes (Minnie) 42, 57
Mission League 17
Mize, Johnny 53
Mizell, Wilmer (Vinegar Bend) 98, 102, 111, 121
Mobile Bears 20
Modesto Reds 9–12
Monahan, Tom 130
Monbouquette, Bill 134–35, 140, 151
Monterey Merchants 17
Montreal Royals 13
Moon, Wally 113
Mooney, John 55, 59
Morehead, Dave 132, 151
Morgan, Nick 58, 202
Morris, Jack 232
Mount Vernon Generals 204
Mullen, Peter 100
Murakami, Masanori 188
Murray, Frank 50
Murray, Jim 78, 149, 170–171
Murtaugh, Danny 1, 3, 54, 65–66, 71–74, 78, 81–84, 86–88, 92–93, 97, 100–103, 106, 108, 112–113, 119–123, 125–126, 129, 131, 141, 156, 169, 172, 184, 196, 232–234
Musial, Stan 73, 77, 79

Napp, Larry 148
Narron, Sam 89
Nashville Volunteers 20, 36
Nathan, Dr. Alan M. 55
Neal, Charley 104–105
Neccai, Ron 48
Neeman, Cal 88
Nelson, Glenn (Rocky) 1, 78–79, 81, 86–87, 89, 90, 92–93, 96, 98–99, 101–102, 105–107, 109, 112–115, 117, 121, 129
Nelson, Lindsey 77
New Orleans Pelicans 20, 21, 44, 46, 65
New York Giants 42
New York Knicks 134, 234
New York Mets 118, 120, 124, 174–180, 183
New York Yankees 1, 2, 36, 105–107, 133, 135–136, 139, 143, 153
Newcombe, Don 190

Newhan, Ross 198
Newman, Willis 99
NFC Services, Ltd. 202, 204
Nichols, Chet 130
Nicholson, Dave 235
Niekro, Phil 230
Nixon, Kent 194, 196
Nixon, Richard 232
Nixon, Russ 136
Nold, Bob 19
Nomo, Hideo 238
Novikoff, Lou 229
Nowak, Jake 21

O'Brien, John 54
Oceak, Frank 13, 26, 51–53, 122
O'Connell, Dick 138
O'Dell, Billy 99
O'Doul, Lefty 190
Ogden Reds 13
Oh, Sadaharu 193
Oldis, Bob 2, 88, 93, 107, 156, 166, 205
Oliva, Tony 227
Olivo, Diomedes 122
Olivo, Federico (Chi-Chi) 233
Olson, Andy 26
O'Malley, Walter 188–189, 238
O'Neill, Paul 12
O'Toole, Jim 115
Ott, Mel 177
Outlar, Jesse 46

Pacific Coast League 12, 18, 26, 31, 36, 38, 40–44, 47, 55–56, 59, 200
Paepke, Jack 22, 24
Pafko, Andy 86
Page, Joe 84
Pagliaroni, Jim 125, 143, 234
Paige, Satchel 195
Paine, Phil 190
Pappas, Milt 135
Parker, Wes 182, 185, 188–189
Parsons, Tom 169
Patkin, Max 14, 15, 28
Patterson, Floyd 50
Pattin, Marty 199
Pell, Gene 129
Pena, Orlando 152
Pendleton, Jim 75
Pepe, Phil 178
Pepitone, Joe 137–138, 143, 149, 153, 191, 235
Perez, George 48
Perez, Tony 227
Perry, Gaylord 227
Pesky, John 4, 125, 129–133, 135–319, 141–145, 147–148, 151–155, 159–160, 164, 168–170, 172–173, 178, 181, 235–236
Petrocelli, Rico 181
Pettit, Paul 21–22, 41–45, 57, 116
Pettitte, Andy 237
Philadelphia Athletics 10, 36
Philadelphia Phillies 39, 74, 154–155, 157–158, 163–166, 169–175, 180, 185–186
Philadelphia Royal Giants 195

Phillips, Harold (Lefty) 200
Phillips, Taylor 66
Phoenix Giants 55–56, 200–201
Picasso, Pablo 179
Pierce, Billy 39
Pinckard, Bill 17, 226
Pinson, Vada 122, 231
Pioneer League 3, 12–17, 22–24
Pipp, Wally 140
Pittsburgh Children's Hospital 233
Pittsburgh Pirates 1–2, 5, 9–11, 13, 17, 20–22, 24–25, 27, 38–44, 51, 53–54, 59–64, 66–68, 70, 73–75, 80–82, 84–89, 92–93, 95, 97, 99–108, 110–111, 113–115, 118, 120–126, 135, 143, 169, 180, 182, 185, 200, 206, 209, 231
Pocatello Bannocks 13–14, 16–17, 226
Pohl, Jude 196
Pomona Tile 17–18
Post, Wally 91
Powell, John (Boog) 179, 186
Power, Vic 197
Powers, John 21
Pratt, Adam 29
Price, Jackie 15, 28, 102
Prince, Bob 72, 82–84, 100–101, 104–105, 153, 232
Pueblo Dodgers 28–29, 32–33, 72
Purkey, Bob 72
Purnage, William (Perk) 33

Quinn, John 159, 168, 173–176

Radatz, Dick 134–135, 139, 143, 145, 151, 160, 173
Ralston, William 9
Ramos, Pedro 140, 150–151
Raydon, Curt 72, 78, 82
Reabe, Don 75
Reagan, Ronald 42
Redwood City, California 8–9, 206, 211
Reese, Harold (Pee Wee) 86
Regan, Phil 184
Reich, Tom 205
Renk, Mrs. R. J. 83
Repoz, Roger 199
Resner, Moe 204
Restelli, Dino 71
Rhodes, Dusty 56
Rice, Bob 96, 231
Rice, Del 79
Rice University 237
Richards, Paul 157
Richardson, Art 237
Richman, Milton 172, 179, 194
Rickey, Branch, Jr. 20, 29, 33, 52
Rickey, Branch, Sr. 13, 17, 21–23, 30, 39–41, 44, 48, 62–64, 77, 108, 125, 227, 229
Riddle, Walt 149
Rigney, Bill 158, 197, 199–200
Rizzuto, Phil 69
Roberts, Dave 195
Roberts, Robin 132
Robinson, Brooks 153, 186

Robinson, Frank 20, 72, 91, 115, 186
Robinson, Jackie 40, 57, 63, 184, 227
Rojas, Cookie 170
Romano, John 140
Rondon, Gilbert 233
Roseboro, John 184, 233, 237
Rosen, Al 42
Rossetto, John 56, 229
Rowe, Don 26, 28, 30, 33, 35, 227
Ruhl, Oscar 40
Runnels, Pete 125, 128
Russo, Neal 108
Ruth, George Herman (Babe) 1–2, 32, 35, 38–39, 53, 57–58, 68, 110, 114–115, 118, 180, 190
Ryan, Bob 22, 116

Saba, Kathy 204
Sadecki, Ray 112, 165
Sain, Johnny 97
Saint Louis Cardinals 82, 184
Salinas Merchants 18
Salt Lake City Bees 13, 35–36, 55–57, 59
Sam Houston State University 21
San Carlos, California 7–9, 11, 17, 68
San Carlos Central School 17
San Carlos Gray Juniors 9
San Diego Padres 43, 174
San Francisco, California 7
San Francisco Giants 55, 68, 88, 96, 99–100, 122, 131, 167, 169–170, 185, 200–201
San Francisco Seals 18
San Jacinto Junior College 237
Sanford, Jack 104
Santa Clara University 8
Sayama, Kazuo 195
Schaffer, Jim 174
Schilling, Chuck 136, 142
Schofield, Dick 3, 75, 94, 100, 102–103, 105, 107, 114, 126, 183
Schreiber, Ted 142
Schulian, John 57
Schwall, Don 125, 129, 143, 169
Scott, Frank 69, 81
Scott, George 180
Scott, Mark 90, 91, 231
Seals Stadium 68
Secory, Frank 64
Seery, Pat 30
Segui, Diego 152
Sequoia High School 7–9, 17
Serena, Bill 227
Shantz, Bobby 31, 109
Shaughnessy, Frank 226
Shea Stadium 169
Shepard, Larry 3, 25–26, 28–29, 33, 35, 48–50, 53, 55–56, 58–59, 156, 190, 200, 226, 234
Sherman Field 25, 27, 30, 32, 34, 48, 70
Sherry, Larry 121, 226–127, 237
Shipp, Leo 15
Short, Chris 157, 165, 183

Shum, Rick 206
Siebern, Norm 137–138, 141, 149
Siegal, Arthur 147, 150
Simon, Neil 207
Simpson, Harry (Suitcase) 75, 88–89
Sinatra, Frank 159
Sinner, Wally 15, 18
Sioux City Soos 29, 31–32, 226
Sisler, George 22, 51–52, 69, 93, 110, 124
Skinner, Bob 40, 51, 69, 71, 80, 87–89, 92, 97–100, 103, 121, 123
Skowron, Bill 153
Small, Mrs. Wesley 26
Smith, Bob 84
Smith, Hal 68, 92, 98, 100, 107, 111
Smith, Lester 61
Smith, Pete 140
Smith Walter (Red) 80
Snider, Duke 177
Sosa, Sammy 206
South Atlantic League 20
Southern Association 20–21, 23, 45–47
Spahn, Warren 73, 77, 80–81, 97, 99, 114, 169–170, 178, 231
Span, Miles 168, 182, 202
Spears, Bill 96, 114, 123, 233
Spencer, Daryl 193
Spencer, Jim 197, 200
Spitzer, Irene 155
Spokane Indians 55
Spooner, Karl 34
Stafford, Bill 133
Stange, Lee 199
Stanka, Joe 190, 192, 239
Stanky, Eddie 39, 82, 142
Stargell, Willie 209
Steiner, Mel 113
Stengel, Casey 106, 138, 173, 177–178
Stephens, Vern 145
Stevens, Bob 232
Stevens, Chuck 32
Stevens, R.C. 54, 59, 81, 96, 109, 232
Stewart, Adiel 56
Stone, Max 28, 35, 50, 226
Strugar, George 116
Stuart, Daryl vi, 7, 31, 120, 166, 205, 208–209, 211
Stuart, Debra 23, 205, 209
Stuart, Diane Mellen 8, 17, 23, 47, 87, 209
Stuart, Laurel vi, 7, 205, 211
Stuart, Lois Murano 58, 61, 80, 84, 92, 95, 129, 174, 188, 205
Stuart, Phyllis Dickerson 7, 208, 209
Stuart, Richard Lee (Dick) vi, 1–5; in Army 1953–4 17–19; with Atlanta 1957 45–47; with Billings 1955 22–24; with Boston Red Sox 1963 128–44; with Boston Red Sox 1964 145–54; with California Angels 1969 197–200; in Dominican Winter

League 91; early life 7-9; with Hollywood 1957 42-45; on Home Run Derby 90-91; home run log 213-221, 225, 226, 228, 229, 230, 231, 233, 234, 236, 237, 238, 239; in Japan 1967-68 190-196; with Lincoln 1956 25-37; with Lincoln 1957 47-52; with Los Angeles Dodgers 1966 182-186; with Los Angeles Dodgers in 1967 training camp 188-189; with Mexico City 1955 21-22; with Modesto 1951 10-11, 12-17; with New Orleans 1955 20-21; with New York Mets 1966 174-181; in 1960 World Series 105-108; in 1966 World Series 186-187; with Philadelphia Phillies 159-173; with Phoenix Giants 1969 200-201; in Pirates training camp 1957 38-41; with Pittsburgh Pirates 1958 61-75; with Pittsburgh Pirates 1959 78-90; with Pittsburgh Pirates 1960 92-105; with Pittsburgh Pirates 1961 109-117; with Pittsburgh Pirates 1962 118-124; post-baseball career 202-211; with Salt Lake City 1958 53-60; traded to Boston Red Sox 124-127; traded to Philadelphia Phillies 154-158
Stuart, Richard Lee, Jr. 81, 161, 205-206
Stuart, Robert 108, 205
Stuart, Roy 7, 211
Stuart Cleaners 7-8
Sturdy, Guy 30, 32
Suguira, Tadashi 191
Sulpher Dell Park 36, 46
Surkont, Max 229
Swoboda, Ron 178-179

Taffell, Tom 57
Taiyo Whales 189-190, 192-193, 196
Tartabull, Danny 12
Tasby, Wille 16, 225
Tatum, Tommy 65
Taylor, Sammy 62, 121, 227
Taylor, Tex 22
Taylor, Tony 172, 233
Tebbetts, George (Birdie) 4, 53
Terrell, Roy 77, 99, 102, 107

Terry, Ralph 2, 107, 133
Terry Park 20
Thomas, Frank 39, 51, 69, 72, 74, 76-78, 88, 116, 157, 161, 164, 167-168, 230, 237
Thomas, Lee 172, 179, 197
Throneberry, Marv 124, 181
Tillman, Bob 145, 151
Timber League 18
Toothman, Ken 26, 28, 30, 34-35, 227
Topeka Hawks 30, 31, 49
Torres, Felix 148
Traceweski, Dick 184
Traynor, Harold (Pie) 81
Triandos, Gus 91, 161-162, 237
Trujillo, Rafael 91, 104
Tucker, Bud 185
Turley, Bob 106-107

Ueberroth, Peter 26
Uecker, Bob 186
University of Nebraska 25, 29
University of Pittsburgh 69
University of San Francisco 8
University of Washington 120, 166

Van Burkleo, Frank (Dutch) 14, 225
Van Burkleo, Ty 225
Vargo, Ed 181
Venson, Tony 97
Vernon, Mickey 93
Virdon, Bill 41, 64, 66, 70-72, 80, 88-89, 105, 109-110, 170, 230
Voss, Bill 198

Wagner, Dick 25-26, 28, 30, 35, 47
Wagner, Leon 56, 88, 148, 150, 200-202, 228, 233
Walker, Fred (Dixie) 79
Wallin, Douglas 16
Walls, Lee 10-11, 38, 53
Walsh, Davis J. 61, 66, 68
Walsh, Dick 197
Waner, Paul 24, 116
Warner, Jim 10-11, 225
Washington Senators 18, 153, 195
Weaver, Earl 21
Webster Hall Hotel 74
Weiss, George 177-178
West, Max 42

West Texas-New Mexico League 35-36
Western League 1, 4, 25, 27-29, 31-35, 47, 51
Westrum, Wes 77, 178, 180-182
Weygandt, Al 30
Whelan, Danny 119
White, Bill 75, 114, 172, 174, 188
Whiting, Robert 191
Wichita Braves 56
Wickersham, Dave 48
Williams, Billy 121-122
Williams, Dick 95, 133, 135-137
Williams, Esther 3
Williams, Joe 106
Williams, Stan 71
Williams, Ted 2, 4, 31, 43, 50, 69, 71, 80, 93, 125-130, 141, 143, 145, 147
Williamsport Grays 25, 65
Wills, Maury 94, 152, 173, 184, 189, 226-227, 238-239
Wilson, Dick 10-11, 225
Wilson, Duane 61
Wilson, Earl 136-137, 149, 151
Wilson, Owen (Chief) 71
Wilson, Pete 18
Wine, Bobby 161
Wirz, Bob 25, 32
Witt, George 72, 78, 82, 96, 107, 231
Wood, Wilbur 135
Woods, Jim 72
Wrigley Field (Chicago) 121
Wrigley Field (Los Angeles) 44, 90

Yakima Junior College 19
Yankee Stadium 106, 137,
Yastrzemski, Carl 4, 125, 129, 131-132, 139-140, 142, 145-149, 151-152, 160, 201, 236
Yawkey, Tom 124-125, 146, 154, 172, 234
Yawkey, William 124
Yomiuri Giants 190-191, 239
Yonamine, Wally 190
Young, Dick 96-98, 149, 173-174, 178, 181, 188, 204

Zavatarro, Joe 33
Ziff, Sid 183
Zminda, Don 231

www.ingramcontent.com/pod-product-compliance
Lightning Source LLC
Chambersburg PA
CBHW060339010526
44117CB00017B/2892